Tourism

Tourism

Concepts, Issues and Impacts

Dillip Kumar Das

Department of Tourism Management, The University of Burdwan, West Bengal

Soumendra Nath Biswas

Indian Institute of Tourism & Travel Management (IITTM), Bhubaneswar, Odisha

Los Angeles | London | New Delhi
Singapore | Washington DC | Melbourne

First published in 2019 by

SAGE Publications India Pvt Ltd
B1/I-1 Mohan Cooperative Industrial Area
Mathura Road, New Delhi 110 044, India
www.sagepub.in

SAGE Publications Inc
2455 Teller Road
Thousand Oaks, California 91320, USA

SAGE Publications Ltd
1 Oliver's Yard, 55 City Road
London EC1Y 1SP, United Kingdom

SAGE Publications Asia-Pacific Pte Ltd
18 Cross Street #10-10/11/12
China Square Central
Singapore 048423

Published by Vivek Mehra for SAGE Publications India Pvt Ltd. Typeset in 10/12 pt Cambria by AG Infographics, Delhi.

Library of Congress Cataloging-in-Publication Data Available

ISBN: 978-93-532-8587-6 (PB)

SAGE Team: Indrani Dutta, Vandana Gupta, Arshita Saxena and Kanika Mathur

DEDICATED TO

OUR PARENTS, FAMILY MEMBERS AND WELL-WISHERS

Thank you for choosing a SAGE product!
If you have any comment, observation or feedback,
I would like to personally hear from you.

Please write to me at **contactceo@sagepub.in**

Vivek Mehra, Managing Director and CEO, SAGE India.

Bulk Sales

SAGE India offers special discounts
for bulk institutional purchases.

*For queries/orders/inspection copy requests,
write to* **textbooksales@sagepub.in**

Publishing

Would you like to publish a textbook with SAGE?
Please send your proposal to **publishtextbook@sagepub.in**

Subscribe to our mailing list

Write to marketing@sagepub.in

This book is also available as an e-book.

Contents

Detailed Contents

List of Abbreviations

ADB	Asian Development Bank
AGM	Annual general meeting
APEC	Asia-Pacific Economic Cooperation
ASEAN	Association of Southeast Asian Nations
ASTA	American Society of Travel Agents
ATOC	Association of Train Operating Companies
AVE	Alta Velocidad Española
B&B	Bed and breakfast
BTA	Bermuda Tourism Authority
CDC	Continuous discharge certificate
CPGI	Country potential generation index
CSR	Corporate social responsibility
EIA	Environmental impact assessment
FHRAI	The Federation of Hotel & Restaurant Associations of India
FRO	Foreigner Registration Office
FRRO	Foreigners Regional Registration Office
GDP	Gross domestic product
GNP	Gross national product
GSA	General sales agents
HIV	Human immunodeficiency viruses
IATA	International Air Transport Association
IATO	Indian Association of Tour Operators
ICAO	International Civil Aviation Organization
ICCA	International Congress and Convention Association
ICE	Intercity express
ICT	Information and communication technology
IFCI	Industrial Finance Corporation of India
IHRA	International Hotel & Restaurant Association
IR	Indian Railways
ITDC	India Tourism Development Corporation
ITTA	International Travel & Tourism Academy
KNP	Khangchendzonga National Park
MDGs	Millennium Development Goals

MICE	Meetings, incentives, conferences and exhibitions
NUC	Neutral unit of currency
PATA	Pacific Asia Travel Association
RORO	Roll-on/roll-off
RTA	Regional Transport Authority
SARS	Severe acute respiratory syndrome
STA	State Transport Authority
TAAI	Travel Agents Association of India
TAR	Trans-Asian Railway
TC	Traffic conferences
TCL	Travel career ladder
TFCI	Tourism Finance Corporation of India
TGV	Train à Grande Vitesse
TIM	Travel Information Manual
TWOV	Transit without visa
UNDP	United Nations Development Programme
UNESCAP	United Nations Economic and Social Commission for Asia and the Pacific
UNESCO	United Nations Educational, Scientific and Cultural Organization
UNWTO	United Nations World Tourism Organization
UT	Union territory
VFR	Visiting friends and relatives
WHO	World Health Organization
WTD	World Tourism Day
WTTC	World Tourism and Travel Council
WWF	World Wide Fund for Nature

Preface

Tourism is not only a fast-growing industry, but also the largest industry worldwide in terms of employment and gross domestic product. In the next few decades, tourism will have a potential role in different ways, such as in employment generation, in social integration, in the economic growth of the country, and in the improvement of human life, wealth and productivity. The impact of tourism on our society is enormous. Each and every destination has its unique products and features like natural and man-made attractions, culture, traditions, food habits, folklore, crafts and languages, all of which would be of great interest to national and international visitors.

Tourism is an exciting and dynamic sector that is constantly changing. It can affect the lives of people in different ways. For tourists, it can be a source of lifelong memories, joy and fulfilment, whereas for businesses, it is a source of income and employment. As tourism has grown considerably and become a prominent activity, tourism studies as an academic field have also developed.

This book is written in a simple language with sufficient examples so that students of different backgrounds of both undergraduate and postgraduate levels, including research scholars, can find it useful for their study. The main feature of this book is that it covers almost all dimensions of tourism studies. All important aspects and impacts of the tourism concept have been discussed thoroughly in this book.

The main objective of this book is to provide complete knowledge about the tourism industry, including its features and importance, to the people/students who are in tourism profession or want to pursue tourism as a study.

The other objectives of this book are as follows:

1. To provide ready-made information regarding the concept, definitions, types, history and so on of tourism.
2. To consider some important aspects of tourism including its demand and supply.
3. To consider the components of tourism industry and their contributions to successful tourism operation.
4. To discuss various impacts of tourism that arise due to the development of tourism.
5. To provide useful information on tourism organizations involved in tourism and hospitality, both nationally and internationally.

One of the objectives of this textbook is to provide a simple and reasonably comprehensive outline of tourism. Suggestions for further reading and bibliography have been given at the end of this book. Each chapter of this book includes learning objectives, learning definitions, figures, tables, pictures and so on.

While writing this book, emphasis has been given on various contents of tourism studies to maintain the quality as per the international standard. This book is planned as a textbook for the students of travel, tourism and hospitality. It would also be helpful for researchers, academicians and industry people. This book thoroughly describes the conceptual framework of tourism in all its dimensions. It takes a global outlook with examples from various countries including India.

Over the years, tourism has grown substantially in the fields of both academics and industry. In the Indian context, this book will prove to be a solid base to understand the concept of tourism and its impact on tourists and businesses. This conceptual framework on tourism will help students, scholars and academicians of different universities, and institutes that are offering tourism and hospitality management disciplines.

This book is broadly divided into 11 chapters. These are as follows:

Chapter 1: It is the introductory chapter which explains the conceptual framework of tourism including definitions; tourism as an industry, a global business and a system; forms of tourism; tourist typology; and components of tourism industry and their characteristics.

Chapter 2: It mainly deals with the historical development of tourism in the international scenario, in general, and India, in particular.

Chapter 3: It discusses the travel motivation including the travel flow pattern, various motivational theories, factors affecting travel and so on.

Chapter 4: It describes tourism demand including meaning, types, levels, measurement and factors.

Chapter 5: It discusses the supply aspects of tourism including the understanding, determinants and significance of tourism supply.

Chapter 6: It mainly deals with the overview of tourism industry including its components such as transportation, accommodation and attractions.

Chapter 7: It comprises travel formalities including passport, visa, customs, currencies, health regulations, immigration rules and so on.

Chapter 8: It deals with tourism impacts including economic, sociocultural and environmental ones.

Chapter 9: It discusses tourist transportation, forms of tourist transportation including water transport, air transport and road transport.

Chapter 10: It mainly deals with various organizations (both domestic and international) related to tourism and hospitality industry including International Air Transport Association (IATA), United Nations World Tourism Organization (UNWTO), Pacific Asia Travel Association (PATA), American Society of Travel Agents (ASTA), International Civil Aviation Organisation (ICAO), International Congress and Convention Association (ICCA), Indian Association of Tour Operators (IATO), Travel Agents Association of India (TAAI), The Federation of Hotel & Restaurant Associations of India (FHRAI), United Nations Educational, Scientific and Cultural Organization (UNESCO) and so on.

Chapter 11: It deals with tourism law. Various laws and legal issues which are directly or indirectly related with tourism business are discussed here broadly. Legal aspects of various tourism conventions and tourism code of ethics are also elaborated here.

This book focuses on a variety of practical application tools, skills, practices, models, approaches and strategies that are important for managing diversity and innovation. This book also gives some recommendations and policy implications to the government as well as private agencies intending to promote destinations in terms of organizational infrastructure, economic development and have positive impacts worldwide.

Acknowledgements

Our humble endeavour would not have culminated in a presentable book had we not been privileged with the generous help, motivation, support, guidance and counselling from several persons of various calibre and numerous organizations at all stages of our work. We are therefore thankful and obliged to all of them. We do not have words to express our heartfelt gratitude to each one of them.

We would like to thank Professor Bijay Kumar Das, Department of English and Cultural Studies, The University of Burdwan, West Bengal, for his guidance, support and cooperation in course of writing this book. We are also grateful to all the authors whose works have enriched our mind to write this book. We thankfully acknowledge the role of our teachers, well-wishers, friends and relatives for their inspiration and encouragement.

Last but not the least, we owe a lot to our parents initiating us into learning and finally choosing teaching as a profession.

About the Authors

Dillip Kumar Das is currently working as an Associate Professor and Head in the Department of Tourism Management, The University of Burdwan, Bardhaman, West Bengal. He has been working in The University of Burdwan since 13 June 2005. The author has also worked in Sikkim University, Gangtok, as an Associate Professor and Head in the Department of Tourism Management for 1 year (on lien). The author has more than 20 years of teaching experience at both undergraduate and postgraduate levels. He was awarded PhD in the year 2008 in tourism management by Utkal University, Bhubaneswar, Odisha, on the topic 'Economic, Socio Cultural and Environmental Impact of Tourism: A Case Study on Puri, Konark and Bhubaneswar'. He has completed masters in tourism management (MTM) from IGNOU, and also qualified UGC-NET (National Eligibility Test for lectureship) twice in December 2003 and in June 2004. He has completed masters degree in economics from Ravenshaw University, Cuttack, and also completed Diploma in Tourism Management from Indian Institute of Tourism and Travel Management (IITTM), Bhubaneswar, Odisha. The author has attended and presented papers in more than 45 national and international conferences, and has 5 books to his credit with the prominent publishers. The author has also published more than 40 research papers on tourism in different international journals and books. He has contributed in many research projects sponsored by Ministry of Tourism, Government of India. The author's areas of research interest are eco-tourism, tourism impact studies and travel agency and tour operation management.

Soumendra Nath Biswas is working as an Assistant Professor (senior scale) at IITTM (an autonomous organization of Ministry of Tourism, Government of India) since 2007. He is from Bhubaneswar, Odisha, India. He has also served as an Assistant Professor in the Department of Tourism Management, Sikkim University (on lien). He was awarded PhD in the year 2010 in tourism management by The University of Burdwan, on the topic 'Food as a Marketing Tool for the Development of Hospitality and Tourism in India, with Special Reference to West Bengal'. He has obtained MTM and bachelor of hotel management (BHM). He has also qualified UGC-NET (National Eligibility Test for lectureship) twice and UGC-JRF. Dr Biswas has 18 years of teaching experience in MBA (Tourism), BBA (Tourism), BHM and diploma in hotel management (DHM), in various government and private institutions including 10 years of research experience. Dr Biswas has contributed a number of research papers in reputed national and international referred, peer-reviewed journals and edited books. He has contributed in many research projects sponsored by UNDP, Government of India and Government of Odisha. The author's areas of research interest include tourism concepts and impacts, tour operation management, tourism geography, tourism marketing, hospitality management and so on.

Tourism: Conceptual Framework

LEARNING OBJECTIVES

After studying this chapter, the reader will be able to understand:

☐ The meaning, concept and importance of tourism
☐ Overview of tourism as an industry
☐ Different forms of tourism
☐ Tourism as a system
☐ Various models of tourist typology
☐ Components of tourism industry
☐ Characteristics of tourism product
☐ Global significance of tourism

CHAPTER OVERVIEW

Chapter 1 is an introductory one which explains the conceptual framework of tourism, including definition of tourism, tourism as an industry, tourism as a global business, tourism as a system, forms of tourism, tourist typology, components of tourism industry, including its characteristics.

1.1. Introduction to Tourism

Since the beginning of time, primitive men have travelled, often traversing great distances, in search of game which provided food and clothing necessary for the survival. Throughout the course of history, people have travelled for several purposes including trade, religion, economic gain, war, migration and other motivations. In the Roman era, wealthy aristocrats and government officials travelled mainly for pleasure. Except during the Dark Ages, an increasing number of people have been travelling, and this has played a vital role in the development of human civilizations.

Tourism is a 'phenomenon', meaning that it is an observable event or occurrence that is constantly evolving, developing and reformulating itself as a consumer activity. The occurrence is most obvious in the destinations that tourists visit because of the infrastructure that it usually requires and the economic, environmental and socio-cultural impacts of tourism activities. The tourist spot/attraction is constantly being developed by the tourism industry and individual businesses to appeal to the consumers. Tourism is not a new phenomenon. Tourism and travel have been part of human experiences for millennia (Smith, 2007).

Tourism is an exciting and dynamic sector that is constantly changing. It can affect people's lives in many different ways such as for tourists it can be a source of life-long memories, joy and fulfilment, and for businesses in the destinations it is a source of income and employment. As tourism has grown considerably and has become a prominent activity, tourism studies as an academic field have also developed.

Tourism is a discretionary activity. In an economy focused on growing service sector industries, many countries see tourism as offering new employment opportunities. Tourism is increasingly becoming associated with quality of life. It is seen as a basic right in the developed countries, and holiday entitlement is enshrined in the legislation with the intention to generate tourism. Tourism studies involve the study of places visited by tourists (where tourism is consumed) and of the factors and conditions in the tourist-generating places (where the demand for tourism is created).

Tourism: A Composite Activity

The fundamental problems in understanding tourism are: what it is, how it occurs, why it occurs, how it affects people and environments, and why it is a very volatile activity that can cease as quickly as it can start? Tourism is a consumer-driven activity and is built on dreams, images and what people like to do. These are bound with notions of enjoyment, feelings, emotions, and intangible and unseen characteristics. Tourism is very difficult to understand as it involves the realms of psychology and trying to read the mind of the individual tourist. This is further complicated because these notions change throughout the life of an individual as a tourist consumer. As a result, understanding what tourism is, how it operates, what it means to people and how to manage it are the key challenges involved in it.

The tourism industry is a composite of organizations, both public and private, that are involved in the development, production and marketing of products and services to serve the needs of travellers. Such a broad definition of the tourism industry raises the question of which agencies, organizations or businesses should be included in the industry and how they should be categorized. It also raises the question of difficulty of dealing with more fluid heterogeneous groups.

1.2. Definition of Tourism

The word 'tourism', although accepted and recognized in common parlance, is nevertheless a term that is subject to a diversity of meanings and interpretations. It is typically used to designate a variety of concepts, partly because tourism studies include a range of disciplines: geography, economics, business and marketing, sociology, anthropology, history, psychology and so on. The differing conceptual structures within these disciplines lead inevitably to contrasts in perspective and emphasis (Williams, 2009).

Not one definition of tourism has gained universal acceptance. Many people believe that tourism is a service industry that takes care of visitors when they are away from home. Some restrict the definition of tourism by number of miles away from home, overnight stays in paid accommodations, or travel for the purpose of pleasure or leisure. Others think that travel and tourism should not even be referred to as an industry (Lowry, 1994, pp. 28–29).

It is extremely difficult to define precisely the words 'tourist' and 'tourism' since these terms have different meanings to different people and no universal definition has yet been adopted. There have been numerous attempts to define tourism and very often the terms 'travel' and 'tourism' are used interchangeably.

In fact, 'there are almost as many definitions of tourism as there are studies of the phenomenon' (Cohen, 1972). There has been no unanimity on the meaning and definition of the term 'tourism' because it has been in the process of evaluation.

Etymologically, the word 'tourist' dates back to 1232 AD. It has come from the word 'tour' which is derived from the Latin word *tornare* and the Greek *tounos*, meaning a lathe or circle, the movement around a central point or axis. Therefore, like a circle, a tour represents a journey that is a round-trip, that is, the act of leaving and then returning to the original starting point, and therefore one who takes the journey can be called a tourist (Theabold, 2005).

Definitions of tourism have evolved into two broad categories—conceptual and technical—each with its own rationale and application. To define tourism, it is helpful to distinguish between the conceptual and technical definitions.

Conceptual Definitions of Tourism

Conceptual definition of tourism was first given by two Swiss professors Hunziker and Krapf during the period between the two world wars and was subsequently adopted by the International Association of Scientific Experts in Tourism.

Burkart and Medlick (1881) mentioned that there are conceptual definitions which attempt to provide a theoretical framework in order to identify the essential characteristics of tourism, and what distinguishes from similar, sometimes related, but different activity.

Swiss professors, Walter Hunziker and Kurt Krapf (1941) defined, 'Tourism is the sum of phenomena and relationships arising from the travel and stay of non-residents, insofar as they do not lead to permanent residence and are not connected with any earning activity'.

Since then the basic concept has been broadened to include various forms of business and vocational travels. Several definitions have evolved since the 1940s as the understanding of tourism has been refined and tourism itself has changed (Mathieson & Wall, 1982). Some other important conceptual definitions are as follows.

According to the **International Association of Scientific Experts on Tourism,** 'Tourism is the sum of phenomena and relationships arising from travel and stay at non-residents, in so far as they do not lead to permanent residence and are not connected with any earning activity.' Hunziker and Krapf (1941).

According to **Cohen (1972),** as quoted in the book *Tourism in India* (Sharma, 1991, p. 24), a tourist can be defined as 'a voluntary, temporary traveller travelling in the expectations of pleasure from the novelty and change experienced on a relatively long and non-recurrent round trip'. According to him, there are four basic criteria one has to take into consideration. These include: purpose of trip, mode of transportation, length of stay and distance travelled.

According to **Ogilvie (1933),** a tourist may be defined as 'any person whose movements fulfil two conditions: first, the person's absence from home is for a relatively short period and second is the money spent during absence is money derived from home and not earned in the place visited'.

According to **Jafri** (1989), 'Tourism is the study of man away from his usual habitat, of the industry which responds to its needs and of the impacts that both he and the industry have on the host socio-cultural, economic and physical environment'.

According to **Ryan** (1991), tourism can be constructed as an economic activity, and might be defined as 'a study of demand for and supply of accommodation and supportive service for those staying away from home, and the resultant pattern of expenditure, income creation and employment'.

Schullard (1910), an Austrian economist, gave one of the earliest definitions of tourism. He defined it as 'the sum total of the operators, mainly of an economic nature, which directly relates to the entry, stay and movement of foreigners inside and outside a certain country, city or region'.

According to **Zivadin** (1999), 'It is a social movement with a view to rest, diversion and satisfaction of cultural needs'.

The Tourism Society of Britain in the year 1976 defines the concept as, 'Tourism is the temporary short-term movement of people to destinations outside the places where they normally live and work, and their activities during the stay at these destinations; it includes movement for all purposes, as well as day visits or excursions' (Tourism Society, 1979, p. 70, www.tourism society.org).

The importance of tourism was acknowledged formally when the XXI United Nations General Assembly designated 1967 as the 'International Tourist Year' with a unanimous resolution recognizing that 'tourism is a basic and most desirable human activity deserving the praise and encouragement of all peoples and governments'.

Gunn (1985) believes that tourism 'encompasses all travel with the exception of commuting' and that it is more than just a service industry.

McIntosh and Goeldner (1984) say that 'tourism can be defined as the science, art and business of attracting and transporting visitors, accommodating them, and graciously catering to their needs and wants'. They also introduced the notion that tourism is interactive, in that they believe that 'tourism may be defined as the sum of the phenomena and relationships arising from the interaction of tourists, business suppliers, host governments, and host communities in the process of attracting and hosting these tourists and other visitors'. D'Amore (1987, pp. 78–81), Taylor (1988, pp. 58–60) and Dann (1988, pp. 25–33) say that *tourism is not only an interactive process but also a vehicle for world peace.*

Mathieson and Wall (1982) said that 'Tourism is the temporary movement of people to destinations outside their normal places of work and residence, the activities undertaken during their stay in those destinations and the facilities created to cater to their needs'.

Hunt and Layne (1991) singularly describe tourism as 'The activity of people taking trips away from home and the industry which has developed in response to the activity'.

The International Labour Organization (ILO) defines Tourism within its framework of the hotel, catering and tourism sector, as defined by the ILO in 1980. It is included within the framework of its sectoral activities, enterprises most of which fall under sections 55 (hotels and restaurants) and 6304 (travel agencies, tour operators and so on) of the International Standard Industrial Classification of All Economic Activities (Sectoral Activities, ILO, 2005, https://www. ilo.org).

From the earlier discussion, it is clear that conceptual definitions of tourism do provide a theoretical framework in order to identify the required characteristics of tourism. It is also proved from the aforementioned definitions of tourism given by different authors who have added different features to provide a wholesome definition of tourism. In these definitions, different activities can have similar, related or different features. However, while defining tourism one has to take note of following five elements:

1. Purpose of the trip
2. Mode of transportation
3. Length of stay
4. Distance travelled
5. Residence of the traveller

Technical Definitions of Tourism

Technical definitions of tourism are important because they help to collect statistical data related with tourism to enable the government to measure tourism and understand its impacts. The data helps those who are employed in the tourism sector to identify trends and anticipate changes in demand. Countries, regions and individual destinations can compare tourism performance with the internationally standardized technical definitions. Clear and standardized criteria to identify tourist and tourism enterprises are important for measuring economic potential of tourism and its interdependence with other industries.

Technical definitions can provide information for statistical and legislative purposes. The several technical definitions of tourism provide meaning or classification that can be applied in both domestic and international perspectives.

According to United Nations World Tourism Organization (UNWTO),

Tourism is defined as the activities of persons travelling to and staying in place outside their usual environment for not more than one consecutive year for leisure, business and other purposes not related to the exercise of an activity remunerated from within the place visited.

Tourism refers to all activities of visitors, including both 'tourists' (overnight visitors) and 'same day visitors'.

The Tourism Committee of League of Nations first officially defined the term 'tourism' in the year 1937. It defined tourism as 'people travelling abroad for periods of at least 24 hours'.

Some Basic Definitions

Tourist: A tourist is a visitor who is motivated to move outside his or her 'beat area' for reasons which have an element of pleasure or recreation for a period of 24 hours or more.

Visitor: A broad definition of the term 'visitor' includes any person visiting a country other than that in which he/she has his/her usual place of residence, for any reason other than following an occupation remunerated from within it.

Excursionist: An excursionist is a person travelling to a place for pleasure for a period less than 24 hours (McIntosh, 1986).

Travel: The act of moving outside one's home community for business or pleasure but not for commuting or travelling to or from school (McIntosh & Goeldner, 1986).

Transit visitor: Any person travelling in a country for a period of less than 24 hours, provided that any stops made are of short duration and for other than tourist purposes.

Domestic tourist: The International Union of Official Travel Organisation defines domestic tourist as 'any person who travels within the country where he resides to a place other than his usual place of residence for at least 24 hours and 1 night, for a purpose other than exercising a gainful activity'. The tourists who travel only within the boundaries of their own country are classified as domestic tourists.

Foreign tourist: The League of Nations defined foreign tourist as 'any person visiting a country, other than in which he usually resides, for a period of at least 24 hours'. The Government of India for the first time adopted on 31 December 1970 that 'a foreign tourist is a person visiting India on a foreign passport for a period of not less than 24 hours and not exceeding 6 months, for non-immigrant, non-employment tourist purposes such as business, pleasures, etc.'

Outbound tourism: It is the tourism of residents of a country visiting outside. Internal tourism is the tourism of visitors coming, both resident and non-resident, within the economic territory of the country of reference.

Inbound tourism: Inbound tourism is a form of tourism which involves non-residents travelling in the country. This can also be defined as incoming tourists from a foreign country to his/her own country.

1.3. Tourism as an Industry

There is a lot of contradiction among the academics and economists whether tourism should be regarded as an industry or not. The tourism fraternity referred tourism supply as the tourism industry to highlight its economic value, to compare its value with other industries and to give credibility to a phenomenon that has struggled to be taken seriously by governments (Davidson, 2005).

There are two definitions of industry. First, the traditional economic view of an industry is of a collection of competing enterprises that produce homogeneous goods. According to this view, tourism cannot be described as an industry because it includes enterprises producing different types of products that complement each other (Davidson, 2005). Second, the Standard Industrial Classification (SIC) regards industry as a group of establishments with the same primary activity whose size is statistically significant (Davidson, 2005). Therefore, tourism as a whole does not fit into this description because the primary activities of transport, attractions and accommodations are not the same.

In conclusion, the authors consider that it is incorrect to define tourism as an industry because tourism is a social as well as economic phenomenon which acts not only as an engine for economic growth but also acts as a social force. Tourism should be considered more than an industry in a broader perspective and a sector comprising a wide range of industries. According to the authors, tourism is a combination of activities of different industries producing different but complementary products. Within each individual industry, suppliers produce the same product and compete with each other but it is not possible to identify tourism as a single industry (Davidson, 2005; Leiper, 1990). Leiper suggests that tourism should be described as a sector that impacts on a diverse range of industries. However, the technical committee of United Nations in 2010 have recommended to use the term 'a tourism industry'. Many tourism professionals including Cooper and Hall (2008), Gunn (1972), Leiper (1979) and Matley (1976) suggested that tourism is most easily understood as a system.

1.4. Tourism as a Global Business

Globalization represents greater integration at a global level in a wide variety of areas, such as trade, finance, communication, information and culture. It comprises a trans-state process that operates across borders. Facilitated by improvements in transportation and information technology, it has led to time–space compression where people, goods and information travel greater distances and cross political borders in shorter periods of time.

Globalization and tourism interact in a variety of dimensions. In the process of globalization associated with tourism, one should keep in mind some important elements including the power and the control issue. Although globalization of tourism industry may have many advantages, including facilitating the arrival of money-carrying guests, there are also many concerns as the local is quickly brought into contact with the global. In 2006, Wall and Mathieson viewed that conflicts result from classes, cultures, religion and family values when shifts occur in the structure of the labour force.

Tourism organizations, including commercial, public sector and non-profit organizations, operate virtually in all countries and communities. In that sense, tourism could be referred to as a 'global industry'. Rather than the single homogeneous market, in globalization cultural differences fade away and diversity of demand is very much present. Tourism can no longer be considered mainly within a domestic context, since the production and consumption of tourism services take place at the global level.

Tourism is part of a global process of development and change which is no longer confined to the developed countries that traditionally provided the demand for world travel. Many tourism analysts of the World Travel and Tourism Council argued that tourism is the world's largest industry. Seeking evidence to substantiate this claim will be particularly difficult until a proper accounting process like tourism satellite account method is developed to provide more reliable and comparable data generated by individual nations related to tourism development in their respective countries.

International Significance of Tourism

The growing international significance of tourism can be explained in many ways. While discussing the reasons why it plays important roles not only in our life but also globally, the following points need to be remembered.

- Tourism is a discretionary activity, that is, people do not need to do it to survive, unlike consuming food and water.
- Many governments view tourism as offering new employment opportunities in a growing sector of the economy.
- Tourism is increasingly becoming associated with quality-of-life issues. It provides the context for rest, relaxation and an opportunity to do something different in a new environment.
- Economic significance of tourism is growing at a global scale—in excess of the rate of growth for many economies.
- Global travel is becoming more accessible in the developing countries for all classes of people.

- Tourism is considered as a basic right in the developed industrialized countries and it is protected in the legislation through holiday entitlement.
- Technologies such as Internet have made accessing travel-related products easy for the tourists who are poor and are willing to organize their own annual holidays.
- Discretionary items such as travel and tourism are being perceived as less costly items in household budgets.

1.5. Tourism as a System

A system can be defined as a combination of individual components that when combined will create a particular phenomenon. In the context of tourism, the system consists of tourists, geographical regions and the resources required for tourism production and consumption. Each element of the system requires different types of production and consumption; they are interrelated and interdependent. Change within one element will cause change within the other elements.

The system defines how the behaviour of the people as tourist creates arrangements of people, places and organization in certain roles (Leiper, 1990) with five basic elements: tourists, generating regions, transit routes, destination regions and tourism industries. These elements operate within and are influenced by physical, cultural, social, economic, political and technological environment.

- **Tourists:** They are the human element of the system who temporarily and willingly move beyond their routine environment through the discretionary use of time and money.
- **Generating regions:** These are the usual places of residence for tourists and the sources of demand for tourism. Generating region is the location of the tourism decision-making process. Consequently, the generating region is the focus of promotional activities. The travel trade has a major presence in generating regions in the forms of travel agencies, wholesalers and tour operators.
- **Transit route:** These are the journeys that must be made to reach the destination region. These determine the destinations that are accessible from the generating regions. Transit routes are important in determining the volume of tourist flow between generating and destination regions as it determines a destination's accessibility to potential tourism consumers.
- **Destination region:** Destination regions are the locations of the resources that attract tourists (Leiper, 1990). This is the most important element according to Leiper. This is because tourism activities are mostly carried out in the destination region and can affect the local economy, environment and society in both positive and negative ways. So keeping in mind the destination, planning and management strategies have to be developed to have positive impacts and to eliminate negative impacts.
- **Tourism industry:** Tourism industry comprises businesses and organizations that provide experiences, services and facilities for tourists. Leiper (1979) describes the tourism sector as a 'linked chain' because it is located in the generating region, transit route and destination region, and it is fragmented across a number of industries and involves both commercial and public sectors. Tourism industry comprises accommodation, transport, and firms and organizations which supply products and services to the tourists.

Leiper first proposed a system for tourism in 1979 with subsequent amendments in 1990 (depicted in the figure here). His model explained how tourism, that is, behaviour of tourists, gives rise to a tourism system and made a major contribution to our understanding of tourism.

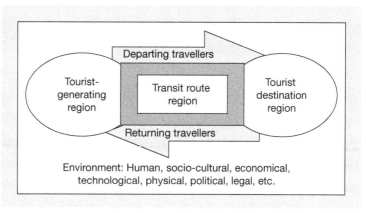

This figure depicts that basically there are two regions, namely **tourist-generating region** and **tourist destination region**. The

Source: Leiper (1990).

tourists normally travel from tourist-generating region to tourist destination region. The **transit route** is the region which connects the two where both departure and return take place. The fourth element is the **tourism industry** which comprises accommodation, transport, and firms and organizations which supply products and services to the **tourists,** which is the fifth and final element of Leiper's model of tourism system.

Tourism System by Mill and Morrison (1992)

While describing tourism as a system, it is important to see tourism as consisting of interrelated parts. This system is like a spider's web—touch one part of it and reverberations will be felt throughout. The tourism system consists of four parts, namely market, travel, destination and marketing.

Figure 1.1 shows the tourism system which comprises four interrelated parts comprising the following elements:

1. **Destination:** It is the first major part of the system. The destination mix consists of the attraction and services used by the traveller. Each part of the destination mix depends upon the others for success in attracting, servicing and satisfying the tourist.
2. **Marketing strategy:** The second part of the system is marketing strategy, planning, promotion and distribution. This is a process by which destination areas and tourism businesses market services and facilities to potential customers by effective use of promotion and services. The development of a marketing plan, the selection of an appropriate marketing mix and the choice of a distribution channel determine the success or failure for the destination.
3. **Demand:** Market demand emphasizes the internal and external influences on travellers including needs, motivation and perception. The demand is created by the factors which influence the travelers make buying decision.
4. **Travel:** Once a person decides to travel, decisions must then be made as to where, when and how to go. The fourth part of the tourism system describes and analyses these choices. The modes of travel are also discussed to determine recent trends and future process. The shape of travel is the combination of who is travelling, where, when and how he or she is travelling.

Figure 1.1   The Tourism System Model

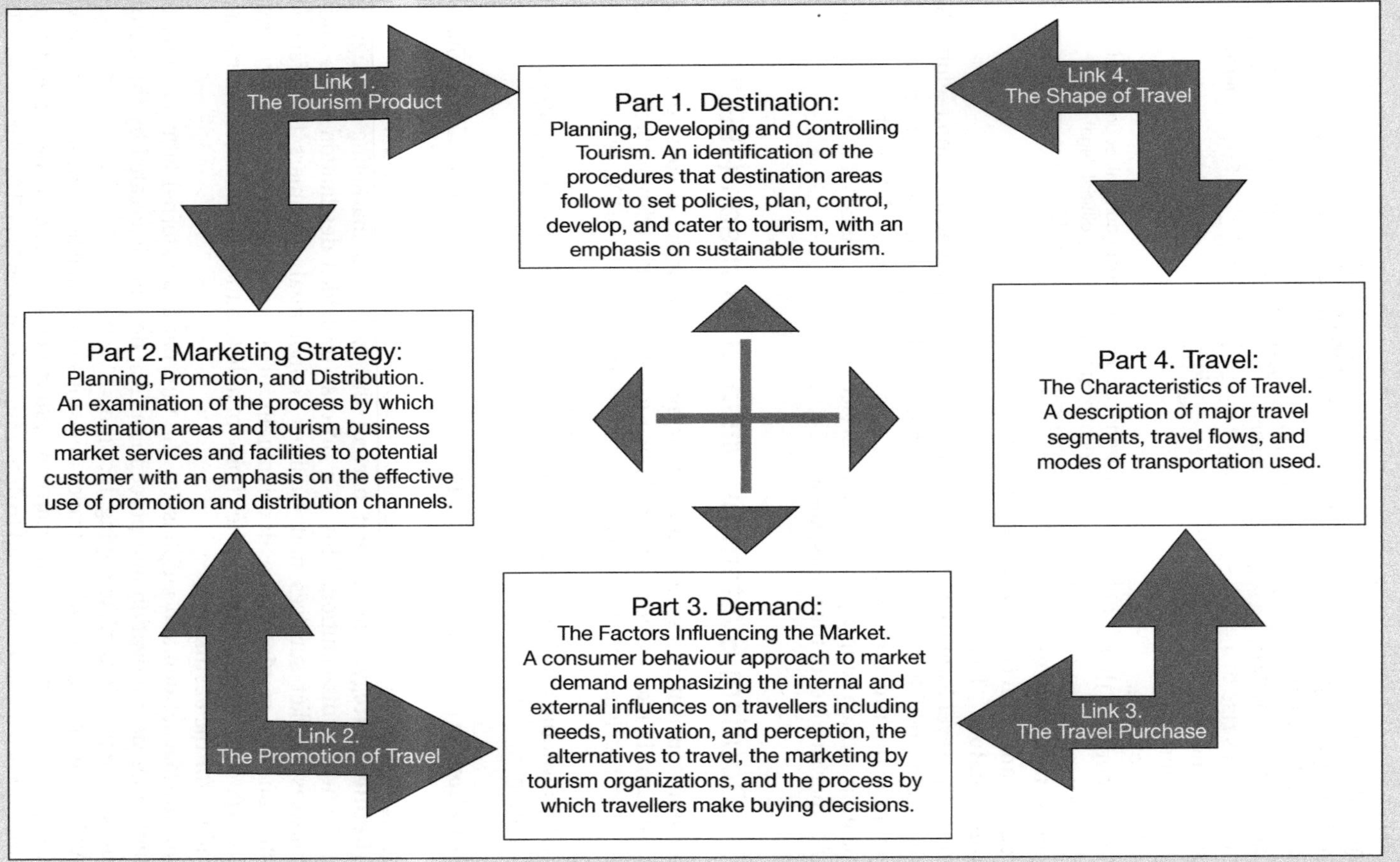

Part 1. Destination:
Planning, Developing and Controlling Tourism. An identification of the procedures that destination areas follow to set policies, plan, control, develop, and cater to tourism, with an emphasis on sustainable tourism.

Part 2. Marketing Strategy:
Planning, Promotion, and Distribution. An examination of the process by which destination areas and tourism business market services and facilities to potential customer with an emphasis on the effective use of promotion and distribution channels.

Part 3. Demand:
The Factors Influencing the Market. A consumer behaviour approach to market demand emphasizing the internal and external influences on travellers including needs, motivation, and perception, the alternatives to travel, the marketing by tourism organizations, and the process by which travellers make buying decisions.

Part 4. Travel:
The Characteristics of Travel. A description of major travel segments, travel flows, and modes of transportation used.

Link 1.
The Tourism Product

Link 2.
The Promotion of Travel

Link 3.
The Travel Purchase

Link 4.
The Shape of Travel

Source: Mill and Morrison (1985).

1.6. Forms of Tourism

Tourism can be described in several ways. According to UNWTO, tourism takes the following three forms:

1. **Domestic tourism:** Domestic tourism involves residents of a given country travelling only within the country.
2. **Inbound tourism:** It involves visit to a country by non-residents.
3. **Outbound tourism:** It involves visit by residents of one country to another country (exporting currency to other countries).

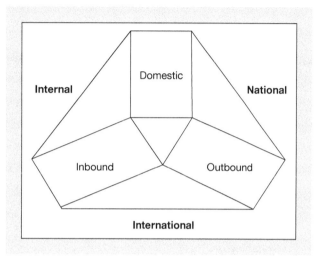

The figure here depicts the forms of tourism identified by the World Tourism Organization in 1991. These forms can be grouped into different ways in order to derive different categories of tourism. These include the following:

Source: World Tourism Organization (cited in Theobald, 1991, p. 15).

- **Internal tourism:** This involves both domestic and inbound tourism.
- **National tourism:** This involves both domestic and inbound tourism.
- **International tourism:** This involves both inbound and outbound tourism.

Types of Tourism (Based on Purpose of Travel) as Given by UNWTO

UNWTO classified different types of tourism based on purpose of travel. According to this organization, on the basis of purpose of travel, tourism can broadly be classified into two types, namely business and personal.

From **business** point of view, the various purposes of visit by a tourist include research, business, and attending conferences, seminars and trade shows.

From **personal** purpose perspective, types of tourism can be further subdivided into eight types:

1. Holiday leisure and recreation
2. Visiting friends and relatives
3. Education and training
4. Health and medical cases
5. Religious/pilgrimage
6. Shopping
7. Transit
8. Others

These eight forms of tourism may further be subdivided into various types as depicted in Figure 1.2.

Figure 1.2   Types of Tourism (Based on Purpose of Travel) as Given by UNWTO

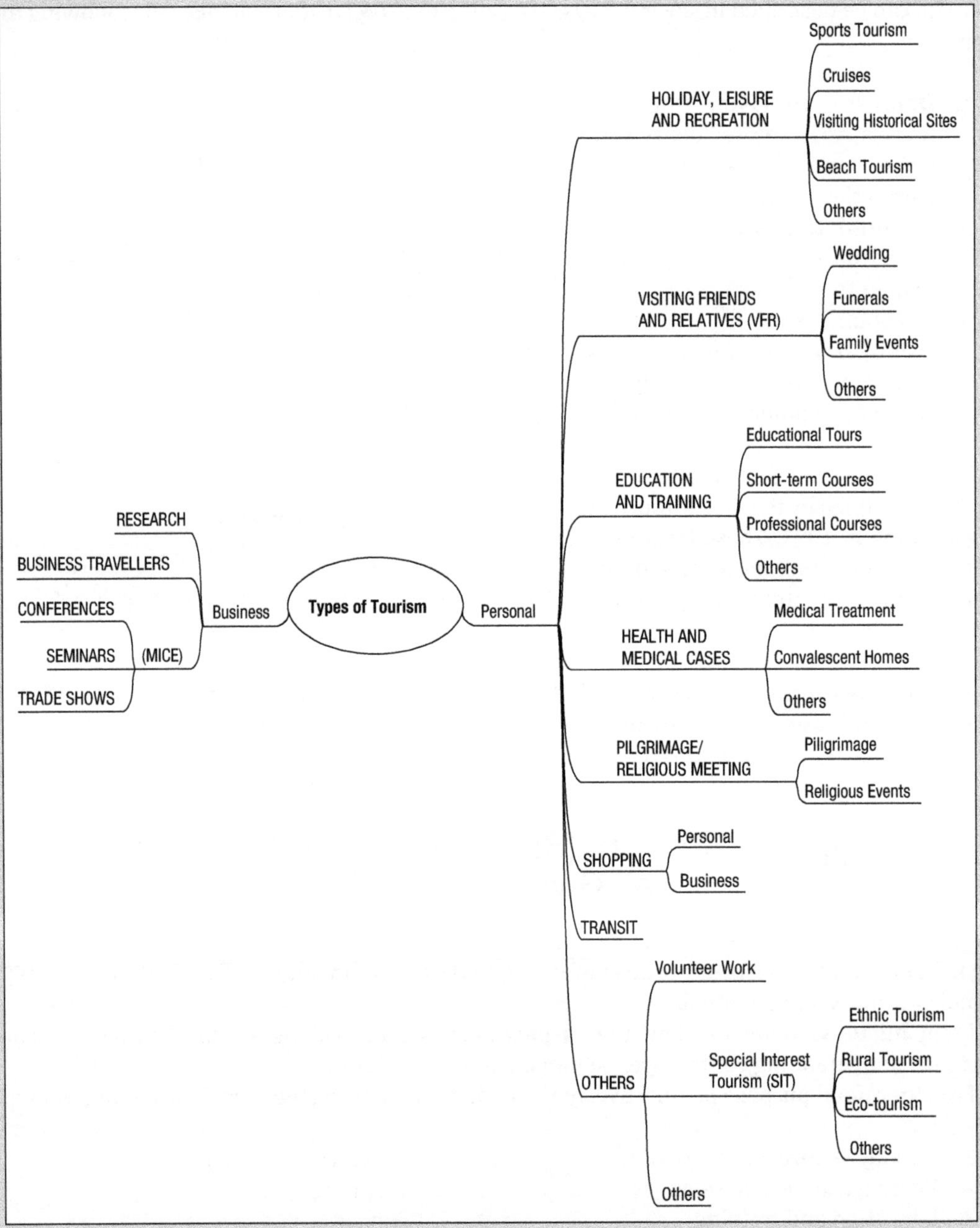

However, the forms of tourism can be categorized depending on the following factors:

1. **The geographical setting of the destination:** Forms of tourism are often characterized by the geographical characteristics of the destination. On this basis, there are three forms of tourism as follows:
   a. *Urban tourism:* Tourism in cities and towns using the resources that are provided primarily by local residents and businesses as attractions for tourists. Transport links to and within urban destinations are usually well developed (Page, 2005).
   b. *Rural tourism:* It is another form of tourism which is practised in small towns and villages or in remote natural areas. Attractions may be natural, cultural and based on specific physical activities. Rural tourism destinations mainly attract holiday, leisure and recreational visitors. Access to the rural tourism areas is limited and requires the use of private vehicles by tourists (Lane, 1994).
   c. *Resort tourism:* This form of tourism attracts large volumes of tourists, especially where the economy and services are dominated by tourism. Resort tourism is usually located in coastal or mountain regions. It may develop in an existing village or town, or be purposely built.
2. **Types of activities engaged in the trip:** Another way to describe forms of tourism is by the type of activity engaged in on the trip. On the basis of the activities, the various forms of tourism are as follows:
   a. *Heritage tourism:* Based on sites of archaeological, cultural, historical or ecological importance in a destination—monuments, buildings and geographical resources.
   b. *Eco-tourism:* Tourism in rural or wilderness environments that actively seeks to educate the tourists about the natural environment with a focus on enhancing the local environment, economy and host society.
   c. *Four S of tourism:* Sun, sand, sea and surf.
   d. *Cultural tourism:* Tourism based specifically on the cultural resources of a destination such as museum, art galleries, architecture, local lifestyle, language, traditions, religion and cultural events.
   e. *MICE tourism:* Tourism for meetings, incentives, conferences and exhibitions (MICE). In this form of tourism, tourists may be associated with companies, businesses, and corporates, or are individuals travelling for business or professional purpose.
   f. *Event tourism:* Tourism to participate or to visit a particular organized event such as cultural events and sports events.
   g. *Dark tourism:* Tourism to visit sites associated with significant sinister events such as battlefields, murder sites and prison camps.
3. **The location of demand and its relationship to the destination from the national perspective:** In this classification, the various forms of tourism include the following:
   a. *Domestic tourism:* In this form, tourism activity by the residents takes place within the borders of their own country.
   b. *Inbound tourism:* It refers to tourism arrivals from residents of other countries.
   c. *Outbound tourism:* It refers to the tourism activity of individuals outside their country of residence.

4. **Characteristics of the trip including how it was organized and the number of tourists:**
   Tourism is often described by using certain trip characteristics relating to the composition
   of the travel party, the method of organization, or the scale and impacts of the trip. On the
   basis of this, various forms of tourism include the following:

   a. *Independent travel:* In this form of travel, the tourists are not travelling with an organized
      group. The purpose for this travel may be research, exploration and so on. Reservations and
      payments are made by the tourists directly to the suppliers via Internet or travel agencies.
   b. *Inclusive travel:* This is also known as package tour. This is a pre-arranged tour consisting
      of transport, accommodation and other travel services sold at one price to groups or to
      individual tourists. It is organized normally by a tour operator or travel agency.
   c. *Group travel:* As the name suggests, the tourist is travelling with an organized group of
      tourists on the same trip. They may or may not be related with each other.
   d. *Corporate travel:* In this form of tourism, the travel is generally organized by the
      company for business or professional purposes.
   e. *Mass tourism:* It includes large-scale holiday offering standardized products and
      experiences. It requires major infrastructural development in destinations.
   f. *Alternative tourism:* This form of tourism is often used to describe specialized forms of
      tourism that attract less numbers of tourists. Host community, environment and society
      are mostly benefited by this form of tourism. This form of tourism is also synonymous
      with green tourism, eco-tourism, soft tourism, sustainable tourism or responsible tourism.

1.7. Tourist Typology

Tourist typology or categorization of tourists is based on a particular theoretical or conceptual
model. These categorizations aim to group tourists with similar characteristics and connect them
to destinations and activities the tourists are likely to choose. Some models also focus on the
underlying values of tourists and the meanings they attribute to travel. By grouping tourists with
homogeneous needs, different market segments can be made.

Tourist Typology by Gray (1970)

One of the first tourist typologies was proposed by **Gray in 1970.** He coined the terms 'wanderlust'
and 'sunlust' tourism. Sunlust tourism is essentially resort based and motivated by three S's—sun,
sea and sand. He described wanderlust tourism as the desire to travel and experience different
places, people and cultures.

Tourist Typology by Cohen (1972)

The distinction between the aforementioned two types of tourists by Gray was expanded by Cohen
in 1972. On the basis of motivation and using the type of experiences, tourists can be categorized
into the following four types:

1. **Organized mass tourists:** Tourists of this type prefer to stay within a tourist bubble in an
   environment that is similar to their natural surroundings. They prefer to travel in groups on

pre-arranged trips. They choose highly organized package holidays and have minimum contact with the host community. Familiarity is at a maximum and novelty at a minimum.

2. **Individual mass tourists:** This type of tourist uses facilities similar to the organized mass tourists but also wants to break away from the norm and visit other sites not covered by organized tours in the destination.

3. **Explorers:** Explorer tourists travel independently and like to experience the social and cultural lifestyle of the destination. They look for novelty but still maintain certain routines and levels of comfort from their normal life.

4. **Drifters:** This type of tourist does not seek any contact with any other tourist or the organized tourism industry. They try to completely immerse themselves in the host culture, that is, live the way they live, eat the food they eat and fully share their customs and traditions. For this type of tourists, familiarity is at a minimum and novelty is at a maximum.

Plog's Model of Tourist Typology (1974)

Plog developed a tourist typology on the basis of tourists' willingness to experience unfamiliarity and novelty on a holiday. He identified two opposite types of tourists. These are allocentric and psychocentric tourists. In between these two extreme kinds of tourists, there exists another category of tourists, namely the mid-centric tourists. The main characteristics of these three kinds of tourists are as follows (Figure 1.3):

1. **Allocentric tourists:** Tourists of this type enjoy travelling independently. They seek adventure on their holidays and are prepared to take maximum amount of risk. They prefer holidays in more exotic locations. They are mostly from the high-income group.

Figure 1.3 Graphical Representation of Plog's Categorization of Tourists

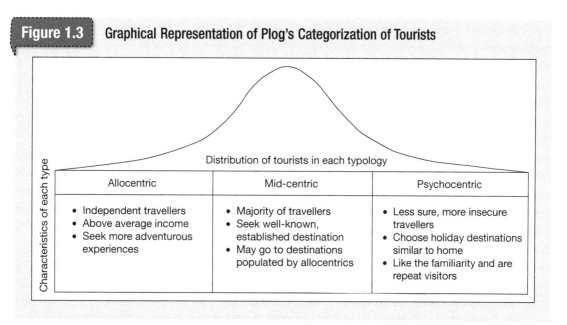

Source: Page (2003, p. 58).

2. **Mid-centric tourists:** Majority of tourist population belong to mid-centric type, which go to known destinations. They may travel to destinations made popular by allocentric tourists. These tourists want to take risk but at a minimum level during their visit to different places.
3. **Psychocentric tourists:** The other extreme form of tourist typology, according to Plog, is psychocentric. These tourists prefer a destination with familiar amenities with tourist infrastructure. They like to visit places similar to their home environment. They do not want to take any risk during their travel to different destinations.

Krippendorf's Tourist Typology (1982)

According to Krippendorf, tourists can be categorized on the basis of their impact on the destination they visited. According to him, since tourism is growing at a rapid pace, tourists are mainly prone to impact negatively on host communities and environments. On this basis, he categorized tourists into two types. These are as follows:

1. **Much maligned tourists:** This is a combination of all the negative stereotypes that exist about tourists. The main characteristics of these tourists are that they are uncultured, spend whole days at the beach and show no interest in local culture and food. They are exploiting and polluting.
2. **Alternative tourists:** These tourists show respect for other cultures and people, and do not conform to the negative stereotype. But they are not without negative impacts. They may have limited negative impacts on the destinations. These tourists include back packers, eco-tourists, adventure tourists and so on.

Smith's Model of Tourist Typology (1989)

In 1989, Smith broadly classified tourist into seven types which are as follows:

1. **Explorer:** These tourists normally travel from one place to another in search of discovery and knowledge. They sometimes desire to interact with the host during their visit. The impacts in the destination by this kind of tourists are less because they can easily accept the local norms and accommodate themselves accordingly.
2. **Elite:** These tourists are characterized by the spending habits during the trip. They normally travel to unusual places, using pre-arranged native facilities. They are small in number, and require high-quality services and facilities.
3. **Off-beat:** These tourists normally travel to destination which is less crowded. Their impacts at the destination are minor because they are willing to adjust with the simple accommodation and services.
4. **Unusual:** These tourists normally go for occasional side trips to explore more isolated areas. They normally undertake more risky activities during their visit to the destinations. They choose temporary simple destinations with availability of full range of services.
5. **Incipient mass:** In this category, the tourists normally travel individually or in small groups and require a combination of both amenities and authenticity at the destination. The

numbers are steadily increasing with the destinations becoming popular. There is a growing demand for services and facilities at the destinations.

6. **Mass:** Mass tourists are characterized by middle-class income group people with common values which lead to the development of a 'tourists bubble' at the destinations. Here tourism is considered as major industry with little interaction with local people beyond commercial links.

7. **Charter:** These tourists normally travel in search for relaxation and good times in a new but familiar environment. In the destination, there is a massive arrival of tourists resulting in requirement of standardized facilities and services to avoid complaints by the tourists.

Perreault and Dorden's Model of Tourist Typology (1979)

In 1979, Perreault and Dorden conducted a survey of 2,000 householders to identify different types of tourists. After conducting the survey, the authors produced a five-group classification of tourists, which is as follows:

1. **Budget travellers:** Who had medium incomes, but sought low-cost vacations.
2. **Adventurous tourists:** Who were well educated and affluent, and showed preference for adventure holiday
3. **Homebody tourists:** Who were cautious people who took holidays but did not discuss their vacation with other people, and spent relatively little time planning it.
4. **Vacationers:** Who were a small group who spent a lot of time thinking about their next holiday and tended to be active people in lower paid jobs.
5. **Moderates:** Who had a high predisposition to travel but were not interested in weekend breaks or sports.

Tourist Typologies	
Gray (1970) • Wanderlust • Sunlust	Cohen (1972) • The organized mass tourist • The individual mass tourists • The explorer • The drifters
Plog (1974) • Allocentric tourists • Mid-centric tourists • Psychocentric tourists	Krippendorf (1982) • Much maligned tourist • Alternative tourists
Smith (1989) • Explorer • Elite • Off-beat • Unusual • Incipient mass • Mass • Charter	Perreault and Dorden (1979) • Budget tourists • Adventure tourists • Homebody tourists • Vacationers • Moderates

1.8. Components of Tourism Industry

The components of tourism industry can be broadly divided into three categories. These are as follows:

1. **Direct providers:** These are the providers which involve directly to fulfil tourist demands. Direct providers include businesses which are generally associated with travel, such as airlines, ground transportation, travel agencies, tour operators, hotels, restaurants and retail shops. These businesses provide services, activities and products which are consumed and purchased by the travellers during their entire course of visit.

2. **Support service providers:** These are those service providers which do not provide primary services but support the principal suppliers providing core products. Examples are service providers such as banks and ATMs, and other financial services such as post offices, sanitations, toilets, healthcare, guide and escort service.

3. **Developmental providers:** These are those organizations that are responsible for developing destinations. Local bodies such as municipalities, local panchayats, NGOs and other private organizations are considered as developmental providers. These include UNESCO, state tourism development corporations, Indian National Trust for Art and Cultural Heritage (INTACH), archaeology departments and so on.

Niagara Falls

Source: httpswww.taketours.comniagara-falls-ny

The components of tourism are the parts of tourism that make the mechanism of tourism industry. There cannot be any tourism activity without **attraction, accessibility, accommodation, amenities** and **activities**. Together, these components are commonly referred to as the five A's of tourism. The components are as follows:

- **Attraction:** These are the features that pull or attract tourists to a destination. There is no easy way to predict or analyse attraction that a place offers because what may appeal to one may not appeal to others. Historical monuments and natural beauty of a place are some of the attractions that lure tourists to a destination. Examples are: Niagra Falls and Red Fort.
- **Accessibility:** Accessibility means if the tourist destination can be easily

Red Fort

Source: https://www.dnaindia.com/india/report-twitter-reacts-to-modi-govt-auctioning-off-red-fort-as-centre-denies-charge-2609674

reached, in terms of transportation. A destination may have all the attractions needed for being a popular destination but if it is not linked properly, it will be avoided by the tourists. Accessibility includes all modes of transport such as road, rail, airlines and waterway that give access to the destination.

Taj Mahal Palace Hotel, Mumbai

- **Accommodation:** The word 'accommodation' is generally used to include boarding and lodging. It is the room or the space provided to the tourists who come from a long distance and is the basic need of any tourist place. The demand for and need of proper accommodation away from one's sweet home is met by a variety of facilities. Sometimes accommodation itself is an important tourist attraction, as in the case of specialty resorts. Example is: Taj mahal Palace Hotel, mumbai.
- **Amenities:** These are the facilities related with the tour provided to the tourists. The facilities could be recreational or it could be infrastructural such as sanitary and hygiene, medical help, travel documentations, foreign currency exchange facilities and telephone.
- **Activities:** These are the actions to be undertaken by the tourists at the destination such as adventure sports, sightseeing, shopping, sun-bathing, golfing, rock climbing and trekking. More the number of activities available for the tourists in a destination, more will be the number of tourists with different interests visiting the destination and longer will be the length of stay of the tourists.

1.9. Characteristics of Tourist Product

Characteristics mean the basic features or qualities that give anything an identity or uniqueness. Tourism industry is commonly referred to as service industry and not consumer goods as it contains all the classic service characteristics. Tourism products are part of the service sector and some of the characteristics are unique to tourism which are as follows:

- **Intangibility:** Intangibility is a distinctive characteristic of the service industry. Things which can be seen, touched and felt are known as tangible products such as consumer goods. Intangible means those products which cannot be seen, tasted, touched, heard or smelled before purchase, but can only be felt and experienced during consumption. Tourism products are intangible in nature and cannot be seen, touched or tasted because they do not exist physically. Tourism products are intangible because:
  - ○ Tourists pay for tourism products and make reservations before their departure for the destination. Therefore, they cannot taste before they reach at the destination. At the end of the trip also they will have no evidence of it except the souvenirs, photographs and memories.
  - ○ The benefits that the tourism product provides are experiential, such as transport, accommodations and attractions, and not physical.

- **Inseparability:** It means that the product cannot be separated from the service provider as often the product is produced and consumed simultaneously. This requires the consumers' direct involvement with the suppliers. For example, the experience of visiting the Red Fort or climbing the Eiffel Tower cannot be experienced sitting in a room. The tourist needs to visit the monument or destination and experience the beauty of the place and its attractions.

- **Perishability:** It is considered to be a feature of a product if the product is lost very quickly or its shelf life is very small. Products such as meat, fish, fruits, vegetables and milk are perishable in nature as they get spoilt very fast. Similarly, all tourism products are perishable and have very short span of time in which they need to be sold or else they are lost forever. It means the life of tourism product is limited to a specific deadline and once that deadline is reached the product ceases to be available for sale. Tourism products are perishable in nature; for example, a hotel room, airlines seat and admission to an attraction cannot be stored indefinitely. If not sold and occupied for the day, the revenue for the day will be lost forever and it cannot be recouped. The characteristic of perishability makes tourism industry very vulnerable to loss in revenue. If it is not sold by a certain time then the opportunity to sell it disappears.

- **Heterogeneity:** It means that each consumer's experience of a product is unique to that consumer. Tourism product is heterogeneous in nature as there is a lot of human element involved in the delivery of the service, and it cannot guarantee that each tourist's experience of the product will be same. Due to the human element involved, the same service provider will be providing different levels of service on different days. For example, the quality of food prepared by the chef in a kitchen of a restaurant cannot be same every day. The experience of travelling by the same coach to the same destination cannot be same every time.

- **Lack of ownership:** Lack of ownership is a typical service characteristic also seen in the tourism industry. Tourists can stay in a hotel room but it does not mean that the tourist is the owner of the hotel room; the consumer has no ownership rights. Whereas, while purchasing consumer goods, customers can own the goods.

- **Seasonality:** Tourism business is seasonal in nature. One destination is not popular to the same extent throughout the year. There are periods when the destination is more popular than other times, also known as peak period. There are lean periods when the destination does not see as many tourists as usual, called off season. For example, peak season for India for foreign tourists is mainly from autumn through winter till spring.

- **Fluctuations of demand:** Tourism service is mainly consumer oriented. The demand of the consumer for a tourist product or attraction varies as taste changes. For example, a popular restaurant may lose flavour for tourists when another restaurant enters in the same place with new styles. New attractions are discovered every day and experienced tourists are looking for newer unexplored attractions. Thus, demand factor changes and accordingly flow of tourist traffic also changes.

- **Interdependence of tourism products:** The total experience of a tour is not only visiting a destination, attraction or shopping for souvenirs at the destination. It also involves the experience of pre-travel experiences with the service provider, during the travel to the destination, the hotel room, meals, fellow travellers, shopping and so on. All these are interdependent to make the tourism product successful. Problem in any one sector affects the entire experience of the tour.

- **Risk in tourism:** Physical ailments or such risks, such as severe acute respiratory syndrome (SARS) and swine flu, can affect the tourism product. Tourist movement stops when the tourists fear physical risks to themselves. Airplane crash, rail accidents and environmental risks during tour are serious concerns. Similarly, terror threats can also affect the tourism industry. Political situations or the image of a country in the media can also affect the desirability of that destination and can affect the whole industry.

- **High ratio of fixed to variable cost:** Tourism products are characterized by the nature of their fixed and variable costs. Fixed costs are those which remain same irrespective of the level of output. Variable costs are only incurred when a unit of capacity is sold. Most tourism products are characterized by high fixed cost and low variable cost.

Some other special characteristic features of tourism products include the following:

- Tourism services are place-dependent.
- Uncertainty and unpredictability in tourism settings.
- Time-specific nature of service delivery.
- The human element of service delivery in creating the intangible experience for the tourist.

Conclusion

A more comprehensive definition would be that tourism is a service industry, comprising a number of tangible and intangible components. The tangible elements include transport systems such as rail, road, waterway and, now, airlines; hospitality services such as accommodation, food and beverages, tours and souvenirs; and related services such as banking, insurance, and safety and security. The intangible elements include rest and relaxation, culture, escape from routine, adventure, and new and different experiences. Some believe that tourism is a service industry that takes care of visitors when they are away from home. Some restrict the definition of tourism by number of miles away from home, overnight stays in paid accommodations, or travel for the purpose of pleasure or leisure. Others think that travel and tourism should not even be referred to as an industry (Lowry, 1994, pp. 28–29).

MODEL QUESTIONS

1. How do you define tourism?
2. How do you distinguish tourists, visitor and excursionist?
3. What are the different forms of tourism?
4. Why is tourism a complex activity?
5. Briefly explain the international significance of tourism.
6. Why is tourism a multidisciplinary subject? Substantiate your answer with a suitable example.
7. What do you mean by tourist typology? Explain various models of tourist typology.
8. Analyse various components of the tourism system described by Mill and Morrison.
9. How do you define tourism system? Explain various components of tourism system developed by Leiper.
10. Briefly explain various characteristics of tourism products with suitable examples.

Student Activity

1. Prepare a project report on new forms of tourism developed in your country to attract both domestic and international tourists.

Suggested Readings

Andreck, L. K., & Vogt, A. C. (2000). The relationship between resident's attitude towards tourism and tourism development options. *Journal of Travel Research, 39,* 27–36.

Bansal, S. P, Sushma, S. K., & Mohan, C. (2002). *Tourism in new millennium.* Chandigarh: Abhishek Publications.

Batra, G. S., & Chawla, A. S. (1995). *Tourism management: A global prospective.* New Delhi: Deep & Deep Publications.

Brukart, A. J., & Medlik, S. (1981). *Tourism: Past, present and future.* London ELBS: Heinemann Professional Publishing.

Chadwick, R. (1994). Concepts, definitions and measurement used in travel and tourism research. In J. R. Brent Ritchie & C. Goeldner (Eds.), *Travel, tourism and hospitality research: A handbook for managers and researchers* (2nd ed.). New York, NY: Wiley.

Chawla, R. (2004). *Heritage tourism and development.* New Delhi: Sonali Publication.

Cohen, E. (2003). Contemporary tourism and host community in the less developed areas. *Tourism Recreation and Research, 28*(1), 1–9.Cooper, C., & Wanhill, S. (1997). *Tourism developments—environmental and community issues.* Sussex: John Wiley & Sons.

Cooper, C., Fletcher, J., Fyall, A., Gilbert, D., Wanhill, S., & Shepherd, R. (1998). *Tourism: Principles and practices* (2nd ed.). London: Pitman.

D' Amore, L.J., & Jafari, J. (1988). *Tourism: A vital force for peace.* Madison: The University of Wisconsin.

Dann, G. (1988), Tourism, Peace, and classical disruption. In *Tourism: Vital force for peace.* Montreal: L. J D'Amore and Associate Ltd.

Davidson, Rob. (2005). *Tourism.* London: Pitman Publishing House.

Gartner, C. W. (1996). *Tourism development: Principles, processes and policies.* New York, NY: Van Nostrand Reinhold.

Gee, C. Y. (1988). *Resort development and management.* East Lansing, MI: American Hotel & Motel Association Educational Institute.

Gee, C. Y. (1994). *Sustainable tourism development: A strategic issue for the Asia Pacific region.* Paper presented before the Commission for Asia and the Pacific of the World Tourism Organization, Kuala Lumpur.

Gee, C. Y., Makens, J. C., & Choy, D. J. L. (1997). *The travel industry.* New York, NY: Van Nostrand Reinhold (a division of International Thomson Publishing).

George, B. P. (2005). Measuring tourist attachment to holidays: Some preliminary results. *Tourism, 52*(3), 229–246.

Goeldner, C. R., & Ritchie, J. R. B. (2009). *Tourism: Principles, practices, philosophies.* Hoboken, NJ: John Wiley & Sons.

Goeldner, C. R., Ritchie, J. R. B., & McIntosh, R. W. (2000). *Tourism: Principles, practices and philosophies.* New York, NY: John Wiley & Sons.

Gray, H. P. (1982). The economics of international tourism. *Annals of Tourism Research, 9*(1), 1–125, (special Issue).

Gunn, C. (1972). *Tourism planning.* New York: Taylor and Francis.

Hall, C. M., & Cooper, C. (2008). *Contemporary tourism: An international approach.* London: Good Fellow Publishers.

Hall, C. M., & Page, S. J. (2006). *The geography of tourism and recreation* (3rd ed.). London: Routledge.

Hernandez, A. S., Cohen, J., & Garcia, H. L. (1996). Resident attitudes towards an instant resort enclave. *Annals of Tourism Research, 23*(4), 755–779.

Holden, A. (2008). *Environment and tourism* (2nd ed.). London: Routledge.

Inskeep, E. (1991). *Tourism planning—an integrated and sustainable development approach.* New York, NY: Van Nostrand Reinhold.

Lane, B. (1994). Sustaining host areas, holiday makers and operators alike. In *Proceeding of the Sustainable Tourism Development Conference*, Queen Margaret College, Edinburgh.

Leiper, N. (1979). *Tourism management.* French Forest, NSW: Pearson.

Likorish, L. J., & Kershaw, A. G. (1958). *The travel trade.* London: Practical Press.

Lowry, L. L. (1994). What is travel and tourism and is there a difference between them: A continuing discussion. *New England Journal of Travel and Tourism,* 28–29.

Lumsdon, L. (1997). *Tourism marketing.* London: Thomson Learning.

Maslow, A. H. (1954). *Motivation and personality.* New York, NY: Harper and Row.

Mathieson, A., & Wall, G. (2006). *Tourism: Economic, physical and social impact* (Reprint). UK: Longman.

Matley, I. M. (1976). *The geography of international tourism.* Washington: Commissioned on College Geography.

McIntosh, R.W. (1986). *Tourism: Principles, practices and philosophies.* Columbus, Ohio: Grid Inc.

McIntosh, Robert W., & Charles, R. Goeldner. (1984). *Tourism: Principles, practices and philosophies.* New York: Willy.

Medlik, S. (1991). *Managing tourism.* Oxford: Butterworth–Heinemann.

Medlik, S., & Middleton, V. C. T. (1973). The tourism product and its marketing implications. *International Tourism Quarterly, 3*, 28–35.

Motiram. (2003). *International tourism—socio-economic prospective.* New Delhi: Sonali Publications.

Negi, J. (1990). *Socio-economic and eco-environmental impact of tourism in the developing countries.* New Delhi: Geetanjali Publishers.

Page, J. S., & Connell, J. (2009). *Tourism: A modern synthesis* (3rd ed.). Hampshire: South-Western Cengage Learning.

Page, S. J. (2005). *Tourism management, managing for change.* Oxford, UK: Elsevier Ltd.

Plog, S. (1974). A carpenter's tools: An answer to Stephen LJ Smith's review of psycho centrism/allocentrism. *Journal of Travel Research, 28*(4), 43–45.

Plog, S. C. (1990). A carpenter's tools: An answer to Stephen L. J. Smith's review of psycho centrism/allocentrism. *Journal of Travel Research, 28*(4), 43–45.

Plumb, J. H. (1959). The grand tour. *Horizon, 2*(2), 73–105.

Pruthi, R. K. (2004). *International tourism—potential measurement and prospects.* New Delhi: Rajat Publications.

Ranga, M., & Chandra, A. (2003). *Tourism and hospitality industry in 21st century.* New Delhi: Discovery Publishing House.

Roday, S., Biwal, A., & Joshi, V. (2009). *Tourism operation and management.* New Delhi: Oxford University Press.

Ryan, C., & Page, S. J. (Eds). (2000). *Tourism management: Towards new millennium.* Oxford: Pergamon.

Sharma, K. K. (1991). *Tourism in India.* New Delhi: Classic Publishing House.

Sharma, P. S. (2004). *Tourism education—theories and practices.* New Delhi: Kanishka Publications.

Sinclair, T. M., & Stabler, M. (1997). *The economics of tourism.* London & New York, NY: Routledge.

Smith, D. M., & Krannich, S. R. (1998). Tourism dependence and residents attitude. *Annals of Tourism Research, 25*(4), 783–802.

Smith, S.J.L. (1989). The measurement of global tourism: Old debates, new consensus and continuing challenges. In A. Lew, C.M Hall and A. William (eds), *A companion to tourism.* Oxford: Blackwell.

Swarbrooke, J., & Horner, S. (2001). *Business travel and tourism.* Oxford: Butterworth–Heinemann.

Taylor, F. F. (1988). The ordeal of the infant hotel industry in Jamaica. *The journal of Imperial and Commonwealth History, 16* (2), 201–217.

Theobald, F. W. (1994). *Global tourism.* Oxford: Butterworth–Heinemann.

——. (1991). *Global tourism, ETD* (p. 15). London: Butterworth and Heinemann (Reprint).

——. (2005). *Global tourism,* ETD. London: Butterworth and Heinemann (Reprint).

Tourism Bill of Right and Tourist Code A/6/11(a), adopted by the Sixth General Assembly, September 17–26, 1985, Sofia, Bulgaria: World Tourism Organization.

Tribe, J. (1995). *The economics of leisure and tourism.* Oxford: Butterworth–Heinemann.

Tribe, J., Font, X., Griffith, N., Vickery, R., & Yale, K. (2000). *Environmental management for rural tourism and recreation.* London: Cassel Publication.

United Nations World Tourism Organisation. (1995). *Concepts, definitions and classifications for tourism statistics.* Madid: UNWTO.

Urry, J. (1990). *The tourist gaze: Leisure and travel in contemporary societies.* London: SAGE Publications.

Vellas, F., & Becheral, L. (1995). *International tourism.* London: Macmillan Press.

William, A. V., & Zelinsky, W. (1970). Some pattern of international tourist flow. *Economic Geography, 46*(4), 549–567.

Williams, S. (1998). *Tourism geography.* London: Routledge.

World Tourism Organization. (1983). *Definition concerning tourism statistics.* Madrid: World Tourism Organization.

Suggested Websites

- United Nations World Tourism Organization: www.world-tourism.org
- World Travel and Tourism Council: www.wttc.org

Historical Development of Tourism

LEARNING OBJECTIVES

After studying this chapter, the reader will be able to understand the following:

☐ The historical development of tourism through the ages
☐ The impact of Industrial Revolution on tourism
☐ The growth and development of tourism during the Thomas Cook era
☐ Development of tourism during the 20th and 21st centuries
☐ The global aspects of tourism

The readers will also be able to define and understand the following terms after going through this chapter:

☐ The Renaissance
☐ Grand Tour
☐ Roaring Twenties

CHAPTER OVERVIEW

Chapter 2 deals with the historical development of tourism in different periods of human civilization, starting from the prehistoric era through the Middle Ages, Renaissance, Grand Tour, Industrial Revolution, era of Thomas Cook and travel during the world wars to travel in the 21st century. This chapter also discusses global significance of tourism and the factors influencing the growth of travel in the international scenario in general, and India in particular.

2.1. Introduction

The word 'travel' comes from the French word *travail*, which means work. Human beings have always travelled in search of food, cloth, territorial expansion and so on. The earliest mode of travel was by foot, but later on different animals were used for transportation. Later on waterways and seaways were also used for travel, mainly for trade and commerce. Travel in those early days was time-consuming and risky.

To understand the history of tourism, two underlying things are important: continuity and change. On one hand, continuity means that tourism has continued to be an important process and influential in the leisure lifestyle of certain social classes. On the other hand, change can be characterized as the evaluation of tourism through the ages. Much of the change is based upon the interaction between the demand for and supply of tourism opportunity through the ages. The discovery and development of many destinations also exhibit elements of continuity and change through time.

2.2. Tourism through the Ages

Travel in Prehistoric Period (40000 BC–10000 BC)

The prehistoric era is one of the longest in terms of the existence of human beings on Earth. Modern man knows little about the period as there is no written record of this period. This period is referred to as prehistory because of lack of written materials. The prehistoric period extends from 40000 BC to 10000 BC. Travel (migration) can be traced back to 40000 BC when Cro-Magnon man moved westward into Europe, as per the earliest archaeological records. Very little is known about why early people travelled because there is no written record. We can assume that the travel was undertaken for survival purpose. It may be for a combination of reasons such as escape from more powerful tribes and search for food.

Early Civilization (10000 BC–500 BC)

Around 10000 BC, human beings began to change their way of life as per some archaeological evidence. This period belonged to the Neolithic man. During this period, man's survival was determined by the occurrence of natural events such as drought, famine and other natural catastrophes. The earliest evidence of domestication of animals is found from this period. Another significant event that occurred in this period was farming. Agriculture was first developed in the Middle East (Mesopotamia, between the Tigris and Euphrates rivers) around 8000 BC. During 5000 BC Sumerians were settled in this area. They are credited with farming and urban life. Sumerian civilization created the cities with a water transportation system that was mainly developed for urban people and also used for irrigation by farmers. The Sumerians also invented money to purchase goods produced by craftsmen. The first known writing on clay tablet is of Sumerian origin dating back to 3100 BC. The wheel was also invented by the Sumerians during 3500–3000 BC. During that period, civilizations also developed in other parts of the world, mostly in India, China and Egypt.

During this time, the Roman empire was beginning to expand from the capital city of Rome, which was founded in 700 BC. Later on, in 508 BC, the Greek civilization was formed, which has been credited with the world's first democracy.

During this period, human civilization created one of the most important requirements for travel. A large number of people decided to settle together in a particular area. Thus, the concept of tourism was developed due to the movement of people away from and return to their homes. Experiencing cultural diversities was a major outcome of travel.

Evolution of Travel (500 BC–500 AD)

Organized travel in the West was started during this period, which was ruled by great empires such as Persians, Greeks, Egyptians and Romans. During this period travel developed mainly for trade, military and government reasons. Travel was also made for the artisans and architects to design and construct the great palaces and tombs which are now still regarded as some of the tourist destinations. Travel led to construct infrastructure of roads, canals, sentinel posts and so on. Ancient Greek people travelled to the Olympic Games which was considered to be the largest event during that period which required accommodation and food services for both the participants as well as audiences. The construction of the Great Wall of China during 214 BC was mainly for defensive structure and to keep invaders out.

The ancient empires became large and difficult to manage. Because of that they crumbled. The established political and economic structures were destroyed and travel became unsafe because there were no soldiers to protect travellers. Roads, communication systems and inns were not maintained properly. As a result travel diminished.

Travel during the Middle Ages (500 AD –1400 AD)

During this period trade declined as people returned to the land, and as a result many of the middle class people disappeared. At the same time the Western civilization entered into a period of decline which is referred to as the Dark Age.

Travel occurred during this period was mainly for trade and pilgrimage; sea and river travel were the most preferred options for travel. Caravan of traders were formed for protection and travel was mainly a day-time activity. Trade fairs were established at major junctions. Inns and other hospitality services were offered at those places.

Church and monasteries acquired wealth, and monks educated the people about miracles and other holy matters and encouraged them to go on pilgrimage. During the 14th century, pilgrimages were the organized mass phenomena served by the charitable networks. In the later period Christian crusades freed the Holy Land and peaceful pilgrimage began by Muslims to Mecca and Christians to Jerusalem and Rome. During the later phase of this period, travel books were written by some eminent authors including Sir John Mandeville's *Travels* printed in 1357.

In the later part of the 13th century, Marco Polo of Venice explored the land routes from Europe to China and other parts of Asia. Probably the first-ever package tour was conducted from Venice to the Holy Land.

Travel during Renaissance (1400 AD–1500 AD)

The Renaissance originated in Italy in 1350 and reached England during the Elizabethan times, and spread then throughout Europe. Francis Bacon described the Elizabethan travellers as merchant of light. The Renaissance or rebirth introduced the view that truth lay outside the mind and spirit. So it created a desire to explore, discover and encourage historic and scientific investigation. During this period, pilgrims were guided by the church, and universities also started giving fellowships.

The Renaissance or rebirth was a period of change and divergent thinking. Independent of Church doctrine, new ideas were the product of the printing press which brought to the period of philosophical change. Because of the reformation movement, the church was substantial power but continued to be a patron of the arts and sponsored famous Italian artists such as Leonardo da

Vinci, Michelangelo and Raphael during the 1500 AD. Their famous works of art were a great inspiration for the Grand Tour. The artistic accomplishments of that period still continue to attract a large number of tourists to these places.

The Grand Tour (1600 AD–1750 AD)

The origin of the modern tourism industry is believed to have begun with the Grand Tour. Many major cities of Europe such as Rome, Milan and Paris had developed superior hotels to serve their guests who wanted to undertake the Grand Tour. During the 18th century, a form of tourism based on social and cultural experiences, and education for young aristocrats became popular which was known as the Grand Tour. The Grand Tour was mainly English in origin, though the historical evidence shows that several nationalities undertook grand tours including the British, French, Germans and Russians. Sometimes it could last for as long as three years and it was available only to the aristocrats. The main objective of the grand tourist was to visit the best places with better facilities. The Grand Tour was an important part of the training of future administrators and political leaders. They normally undertook the Grand Tour to gain knowledge of different languages, cultures and so on. The main purpose was exposure to the cultural attractions of the European main land. The primary reasons for travel during the Middle Ages were trade and pilgrimage. The focus now shifted to attaining cultural enrichment. In the Grand Tour, the participants were accompanied by a guardian mentor and they were expected to observe the arts, literature, music, science and other cultural refinements of Europe along with an increased ability to utilize the knowledge gained in their travel while returning home. England was growing steadily in terms of economic development and rich culture; as a result, the Grand tour was become more popular.

In Italy the Grand Tour started in Turin. From there the tourists went to Milan, Venice, Naples, Florence and finally Rome. In Rome, facilities for English tourists were created with English-style inns, restaurants and coffee houses. In 1778, the first travel guide book for the travellers of the Grand Tour was published. The name of the book was *The Grand Tour* by Thomas Nugent. The Grand Tour produced a real revolution in British taste including Renaissance architecture and inspired many noble houses such as Burlington House and Blenheim Palace.

In 1789, *The Ground Tour* was severely disrupted by the French revolution, and later the Napoleonic war of the early 1800 AD effectively ended the Grand Tour for the English elite.

The Age of Industrial Revolution (1750 AD–1850 AD)

The Industrial Revolution started in Britain in the mid-1700 AD, and accelerated and spread throughout the world. The shift from hand to machine resulted in labour-free time for the people. This created the base for mass tourism. This period brought economic and social changes, and many workers changed their occupation from agriculture to factory work, and urban life compelled them to travel on a mass basis.

The Industrial Revolution introduced the steam engine, machinery especially the new kind of technology to run vehicles including trains and ships. All of these developments required scientific learning and these new occupations led to the rapid expansion of the middle class' education and wealth. This resulted in increase in leisure time and demand for recreational travel activities for middle class people which also led to the decline of the elite class' Grand Tour (Figure 2.1).

The first locomotive steam engine was used in Britain in 1813. In 1835 enough refinement had been made to build the first passenger railway. By 1835 the use of locomotive steam engine spread

Figure 2.1   Cities Usually Travelled as a Part of the Grand Tour

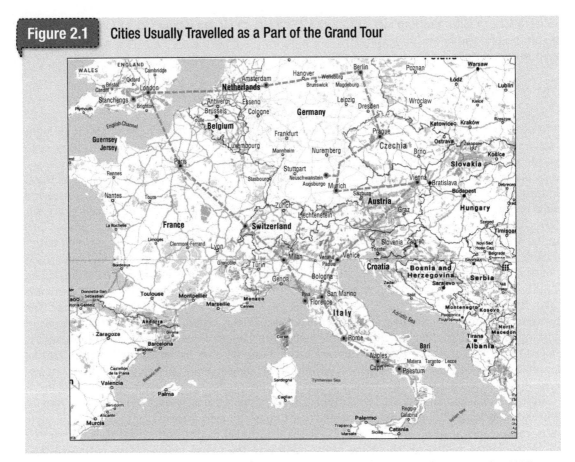

Source: http://www.texaschapbookpress.com/magellanslog15/grandtourmap.htm (accessed on 4 December 2018).
Disclaimer: The above image is for representation purpose only.

throughout Europe and America. Initially rail travel was undertaken for pleasurable purposes, especially to visit family and sea coast, and not for leisure travel. In 1840, Thomas Cook, while walking down a rail line to a temperance meeting decided to use convenient and affordable rail travel to increase attendance at the meetings. In this way the experience gained from using rail transportation led to the development of a large-scale travel agency.

Initially recreational trips were only for day trips as many people still had only limited discretionary income and weekends off. Later on, workers began to take annual vacations to escape from the rapidly growing urban life. During this period the major destinations were spas and seaside resorts.

The Era of Thomas Cook (1843–1900)

Tourism also greatly benefitted from the steam engines which lead to rail travel as well as travel by steamboats and ships. Railways first started carrying passengers in 1830 in England, between Liverpool and Manchester. This was the mode of travel that led to the first organized tour in the tourism industry. The credit for the first organized tour goes to Mr Thomas Cook. He organized an excursion trip from Leicester to Loughborough, England, on 5 July 1841 with 570 passengers, where each passenger paid a shilling each for the excursion tour. The group travelled on the chartered train, complete with picnic lunch and brass band. The tour was so popular that Thomas Cook took up arranging for travel services, and in 1843 nearly 3,000 students took a trip from Leicester to Derby. Cook conducted circulars tours to Scotland between 1848 and 1863 and approximately 5,000 tourists undertook these tours in one season. Thomas Cook is also credited with coming up with the first hotel voucher in 1867 and adding the foreign currency exchange to the travel business. It is no wonder that sometimes Thomas Cook has been referred to as the father of tourism industry.

Thomas Cook

Source: http://ilovetravel.ro/en/thomas-cook-si-povestea-primei-agentii-de-voiaj-din-lume/

Tourism in the 20th Century (1900–1939)

Tourism in Modern Times

It is impossible to pin point the date when modern tourism began; rather it evolved through time building on the needs and desires of society, and the opportunities that were available. However, the authors feel that the modern tourism came into being in the 20th century.

The development of tourism in the early 20th century displayed impact on economic, social and political environment. Technological advancement, economic affluence and holiday entitlement were the positive factors for tourism development during this period.Travel was expanding in the early 20th century mainly due to growing affluence and transport system. Holiday brochures were mainly developed with special emphasis on different destinations and modes of transportation.

War has an adverse effect on nations, in many ways. This happened during the First World War (1914–1918) and the Second World War (1939–1945).

First World War (1914–1918)

The Industrial Revolution had made it possible to establish effective military powers for the destruction of human life and property. As a result of the war, huge amount of resources were used to produce military hardware. Advancement of research and development led to the development of radio communication, air and ground transportation. Those resources were later on used for the development of tourism.

Just after the war was over, the historical development of tourism was directly affected by economic austerity, unemployment and financial hardship. Later on there was prosperity in some parts of Europe and United States of America, and that period was commonly referred to as Roaring Twenties. Development in transport, increased leisure time and paid holidays inspired many people to travel. In many countries the geographical extent of domestic tourism was extended as per the availability of transport infrastructure. Wealth generated through the technological advancement made during the First World War fuelled an increase in pleasure travel. There were advances in automobile transportations, small-scale lodging properties, camping and resort development in the coastal mountain and lake areas especially in United States of America and Europe.

Great Depression

The aforementioned Roaring Twenties came to an abrupt halt due to the collapse of world financial market in New York in 1930. There was fluctuating prosperity, depression and recovery. The Wall Street crashed and international tourism slowed down during 1929–1934. Tourism business specially related with high-rolling tourists and upscale hotels disappeared. During that period there was a mass migration of people from one region of the country to another in search of employment. As a result of that migration, people left their family and friends behind, which led to future travel to renew interpersonal relationships—which is popularly known as visiting friends and relatives (VFR).

Second World War (1939–1945)

Just after the Great Depression of the 1930s, the Second World War (1939–1945) began when Germany invaded Poland in 1939 and ended with the surrender of Japan in 1945. During the 6 year period of the Second World War, technology was accelerated rapidly and was never as noticeable as when the nuclear bomb was dropped at Hiroshima and Nagasaki in 1945. The great economic depression ended throughout the western world as industry expanded to produce weapons of war.

After 1945 the war-time industry was converted to produce consumer goods such as automobiles, interstate highway systems and air transportation. The wealth created through the production of consumer goods resulted into a growing middle-class population. The advancement of the labour unions occurred during that period. All these factors were responsible for the growth in the number of tourists.

Tourism during Post-World War Period (1945–1970)

In many western countries, including the United States of America, there was a rapid growth in tourism after the Second World War. During that period air transportation flourished. Many of the surplus military aircrafts were converted to passenger aircrafts after the world war. After 1950, jet airliners were introduced. The use of jet engines reduced travel time considerably and the use of larger aircrafts reduced the relative price for air transportation. Long-distance flight, sleeping berths, flight attendance, and in-flight meals were also offered. Due to the introduction of new jet airliners, older aircrafts became available for charter holiday companies to operate services in holiday destinations.

There was a substantial rise in international tourist movement during the 1960s, particularly in Britain and Spain. By 1965, Spain had become Europe's leading tourist destination with 14 million visitors annually. Its tourist inflows increased from 6 per cent to 30 per cent from 1951 to 1968.

During this period radio and television were major forms of leisure entertainment. Therefore, advertisements in television and radio channels were gradually introduced by the tour operators to promote overseas and domestic tourism. The concept of holiday camp flourished in that period. It may be noted that the entrepreneur Billy Butlin is often credited with the concept and development of holiday camps after developing amusement parks in the United Kingdom during 1925–1927.

In 1957, the Soviet Union sent the satellite 'Sputnik' into orbit. Yuri Gagarin became the first citizen of the world to enter space in 1961. The space race started. By the time man reached the moon in 1969, space was crowded with satellites and debris of space flights. The space race resulted in technological advancement which resulted in support to global communication system. Because of that almost every part of the world was in contact with each other. Today's tourism industry has been made possible by the advancement in telecommunication from airlines reservation system to international weather report, cable television programme and so on.

Tourism during 1970–1999

Although tourism flourished during the 1960s, the beginning of the 1970s experienced a slowdown due to the Arab–Israeli War followed by the oil crisis and the oil embargo of 1973, which caused an increase in fuel prices and drop in package holidays. This led to a massive reduction in tourist inflow. Except this, in the 1970s, the 1980s and the 1990s there was an increase in tourism products, experiences and growing global reach for travel.

This era experienced changes in demand for domestic and international travel, particularly business travel, VFR and for new travel experiences. Due to the improvement of transportation especially the introduction of jumbo jets and the rise of high speed trains, the world became a global village. Some of the significant developments that occurred during that period which led to the change in both demand and supply of tourism are as follows:

- **Changes in technology:** Development of transport was highly influenced by the improvement in technology. It was more significant particularly in the airlines industry. Due to that advancement, more people were able to travel more frequently, cheaply, easily and cover greater distances within a short span of time. Technological breakthrough in air transportation industry led to the introduction of bigger aircrafts such as Boeing 747 and DC–10 on a global scale. Towards the end of the 20th century interest in rail travel regained with the introduction of high-speed train networks connecting major urban cities. Those networks also gave tough competition to the airlines. Some of the examples are Shinkansen or bullet train in Japan, Train à Grande Vitesse (TGV) in France, Intercity-Express (ICE) in Germany, Pendolino trains in Italy, Alta Velocidad Española (AVE) in Spain and Amtrak in the United States of America. Apart from that some advancement in technology was also seen in the field of tunnel transport system both under sea and mountains.
- **Rise in consumer spending:** Since 1970, there has been an extensive growth noticed in affluence of many people. As a result there was a substantial increase in consumers' disposable income. Other exogenous factors affecting society also influence the tourism industry. Those exogenous factors include:
  - Increase in life expectancy
  - Retirement at a younger age
  - And the elderly as a single groups

  Early retirement and financial affluence is often synonymous with a higher propensity to travel. All the aforementioned factors were responsible for the growth and volume of tourism both in domestic and international tourism.
- **Change in legal environment:** During that period political reorganization of tourism was a significant part for many developed nations' economy. In many countries, within a legislative structure, the government policy for tourism was set out. In Europe, during the 1980s legislation for the tourism industry was one of the most important features for development. That legislation had affected the private sector. For example, from 1970, tour

operators have required to have an Air Travel Organizers License (ATOL). The legislation also had introduced measures to liberalize air and road transport, relaxing of frontier controls, duty-free regulations and harmonization of hotel classifications to remove the barriers in tourism.

- **Increasing recognition of political and economic impacts of tourism:** Certain events that affected the tourism industry occurred due to the combination of both political and economic factors. Variations in the economy have a direct impact on tourism demand, as tourism is demand inelastic. The factors that impact tourism demand are unemployment, high interest rates and high levels of inflation. Economic uncertainty occurred mainly due to the high interest rates and fear of redundancy may have caused many tourists to abandon plans for expensive tours. Politics can also influence the tourism industry in many ways. Disputes can seriously impede travel.
- **Changes in types of products:** The period from 1970 to 1999 was considered as a growth in tourism destination and activity. Due to the new technological advancement especially in airlines, there was greater accessibility to a wide variety of destinations to a greater number of people. Many domestic resorts declined due to their lack of cost competitiveness and attraction compared to cheap overseas holiday destinations. In the later period, niche products emerged and developed including eco-tourism, adventure tourism, heritage tourism, film tourism and so on. Differentiation of products and segmentation of the tourist market has resulted in a huge variety of tourism forms. That period also experienced the formation of powerful tour operators and travel agents to shape the tourism industry.
- **Greater internationalization and globalization of tourism:** Globalization of tourism flourished during this period mainly due to declining relative costs of travel, increased consumerism in tourism and constant innovation in tourism products. Tourists became more adventurous with long-haul travel to different parts of the globe. Places such as Asia Pacific, Australia, North America and Europe have gained a prominent position in respect to long-haul travel. Wide geographic range of destinations emerged in this period including areas which offered diverse products, such as Africa, East Asia and Pacific, and Antarctica.

Tourism in the 21st Century

Tourism enterprises and destinations must respond effectively to contemporary forces that shape the economy and environment for successful tourism. These contemporary forces include: globalization, sustainability and developments in information and communication technology (ICT). We can refer to these factors as the three pillars of tourism in the 21st century.

Globalization

In simple terms, globalization means crossing the borders. It is about increasing mobility across frontiers in terms of people, goods and commodities, products and services, and information and communication. According to Wahab and Cooper (2001), 'Globalization is an all-encompassing term that denotes a world which due to many politico-economic, technological and informational advancements and developments is on its way to becoming borderless and an interdependent whole'.

The process of globalization is facilitated by a number of trends including increased market liberalization and trade, foreign investment, privatization, financial deregulation, rapid technological change, automation, changes in transportation and communications, standardization, immigration and so on. In the 21st century globalization has increased rapidly due to new technology such as jet planes and Internet which have led to global economic, politics and communications. Nowadays any occurrence anywhere in the world has an impact somewhere else.

Globalization and Tourism

Tourism can be seen as part of the process of globalization. According to Hoogvelt (2001), there are three key features to economic globalization which are evident in tourism:

1. There is a global market discipline in terms of global competition, individuals, groups and national government which have to compete with international standards for price and quality.
2. Flexible accommodation through global website: Companies are organizing through global webs or networks where tourism services are often managed electronically.
3. Financial deepening: Money is quickly moved across borders and profits are being made out of the circulation of money.

Tourism is a sector with globalized supply and demand. It is also a social phenomenon that can influence communities around the world. Many tourism suppliers such as hotel chains and tour operators have expanded across the borders which give confidence that the level of service and comfort will be the same across the globe.

Globalization also has resulted in a growth in international tourism demand. According to Macleod (2004), visitors have an increasing number of destinations to choose from—they can find out about them via 'a globalized world of communications and advertising'. Globalized tourism also has far-reaching economic, socio-cultural and environmental impacts on host communities.

The following factors are significant to understand the globalization of tourism in the 21st century.

- The developments of new forms of holiday accommodations such as the change from holiday camps to timeshare, self-catering and second homes, and hotels to home stay.
- The developments of new forms of tourism such as the change from mass tourism to alternative tourism, eco-tourism to sustainable tourism, urban tourism to rural tourism, and cultural tourism to ethnic tourism.
- Innovations by tour operator including the rise of the tour brochures, new forms of retailing such as direct selling, selling via Internet, evolution of single window retailing, and more competitive pricing including credit payments and making payments in instalments.
- Greater availability of information on destinations from the media, Internet, travel talks, travel shows, travel channels, guide books and so on.
- Growing consumer protection to ensure greater regulations.
- Developments of travel blocks and forums such as SAARC—such as the Association of Southeast Asian Nations (ASEAN), Pacific Tourism Commission and European Union Tourism, and SAARC Chamber of Commerce and Industry.
- Reducing frontier formalities such as visa on arrivals and Shenzhen visa.

Sustainability

The term 'sustainability' is mainly used to bridge the gap between developments. It also integrates environmental considerations into economic policy.

The concept of sustainable development first commenced in 1987 when Gro Harlem Brundtland, the then Norwegian prime minister, published a report in a convention organized by United Nations World Commission on Environment and Development, popularly known as **Brundtland report**. According to this report, sustainable development is the development that meets the need of the present without compromising the ability of future generation to meet their needs.

Further, the concept of sustainable development was discussed by United Nations Conference on Environment and Development, also known as the 'Earth Summit', in Rio de Janeiro in 1992 where **Agenda 21** was produced.

The concept of sustainable development again got its importance in 1997 when a United Nations Treaty was signed by more than 140 countries of the world popularly known as **Kyoto protocol.** This protocol concentrates mainly on the relationship between sustainability and climate change exclusively on reducing greenhouse gas emission.

Aspects of Sustainability

According to Rogers et al. (2008), sustainability has the following three aspects:

1. **Economic:** Maximizing income while maintaining a constant or increasing level of capital.
2. **Socio-cultural:** Maintaining and maximizing the robustness and resilience of social system and culture.
3. **Environmental/ecological:** Maintaining and maximizing robustness and resilience of the natural environment.

Determinants of sustainable development   According to Rogers et al. (2008), there are three determinants of sustainable development:

1. **Consumption:** In sustainable development, the aim is not to use resources beyond the reasonable limit set by the nature through its regeneration capacity.
2. **Production:** Sustainable development recognizes the need for new production patterns that take into account not only the economic benefits of production but also the social and environmental benefits.
3. **Distribution:** Sustainable development aims to reduce poverty and inequality—the socio-economic aspects of sustainability are particularly important.

Tourism and Sustainability

Sustainable tourism is designed to minimize tourism's negative impact while optimizing benefits to the destination. According to Bramwell and Lane (1993), 'sustainable tourism is the positive approach intended to reduce tensions and friction created by the complex interaction between the tourism industry, visitors, the environment and the communities which are host to holiday makers'. In Globe '90 conference and trade fare, held on 19–23 March 1990 in Vancouver, Canada.

Following three basic principles were adopted to guide tourism planning and management for maintaining sustainability:

1. Tourism must be a recognized sustainable economic development option, considered equally with other economic activities.
2. There must be a relevant tourism information base to permit recognition, analysis and monitor the tourism industry in relation to other sectors of the economy.
3. Tourism development must be carried out in a way that is compatible with the principles of sustainable development.

The sustainable use of natural resources and the development of tourism within physical and socio-cultural capacities are at fundamental importance for the development of sustainable tourism. The term 'sustainable tourism' is sometimes used synonymously with different forms of tourism including green tourism, low impact tourism, rural tourism, eco-tourism, nature tourism, soft tourism and responsible tourism.

Information and Communication Technology

ICT is the use of computer hardware, software, telecommunication, Internet and satellite technologies for storing, processing, retrieving and transmitting information. It is used by the organization to collect and record data for processing information efficiently and accurately to communicate internally between departments, and externally with partners and existing or potential customers.

According to Buhalis (2003), 'ICT is the entire range of electronic tools that facilitate the operational and strategic management of organizations by enabling them to manage their information, functions and processes as well as to communicate interactively with their stakeholders, enabling them to achieve their mission and objectives.'

ICT speeds up internal process to allow quicker decision-making and reduces staff costs by automating some functions. In tourism the handling of huge amounts of data related with availability and reservations, price information and the production of travel documents is an extremely complex, time-consuming, labour-intensive process which is vulnerable to errors. These problems can be solved by effectively utilizing this ICT. The internet has transformed consumer's ability to access information about a product and compare prices of competitors. Social media has also revolutionized the way consumers communicate about products and organizations with the help of ICT. Websites have caused a major shift in power towards consumer. In tourism, customer's review sites are important to the tourists, who can check other tourists' opinions and experiences about the services provided by different tourism suppliers.

2.3. History of Tourism in India

History of India goes back to more than 5,000 years, making it one of the oldest civilizations of the world. India has an ancient tradition of travel and tourism; and has existed informally since ancient times and was indulged in by all classes of people. In Aitareya Brahmana of the Rigveda, written about 3,000 years ago, the prime motto was to be like the sun and keep on travelling tirelessly—travel and move on. In Sanskrit literature there are three terms for tourism derived

History of Tourism

Unconscious—uncultured—unrecorded
↓
Conscious—cultured—recorded
↓
Babylonians and Sumerians (concept developed in their minds for the construction of road and other facilities)
↓
These people travelled for the purpose of trade and commerce
↓
Market came into existence (around 4000 BC)
↓
Then Romans (Roman Empire) came. They were affluent and more cultured people.
They travelled for the following different purposes:

- Pleasure
- Spas
- Entertainments (opera/theatres)
- Sports (Olympics in 776 BC)
- Cultural exchange

Romans also pioneered in introducing coinage system. It was the universal coinage system and its modified nomenclature is neutral unit of construction (NUC) today
↓
5th Century AD: Fall of Roman Empire. Dark Age for travel.
↓
The concept of mass travel started.
The concept of mass travel was introduced in that period in the shape of religious travel.
The whole of central Europe was involved in pilgrimage activity. People moved around in search of solace. Christianity was introduced around that time.
↓
Industrialization helped in better road facilities and security facilities.
↓
Travels to the Orient, especially the Indian subcontinent, in search of wealth and moral courage.
During those days this subcontinent was very rich with

- Religion/knowledge/culture
- Education
- Science
- Wealth

Christopher Columbus discovered America due to India only.
↓
Forerunner of Passport was introduced by King Richard–II in 1388.
↓
Chinese contribution: They introduced the concept of accommodation/catering (1300–1400).
They also introduced the concept of registration of services.
↓
During the later part of 1400 AD the concept of trade fair was introduced in Europe.
↓

During that period, the concept of educational tour was introduced for learning (French).
The British Aristocrats travelled to France to learn French.
This period was termed as the Middle Age of travel.
↓
Resurgence of Roman people and they attracted people from around the world for

- Trade and commerce
- Art, culture and sculptures
- Foods

They introduced the printing of catalogue for trade fair.
↓
Industrial Revolution (Later 1700 AD to 1800 AD)
↓
The concept of package tour came.
↓
Railways: A major breakthrough in travel

- Liverpool to Manchester
- Paris to Versailles
- Nuremburg to Furth

↓
Then the father of Package Tour came: (Sir THOMAS COOK) the creation of modern age of travel.
He started the first package tour (from Leicester to Loughborough and back) to attend a rally in 1841.
The total distance was 22 miles. The package included travel + lunch + music + tea
↓
Another breakthrough (1832–1860) was the introduction of steamer hotels (Flotels).
↓
In 1889, the Americans travelled to Europe in large scales in search of wealth and because of curiosity.
↓
During the First World War all-inclusive tour started from the United States of America to Europe.
↓
Introduction of jet airliners in 1958. The concept of global village came into existence.
The globe became synchronized.
↓
Democratization of travel (poor can also think of travel).
↓
Then the modern travel flourished for various reasons such as economic, social,
environmental, education, relaxation and leisure.
↓
The concept of paid holiday starts.

from the word *atna*, which means 'going or leaving home for some other place for a short period'.
The three words are:

1. **Tirthatan** means going out to places of religious merits.
2. **Deshatan** means going out of the country, primarily for economic gains.
3. **Paryatan** means going for pleasure and knowledge.

Tirthatan, that is, pilgrimage, was and still now remains one of the major types of tourism in India. Pilgrimage is sacred to all religions in India, a country with diverse cultures and religions. Pilgrimage such as followers of Hinduism visit the *Char Dham* (four religious centres) and have a holy dip in all the sacred rivers of the country. While followers of Buddhism on the other hand visit places associated with Buddhism such as *Bodh Gaya, Sarnath* and *Kushinagar*. Followers of Sikhism visit Golden Temple of Amritsar and so on. Travel for pilgrimage was also facilitated by the kings and emperors of the time. For example, the great king Ashoka travelled a great deal to spread the doctrines of Buddha. He was the one who planted trees along the roadsides and built rest houses along the way. Emperor Harshabardhan also built many institutions, monasteries and *dharamshalas* to facilitate travel, especially for pilgrimage. Emperor Sher Shah Suri constructed many *sarais* (inn) besides Grand Trunk Road.

The *Arthashastra* also reveals the importance of travel infrastructure for the state, and the presence of well-developed mode of travel for military, commercial travellers and civilians. In ancient times, commerce and trade was another reason for travel. Silk route was one of the examples of travel for trade and commerce during that period. Account of travellers and history tells us that well-maintained road with trees planted on both sides and *dharamshalas*or rest houses along the way facilitated travel. During the rule of the Mughals, the emperors travelled extensively in the kingdom. Travel in early times was not just limited to Indians travelling abroad but it also involved visitors visiting our country due to its rich trade links as well as the stories about India's culture and riches.

Famous Travellers in India

- **Herodotus,** a Greek traveller to India, wrote *Historica* which gives a lot of information about Alexander's invasion of India.
- **Megasthenese,** the Greek ambassador to the court of *Mauryan* emperor Chandragupta Maurya, wrote an account of the life during the time of the Chandragupta Maurya.
- **Fa-hien**, a Chinese traveller to India in the 5th century AD, gave an account of the social life, Buddhism and the political events of that period.
- **Yuan Chwang,** another Chinese traveller, visited India in 7th century AD and spent 16 years in India and described religious and cultural life of that period along with the political events.
- **Hiuen Tsang** (or 'Xuangzang', as he is referred to in China), the celebrated Buddhist scholar-pilgrim from China spent 14 years of his life, from 630 to 644 AD, in India.
- **Al-Masudi,** an Arab traveller, visited India between 941 and 943 AD and wrote about the Rashtrakutas.
- **Abu Ryham** or **Alberuni** was a famous Arab traveller and a contemporary of Mahmud of Ghazani. He left a graphic, objective and unbiased description in his written work *Tahqiq–ul–Hind*.
- **Marco Polo,** a Venetian traveller, visited South India in 1294 AD and gave valuable information on the economic history of India.
- **Ibn–Battuta** from Morocco visited India between 1333 and 1342 and wrote a *Rihla*, that is, travelogue, wherein he gave a vivid account of the places in India that he had visited; he had visited length and breadth of India.

Tourism as we know today started quite late in India. The extensive railway network has helped people with time and resources to travel. Air travel was made easy by the Air Corporations Act, 1 August 1953, when the entire air transport industry in India was nationalized and subsequently, the Indian sky was opened to private players in 1993, which has helped people with means to travel in short time. The India Tourism Development Corporation (ITDC) was started to provide modern infrastructure and comfort to the guests, especially foreign tourist.

The clowning glory of India is reflected by its splendid monuments in the form of forts, havelis, palaces, temples, churches and mosques. The northern part of India is covered by the great Himalayas and Indo-Gangetic Plains. The western part is covered with The 'Thar Dessert', followed by the great Indian Peninsula and Deccan Plateau. Eastern India is bestowed with beautiful beaches of Bay of Bengal, natural scenic beauties and attractive monuments.

The Northern part of India is famous for its pleasant hills and valleys, the home of variety of wildlife, hill retreats and so on. The major hill stations of northern India include Kashmir, Dehradun, Mussoorie, Nainital, Kausani, Gangotri, Kullu, Manali, Shimla, Kangra Valley and so on. Destinations having monumental importance include Agra, Fatehpur Sikri, Delhi, Amritsar and so on. Famous pilgrimage destinations include Mathura, Vrindavan, Ayodhya, Allahabad, Varanasi, Haridwar, Rishikesh, Kedernath, and Badrinath. Buddhist destinations include Sravasti, Kushinagar, Bodhgaya, Nalanda, Rajgir, Vaishali and so on.

The Western part of India is famous for royal cities, forts and havelis, deserts, pilgrimage sites and so on. The romantic desert state of Rajasthan with its legends of chivalry and valour is one of the most exiting destinations of India. Splendid desert forts, colourful costumes and crafts, exuberant festivals, lake palaces and temples are some of the important attractions for the tourists. Some of the important tourist destinations include Jaipur, Jaisalmer, Jodhpur, Bikaner, Barmer, Udaipur, Chittorgarh, Mount Abu, Ahmedabad, Surat, Mumbai, Pune, Lonavla, Khandala and so on.

The Southern part of India is famous for ancient temples, hill stations, sea beaches, spice gardens, Ayurveda and many more. Temples of Dravidian architecture such as Mamallapuram, Thanjavur, Trichy, Rameswaram, Darasuram, Gangaikondan and Cholapuram are world famous heritage sites in Tamil Nadu. Tirupati in Andhra Pradesh is one of the richest temples in the world. Popular hill stations such as Ooty (Ootacamund) and Kodaikanal are attracting good numbers of tourists every year. Sea beaches such as Kovalam, Marina and those in Pondicherry are popular among the tourists. Spice gardens in Thekkedy, Alleppey, Munnar tea garden and so on, are also hotspots for the tourists.

The Eastern part of India is mainly constituted of the states West Bengal, Bihar, Jharkhand and Odisha. Popular hill stations such as Darjeeling, Karseong, Kalimgpong and Dooars are attracting huge numbers of tourists. World famous Sundarbans is situated in southern West Bengal. Sea beaches such as Digha, Shankarpur, Puri, Chandipur and Gopalpur are famous among the tourists. Puri is a well-known Hindu pilgrimage site and is among the four Dhams of India. Car festival of Lord Jagannath attracts millions of tourists every year. Other Hindu pilgrimage centres such as Deoghar in Jharkhand, Gaya in Bihar, Tarapith, Dakshineswar and Kalighat in West Bengal are popular destinations in this region. This region is also famous for Buddhist pilgrimage cites. Destinations such as Bodh Gaya, Vaishali, Nalanda, Rajgir, Dhauli, Ratnagiri, Lalitgiri and Udayagiri are attracting huge numbers of foreign Buddhist pilgrimage tourists.

Although international tourist arrivals are very important for any country, for India domestic tourism was and always will be the mainstay of Indian tourism. This is due to the vast population of the country and the vast expanse and tourism attractions of our country. The movement of domestic tourists is always important for a country as foreign tourist arrival may get affected by various crisis situations but domestic tourism continues even in the face of adversities. The government also encourages domestic travel by giving paid leave to its employees under a scheme known as leave travel concessions or LTC. International tourist arrivals and tourism receipts of India are also showing an appreciable increase since the last couple of decades or so. India is being promoted as a destination of choice among the international tourists and the result is finally noticeable.

Conclusion

History reveals the realities of travel and development of tourism from ancient times to the modern civilization. By studying history we can understand that how searching the basic necessities of life such as food, water, shelter and safe environment, the ancient people especially hunters from Palaeolithic era, Neolithic era to the later periods used to move from one place to another and settled there. Travel started from that time. In that period, travel was difficult and dangerous for ancient human beings. People used to travel with families or entire communities. Due to the absence of organized roads and technical modes of transportation, people used to travel by foot or by riding animals. When people developed tools, slowly they built shelters and enabled ancient people to travel to new hunting grounds. In that period, travel was mainly to fulfil primary needs. Slowly their needs were transferred from basic needs to business through silk routes, pilgrims and education. People from distant lands in large numbers started moving and visiting many places for the purpose of commerce. History revels that early travel in India and China was mainly depended on commerce and trade. This unit mainly highlights travel in various ages of human civilization from ancient period through middle ages to the modern ages. The Grand Tour, Renaissance and era of Thomas Cook also have been described here in detail. Tourism in the 21st century and history of tourism of India are also highlighted in this unit.

MODEL QUESTIONS

1. Discuss how Roman Empire affected early travel.
2. Explain the reasons for the decline in travel during the early Middle Ages.
3. Write a note on the contribution of Industrial Revolution in the development of tourism.
4. What was Renaissance? Explain its origin and its impact on tourism.
5. Describe the concept of Grand Tour.
6. Discuss the impact of the Second World War on mass tourism.
7. Explain various factors that led to the development of mass tourism worldwide.
8. Analyse the growth of historical significance of tourism in India.
9. Write in detail about the reasons for the growth of tourism in the 21st century.
10. Analyse the effect of globalization on tourism business.

Student Activities

1. Find out the Seven Wonders of the world and their importance in tourism.
2. List out different historical sites/monuments of your own state/region.

Suggested Readings

Balsdon, J. P. D. (1969). *Life and leisure in ancient Rome*. London: Bodley Head.

Banister, D. (1995). *Tourism and urban development*. London: Spon Press.

Batra, G. S., & Chawla, A. S. (1995). *Tourism management: A global prospective*. New Delhi: Deep & Deep Publication.

Bhatia, A. K. (2002). *Tourism development: Principles and practices*. New Delhi: Sterling Publications.

Brukart, A. J., & Medlik, S. (1974). *Tourism—past, present and future*. London: ELBS-Heinemann.

Burgess, A., & Frances, H. (1967). *The age of grand tour*. London: Paul Elek.

Casson, L. (1974). *Travel in the ancient world*. London: Allen & Unwin.

Chapman, K. (1979). *People, pattern and process: An introduction to human geography*. London: Edward Arnold.

Chawala, R. (2004). *Heritage tourism and development*. New Delhi: Sonali Publication.

Coltman, M. Michael (1989). *Introduction to travel and tourism: An international approach*. New York, NY: Van Nostrodam Reinhold.

Cook, A. R., Yale, J. L., & Marqua, J. J. (2012). *Tourism: The business of travel* (3rd ed.). New Delhi: Pearson.

Cooper, C., & Wanhill, S. (1997). *Tourism developments—environmental and community issues*. London: John Wiley & Sons.

Cooper, C., Fletcher, J., Fyall, A., Gilbert, D., Wanhill, S., & Shepherd, R. (1998). *Tourism: Principles and practices* (2nd ed.). London: Longman.

Douglas, N., & Douglas, N. (1996). Tourism in the pacific: Historical factors. In C. M. Hall & S. J. Page (Eds.), *Tourism in the Pacific: Issues and cases*. London: Thomson Learning.

———. (2000). Tourism in South and Southeast Asia: Historical dimensions. In C. M. Hall & S. J. Page (Eds.), *Tourism in South and Southeast Asia: Issues and cases*. Oxford: Butterworth–Heinemann.

Feifer, M. (1985). *Going places: The way of the tourists from imperial Rome to the present day*. London: Macmillan.

———. (1986). *Tourism in history: From imperial Rome to the present*. New York, NY: Stein and Day.

Gartner, C. W. (1996). *Tourism development: Principles, processes and policies*. New York, NY: Van Nostrand Reinhold.

Gee, C. Y. (1994). *Sustainable tourism development: A strategic issue for the Asia Pacific region*. Presented before the Commission for East Asia and the Pacific of the World Tourism Organization, Kuala Lumpur.

Gee, C. Y., Makens, J. C., & Choy, D. J. L. (1997). *The travel industry*. New York, NY: Van Nostrand Reinhold (a division of International Thomson Publishing).

George, B. P. (2005). Measuring tourist attachment to holidays: Some preliminary results. *Tourism, 52*(3), 229–246.

Goeldner, C. R., Ritchie, J. R. B., & McIntosh, R. W. (2000). *Tourism: Principles, practices and philosophies*. New York, NY: John Wiley & Sons.

Hall, C. M., & Page, S. J. (2002). *The geography of tourism and recreation: Environment, place and space* (2nd ed.). London: Routledge.

Hibbert, C. (1974). *The grand tour*. London: Spring Books.

Hoogvelt, A. (2001). *Globalization and the postcolonial world* (2nd ed.). Basingstoke: Palgrave.

Hunt, J. D., & Layne, D. (1991). The evolution of travel and tourism terminology and definitions. *Journal of Travel Research, 29*(4), 7–11.

Lickorish, L. J., & Jenkins, C. L. (Eds.). (1997). *An introduction to tourism*. Oxford: Butterworth–Heinemann.

Medlik, S. (1991). *Managing tourism*. Oxford: Butterworth–Heinemann.

Meethan, K. (2001). *Tourism in global society: Place, culture, consumption*. Basingstoke: Palgrave.

Murphy, P. E. (1985). *Tourism—a community approach*. New York, NY: Methuen.

Nash, D. (1979). The rise and fall of an aristocrat tourist culture: Nice, 1763–1936. *Annals of Tourism Research, 6*(1), 61–76.

Norval, A. (1936). *The tourism industry: A national and international survey*. London: Pitman.

Plumb, J. H. (1959). The grand tour. *Horizon, 2*(2), 73–104.

Roday, S., Biswal, A., & Joshi, V. (2009). *Tourism operation and management*. New Delhi: Oxford University Press.

Rugof, M. (1960). *The great travelers*. New York, NY: Simon and Schuster.

Ryan, C., & Page, S. J. (Eds.). (2000). *Tourism management: Towards new millennium*. Oxford: Pergamon.

Sharma, P. S. (2004). *Tourism education—theories and practices*. New Delhi: Kanishka Publications.

Smith, S. J. L. (2007). The measurement of global tourism: Old debates, new consensus and continuing challenges. In A. Lew, C. M. Hall & A. William (Eds.), *A companion to tourism*. Oxford: Blackwell.

Stephen, L., & Smith, J. (1995). *Tourism analysis: A handbook* (2nd ed.). Harlow: Longman Book.

Theobald, F. W. (1994). *Global tourism*. Oxford: Butterworth–Heinemann.

Towner, J. (1985). The grand tour: A key phase in the history of tourism. *Annals of Tourism Research, 12*(3), 297–334.

Twain, M. (1869). *The innocents abroad*. New York, NY: Harper.

Vellas, F., & Becheral, L. (1995). *International tourism*. London: Macmillan Press.

Wahab, S., & Pigram, J. J. (Eds.). (1997). *Tourism development and growth: The challenges of sustainability*. London: Routledge.

Suggested Websites

United Nations World Tourism Organization: www.world-tourism.org
World Travel and Tourism Council: www.wttc.org
http://www.texaschapbookpress.com/magellanslog15/grandtourmap.htm
World Travel and Tourism Council Report: www.wttc.com

3 Tourism Motivation

After going through this chapter, the reader will be able to understand the following:

☐ **Interrelation between tourism and motivation**
☐ **Importance of tourist motivation**
☐ **Different types of tourist motivation**
☐ **Factors influencing tourist motivation**
☐ **Various models of tourist motivation**
☐ **Travel flow pattern**

CHAPTER OVERVIEW

Chapter 3 mainly deals with understanding tourist motivation and its important propositions. Different aspects of tourist motivations including their importance, types and interrelationship are discussed in this chapter. Motivations related to destination and not related to destination are discussed here. This chapter also discusses intrinsic and extrinsic motivations including factors influencing tourist motivations. Different motivational theories which are relevant to the tourism business are also discussed chronologically in detail.

3.1. Introduction

The movement and the concentration of people—as tourists—at preferred destinations is not an accidental process, but is shaped by individual or collective motives and related expectations. A motive can be defined as a person's basic predisposition to reach for and to strive towards a general class of goals. Motives may change with time. The underlying motive for many of the tourist activities is escape—sometimes physical and sometimes mental. However, tourists can have multiple motives for travel. A motive can be specific or general. A general motive would be the end objective, and a specific motive would be a means to reach that end objective. Motivation occurs when an individual wants to satisfy a need. A motive implies action, that is, an individual is moved to do something. People are motivated to satisfy the need that may be innate or learned.

3.2. Motivation and Tourism

Understanding tourist motivation is not best served by static models, but by recognizing the dynamic and changing elements, with time, of tourism motivation. According to Moutinho (1987), 'motivation is a state of need, a condition that exerts a push on the individual towards a certain type of action that are seen as likely to bring satisfaction'. In relation to tourism, motivation is a part of the consumption process and is stimulated by a complex mixture of economic, social, psychological, cultural, political, environmental and industry-related activities. Motivation is an integral part of consumer behaviour in tourism. Hall and Page (2002) noted that 'the factors which shaped the tourist decision-making process to select and participate in specific forms of tourism are largely within the field of consumer behaviour and motivation'.

There are two important propositions of tourist motivations. They are as follows:

1. Tourist motivations are formed around a combination of stimuli. On one hand, it encourages tourist behaviour (push factors), and on the other hand, it attracts tourists to a particular destination (pull factors).
2. Tourists expect to derive benefit or reward from the activities undertaken.

3.3. Definitions of Tourist Motivation

The motivation for tourism has been defined by many authors in different ways. Pearce and Lee (2005) mentioned that tourist motivations are not the same as the purpose of travel. Travel motivators are also related to an individual's socio-economic or psychological circumstances.

- According to **Backman** et al. (1995, p. 15), 'motivation is a state of need, a condition that serves as a driving force to display different kinds of behaviour towards certain types of activities, developing preferences, arriving at some satisfactory outcome'.
- According to **Pearce and Lee** (2005, p. 226), 'tourist motivation is the driving force behind all actions'.
- According to **Piznam and Mansfield** (1999, p. 07), 'tourism motivation is a set of needs, which predispose a person to participate in touristic activity'.

3.4. Motivation and Destination

Travel motivations are critical aspects in understanding travel behaviour of the tourists. Tourists generally have a very little or limited knowledge about a destination, especially if they have not previously visited the location, and are often dependent upon symbolic information acquired from either the media or from social groups. Motivation or motive is explained as to why an individual does something. Travel motivators can be classified into two types in relation to a destination. These are destination-related travel motivators and non-destination-related travel motivators.

Destination-related Travel Motivators

They are otherwise known as destination-specific motivators. These motivators allow tourists to select destinations where they want to visit or travel. In this type of motivation, tourists are not restricted to a specific destination. Destinations can be compared in terms of costs involved in the entire travel experience and then deciding the appropriate destination. Destination-specific travel motivators include curiosity about other cultures, people, places, religion, political systems and so on, and desire to see attractions such as art, drama, music and folklore. This type of motivation may include romance of travel, use of leisure time to escape, the desire for change of routine, social contact and to take part in various recreational and adventure activities and so on.

These types of tourist motivators allow the tourist to choose the destination where the tourists want to visit. Since in some cases tourists are not confined to choose a destination, they normally choose a destination in terms of appeal, cost, distance and so on.

In comparison to non-destination-related travel motivations, this type of motivation is normally difficult to determine. The main source of motivations to visit a destination in this category includes curiosity about others culture, religion, lifestyle, people, political systems and so on; this also includes motivations to see attractions such as art, drama, music and folklore. People in this kind of motivation normally want to interact with the host populations to fulfil their ego or self-esteem needs, which is considered to be a trend in specific destinations. The main sources of motivation in this category include the following:

- To enjoy the romance of travel
- To use leisure time to escape
- The need to improve social contact
- The wish for change of routine
- To experience doing new things in a new destination
- To watch sports
- To experience the gamble
- To participate in sporting events, especially in adventure sports
- To watch and experience the entertainment facility and so on

Non-destination-related Travel Motivators

This type of tourist motivators is easy to identify. Here, rather not the destination, the cause of travel is the determining factor for identifying travel motivation. These factors are as follows:

- Business
- Education
- Visiting friends and relatives
- Religion
- Health

3.5. Factors Influencing Tourist Motivation

Factors influencing tourist motivations can be categorized under the following two headings.

1. **Personal and family influence:** These include age, gender, stage in the family life cycle, nationality and so on.
2. **Social and situational influence:** These include tourism and work relationship, social class and income issues (Page & Connell, 2009).

3.6. Types of Tourist Motivation

There is no common theoretical approach to understand tourist motivations. Various models are developed to emphasize what really motivates tourist. The subject motivation has enjoyed widespread and diverse treatment in the tourism literature. It represents one of the most important and complex areas of tourism research. Tourist motivation is dynamic, potentially determined including person-specific psychological factors and extrinsic social forces.

Intrinsic and Extrinsic Motivation

- Intrinsic motivation recognizes that individuals have unique personal needs that motivate them to pursue tourism. Some of these needs are associated with the desire to satisfy himself or herself.
- An extrinsic motivation identifies the broad conditioning factors that save the individual's attitude, perceptions and preferences, which are more externally determined.

Motivation can be described as a state of need, a condition that exerts a push on the individual towards a certain type of action that is seen as likely to bring satisfaction. Motivation can also be described as a driving force within individuals that impels them to action.

- According to Hudman (1980), the following are the 10 types of tourist motivations:
  o Health
  o Curiosity
  o Sports (participation)
  o Sports (watching)
  o Pleasure
  o Visiting friends and relatives
  o Professional and business
  o Pursuit of roots
  o Self-esteem
  o Religion
- According to Schmoll (1977), there are five general travel motivators. These are as follows:
  o Educational and cultural
  o Relaxation, adventure and pleasure
  o Health and recreation
  o Ethnicity and family
  o Social and competitive (including status and prestige)

3.7. Tourism Motivation Models

Cohen's Model of Motivations (1979)

So far as tourism motivation is concerned, Cohen's model is one of the oldest models. Cohen emphasized that the motivation for travel is the search for certain tourist experience in relation to a 'centre'. He defined 'centre' as a theoretical concept that refers to values and meanings which are important and valuable for the individual. He identified five types of tourist experiences and their motivation and relationship to the centre. These five types of tourist experiences are as follows:

1. **The recreational mode:** The main motive of this experience is to take a break from daily life and come back refreshed and positive. In real life when everything related to the centre becomes stressful, a holiday takes the pressure off. Here tourists may not be concerned with authenticity, rather they want the pleasure of entertainment experienced by them.
2. **The diversionary mode:** Cohen explained that this form of motive may be seen as an escape or diversion from boredom and meaningless routines. Unlike the recreational mode, in this case some people accept the view that tourism is a way to find temporary oblivion because their professional and personal life is unrewarding. Here the motivation for travel is superficial and not because of any commitment and is entirely a search for meaningless pleasure.
3. **The experiential mode:** In this mode people who have lost their 'centre' start looking for meaning in the life of others via tourist experiences. This search for meaning is outside their own society and culture. This mode is more profound than the previous two but does not generate real experiences.
4. **The experimental mode:** This mode refers to travellers who try to participate in the authentic life of others as part of their pursuit for an alternative cultural centre.
5. **The existential mode:** According to Cohen, this mode refers to individuals who are already committed to an elective center. This is culturally and geographically external to the tourist's own society.

Dann's Model of Tourism Motivation (1981)

Dann (1981), in his approach to provide a comprehensive view on tourist motivation, mentioned that 'leisure' is considered to be the most important source of tourist motivation. According to him, apart from leisure different tourist motives like VFR, business travel sometimes dominates the main purpose of travel motivation. According to Dann, there are seven perspectives of tourist motivations which prove a better in-depth study to various elements of tourist motivations. These are as follows:

Principal Elements of Tourist Motivation	Characteristics
Travel as a response to what is lacking yet desired	Tourist motivation may result from a desire for something new or different that cannot be provided in the individual's home environment.
Destination pull in response to motivational push	The distinction between the needs, wants and desires (push factors) of the individual and how these are shaped by perceptions of the destination (pull factors).
Motivation as fantasy	Tourists may be motivated to travel to engage in forms of behaviour or activities that are not culturally acceptable in their home environment. For example, gambling, drugs or prostitution and so on may be illegal in the home country but not in some other countries. This creates the desire to travel.

Principal Elements of Tourist Motivation	Characteristics
Motivation as a classified purpose	Some people are motivated to travel by the nature or the purpose of the trip such as VFR and the opportunity to undertake specific leisure activities.
Motivational typologies	Different types of tourists may influence the motivation to travel.
Motivation and tourist experiences	Tourism often involves travel to places not visited previously. For example, some people are motivated to travel by what they expect to experience in contrast to their home area and other holiday experiences.
Motivation as auto-definition meaning	The ways in which tourist defines their situations and responds to them may provide a better understanding of tourist motivation. This approach is seen in contrast to simply observing behaviour as a means to explain tourist motivation.

The Travel Career Ladder (TCL) Model by Pearce (1993)

Pearce in his model suggested that individuals exhibit a 'career' in terms of tourism behaviour. He developed this model based on Maslow's five levels of the motivation theory. According to this model, individuals start out at different levels and change levels as they progress through the various life cycle stages. This life cycle progress sometimes gets hampered by money, health and other people. Here lower order needs are satisfied first and the tourist gains the experience, and higher order motives are accessed. Pearce proposed and empirically tested his model that emphasizes the tourist's patterns and motives rather than a single motive for travelling (Figure 3.1).

The five levels described by Pearce are as follows:

1. Relaxation or bodily needs (concern with biological needs)
2. Stimulation (safety and security needs)
3. Relationship development and extension needs
4. Self-esteem and development (special interest and self-development needs)
5. Fulfilment or deep involvement needs akin to self-actualization

In addition, he advocates that these travel goals may be self-directed that travel may be a solo or group experience. As per careers in general and the TCL model specifically, people may start at different levels.

According to Pearce, every individual normally exhibits a career in terms of tourism behaviour. The TCL model suggested that tourists can 'retire' from the travel career by not taking holidays at all and may be considered as not a part of the system (Pearce, 1993). According to Pearce, motivation is an ever-changing process and individuals who move up the ladder can modify from TCL to travel career patterns (Pearce, 2005). The concept of travel career patterns according to him is nothing but consists of three layers of travel motivations.

Figure 3.1   The Ladder Model

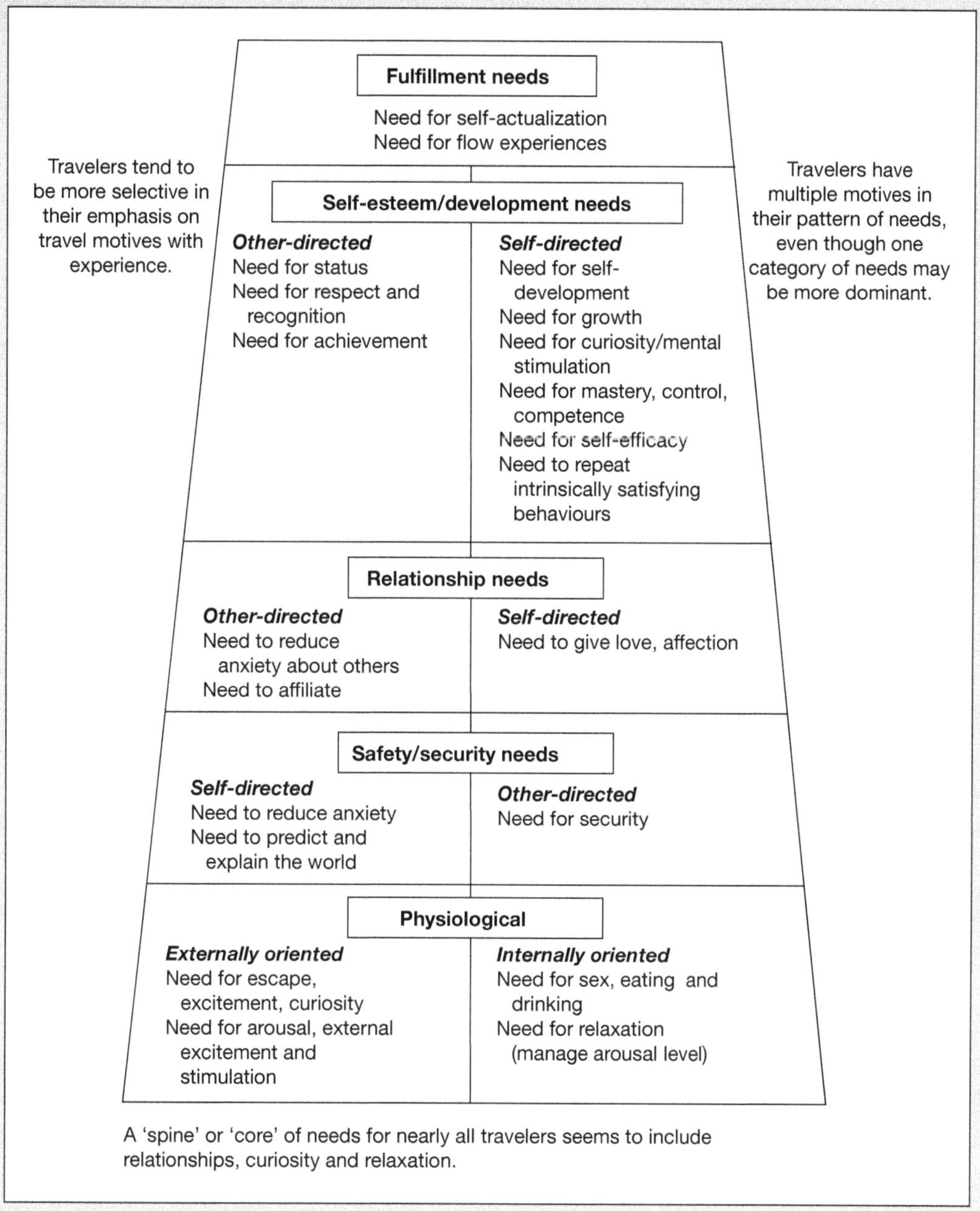

<table>
<tr><td colspan="2" align="center">**Fulfillment needs**</td></tr>
<tr><td colspan="2" align="center">Need for self-actualization
Need for flow experiences</td></tr>
</table>

Travelers tend to be more selective in their emphasis on travel motives with experience.

Travelers have multiple motives in their pattern of needs, even though one category of needs may be more dominant.

Self-esteem/development needs

Other-directed	*Self-directed*
Need for status Need for respect and recognition Need for achievement	Need for self-development Need for growth Need for curiosity/mental stimulation Need for mastery, control, competence Need for self-efficacy Need to repeat intrinsically satisfying behaviours

Relationship needs

Other-directed	*Self-directed*
Need to reduce anxiety about others Need to affiliate	Need to give love, affection

Safety/security needs

Self-directed	*Other-directed*
Need to reduce anxiety Need to predict and explain the world	Need for security

Physiological

Externally oriented	*Internally oriented*
Need for escape, excitement, curiosity Need for arousal, external excitement and stimulation	Need for sex, eating and drinking Need for relaxation (manage arousal level)

A 'spine' or 'core' of needs for nearly all travelers seems to include relationships, curiosity and relaxation.

Source: Pearce (1993, 2005).

These three layers of travel motivations are the following:

1. **The core motives:** These are the most important motives consisting of novelty of escape, pleasure and relaxation, and willingness to make relationships.
2. **A layer surrounding the core:** The second layer of travel motivations consists of comparatively moderate important travel motives such as self-actualization, which vary from inner focused motives to outer focused motives.
3. **An outer layer:** These motives are characterized by some of the most commonly cited and less stable motives which have less importance. The main example in this category of motives includes nostalgia and pursuit of isolation.

The TCL depicts that tourists become more and more experienced as they climb the higher ladders; as a result their moderately important motives will shift from the inner to outer focused needs such as experiencing the environment as well as interaction and involvement with the local people.

3.8. Tourism Motivation Theories

The importance of motivation in tourism is quite obvious. Motivations act as a focal point that set off all the events involved in travel. However, there is no commonly agreed theoretical approach to understand tourism motivations.

Maslow's Need Hierarchy Theory (1954)

Maslow's need hierarchy theory was introduced in 1954. This theory is considered to be one of the most widely used theories on motivation. According to Abraham Maslow, there are five categories of needs, namely:

1. Physiological needs
2. Security and safety needs
3. Love or belongingness needs
4. Self-esteem needs
5. Self-actualization (self-fulfilment) needs

According to this theory, the individual's future actions are mainly governed by the degree of satisfaction derived within each preceding need category. He argued that once the lower order need will be satisfied, the individual will strive for the next higher order needs. According to the sequence of motivation provided by him, he identified the following two types of motives:

1. Deficiency or tension-reducing motives
2. Inductive or arousal-seeking motives

Cooper et al. (1993, p. 21), in their study, mentioned that Maslow's theory of motivation model could be applied to both work and non-work (tourism and leisure) context.

Maslow stated that one did not have to be satisfied fully at one level before switching over to the next level of needs. This reflects that an individual could be partially satisfied and partially

Figure 3.2 Maslow's Need Hierarchy and Its Application in Tourism (1954)

Self-actualization: Tourism may play an important role in the self-fulfilment of the individual.

Esteem: This takes the form of different kinds of experiences through which tourism can build our confidence. Travelling can also build social esteem.

Relationships/Belongingness: The need to establish relationships with other people is essential for our psychological well-being. Tourism provides opportunities to develop relationships with family and friends. It also offers opportunities to make new friends and acquaintances.

Safety: These needs are likely to manifest themselves for most people by choosing destinations that they feel are safe and secure to visit. Acts of terrorism or high crime rates act as a deterrent to tourism. Conversely, some individuals who feel that the risk has been removed from their daily lives may search for 'risk' through tourism. However, this is likely to be in a managed form, largely under the control of the individual.

Physiological: In Maslow's original model emphasis was placed upon the meeting of basic needs such as food, sex and shelter. In the case of tourism, the need for relaxation and recuperation is often given as a key reason for the taking of holidays or vacations. Example: Provision for clean drinkable water, food and hygiene at the destination.

dissatisfied at all levels in the need hierarchy at the same time. This denotes that for each individual there should be different threshold levels in each need category. As a result, any individual can enter into the next higher order needs when they become cognitively aware of the desire to satisfy new needs (Figure 3.2).

Nature of Needs According to Maslow

Maslow has explained nature of needs as follows:

- A human need is a state of felt deprivation of some basic satisfaction (food, clothing, shelter, safety, belonging, esteem and so on).
- Abraham Maslow noticed that some needs take precedence over others. Maslow took this idea and created his now famous hierarchy of needs. Beyond the details of air, water, food and sex, he laid out five broader layers.

Maslow's Hierarchy of Individual Needs

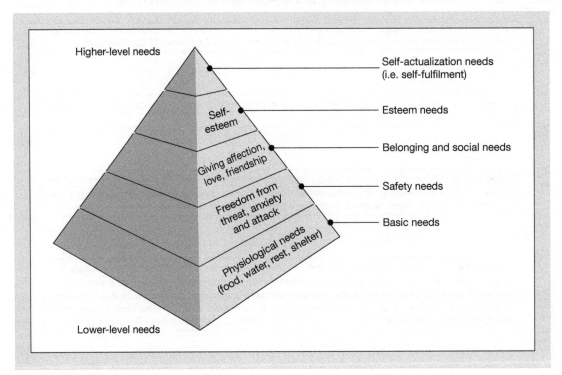

Maslow has described the hierarchy of needs as follows:

1. **Physiological needs:** These include the needs we have for oxygen, water, protein, salt, sugar, calcium, and other minerals and vitamins. They also include the need to maintain a pH balance (getting too acidic or base will kill you) and temperature. Also, there's the need to be active, to rest, to sleep, to get rid of wastes (CO_2, sweat, urine and faeces), to avoid pain and to have sex.
2. **Safety and security needs:** When the physiological needs are largely taken care of, this second layer of needs comes into play. You will become increasingly interested in finding safe circumstances, stability and protection. You might develop a need for structure, for order and some limits.
3. **Love and belonging needs:** When physiological needs and safety needs are, by and large, taken care of, a third layer starts to show up. You begin to feel the need for friends, a sweetheart, children; affectionate relationships in general, even a sense of community.
4. **Esteem needs:** Maslow noted two versions of esteem needs, a lower one and a higher one. The lower one is the need for the respect of others, the need for status, fame, glory, recognition, attention, reputation, appreciation, dignity, even dominance.

   The higher form involves the need for self-respect, including such feelings as confidence, competence, achievement, mastery, independence and freedom. Note that this is the 'higher' form because, unlike the respect of others, once you have self-respect, it's a lot harder to lose.

All of the preceding four levels he calls deficit needs, or D-needs. If you do not have enough of something—that is you have a deficit—you feel the need. But if you get all you need, you feel nothing at all. In other words, they cease to be motivating. 'You do not miss your water till your well runs dry'.

5. **Self-actualization or Self-fulfilment need:** It is the need for understanding one's own abilities and potentials, and using them to the maximum. The person becomes growth oriented, self-directed and creative.

According to Maslow, 'a musician must make music; an artist must paint, a poet must write, if he is to be ultimately happy. What a man can be he must be. This need we may call self-actualization' (Exhibit 3.1).

[A man must be what he likes to be]

Exhibit 3.1   Maslow's Need Hierarchy Theory and Its Application in Tourism

Need	Motive	References
Physiological	Relaxation	• Escape • Physical relaxation • Relief of tension • Sunlust • Mental relaxation
Safety	Security	• Health • Recreation • Keep oneself active and healthy for the future
Belonging	Love	• Family togetherness • Enhancement of kinship relationships • Companionship • Facilitation of social interaction • Maintenance of personal ties • Roots • Ethnicity • Show one's affection for family members • Maintain social conflicts
Esteem	Achievement status	• Show one's importance to others • Prestige • Social recognition • Ego enhancement • Status and prestige
Self-actualization	Be true to one's own nature	• Exploration and evaluation of self • Self-discovery • Satisfaction of inner desires
To know and understand	Knowledge	• Cultural • Education • WanderlustInterest in foreign areas
Aesthetics	Appreciation of beauty	• Environmental • Scenery

Criticism of Maslow's Need Hierarchy Theory

Maslow's hierarchy of needs in the context of tourism has been criticized by some tourism professionals. Witt and Wright (1992) criticized the theory on the ground that some important needs such as dominance, play and aggression have not been considered in this theory, which play a major role in the field of tourism motivation.

Another criticism of the theory is that it has been tested only to western culture and thereby ignores the other cultures' applicability. No time dimension has been incorporated in this theory. This theory has also been criticized on the ground that some needs are not in reality hierarchical because they may occur simultaneously at different levels.

The theory is also criticized on the ground that it is difficult to justify five discrete levels of needs as these are not based on any extensive empirical research.

Mill and Morrison (1992) criticized this theory that the assumed relationship between physical, psychological and intellectual needs all in terms of the discreetness of each level and the order. Both of them considered that it is more realistic to accept the degree of interdependence between the levels. According to them, those seeking higher order needs at the same time require equal satisfaction of lower order needs. They argued that the theory developed by Maslow would be better illustrated as a series of nested triangles rather than a pyramid formation. They have identified two higher order needs. These are knowledge and understanding, and antithetic appreciation. According to them, these two higher dimensions of needs are of greater importance in the field of tourism because these are appropriate to tourism behaviour, but could possibly be subsumed as an integral part of self-actualization.

Conclusion

In spite of these criticisms, this model is very popular in the sense that it has considered both the psychological and physiological needs as important factors for tourist motivation. Apart from that it has also taken into consideration wider environmental and social factors including its greater acceptability to a wider audience. This theory considers the developmental need of humans with individuals striving towards personal growth and this can be very much understood in the context of tourism.

Beard and Ragheb's Theory of Motivation (1983)

According to Beard and Ragheb, there are four major components of motivational typology:

1. **Intellectual component:** This motivates people to use tourism to undertake mental activities such as learning, exploring, thinking and imagining.
2. **Social component:** In this type of motivation, people undertake tourism and leisure activities for social reason: to make friends, gain people's esteem or to build interpersonal relationships.
3. **Competence-mastery component:** This type of motivation refers to physical activities: People engage in these to master new skills, compete with others or challenge themselves.
4. **Stimulus-avoidance components:** These motivators relate to getting away from stressful or problematic environments. For example, after work people engage in tourism to relax and unwind.

McIntosh's Theory of Motivation (1995)

In 1995, McIntosh established a model with four categories of motivations. These are as follows:

1. **Physical motivators:** These are related to refreshment of body and mind, health purposes, sports and leisure. They are usually engaged in to reduce tension.
2. **Cultural motivators:** These are concerned with the desire to learn about new cultures or the music, art, architecture and lifestyles of a destination.
3. **Interpersonal motivators:** These are concerned with meeting new people or visiting friends and family. They can also refer to escape from the home environment or spiritual reasons.
4. **Status and prestige motivators:** These are linked with the desire for attention and recognition for others in order to boost personal ego. They may include a desire for the continuation of education or personal development in the pursuit of a hobby.

Tourist Motivation by Mayo and Jarvis (1981)

Mayo and Jarvis suggested that travel motivation is mainly based on the tourist's wish to gain, see or experience in the trip, which is mainly divided into the following four types:

1. **Physical motivators:** The desire for physical rest, participation in sports, beach recreation, relaxing entertainment and health consideration.
2. **Cultural motivators:** The desire for knowledge of other countries including their art, dances, folklore, music, painting, religions and so on.
3. **Interpersonal motivators:** The desire to meet new people, to visit friends and relatives, to escape from routine life, to experience anomie and so on.
4. **Status and prestige motivators:** The desire for recognition, appreciation, good reputation among friends and family, and so on.

3.9. Factors Affecting Tourist Motivation

Travel motivators are generally related to an individual's socio-economic or psychological circumstances, and are sometimes called as background characteristics (Stankery & Schreyer, 1985). There are several factors which affect tourist motivations in different ways. The factors which influence tourism motivations can be broadly classified into the following two categories:

1. **Personal and family influence:** This includes age, standard of living, family cycle stages, gender issues and nationality, and so on.

   a. **Age:** Age is one of the most important demographic and socio-economic factors which affect tourist motivation. Although there are different views in relation to age.
   b. **Standard of living:** There is a direct relationship between standard of living and motivation to travel. A high standard of living leads to a high disposable income, which will lead to reduction in working hours and as a result the length of holiday increases with good purchasing power. This can be considered as the strongest determinants of travel.

Table 3.2		Interrelationship between Stages of Life Cycle and Travel Motivation

Serial No.	Stages of Life Cycle	Main Travel Motivations and Their Characteristics
1.	Teenagers	Adventure and fun-related tours; income is less, mainly single and not employed; dependent on parents
2.	Single in employment	Adventure, action-oriented tours; disposable income normally high
3.	Newly married	Family-type holiday with resort accommodation; little disposable income
4.	DINKS (double income with no kids)	Choose pleasure travel mostly to hill stations; maximum disposable income; comparatively short duration trip; avail luxury accommodation
5.	Family with babies	Opt for repeat holiday visit with same accommodation; little disposable income
6.	Family with young children	More activity-based diversified holiday; avail resort-type accommodation
7.	The broken marriage	Travel for short duration with escort, divorced with single parents or just separated
8.	Family with older children	Choose multi-destination holidays with special interest tours; they are getting older and children still dependent
9.	Alone age	Older and married without their children; they are wealthy and normally prefer cruise holidays and special tours
10.	Survivors/widows	Special interest tourist; single and alone and normally want to travel in groups

c. **Family cycle stages:** Different stages of family life cycle have strong influence on various travel motivations in different stages. A typical stage of family life cycle can be differentiated into the following types (Table 3.2).

Apart from the earlier categorization of age and its impact on tourist motivation, age exercises many other influences on a person's motivation. Sometimes, a person's need as well as taste changes with the change in stages of life. For example, younger people want to do various activities/works in comparison to married couple with kids and also the elderly people who do altogether different things.

d. **Gender issues and nationality:** Gender is considered to be one of the important variables which influence the travel motivation. Both men and women may have different types of needs and wants. These have to be identified and fulfilled according to their demand during the entire course of the tourism activity.

Every nationality has its own language and many distinctive preferences and patterns of behaviour. Since tourism is a multidimensional activity, mixing of culture is obvious. However, sometimes people of the same culture, nationality want to share the same resource without any involvement of other culture people. In this case tour operators/organizers have to take care of this factor with utmost priority. In case there is a mixing of culture or sub cultures from the same country, there has to be a very good understanding of the ways in which groups of people differ and how they will mix together. Since people from different regions differ in the educational level, cultural values and income, they may not mingle together instantly. So these things must be taken care of by the operators/organizers to provide the opportunity and facility to minimize the hiccups arising due to nationality issues.

From a business point of view, both the supplier and the organizers should be ready to provide services and facilities not only to one nationality but to different nationalities, thereby increase the business opportunities as well as capture different markets to increase their business endeavour.

2. **Social and situational influence:** This influence includes social class and income issue, and relationship between tourism and work:

a. **Social class and income issue:** This is one of the most important external factors which influence motivation. This is mainly assessed by occupation and level of income (Lumsdon, 1997). The concept of social class is associated with different dimensions. These include: power, money, prestige, culture, background and so on. However, in social science research, social class means segmenting the population on the basis of gender, age and occupation for the purposes of conducting surveys, opinion polls and so on.

Tourism is price elastic because a small increase in price will lead to more people wanting cheaper alternatives. Since income is generally synonym with occupational groups, these classifications have a positive influence on tourism patterns. Research in this regard already suggested that professional occupations enjoy a more active and varied range of leisure activities in comparison to unemployment dependants. Since, tourism has been traditionally associated with certain destinations, and marketers are often charged with repositioning a destination as part of a wider tourism strategy. It is also evident that the higher status consumers tend to travel independently more often and for a short period which is dominated by the high income bracket people.

b. **Relationship between tourism and work:** There is a close relationship between tourism and work. Work is sometimes used as a means of tourism and escaping from work provides a motivation for the tourist. The relationship between work and tourism is indirect, that is, if one increases, the other one decreases. Tourism is mainly influenced by the nature of work. When an individual's work is boring and monotonous tourism can be a form of escape, but when the work is exciting, enjoyable and difficult to disassociate from leisure, holiday may be seen as a means to extend one's interest.

According to Zuzanek and Manneal (1983), the relationship between work and leisure can be established by studying the following four hypotheses:

i. **The trade-off hypothesis:** According to this hypothesis, work and leisure are competitors for time and an individual has to choose between them.

ii. **The compensation hypothesis:** According to this, leisure and holiday compensate for the boredom and troubles associated with work and everyday life.

iii. **The spin-off hypothesis:** This hypothesis states that the nature of individual's work produces a similar pattern of leisure activities.

iv. **The neutralist-hypothesis:** According to this hypothesis, there is no discernible relationship between leisure and work.

From the discussion we may conclude that different types of work produce different levels of satisfaction, which in turn influence individual needs and wants, and hence leisure and tourism motivations.

3.10. Travel Flow Pattern

William and Zelinsky (1970) mentioned in their study that there is no random distribution of tourist flow. According to them, there are some distinct features which are responsible for tourist flow from one place to other. These are as follows:

- **Special distance:** This is one of the important factors which affect the travel flow pattern. Here the relationship is indirect, that is, the more the distance between two countries, the less will be the travel flow and vice versa.
  Example: The important reason for which India is receiving less number of tourists is the distance from the tourist-generating countries. Whereas France, being a very small country, receives maximum numbers of tourists.
- **Presence and absence of past and present international connectivity:**
  The travel flow between two countries or among countries is mainly dependent upon the communication facility developed between them as well as the connectivity to various destinations of different countries.
  Example: Historically, due to the presence of international connectivity such as Nathu La and Jelep La the travel flow between India, China and Nepal is comparatively high from the beginning. So the relationship between the two is direct, that is, if there is any presence of international connectivity, the travel flow will be more and vice versa.
- **Reciprocity of travel flow:** According to **William and Zelinsky**, if the travel flow between one country will be more to the other then obviously the travel flow between the destination country to the originating country will also high. The relationship is direct in this case.
  Example: Nowadays, in recent years as most of the Australian tourists are visiting India, as a result the statistical figures indicates that now most of the Indians are also visiting Australia in recent years.
- **Attractiveness of one country towards other:** Another important factor which can influence the travel flow pattern is the attractiveness of one country towards the other. This has been experienced that every tourist has certain preferences or strong weakness to travel to a particular destination/country. Even if the country may not be destination wise so diverse, still the tourist has certain weakness to visit the country again and again (if given the chance to visit).
  Example: Given the opportunity to visit, in case of Indian tourist, if we ask them to which country they prefer to visit, then one must observe that maximum tourists are preferring Switzerland in comparison to other countries as most of the Indians have in their mindset that this is one of the best tourist destination to visit in the entire world.
- **Known or presumed cost of visit to a attraction:** In continuation with the previous discussion, if we consider Switzerland as an important tourist destination, no doubt that the cost of living, accommodation, food, as well as transportation cost of that country is very high, still people are travelling to that country because of the attractiveness of one country

for the other. However, in general circumstances, if the cost of visit to attraction is high then the tourist flow to that place will be less and vice versa.

- **Influence of intervening variables and opportunity:** Intervening variables are those factors which are responsible for compelling the tourist to visit different destinations because they are in the profession and staying in the profession, they as getting this opportunity to visit/travel.
  Example: Multinational companies nowadays organize seminars/conferences/workshops/ launch their product in different tourist destinations/countries, and thereby take their employees to participate in the event and as a result the travel flow pattern is affected by this.

- **Impact of specific non-recurring events:** A non-recurring event means an event which is not held regularly, rather organized every three to four or five years. Such events have the power/impact to attract a huge number of people from different parts of the world to visit or enjoy the events.
  Examples: Countries are organizing World Cup football, World Cup cricket, World cup hockey, Assess cricket series between England and Australia, and so on. These specific non-recurring events resulted in a huge scale movement of tourists from one country to other, thereby influencing the travel flow to that country.

- **National characteristic of citizen of the visiting country:** According to the authors, when the tourists visit a particular country, they normally carry sensory information about the people of the visiting country. This is regarding the study of the host country's behaviour, their standard of living, way of talking, language they speak and understand, hygiene conscious or not, hospitable or not and so on. On the basis of these factors, they normally visit a destination/country. If the tourists carry a good impression about the host country's people, then obviously the tourist flow to the state will be more or vice versa.

- **Mental image of the destination country on the mind of the citizen of the originating country:** This is one of the most important factors which influence the travel flow pattern of any country. The people in the originating country have always a pre-mindset regarding the tourists those who are coming to that country. So, if the mental image of the persons originating country is good then they will be more hospitable, humble, caring and always want to have a healthy interaction with the guests/tourists. Otherwise the case will be reverse. So when the tourists want to visit the place they normally look into this aspect which has a strong influence on the travel flow pattern to that country.

Conclusion

Travel motivations are those factors which create a person's inclination to travel to a destination. Motivation changes over time, over the course of a life time, from one trip to the other and from one activity to the other. Many tourists are not aware of what motivates them to go to a particular trip. Tourism motives are multidimensional and sometimes contradictory, including a range of push and pull factors. Tourist motivations are complex and are highly personal construes. The tourism market is a dynamic one, different factors including demographic characteristics and change in lifestyles continue to affect the travel flows, including the development of new travel-related products. As a result, travel motivations are increasingly important to identify the current trends and analyse the market effectively to measure travel and tourism.

MODEL QUESTIONS

1. What do you mean by motivation?
2. Define tourist motivation.
3. Explain various theories of travel motivations with suitable examples.
4. Analyse various factors influencing tourist motivations.
5. Write a note on types of tourist motivations.
6. What are the factors that have influenced the recent growth of pleasure travel?
7. How is Maslow's theory used to explain travel motivations and behaviour?
8. Critically examine different theories of travel motivations.
9. What do you mean by travel flow pattern? Briefly explain the factors influencing travel flow pattern described by William and Zelinsky.
10. Explain how does destination-related travel differs from non-destination-related travel? Substantiate your answer with suitable example.

Student Activity

1. Visit a nearby tourist destination of your choice. Find out what are the factors that motivated you to visit the destination.

Suggested Readings

Andreck, L. K., & Vogt, A. C., (2000). The relationship between resident's attitude towards tourism and tourism development options. *Journals of Travel Research, 39,* 27–36.

Backman, K. F., Backman, S. J., Uysal, M., & Sunshine, K. M. 1995. Event tourism: An examination of motivations and activities. *Festival Management and Event Tourism, 3*(1): 15–24.

Banister, D. (1995). *Tourism and urban development.* London: Spon Press.

Bansal, S. P., Sushma, S. K., & Mohan, C. (2002). *Tourism in new millennium.* Chandigarh: Abhishek Publications.

Batra, G. S., & Chawla, A. S. (1995). *Tourism management a global prospective.* New Delhi: Deep & Deep Publishing.

Brukart, A. J., & Medlik, S. (1981). *Tourism—past, present and future.* London: ELBS-Heinemann Professional Publishing.

Butler, R. W. (1980). The concept of tourist area cycle of evolution: Implications for management of resources. *Canadian Geographer, 14,* 351–384.

Coltman, M. (1989). *Introduction to travel and tourism: An international approach.* New York, NY: Van Nostrand Reinhold.

Connell, J. (2004). The purest of human pleasure: The characteristics and motivations of garden visitors in Great Britain. *Tourism Management, 25*(2), 229–247.

Cook, A. R., Yale J. L., & Marqua, J. J. (2012). *Tourism: The business of travel* (3rd ed.). New Delhi: Pearson.

Cooper, C., Fletcher, J., Fyall, A., Gilbert, D., Wanhill, S., & Shepherd, R. (1998). *Tourism: Principles and practices* (2nd Ed.). London: Pitman.

Cooper, C., Fletcher, J., Gilbert, D., & Wanhill, S. (1993). *Tourism: Principles & practice.* Harlow, UK: Longman.

Faulkner, B., Moscardo, B., & Laws, E. (2000). *Tourism in the 21st century.* London: Continuum.

Feifer, M. (1985). *Going places: The way of the tourists from imperial Rome to the present day.* London: Macmillan.

Frechting, C. D. (1996). *Practical tourism forecasting.* Oxford: Butterworth–Heinemann.

Gartner, C. W. (1996). *Tourism development: Principles, processes and policies.* New York, NY: Van Nostrand Reinhold.

Gee, C. Y., Makens, J. C., & Choy, D. J. L. (1997). *The travel industry.* New York, NY: Van Nostrand Reinhold (a division of International Thomson Publishing).

George, B. P., Inbakaran, R., & Poyyamoli, G. (2010). To travel or not to travel: Towards understanding the theory of nativistic motivation. *Tourism, 58*(4), 395–407.

Goeldner, C. R., Ritchie, J. R. B., & McIntosh, R. W. (2000). *Tourism: Principles, practices and philosophies.* New York, NY: John Wiley & Sons.

Hibbert, C. (1974). *The grand tour.* London: Spring Books.

Holloway, J. C. (1994). *The business of tourism* (4th ed.). London: Pitman Publishing.

Hudman, L.E. (1980). *Tourism: A shrinking world.* Ohio: Grid Publishing.

Hunt, J. D., & Layne, D. (1991). The evolution of travel and tourism terminology and definitions. *Journal of Travel Research, 29*(4), 7–11.

Inskeep, E. (1991). *Tourism planning–an integrated and sustainable development approach.* New York, NY: Van Nostrand Reinhold.

Krippendorf, J. (1987). *The holidaymakers: Understanding the impacts of leisure and travel.* London: Heinemann.

Laws, E. (1995). *Tourist destination management: Issues, analysis and policies.* London: Routledge.

Leiper, N. (1990). *Tourism systems: An interdisciplinary perspective* (Occasional paper 2, Massey University, Department of Management System). New Zealand: Palmerton North.

Maslow, A. H. (1943). A theory of human motivation. *Psychological Review, 50,* 370–396.

Mayo, E., & Jarvis, L. (1981). *The psychology of leisure travel.* Boston, MA: CBI Publishing.

McIntosh, R. W., Goeldner, C. R., & Ritchie, J. R. B. (1995). *Tourism: Principles, Practices, Philosophies.* New York: John Wiley and Sons.

Meethan, K. (2001). *Tourism in global society: Place, culture, consumption.* Basingstoke: Palgrave.

Motiram. (2003). *International tourism—socio-economic prospective.* New Delhi: Sonali Publications.

Norval, A. (1936). *The tourism industry: A national and international survey.* London: Pitman.

Page, S. J. (2003). *Tourism management, managing for change* (1st ed.). Oxford: Elsevier.

Pearce, P. L. (2005). *Tourist behaviour: Themes and conceptual schemes.* Clevedon: Channel View.

———. (1982). *The social psychology of tourist behaviour.* Oxford: Pergamon.

Pearce, P. L., & Lee, U. (2005). Developing the travel career approach to tourism motivation. *Journal of Travel Research, 43*(3), 226–237.

Pearson, C. S. (2000). *Economics and the global environment.* Cambridge: Cambridge University Press.

Pitts, R. E., & Woodside, A. G. (1986). Personal value and travel decisions. *The Journals of Travel Research, 25*(1), 20–25.

Pizam, A., & Mansfeld, Y. (1999). *Consumer behavior in travel and tourism.* Binghampton: Haworth Hospitality Press.

Plog, S. C. (1973, November). Why destination areas rise and fall in popularity. *HRA Quarterly,* 14, 13–16.

———. (1974). A carpenter's tools: An answer to Stephen L. J. Smith's review of psycho centrism/allocentrism. *Journal of Travel Research, 28*(4), 43–45.

Poon, A. (2003). Competitive strategy for a new tourism. In C. Cooper (Ed.), *Classic review in tourism* (pp. 130–142). Clevedon: Channel View.

Prentice, R. (2004). *Tourism motivations and typologies.* In A. Lew, C. M. Hall, & A. Williams (Eds.), *A companion to tourism* (pp. 261–279). Oxford: Blackwell.

Ray, N., & Ryder, M. (2003). E-abilities' tourism: An exploratory discussion of the travel needs and motivations of the mobility disabled. *Tourism Management, 24*(1), 57–72.

Ryan, C. (Ed.). (1997). *The tourist experience: A new introduction.* London: Cassell.

Ryan, C., & Page, S. J. (Eds.). (2000). *Tourism management: Towards new millennium.* Oxford: Pergamon.

Schmoll, G. A. (1977). *Tourism promotion: Marketing background, promotion techniques and promotion planning methods.* London: Tourism International Press.

Sharpley, R. (1994). *Tourism, tourist and society.* Huntingdon: Elm.

Smith, D. M., & Krannich, S. R. (1998). Tourism dependence and residents attitude. *Annals of Tourism Research, 25*(4), 783–802.

Stankey, G. H., & Schreyer, R. (1985). Attitudes toward wilderness and factors affecting visitor behavior: A state of the knowledge review. In R.C. Lucas (compiler), *Proceedings, National wilderness research conference: Issues, state of knowledge, future directions,* Fort Collins, Colorado, 23–26 July 1985.

Stewart, C. D., & Calantone, R. J. (1978). Psychographic segmentation of tourists. *Journal of Travel Research, 16*(3), 14–20.

Swarbrooke, J., & Horner, S. (1999). *Consumer behavior in tourism.* Great Britain: Butterworth–Heinemann.

Thornton, P., Shaw, G., & Williams, A. (1997). Tourist group holiday decision making and behaviour: The influence of children. *Tourism Management, 18*(5), 287–298.

Tinesely, H. E. A., & Kass, R. A. (1978). Leisure activities and need satisfaction: A replication and extension. *Journals of Leisure Research, 10*(3), 191–202.

Vellas, F., & Becheral, L. (1995). *International tourism.* London: Macmillan Press.

Wahab, S., & Cooper, C. (2001). *Tourism in the age of globalisation.* London: Routledge.

Wahab, S., & Pigram J. J. (1997). *Tourism development and growth: The challenges of sustainability.* London: Routledge.

Williams, Anthony V., & Zelinsky, Wilbur. (1970). On some patterns in international tourist flows. *Economic Geography, 46* (4), 549–567.

Witt, C. & Wright, P. (1992). Tourist motivation: Life after Maslow. In P. Johnson and B. Thomas (eds.), Choice and demand in tourism (pp. 33–55). London: Mansell.

Tourism Demand

LEARNING OBJECTIVES

After going through this chapter, the reader will be able to understand:

- ❏ The meaning, concept and importance of tourism demand
- ❏ Various levels and elements of tourism demand
- ❏ Different forms of tourism demand
- ❏ The concept of law of demand and its application in tourism
- ❏ The measurement of tourism demand
- ❏ The factors influencing tourism demand
- ❏ The concept of travel propensity and its application in tourism business
- ❏ Issues involved in managing tourism demand

CHAPTER OVERVIEW

Chapter 4 describes tourism demand including its meaning, types, levels, measurement and factors influencing it. Demand is the basis on which all tourism-related business decisions ultimately depend. It also provides a framework on which the tourists choose and pursue a range of opportunities during the tour. It is a useful indicator of changing trends in tourism business. It provides answers to different questions related to tourism development, including why tourism developed in a particular destination, what influences the tourists to visit the destination and so on.

4.1. Introduction

What Is Demand?

Demand is the desire or want for something. It is the human want which is backed by purchasing power. In economics, demand refers to effective demand. Demand is the desire or want backed up by money. It means effective desire or want for a commodity which is backed up by the ability to pay and willingness to pay for it.

Demand is not an absolute term. It is a relative concept. It is always related to price and time. Demand for a product can be defined as the ability and willingness to purchase a particular product in a given time period at a constant price. It may be viewed as **ex-ante** or potential demand or intended demand and **ex-post** or actual demand, what is already purchased.

Demand is one of the most important requirements for the existence of any business enterprise. A firm is always interested in its own profit and/or sales, both of which depend partially on the demand for its product. The decisions which management takes with respect to production, advertising, cost allocation, pricing and so on, call for an analysis of demand.

Demand for a Commodity

Demand for a commodity implies the following:

- Desire to acquire it
- Willingness to pay for it
- Ability to pay for it

Demand = Desire + Ability to pay + Willingness to spend

Individual Demand and Market Demand

Consumer demands for a product can be categorized into two types: individual demand and market demand.

Individual Demand

It refers to the demand for a commodity from an individual point of view. The consumer who purchases a quantity of product at a given price over a given period of time is his or her individual demand. It is considered from a person's point of view or from the point of view of a family or a household. It is a single consumer's demand.

The factors influencing individual demand are as follows:

- Price of the product
- Income
- Tastes, habits and preferences
- Relative prices of other products (substitute and complementary products)
- Consumer's expectation
- Advertisement effect

Market Demand

Market demand for a product refers to the total demand of all the buyers taken together. It is the sum total of all individual demands and is derived by aggregating all individual buyer's demand function in the market. It is an aggregate quantity of a product demanded by all the individual buyers at a given price over a given period of time.

The factors influencing market demand are as follows:

- Price of the product
- Distribution of income and wealth in the community
- Community's common habits and scale of preferences

- General standards of living and spending habits of the people
- Number of customers in the market and the growth of population
- Sex ratio and age structure of the population
- Level of taxation and tax structure
- Fashion and customs
- Advertisements and sales propagandas
- Inventions and innovations
- Climate and weather conditions
- Future expectations

Demand Functions and Demand Curve

In mathematical terms, a demand function represents a functional relationship between the demand for the product and its various determining variables. In demand analysis, at any point in time, the quantity of a given product that will be purchased by the consumer depends on a number of key variables or determinants. It is stated in terms of demand function for the given product.

Demand function is a comprehensive formulation which specifies the factors that influence the demand for the product.

Mathematically, it can be explained as follows:

$$D_x = f(P_x, P_y, P_z, Y_d, B, A, E, T, U, N)$$

where
D_x Demand for product x
P_x Price of product x
P_y Price of substitute good
P_z Price of complementary good
Y_d Disposable income of the consumer
B Income of consumer
A Advertisement effect
E Price expectation of the user
T Taste or preference of user
U All other factors
N Number of buyers

Demand Schedule and Demand Curve

Price x P_x (per Unit Price)	Quantity x Demanded D_x (in Unit Demand for x)
2.5	1
1.5	2
1.0	3
0.5	5

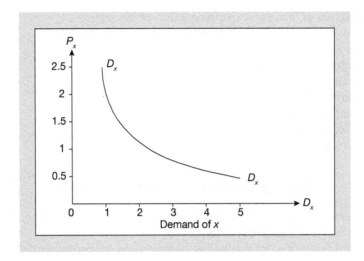

The above figure depicts how the demand curve is formed with the help of the demand schedule given in the table. D_xD_x is the demand curve which is slope downward to the right. The x-axis measures the quantity demanded of good x and y-axis measures the price of good x.

Shift in Demand Curve

If any of the components is held constant in drawing a demand curve change, there is a shift in the demand curve. It is of two types:

1. **Increase in demand:** An increase in demand indicates either that more will be demanded at a given price or same will be demanded at a higher price. This point can be understood with the help of following diagram:

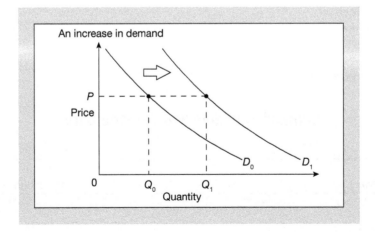

The above figure shows how the demand curve shifts with the increase in demand. Here, x-axis measures the quantity demanded and y-axis measures the price of the product. Initial demand curve is D0. With the increase in demand, the demand curve is shifting to the right, that is, from

D0 to D1. In this case, the movement from D0 to D1 indicates that the price remains same at 0P, but more quantity 0Q1 is demanded instead of 0Q0. Hence, the increase in demand is Q0Q1.

2. **Decrease in demand:** A decrease in demand indicates there is either a decrease in consumer's income or fall in the price of substitute product or unfavourable change in consumer's preference or aggressive advertisement expenditure by the competitive firms. This point can be understood with the help of the following diagram:

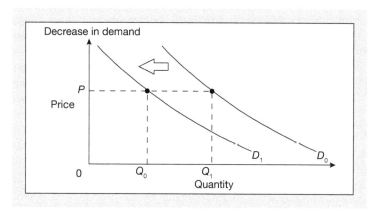

The above figure shows how the demand curve shifts with the decrease in demand. Here, x-axis measures the quantity demanded of the product and y-axis measures the price of the product. Initial demand curve is D_0. With the decrease in demand, the demand curve is shifting to the left, that is, from D_0 to D_1. In this case, the movement from D_0 to D_1 indicates that the price remains same at 0P, but less quantity $0Q_1$ is demanded instead of $0Q_0$. Hence, the decrease in demand is Q_1Q_0.

Relationship between Individual Demand and Market Demand

The relationship between individual demand and marketing demand can be depicted as follows:

Market Demand = Sum Total of Individual Demand

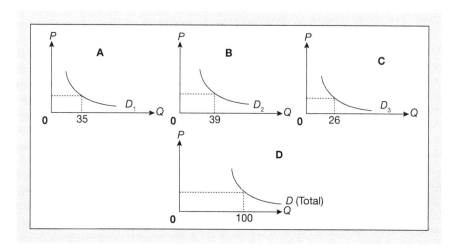

In the above diagrams, figure A denotes individual demand for A, figure B denotes individual demand for B and figure C denotes individual demand for C. If we combine these three demands of A, B and C, then we have market demand D.

4.2. Understanding Tourism Demand

The reasons why people choose to engage in tourism are diverse and multifaceted. In this context, no single explanation can be sufficient to attribute the demand for tourist motivation. Tourism demand can be conceptualized as how visitors choose and pursue a range of opportunities in their leisure time. The principles of tourism development have both demand- and supply-side dimensions. The study of tourist behaviour constitutes the demand side. Hall and Page (2006) explained that 'an understanding of tourism demand is a starting point for the analysis of why tourism develops, who patronizes specific destinations and what appeals to the client market'.

Tourism demand is the foundation on which all decisions related with tourism business are taken into consideration. Tourism demand has been defined in numerous ways. 'Geographers' examine tourism demand in a spatial context, whereas the 'economists' examine the tourist propensity to purchase tourism products or services at a specific price within a given timeframe. However, a 'psychologist' defines tourism demand on the basis of motivation and behaviour. On the other hand, the 'anthropologists' and 'sociologists' define tourism demand in terms of society hosting tourist and the social dimension of tourist visiting the destination.

The demand for tourism depends on the total budget which is available for spending and on the preference of tourism relative to other goods and services. In the case of tourism, both the expenditure budget and people's preferences are key variables underlying tourism demand.

- **Pearce** (1995) stated that tourism demand is the relationship between individuals' motivation to travel and their ability to do so.
- **Mathieson and Wall** (1982) mentioned that tourism demand is the total number of persons who travel, or wish to travel, to use tourist facilities and services at places away from their places of work and residents.
- **Cooper et al.** (1993) defined tourism demand in terms of the economic context as 'the schedule of the amount of any product or service which people are willing to have and ability to buy at each specific price in a set of possible prices during a specified period of time'.

4.3. Levels of Tourism Demand

In tourism, demand has to be analysed for studying market segmentation for the destination. Accordingly, the product will be developed to meet the needs of those segments. Each and every product segment in tourism has distinctive characteristic feature to match the needs of its market segment.

Smith (1995) described that tourism demand occurs at four different levels. These are:

1. Amount of products that will be consumed at various prices
2. Actual levels of participation
3. The unsatisfied components of participation
4. The desire for emotionally and psychologically based experiences

Roger Doswell mentioned four levels of demand. These are:

1. **Basic:** The basic demand is an existing demand which is not being completely satisfied. It is also referred to as an unfulfilled need.
2. **Displacement:** This level of demand occurs when people are persuaded to stop using one product in favour of another product which better satisfies their needs. For example, sometimes it is seen that construction of good hotels and better tourist facilities for the tourists result in displacement demand for one destination towards the other.
3. **Created:** This level of tourism demand arises when the creation of a new product creates a demand which did not exist before. Here, new needs are generated.
4. **Future:** This means the need which is yet to come in future. This demand will be generated by the future changes and developments. For example, future demand becomes a part of a basic demand by increasing standard of living, increasing population, economic growth and by a general growth in tourism.

4.4. Elements of Tourism Demand

The elements of tourism demand can be categorized under the following headings:

- **Actual/effective/aggregate demand:** Actual demand may be referred to as the demand which is materialized. Sometimes it is also used as a synonym for effective demand or aggregate demand. It is the number of tourists recorded in a given location for a particular time period. Actual demand is the number of people who are participating in tourism activity, commonly expressed as the number of travellers. Within a population, effective tourism demand can be measured by means of gross and net travel propensity (total number of tourism trips as a percentage of travel population). It means the absolute number of participants who actually travelled and experienced during the entire course of their entire tourism activity.
- **Suppressed demand:** This type of demand consists of the population who cannot travel because of various circumstances such as limited holiday entitlement and lack of purchasing power. Cooper et al. (1998) suggested that suppressed demand can be further sub-divided into **'potential'** and **'deferred'** demands.
  - **Potential** demand can be converted to effective demand if the circumstances are favourable. This demand relates specifically to factors associated directly with the individual.
  - **Deferred** demands are those demands where constraints can also be converted to effective demand if a destination can accommodate the demand. Deferred demand is not attributed to any failing or bottleneck on the part of the tourist rather it can be due to the shortcomings in the supply-side environment. The reasons for the suppression are down to problems mainly from the supply side such as shortage of accommodation, problems in transportation and adverse climate to the preferred destinations. If this problem can be overcome, then it can be converted into actual or effective demand.
- **No demand:** There are some distinctive categories of population who have no desire to travel or not interested to participate in any kind of tourism activity. Reasons for not travelling may be due to the lack of money, family obligations, unwillingness or inability to find the time or a desire to enjoy holiday and so on.

Apart from these three elements, there is also another element of demand which is popularly known as '**substitution of demand**'. Cooper et al. (1998) referred this demand as the demand for an activity which is replaced by another form of activity. For example, eating in a restaurant rather than using self-catering.

4.5. Determinants of Tourism Demand

Determinants of tourism demand provide a general idea which is associated with the area of consumer behaviour and motivation. This may not exactly explain how and why people decide to select and participate in specific forms of tourism. There are numerous factors which may influence the demand in the tourist-generating area which was summarized by Uysal (1998):

- **Economic determinants:** The availability of money is the most influencing determinant for tourism demand. Income of the tourist and tourism expenditure are closely linked. This relationship can be examined through statistics on economic trends and tourism activity in any country. These determinants are disposable income, gross national product (GNP) per capita income, private consumption, cost of living, exchange rate difference, price with physical distance, transportation cost and so on.
- **Socio-psychological determinants:** These determinants may include demographic variables, holiday entitlements, images and perceptions of destinations, attitude about destinations, amount of travel and leisure time, past experience, life expectancy and so on. A range of demographic variables such as age, gender, family size and education affect demand. The impact of education can also become a major determinant for the type of employment and income. Other factors such as occupation, ownership of home and ethnic groups are recognized as major determinants of demand. Holiday entitlements including public holidays and holidays for school children give seasonal pattern of tourism demand.
- **Exogenous determinants:** These determinants may include political environment, economic growth and stability, availability of supply resources, recession, levels of infrastructural development, natural disaster, degree of urbanization, rules regulations and restrictions, technological advancement and so on. The government controls such as policies, and rules and regulations have greater impact on tourism demand. The government tax policies and control policies can affect tourist flow to a specific destination.

4.6. Law of Demand

The law of demand is one of the most important aspects in economic analysis. The law of demand explains about the general tendency of consumer's behaviour in demanding a good/commodity in relation to the changes in its price. It expresses the functional relationship that between price and quantity demanded. It simply states that there is an inverse relationship between these two, whereas other things remain the same. The nature of this inverse relationship explained by the law of demand is one of the best known and most significant laws in economics.

Statement of the law of demand
According to the law of demand, 'other thing being equal, the higher the price of a commodity, the smaller the quantities demanded and lower the price, higher the quantity demanded'.

In other words, if the price of a commodity rises, then its quantity demanded falls and vice versa.

Explanation of the law of demand

From economist viewpoint, let's consider that the law of demand should be referred to as the market demand. This law of demand can be explained with the help of following imaginary table. According to the table given below, when the price of commodity decreases, the corresponding quantity demanded for that commodity increases and vice versa.

A Market demand schedule

Price of Commodity X (in ₹)	Quantity Demanded Units per Week
5	100
4	200
3	300
2	400
1	500

The above table describes about the hypothetical demand schedule for commodity X. From the above table, we can see that with a fall in price of commodity X, the quantity demanded tends to increase. This shows that there is an inverse relationship that exists between these two.

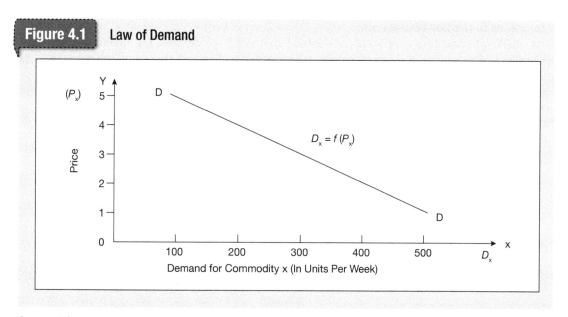

Figure 4.1   **Law of Demand**

Source: Mithini D. M. (2000).

The pictorial presentation of the law of demand can be seen in Figure 4.1, where DD is the demand curve. In the x-axis, we measure the quantity demanded and in the y-axis we measure the price. This demand curve indicates that there is an inverse relationship that exists between price and quantity demanded. Mathematically, the demand function can be expressed as $D_x = f(P_x)$.

The law of demand is based on following assumptions:

- The consumers income should remain constant.
- Consumer's tastes, habits and preferences should remain constant.
- No change in fashion and custom.
- There should not be any change in price of related goods.
  - No change in size, age composition and sex ratio of the population.
  - No changes in future price of the product.
  - No change in the government policy.
  - No change in weather condition.

It should, however, be noted that demand schedule or a demand curve does not tell us what price is; it only tells us how much quantity of good would be purchased by the consumer at various possible prices. Further it is seen from the demand schedule and the demand curve that as the price of commodity falls, more quantity of it is purchased or demanded. Since more is the demand at lower price and less is the demand at higher price, the demand curve slopes downward the right. Thus the downward slopping demand curve is in accordance with the law of demand which, as stated above, describes an inverse price–demand relationship.

It is also important to note that the taste and preference of the consumer, income of the consumer, the price of substitute goods and complementary goods are assumed to remain constant behind this price–demand relationship or demand curve.

Exceptions to the law of demand
It is universal according to the law of demand that when price falls, the quantity demanded increases and vice versa. But sometimes, in rare cases it is observed that when the price falls, its quantity demanded also falls and when the price rises, the quantity demanded also rises. These are known as exceptions to the law of demand. In this case, the demand curve is upward sloping which is depicted in the figure given below.

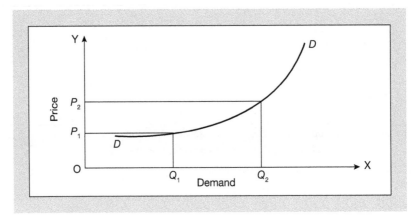

The figure on the previous page depicts the upward sloping demand curve which implies even if the price of the products increases from P1 to P2 the quantity demanded of the product increases from Q1 to Q2 which is contradicting the law of demand. Exceptions to the law of demand can be understood with the help of following examples:

- **Giffen goods:** According to Sir Robert Giffen, in the case of certain inferior goods, when the price decreases, sometimes the quantity will be purchased less than before because of the negative income effect and people's increasing preference for superior commodity with the rise in their real income. Some of the examples in this regard are cheap potatoes, vegetable ghee, cheap bread and so on.
- **Article of snob appeal:** In some cases, certain commodities such as diamond and gold are demanded just because not only they are expensive but also happen to represent prestige or status symbol. These articles satisfy the aristocratic desire to preserve exclusively for unique goods. It is also seen that when the prices of such article increase, instead of decrease in demand, the demand for the above goods still increases.
- **Speculation:** As we know that money can be demanded for three reasons, namely transaction demand, precautionary demand and speculative demand. In speculative demand for money, people generally invest money in bonds, shares, debentures and so on. However, in stock market, when the price of bonds, shares or debentures increases, the quantity demanded also increases with an expectation that the price will further increase so that they can get more return. So, here, the law of demand does not work.
- **Consumer psychological bias or illusion:** In certain cases when the consumer is wrongly biased against the quality of commodity with the price change, he/she may reduce the demand with a fall in price. For example, some sophisticated consumers do not buy when there is a stock clearance sale at reduced price, thinking that the good may be of bad quality.

4.7. Measurement and Forecast of Tourism Demand

Adequate measurement and forecast of tourism demand help tourism manager in planning, marketing and selling of their products. Demand must be understood to successfully design, develop and promote a tourism product. Witt and Witt (1992) mentioned that international tourism demand is measured in terms of the number of tourists from an origin country who visit a foreign destination; or in terms of tourist expenditures by visitors from the origin country in the destination country.

Tourism demand can also be measured by counting tourist nights in the destination country. Tourist visits are usually recorded at the border (inbound) or by serving by a sample of travellers. For counting the number of visitors and number of nights at the destination, records of accommodations establishments can be used.

Measuring Tourism Demand

There are number of ways by which tourism demand can be measured both nationally and internationally. *Latham and Edwards* (2003) explained that most tourism statistics are typically measurements of arrival, trips, tourist nights and tourist expenditure. In the case of measuring

domestic tourism demand, *Pearce* (1995) acknowledged that the scale and volume of domestic tourism exceed that of international tourism. It is difficult to calculate domestic demand because domestic tourism statistics often underestimate the scale and volume of tourist flows or are sometimes ignored in official statistics.

The VFR, staying in supplementary accommodations and travel to the countryside destination or remote destinations by a large number of travellers are not sometimes included in calculating the domestic tourist statistics. That is why the collection of domestic tourism statistics requires the use of data from all sources besides the traditional sources such as collecting statistics from hotel records and entry tickets.

WTO in 1981 identified the following four uses of calculating domestic tourism statistics:

1. To calculate the contribution of tourism to the country's economy, whereby estimates of tourism's value to the gross domestic product (GDP) estimated due to the complexity of identifying the scope of tourism contribution.
2. To assist in the promotion and marketing of tourism, where the government-sponsored tourism organizations seek to encourage the population to take domestic holidays rather than to travel.
3. To help the regional development policies of the governments which harness tourism as a toll for area development where domestic tourists in congested environment are encouraged to travel to less developed areas and to improve the quality of tourism in different environments.
4. To achieve social objectives where socially oriented tourism policies may be developed for the underprivileged: this requires a detailed understanding of the holiday-taking habits of a country's nationals.

International tourism can be measured in terms of a number of tourist visits to a foreign destination or in terms of tourist expenditure incurred during their visit to the destination country. It can also be calculated by counting tourist nights spent by the tourist in the destination country. Tourist's visits are usually recorded at the border. International tourist expenditure statistics are collected by the bank reporting method or by conducting specialized survey. Bank reporting method is the buying and selling of foreign currency by the travellers. Latham, in 1989, suggested that the international tourism statistics are collected in relation to:

- Volume of tourist
- Expenditure by tourist
- Profile of the tourist
- Characteristics of the tourist's trip

International tourism statistics are collected by the following:

- The counting of all travellers entering or leaving the country. Interviews are carried out at different entry points of the international border to obtain a more detailed profile of visitors and their activities during tour.
- Collecting international tourism statistics is by answering a self-administered questionnaire.
- Sample survey of an entire population of a country, both travellers and non-travellers.
- Calculating the nights spent by the tourists at different accommodation establishments.

Benefits of Measuring Tourism Demand

Statistics are necessary features for measuring the effective tourism demand. Burkart and Medlik (1981) identified three principles for statistical measurement in tourism demand. These are:

1. To evaluate the magnitude and significance of tourism to a destination area or region.
2. To quantify the contribution to the economy or society, especially the effect on the balance of payments.
3. To assist in the planning and development of tourism infrastructure, and the effect of different volumes of tourists with specific needs to assist in the evaluation and implementation of marketing and promotional activities, where the tourism marketers need information on actual tourist arrivals and their characteristics.

For measuring tourism demand, statistics are essential in terms of volume, scale, value and impact of tourism at different geographical scales.

Forecasting Tourism Demand

Forecasting refers to the process of organizing information about a phenomenon's past in order to predict its future (Frechtling, 2001). Witt and Witt (1995) explained that forecast can have different time scales such as short-term forecasts and long-term forecasts. For example, short-term forecasts are needed for scheduling and staffing, whereas long-term forecasts can influence the level of investment in airplanes and hotels.

In forecasting tourism demand, two types of methods are used. These include:

1. **Causal method of forecasting tourism demand:** This method links forecasting to a set of determining factors. These determining factors include arrival and expenditure of visitors, size of the origin population, the income of the origin country per capita, the price of products at the destination and other comparable destinations. In this method, forecasts are made up of each of these determining factors depending on their impact on tourism demand. This is also called as econometric forecasting method. This type of forecasting is more expensive as well as complex and may be difficult to find forecasts for all the determining factors.
2. **Non-causal method of forecasting tourism demand:** Non-causal methods look at the past development of a phenomenon and predict the future of the phenomenon by extrapolating the trend. This method starts from the principle that a variable may be forecasted without reference to the factors which determine the variable. In the case of tourism, if it was growing at a certain rate in the past, it can be predicted that tourism demand will grow based on past trend. The benefit of this method is that it is easy to apply at a low cost. The problem of this method is that it presumes the cause of growth and decline will be same in future as it was in the past. This may not be always true. As described by Frechtling (2001), tourism demand is highly volatile and can be severely affected by events like war or crisis. Demand is thus not stable enough to assume that it will just continue to grow or decline.

4.8. Factors Influencing Tourism Demand

There are several factors which are responsible for influencing the tourism demand of a destination. However, these factors can be broadly categorized as follows:

- **Economic factor:** The main economic factor which can influence the tourism demand of a destination is **price.** The relationship between price and demand is an inverse one. Higher prices result in lower demand and vice versa. As Burkart and Medlik (1981) pointed out that tourism suppliers, such as in the accommodation and transport sectors, may effectively price their products independently, but a close watch on the behaviour of their competitors is clearly necessary. Though the price is considered as a central part of the tourist product, the demand for tourism is also influenced by other forms of expenditure associated with the tour. Tourists are very much sensitive to the cost of the tour. Any changes in the price, especially a reduction may be perceived as the quality of product compromised during the visit.
- **Supply-related factor: Competition** among the suppliers is one of the important factors which can influence the tourism demand at the destination. If the number of suppliers in the destination increases, the level of competition among the suppliers also increases. The extent of this competition among the suppliers will relate to the number and size of the suppliers. Price competitiveness between the destinations is also an issue which can influence tourism demand.
- **Political factor:** Political factors especially the government controls at the destinations and in the tourist generating area can influence the tourism demand. The government regulation regarding the tourist movement can directly influence the tourist flow. Frontier formalities such as passport, visa, health regulations, customs and currency are some of the best examples of political factors which affect the tourism demand of a destination. Sometimes at tourism destination, the government can control carrying capacity through planning regulation which may restrict tourist flow.
- **Other factors:** Apart from the above important factors, there are some other factors which can influence the tourism demand at the destination. These include:
  - *Seasonal variations:* The demand for tourism may be affected by environmental factors such as climate and weather. Climate (sunshine, wind, temperature, precipitation, snow fall and so on) may be the key determinant of tourist activities in many destinations. It helps to shape seasonal patterns of tourist's movements. Seasonality is an important determining factor for influencing tourism demand to escape from unfavourable climate. Pricing policies of different tourist providers (airlines, hotels, transporters and so on) are affected by the seasonal variations. Vacations and holidays, and sport activities are some of the elements of seasonal variations which affect the tourism demand.
  - *Promotional efforts of the destination:* In today's competitive world, promotion for the destination is one of the important factors for creating demand for the destination. Due to the intangible nature of the tourist product, the promotional effort is more important in selling the tourist product. Before visiting a destination, the information normally sought by the tourist must be provided to create demand for the destination. The success of promotional effort can influence tourism demand. This may be in the form of

brochures, pamphlets, leaflets, provision of online information, advertisement in print and electronic media and so on.

○ *Safety, security and health issues:* Safety and security issues are more important to create tourism demand at the regional and international levels. In this context, some of the recent incidents such as 9/11 attack at the World Trade Center, New York; terrorist attack at Indian Parliament, New Delhi; and war-like situation in different parts of the world especially in the Middle East, Afghanistan, Pakistan and so on are major security and safety issues causing considerable influence on tourism demand. Some health-related issues such as SARS, plague, foot and mouth diseases, yellow fever, cholera and human immunodeficiency viruses (HIV) are major constraints for tourist inflow to different countries causing influence on tourism demand.

○ *Time and cost consideration:* Both time and cost components involved in travel may influence tourism demand in a considerable manner. Destinations in Europe, United States of America–Canada, South Asia and so on are attracting tourists from their neighbours because of these factors.

4.9. Travel Propensity

Propensity is an important term frequently used in the study of travel and tourism. The main aim of studying travel propensity is to define the extent of participation in travel activity in a given population. Proper calculation of travel propensity can be made by using national and other tourism survey regarding the trips taken in a specified period. Travel propensity is a useful tool to calculate the effective demand for travel. Travel propensity means the percentage of a population that is actually engaged in tourism.

For example, while calculating holiday propensity, we have to measure the proportion of population which normally undertake holiday in a given year. There are instances where some people may take one holiday, while others take three or more. So to calculate the travel propensity properly we have to distinguish between net travel propensity and gross travel propensity.

- **Net travel propensity:** It can be calculated as the proportion of a population which takes at least one holiday in a year, that is, within 12-month period.

  Net travel propensity = Number of population taking at least one trip/Total population

- **Gross travel propensity:** It can be calculated as the total number of holidays taken, expressed as a proportion of a population (proportion taking any holidays multiplied by the average number of holidays taken).

  Gross travel propensity = Number of total trips/Total population

- Similarly, travel frequency can be calculated as:

  Travel frequency = Gross travel propensity/Net travel propensity

- Similarly, if we want to calculate the country potential generation index (CPGI) as a whole, then the formula will be

CPGI = Number of trips generated by country/Number of trips generated in the world

$$CPGI = \frac{Nc \, / \, Nw}{Pc \, / \, Pw}$$

where
Pc = Population of the country
Pw = Population of the world
CPGI = Country Potentials Generation index
Nc = Number of trips generated by the country
Nw = Number of trips generated by the world

Determinant of Travel Propensity

Travel propensity is determined by a variety of factors which can be broadly classified into two types. **The first category** is the influences that lie at the national level of generalization and comprised the view of travel propensity, including economic development, population characteristics and political regimes. **Second category** includes a personal view of variation in travel propensity that can be envisaged in terms such as lifestyle, life cycle and personality factor.

In fact, **a third category** of factor relating the supply of tourist services is also important. This group encompasses technology, price, frequency and speed of transport as well as the characteristics of accommodation, facilities and travel organizers.

Based on these above determinants of demand, mainly the **socio-economic aspects**, propensity can be of two types, namely low propensity and high propensity.

Low propensity includes:

- Low income per household
- Single parent household
- Rural community dweller
- Educated to minimum wage
- Older people
- No private transport availability
- Less than two weeks of holiday

High propensity includes:

- High income per household
- Families with two parents employed
- Large city dwellers
- Younger people
- Two or more vehicles in the household
- Four or more week holidays with pay

An index of 1.0 reveals an average generation capability to travel. A country with an index more than 1.0 indicates that the country is generating more tourist than expected. Similarly a country with an index value of less than 1.0 indicates that the country is generating fewer trips than expected.

4.10. Tourism Demand Process

To study the nature of tourism demand process is really a complex issue. Sometimes, the demand for tourism is synonymous with the consumption of tourism. As described by Pearce (1992, p. 114), tourism demand is characterized as discretionary, episodic, future oriented, dynamic, socially influenced and evolving. The demand for tourism is nothing but to make a choice about how to spend specific period of leisure time. The choice of destination as well as time period is mainly influenced by various factors. Sometimes these factors may vary with the change in time as well. The most important things are to know exactly:

- How and why people decided to participate in tourism?
- How the people behave as tourists during their visit?
- Why did they choose a particular type of tourism?

These questions may be answered properly if we study the consumption/demand process of the tourists. Despite the complex process of consumer demand, tourism demand process can be explained with the help of following stages:

Stage 1: Problem identification of the tourists (identifying the basic/felt need)
Stage 2: Information search and evaluation
Stage 3: Purchase (travel) decisions
Stage 4: Travel experience
Stage 5: Evaluation of travel experience

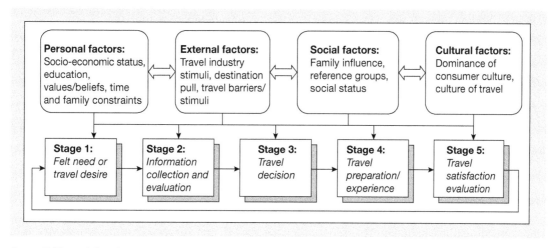

Source: Telfer and Sharpley (2008).

Each stage of the above demand process may be influenced by both personal factors and external factors. These factors include:

- Time
- Money constraints
- Social stimuli

- Media influences
- Image about the destination
- Marketing techniques

According to Pearce (1992), tourism demand is not a one-off event. According to him, people consume tourism product over a lifetime, during which tourist may climb a travel career ladder (discussed in Chapter 3) as they become more experienced. As a result, a tourist's travel needs and expectations may vary and evolve, but these may be influenced by several factors such as social relationship, lifestyle factors and constraints, and emerging values and attitudes. Tourism demand/consumption process is an appreciation of the factors that may influence the demand process which can be categorized under four headings:

1. **Energizers of demand:** These factors are popularly known as push factors which motivate the tourist to travel to go for holiday. This initiates the demand process.
2. **Effectors of demand:** This is the subsequent stage of demand process which influences the travel purchase. This is influenced by tourist knowledge and perception of a particular destination. These are popularly known as pull factors which influence the tourist to make decision on travel.
3. **Filters/Determinants of demand:** These are the economic, sociocultural and demographic factors which filter out the negative factors from the lot and make provision to travel. These include mobility, income, employment, age, gender, race, stages of family cycle and so on. These are also influenced by psychographic variables such as value, attitude, belief and lifestyle.
4. **Roles:** These are related to the members/persons who are taking final decisions (choice) on travel in choosing the holiday.

It is evident from the above that no doubt predicting tourist behaviour is very difficult but it is not an impossible one. There are several variables which can be taken into consideration while taking a decision on how, when and where tourism is consumed by the tourists.

- According to Krippendrorf (1987), 'sometimes many tourists they themselves are unable to explain precisely why they are participating in a particular type/form of tourism'.
- According to Ryan (1997), 'tourism mostly shows an irrational form of behaviour because of its complexity'.

So to study the tourism demand process, one has to give importance to three issues, namely, tourist motivation, the influence of value on consumption and the consumer culture.

Conclusion

Understanding tourism demand is essential for the growth and survival of tourism industry. It is also important in fixing the price of the products as well as various promotional efforts required to market the product. It is one of the most complex issues involved in tourism business. There are various factors which influence the demand and sometimes are beyond the control of those within the tourism industries, called as exogenous factors. A lot of problems and challenges are involved in measuring demand because of its complexity and accuracy. Study of tourism demand will help in getting practical application and principles of understanding what motivate a tourist as a consumer. Understanding why do people travel and why they choose to go for a holiday though seems to be a very simple proposition but practically it is a very complex issue which needs to be tackled carefully. Demand theories will help in finding the reasons behind both the development and intensity of tourism flow within a country as well as between countries. As tourism demand represents the quantity of touristic goods and services that are consumed in a given period of time, it helps in calculating the population's interest in undergoing trips.

The role of demand can be studied at both domestic and international levels. In the case of domestic level, the study of tourism demand will determine the level of international tourism in a country. It is a well-known fact that a high domestic tourism demand may create an environment and condition which is favourable for the development of international tourism. Keeping this in mind, a country should develop transport, accommodation, infrastructure and super structure including natural, historical and cultural sites to increase the demand of the tourist to visit that country. In the case of international level, the role of demand can be measured both qualitatively and quantitatively. Attempt has also been made in this chapter to define tourism demand in terms of levels, elements and determinants.

MODEL QUESTIONS

1. How do you define demand?
2. Explain the law of demand and its exceptions.
3. What do you mean by travel propensity? Explain various methods of calculating travel propensity.
4. Explain different types of tourism demand.
5. State and explain factors affecting tourism demand.
6. Write a note on levels of tourism demand.
7. Briefly explain the major issues involved in forecasting tourism demand.
8. Write short notes on elements of tourism demand.
9. Explain in brief various determinants of tourism demand with suitable examples.
10. What is tourism demand? Explain various methods of calculating tourism demand.

Student Activities

1. Visit different tourist destinations and provide suggestions by which future tourism demand of these destinations can be increased.
2. Study the role played by the government to increase the tourism demand of your state during the lean season.

Suggested Readings

Cooper, C., Fletcher, J., Fyall, A., Gilbert, D., Wanhill, S., & Shepherd, R. (1998). *Tourism: Principles and practices* (2nd ed.). London: Longman.

D. Ioannides & K. G. Debbage (eds), *The economic geography of the tourist industry: A supply-side analysis* (pp. 79–95). New York: Routledge.

Frechting, C. D. (1996). *Practical tourism forecasting*. Oxford, London: Butterworth–Heinemann.

Frechtling, Douglas C. (2001). Forecasting tourism demand: Methods and strategies. Oxford, UK: Butterworth Heinemann. Published in *Journal of Travel Research, 41*, 3 (February 2003), 332–334.

Karma, K. K. (2006). *Economics of tourism: Pricing, impact and forecasting* (Rev. ed.). New Delhi: Kanishka Publishers, Distributors.

Mithani, D.M. (2000). *Managerial Economics Theory and Applications*. New Delhi: Himalayan Publishing House.

Moutinho, L. (1987). Consumer behaviour in tourism. *European Journal of Marketing, 21*(10), 3–44.

Pearce, D. (1992). *Tourism today a geographical analysis*. London: Longman, Scientific & Technical.

Pearce, P. (1982). *The social psychology of tourist behaviour*. Oxford: Pergamon.

Ryan, C., & Page, S. J. (Eds.). (2000). *Tourism management: Towards new millennium*. Oxford: Pergamon.

Smith, S. J. L. (2007). *The measurement of global tourism: Old debates, new consensus and continuing challenges* (reprint). Oxford: Blackwell.

Tefler, D. J., & Sharpley, R. (2008). *Tourism development in the developing world*. London: Routledge.

Uysal, M. (1998). The determinants of tourism demand: A theoretical perspective. In

Wahab, S., & Pigram, J. J. (Eds.). (1997). *Tourism development and growth: The challenge of sustainability*. London: Routledge.

Witt, S. F., & Witt, C. A. (1995). Forecasting tourism demand: A review of empirical research. *International Journal of Forecasting, 11*(3), 447–475.

5   Tourism Supply

CHAPTER OVERVIEW

Chapter 5 discusses various components of tourism supply and their importance in tourism business. This chapter mainly deals with understanding of the tourism supply determinants and their significance. Various issues involved in tourism supply chain management are discussed in this chapter. Different models of tourism supply chain (TSC) including features and elements are also explained.

5.1. Introduction

Supply in terms of pure economics implies the quantities of goods which are offered for sale at a particular price at a given period of time. Supply of goods/commodities can be defined as 'the amount of commodity which the seller/producer is able to or willingness to offer for sale at a particular price during a certain period of time'.

The law of supply describes a relationship between price and quantity supplied of a commodity on the assumption that the conditions of supply remain constant. The supply of a good/commodity depends not only on the price of the commodity but also on several other factors collectively known as the conditions of supply. The main determinants of supply are as follows:

- **The cost of factors of production:** The cost of production of a commodity depends on the prices of the various factors of production. If the price of factor of production rises, the production costs would be higher for the same level of output. Conversely, a fall in the price of a factor would reduce the cost of production. In both the cases, the supply will be affected. When costs fall, a new line will have to be drawn to the left of the old one while depicting a supply curve.

- **The state of technology:** The supply of a commodity depends on the methods of production. Advances in science and technology are the most powerful forces influencing the factors of production. Most of the inventions and innovations in chemistry, electronics, atomic energy and so on have greatly contributed to the increased supplies of commodities at lower costs.
- **Factors outside the economic sphere:** Weather conditions, floods, droughts, epidemics and so on do cause fluctuations in the supply of goods, particularly of agricultural goods. Fire, war and earthquakes may destroy productive assets of a commodity and curtail future supplies.
- **Tax and subsidy:** Tax on a commodity or a factor of production raises its cost of production; consequently, production is reduced. A subsidy, on the other hand, provides an incentive to production and augments supplies.

Supply function

In a supply function, the determinants of supply can be summarized as under:

$$Sx = f (Px, Pf, Py, ..., Pz, o, T, t, s)$$

where

Sx   the supply of commodity X
Px   the price of X
Pf   the set prices of the factor inputs employed for producing X
O   factors outside the economic sphere
T   technology
t   tax
S   subsidy

The Law of Supply

The law of supply explains the general tendency of the sellers in offering their stock of a commodity for sale in relation to the change in prices. It indicates sellers' supply more with a rise in prices.

Statement of the law

Under the ceteris paribus assumption, the law of supply may be defined as 'other things remaining unchanged, the supply of a commodity expands (i.e., rises) with a rise in its price, and contracts (i.e., falls) with a fall in its price'.

The law, thus, suggests that the supply varies directly with the changes in price. So, a larger amount is supplied at a higher price than at a lower price in the market.

Explanation of the law

The law can be explained and illustrated with the help of a supply schedule as well as a supply curve, based on an imaginary data, as shown in Table 5.1 and Figure 5.1.

When the data of Table 5.1 is plotted on a graph, a supply curve can be drawn as shown in Figure 5.1. From the supply schedule, it appears that the market supply tends to expand with a rise in price and vice versa. Similarly, the upward sloping curve also depicts a direct covariation between price and supply.

Assumptions underlying the law of supply

The law of supply is conditional, since we have mentioned it under the assumption 'other things remaining unchanged'. It is based on the following ceteris paribus assumptions:

- **Cost of production is unchanged:** It is assumed that the price of the product changes, but there is no change in the cost of production. If the cost of production increases along with the rise in the price of product, the sellers will not find it worthwhile to produce more and supply more. Therefore, the law of supply is valid only if the cost of production remains constant. It implies that the factor prices such as wages, interest and rent are also unchanged.

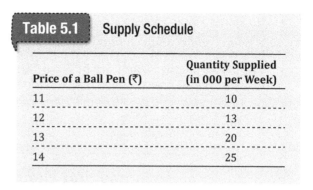

Table 5.1	Supply Schedule

Price of a Ball Pen (₹)	Quantity Supplied (in 000 per Week)
11	10
12	13
13	20
14	25

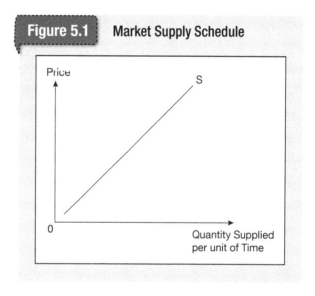

Figure 5.1   **Market Supply Schedule**

- **No change in technique of production:** The technique of production is assumed to be unchanged. This is essential for the cost to remain unchanged. With the improvement in technique, if the cost of production is reduced, the seller would supply more even at falling prices.
- **Fixed scale of production:** During a given period of time, it is assumed that the scale of production is held constant. If there is a change in the scale of production, the level of supply will change, irrespective of the changes in the price of the product.
- **The government policies are unchanged:** The government policies such as taxation policy and trade policy are assumed to be constant. For instance, an increase in or totally fresh levy of excise duties would imply and increase the cost or in case there is fixation of quotas for the raw materials or imported components for a product, then such a situation will not permit the expansion of supply with a rise in prices.
- **No change in transport costs:** It is assumed that the transport facilities and transport costs are unchanged. Otherwise, a reduction in transport cost implies lowering of cost of productions, so that more would be supplied even at a lower price.

- **No speculation:** The law also assumes that the sellers do not speculate about the future changes in the price of the product. If, however, sellers expect prices to rise further in future, they may not expand supply with the present price rise.
- **The prices of other goods are held constant:** The law assumes that there are no changes in the prices of other products. If the price of some other product rises faster than that of the given product in consideration, producers might transfer their resources to the other product which is more profit yielding due to rising prices. Under this situation, more of the product in consideration may not be supplied, despite the rising prices.

Increase and Decrease in Supply

These two terms are introduced to explain the change in supply without any change in price. Sometimes, more supply might be forthcoming in the market without a change in price, in which case it is called increase in supply. If there is less supply forthcoming in the market without a change in price, then it is called decrease in supply. The change in supply due to causes or determinants other than price is called 'decrease' or 'increase' in supply and can be shown on a different supply curve.

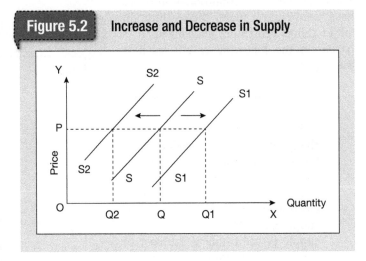

Figure 5.2   **Increase and Decrease in Supply**

In Figure 5.2, at point OP, the supply is 00; at the same price when the supply increases from 0Q to 0Q1, it is called increase in supply. It cannot be shown in the initial supply curve. Likewise in the same figure, when the price is at OP, the supply becomes 0Q2 instead of 00. It means there is a decrease in supply. This can be shown by shifting the supply curve to the left (S2S2 curve). It should be noted that the shifts need not be parallel.

Causes for Change in Supply

There are many causes which bring about a change in the conditions of supply. The important factors are:

- **Cost of production:** Given the price, the supply changes with the change in the cost of production. If the cost of production increases because of higher wages to workers or higher prices of raw materials, there will be decrease in supply. If the cost of production falls due to any of the above reasons, the supply will increase.
- **Natural factors:** There might be a decrease in the supply due to floods, paucity of rainfall, pests, earthquakes and so on; absence of the above calamities or an exceptionally good as well as timely monsoon might increase supply.

- **Change in technique of production:** This has an important influence on supply. An improvement in the technique of production might go a long way in increasing the supply. For instance, introduction of highly sophisticated machines increases the supply of goods.
- **Government policies:** Taxes on production, sales, import duties and import restrictions may reduce supply. It may also be delicately reduced by the government policies.
- **Development of transport:** Improvement in the means of transport obviously increases the supply of goods as they facilitate the movement of goods from one place to another.
- **Business combines:** The producers might also reduce the supply by entering into an agreement among themselves through their business combines such as trust and cartel or a syndicate with a view to raising prices in the market.

5.2. Understanding Tourism Supply

Tourism suppliers are providers of the travel products that are consumed by tourists during their trip. In any buying decision for a tourism product, there has to be some provision of product by the business organizations to meet the visitor's demand. **Sessa** (1983) mentioned that 'tourism supply is the result of those productive activities that involve the provision of goods and services required to meet tourism demand and which are expressed in tourism consumption'. Tourism suppliers can be defined by the sectors within which they operate. These include transport, accommodations, attractions, destination facilities and services, and so on. Each of the sectors is highly fragmented and consists of a broad range of distinct suppliers.

Various issues related to tourism supply, according to **Sinclair and Stabler** (1992), can be classified into the following:

- Descriptions of the industry, and its operation, management and marketing
- The spatial development and interruptions which characterize the industry on local, national and international scales
- The effects which result from the development of the industry

In order to manage the business organizations' resources in an efficient and profitable manner, the following questions need to be addressed:

- What should be produced by the organization to meet the tourism demand?
- How should it be produced by the business organizations?
- Where, when and how the organization produce the tourism product?
- What destinations should be given importance?
- What form of business is needed to produce the tourism product?

5.3. Features of Tourism Supply

Tourism supply is a complex phenomenon due to its nature of the product and the process of delivery. Basically, tourist product is a complex product which includes transportation, accommodation, catering, natural resources, entertainments, and other facilities and services such as travel agents, tour operators, foreign exchange companies, banks and shops.

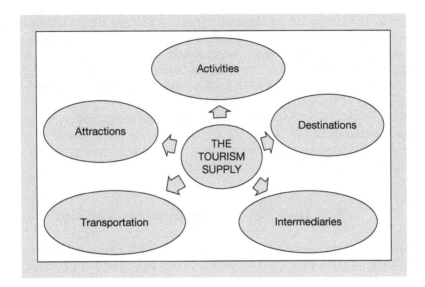

The key features of tourism supply examine the interrelations between the structure of tourism supply, and the degree and types of consumptions that prevail between firms, particularly the tourism sector. Different theoretical models have been developed to describe the criteria needed for the context of specific tourism sectors in different countries, thereby giving importance to the types of market structures (perfect competition, monopoly, monopolistic, oligopoly and so on) prevailing in this sector, as well as to study the nature of inter-firm competition. These studies are important because they provide useful information on the implications of different market structures for determining the profit, break-even level and hence helps in providing measures to achieve consumers' welfares. The main reasons for which both technical model and the overview of tourism business are identified include the following:

- Number and size of firms
- Degree of market concentration, and the level of entry and exit barriers
- Economics and diseconomies of scale, and economics of scope
- Capital individualities, fixed capacity and associated fixed costs of operations
- Price discriminations and product differentiations
- Pricing policies—leadership, war and market share strategies

From the above criteria, the first four points will determine the market structure and the last two will determine the strategies the firms will pursue within imperfect competitive market.

5.4. Elements of Tourism Supply

Tourism supply consists of an amalgamation or admixture of attractions that help in shaping the demand for tourism in a country. Elements of tourism supply include the following:

- **Tourism resources:** Both natural and man-made resources
- **Tourism infrastructure:** Roads, buildings, drainage systems, airports, electricity and so on

- **Facilities:** Food and beverage, accommodations, shopping, souvenirs and so on
- **Entertainment facilities:** Leisure, recreation, amusements and so on
- **Tourism service providers:** Tour operators, travel agencies, car rental companies, guides and so on

5.5. Determinants of Tourism Supply

Tourism is a composite product which includes accommodation, transportation, food service, natural and man-made resources, and other supplementary services such as tour operators, travel agents, tourist guides, banking and other financial institutions, and shops. Tourism supply, as we know, is a complex phenomenon because of its peculiar product characteristics and the process of service delivery. Basically tourist products are perishable and intangible in nature. There are basically three types of business organizations involved in tourism supply business. These are as follows:

1. **The public sector:** These are the government organizations which provide services, facilities and infrastructure by imposing taxes to facilitate and manage tourism activity. The major roles of public sector include:
   i.   Provide necessary infrastructure.
   ii. Support tourism product at local level.
   iii. Provide sufficient information on local events, attractions and so on.
   iv. Maintain safety and security at the destination.
   v.   Develop new tourism products.
   vi. Maintain good quality environment.
2. **Private sector:** In the case of tourism supply, the private sector plays a very crucial role although it is mainly driven by profit motive. In tourism sector, mainly the small sectors are dominated by the private sector.
3. **The non-profit/voluntary sectors:** NGOs and voluntary organizations work in tourism business which includes maintenance of heritage property, national historic assets and so on. They are also facilitating the community in terms of providing employment, skill development, awareness creation, educating the local community, including the service providers, as well as protecting the environments and so on.

5.6. Factors Affecting Tourism Supply

We know that tourism supply is the supply of all goods and services to be enjoyed or bought by the tourists during the entire course of his/her journey. There are several factors which affect the tourism supply. These factors may be categorized under the following headings:

- **Individual factors:** These factors include mobility, age, gender, family influence, composition of family, stages of family life cycle, religion, education and awareness, income and so on.
- **Economic factors:** The main economic factors which influence the tourism supply include cost of products (package), cost of travel, competition that prevails in the market, exchange rate and so on.

- **Geographical factors:** Geographical factors which influence the tourism supply include distance, accessibility, location, seasonality, availability of attractions and urban or rural economies.
- **Destination factors:** Major destination factors which affect the supply of tourism are image of the destination, awareness and promotion of the place/destination, technological advancement, credibility of the destination, safety and security aspects, quality of tourist products, availability and travel formalities, and so on.
- **Political factors:** These factors include the provision for the government regulation on tourists and supply, visa, foreign exchange, customs and currencies, bilateral agreements, transport regulations and so on.

5.7. Tourism Supply Chain

Tourism products are often perceived by the consumers as combinations of value added chain of different service components. As a result, various firms in order to gain competitive advantages over others tried to effectively and efficiently manage their business to meet the expectations of the consumers as well as accomplish their business goals. Different stakeholders in tourism industry generally communicate with each other to sort out their business objectives with different operating scopes. Due to this, the benefits sought by will be enjoyed not only by the individual enterprise but also by the entire enterprises involved in this business.

Need for Supply Chain in Tourism

Tourism is normally operating in a highly competitive environment in different destinations and in different countries. So to increase the competitiveness, new firms particularly focus on tourism supply chain management to enhance their business and thereby meet the customer needs as well as improve business operations.

Tourism supply chain management may be referred to as a set of approaches used to manage efficiently and effectively the operation of TSC within a specific tourism destination not only to meet the needs of the tourist but also to increase the business operations of different firms within the supply chain. Tourism supply chain management generally helps in finding ways to maintain competitive advantages over other rivals.

In the field of tourism, tourism researchers including Buhalis (2000), Middleton and Clark (2001), Pearce and Schott (2005), Stuart et al. (2005) and Pearce et al. (2007) used the concept of supply chain management in marketing management perspective particularly to investigate the tourism distribution channel.

In comparison to the demand side, the supply-side aspects of tourism have always been ignored. This supply network consists of involvement of inter-firm relationship and product development which are crucial in studying the distribution channels where the involvement of promotional and marketing activities is more. Since only improvement of distribution side seems to be not enough to benefit the single tourism firm or industry as a whole, there is a greater need for analysing the entire industry from an integrative perspective, which can be seen as a TSC. Some prominent researchers in tourism used this supply chain management in the name of tourism value chain. Kaukal et al. (2000) pointed out that a typical tourism value chain consists of four components, namely **tourism supplier, tour operator, travel agent and customer**, and they are in a single-link chain.

The concept of supply chain is very popular in manufacturing industry which acts as a strategy to counter the uncertainty and complexity of tourism market place, and increase efficiency by reducing inventories along the entire supply chain. Taking into consideration the specific nature and characteristics of tourism industry as well as due to the complex interaction among various stakeholders who are having divergent goals, scopes and objectives, the need and importance of tourism supply chain management is definitely huge.

Concept of Tourism Supply Chain

The first conscious effort to study the concept of supply chain management was made by UNWTO in the year 1975, when it published a report on the distribution channels of the tourism industry (UNWTO, 1975). The term *distribution channel* is a supply chain; in a different appearance, it could be narrowly defined as a supply chain that focuses mainly on the distribution and marketing activities in the chain. Some other studies regarding TSC including UNWTO (1994), Sinclair and Stabler (1997), Buhalis and Laws (2001), and Page (2003). Sinclair and Stabler (1997) emphasized the importance of the supply side of tourism industry.

Identifying the features of the tourism industry and its products is of great importance when describing a TSC. For instance, tourism products are normally rooted in a specific territory and provided to tourists from a specific source market, so they often vary according to destinations and source markets.

TSC includes all suppliers of goods and services directly or indirectly. These supply chains are managed by business-to-business relationship. So the management of supply chain is important to improve the performance and output. Tourism supply chain consists of four components: a tourism supplier, a tour operator, travel agent and customer. Supply chain is one of the critical elements both in the management and in the development of tourism sector.

Components of Tourism Supply Chain

TSC involve not just accommodation, transport and excursions, but also bars, restaurants, handicrafts, food production, waste disposal, and the infrastructure that supports tourism in destinations. These all form a part of the holiday product that is expected by tourists when they purchase holidays—whether or not the suppliers of those components are directly contracted by a tour operator. Just as no tour operator would provide 1-star transport to take customers to a 5-star holiday hotel, the sustainability of a holiday, like quality, depends on the performance at all the links in the TSC.

One more aspect of the TSC is the activities of customers while on holiday, particularly in relation to their behaviour, and what they source for themselves in destinations. Tour operators are marketing the whole holiday experience to customers, and this includes opportunities to experience a destination's local products and services. Tour operators can play a significant role in providing appropriate advice to their customers about local products and services, and in ensuring that local producers and service providers have access to tourists on a fair basis. Many tour operators already supply some information on these aspects, but there is scope to do more.

Definitions of Tourism Supply Chain Management

Tourism supply chain can be defined in two ways. One is by macro level and the other is by micro level. In **macro perspective**, tourism supply chain management is a network of enterprises which are engaged in different functions starting from the supply of raw materials to the production and delivery of end products to its target customers. From the viewpoint of **micro perspective** of a firm, TSC is a network of nodes which perform functions starting from the process of raw materials to production and delivery of finished products to the regional distribution centres. Tourism supply chain management is characterized by a forward flow of goods and a backward flow of information.

The supply chain comprises the suppliers of all the goods and services that go into the delivery of tourism products to consumers. Supply chains operate through business-to-business relationships, and supply chain management delivers sustainability performance improvements alongside financial performance, by working to improve the business operations of each supplier in the supply chain. The most popular definition of supply chain management was given by **Simchi-Levi et al.** (2000). According to them, tourism supply chain management can be defined as 'a set of approaches utilized to efficiently integrate suppliers, manufacturers, warehouses, and stores, so that merchandise is produced and distributed at the right quantities, to the right locations, and at the right time, in order to minimize system-wide costs while satisfying service level requirements'.

Tapper and Font (2004) defined a TSC as a chain which 'comprises the suppliers of all the goods and services that go into the delivery of tourism products to consumers'.

According to **Porter** (1980), every industry has an underlying structure, or a set of fundamental economic and technical characteristics, that gives rise to its operational and competitive characteristics. That is, every supply chain varies according to the type of products supplied.

A TSC can be defined as a network of tourism organizations supplying different components of tourism products/services such as flights and accommodation for the distribution and marketing of the final tourism products at a specific tourism destination, and involves a wide range of participants in both the private and public sectors.

5.8. Managing Tourism Supply Chain Business

The supply chain concept originates from the subject matter of economics. It is used to explain how different businesses enter into contractual relationship to supply services and goods, and how these goods and services are assembled into products at different points in the supply chain. On the basis of the above, tourism can be well fit into a supply chain because the tourism product or experience that is consumed is assembled and consists of wide range of suppliers.

TSC includes all suppliers of goods and services directly or indirectly. These supply chains are managed by business-to-business relationship. So the management of supply chain is important to improve the performance and output. TSC consists of four components: tourism supplier, tour operator, travel agent and customer. Supply chain is one of the critical elements in the both management and development of tourism sector. These supply chains contain both tourism and non-tourism sectors which determine the overall experience of the destination in relation to those elements of supply chain they communicate with. This supply chain will help different major players

TSC Structure

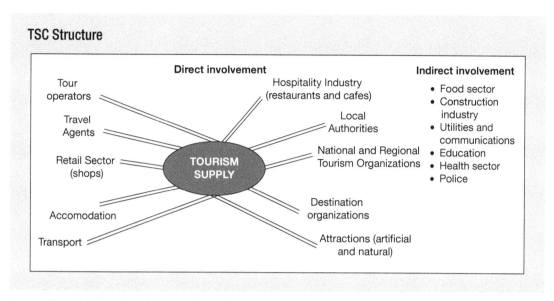

Source: TSC model taken from Connell and Page (2009, 110).

of supply chain to evaluate their performance in terms of efficiency, investment, cost savings and gains so that they can add value to their service to achieve sustainable business performance by providing maximum satisfaction to the tourist in terms of fulfilling tourist experiences.

Tourism Supply Chain

TSC represents the functional relationship that exists among different interests, activities, stakeholders and business to experience tourism activity. Although the concept of supply chain was a subject matter of economics initially, this concept is very much suited in tourism because the goods, services or experiences that are consumed and assembled are supplied by a wide range of suppliers.

The figure on the next page depicts that whenever a tourist/consumer selects a destination and product, the decision to purchase involves contacting a tourism retailer (can be a small travel agency or tour operator etc.), and then the retailer offers him/her a package. Once the package has been purchased by the tourist, the travel agent/tour operator contact with the tourism suppliers including airlines, hotels, other support service providers, tourist guides and so on.

The tourism suppliers in turn contact with other specialist suppliers such as in-flight caterer, airport terminal service providers, baggage handlers and so on; in some cases, the service providers may also need some specialized service at the destination also. This will lead to the generation of additional income/revenue for the tour operators and travel agencies, and other tourism service providers in terms of commissions and so on.

We may conclude that at the time of providing services, not only formal contacts/relationships exist among them but also informal alliance does exist between recommenders (transfer boy, tourist guides, tour representatives and so on) at every stage of travel distribution system.

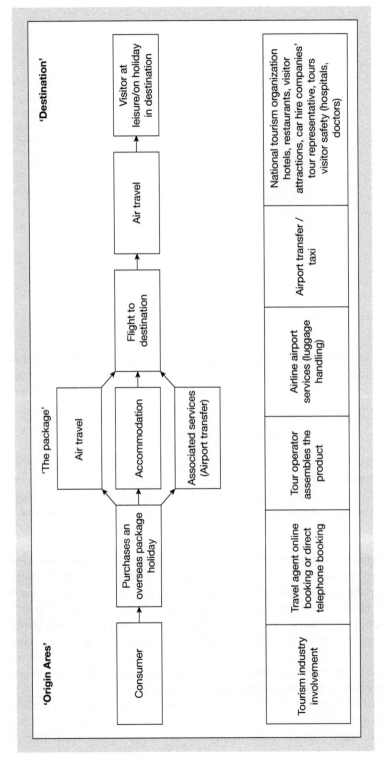

Source: TSC by Page (2003, 80).

Tourism supply must be customer-oriented. It should act strategically and focus on immediate operation and management issues for maintaining profitability. Tourism supply must use sophisticated information technology, innovative advertising and recognizable brands to motivate the consumer. In tourism supply business, the combination of transport, accommodations, attractions and associated services are needed to co-exist to attract the visitors to the destination. A proper management of TSC is essential to ensure that the tourism services are delivered in an appropriate manner as per the demand of the visitors.

To understand the key challenges faced by the successful management of TSC, it is important to know some special characteristics of tourism products as well as tourism industry. Being a part of the services sector of the global economy, tourism possesses a number of special characteristics which are different from the manufacturing and primary sectors. **Six special characteristics** of tourism can be identified in this regard which are as follows:

1. Tourism is a *coordination-intensive* industry where different products/services (transportation, accommodation and so on) are bundled together to form a final tourism product.
2. As service cannot be stored for future use, tourism as a product is *perishable*.
3. Tourists generally need to travel to the destinations where tourism products are produced to consume these products. Tourism products cannot normally be examined prior to their purchase, which means that the sale of tourism products is very much dependent on the presentation and interpretation of the products. Therefore, the tourism industry is a very information-intensive or information-dependent industry (Ujma, 2001).
4. Tourism products are *complex* in nature.
5. Tourism products are *heterogeneous* and compound, consisting of many different service components such as accommodation, transportation, sightseeing, dining and shopping.
6. The tourism industry often faces higher *demand uncertainty* and more complex *dynamics* than its counterparts because of the intensive competition among service providers. Many factors contribute to market uncertainty in terms of the demand for tourism products.

The following seven key tourism supply chain **management issues are identified:**

1. Demand management
2. Two-party relationships
3. Supply management
4. Inventory management
5. Product development
6. TSC coordination
7. Information technology

The above issues are to be dealt with carefully so that the benefits sought by the firms in adopting tourism supply chain management can be enhanced. While dealing with these issues, the firm has to take care of economic, sociocultural and environmental aspects.

Socio-economic and cultural issues include a number of aspects, including contribution to the economic development and the well-being of local communities; preservation of local cultural identity; respect for human rights of local communities and indigenous peoples' rights; and so on.

Environmental aspects include sustainable transport development and sustainable use of resources; reducing, minimizing and preventing pollution and waste (e.g., solid and liquid waste, and emissions to air); conserving plants, animals, ecosystems and protected areas (biodiversity); and conserving landscapes, cultural and natural heritage. Examples of practices here include environmental auditing and management in hotels as well as supply chain management actions. The principles embodied in the various actions and policies advocated in making tourism more sustainable.

Benefits of Supply Chain Management in Tourism

Tourism supply must be customer-oriented. It should act strategically and focus on immediate operation and management issues for maintaining profitability. Tourism supply must use sophisticated information technology, innovative advertising and recognizable brands to motivate the consumer. In tourism supply business, the combination of transport, accommodations and attractions and associated services are needed to co-exist to attract the visitors to the destination. A proper management of TSC is essential to ensure that the tourism services are delivered in an appropriate manner as per the demand of the visitors.

There is no doubt that adoption of a proper supply chain management will provide business benefits as well as increase competitiveness. Major benefits include the following:

- More retention of clients
- Increased revenue
- Operational efficiency improved due to decrease in costs
- Competitive to assess, and respond to risks and opportunities in the market
- Enhanced staff performance
- Achievement of better recruitment and staff retention
- Improved environment culture and climate; as satisfied staff is a key asset, protection of the core assets of the business
- Enhanced brand value, reputation and market share
- Protecting image and status, particularly for companies publicly quoted on stock markets

Conclusion

It is observed from the past that economists, knowingly or unknowingly, have a tendency to neglect the service sector in general and tourism in particular. As a result of this, difficulties arise due to a large-scale gap in the empirical evolution of the parts of the industry. It is revealed from the above discussion that tourism sector which mainly comprises accommodation, intermediary and transportation service is heterogeneous with the presence of competition within each sector. This sector is primarily characterized by:

- Presence of a wide range of competitive firms
- Market segmentation
- Product differentiation
- High rate of entry and exit
- Some scale of economics
- Significance of variation in degree of regulations

As a result of these, there is a considerable change in the structure of tourism supply. These changes may be in terms of number of firms, size and market share in intermediary sector. Two main questions arise which need to be answered:

1. How far the neoclassical theories of the firm and the competitive structure have been identified in tourism supply?
2. Does heterogeneity in the specific sector suggests that the theory of firm is inadequate or does it merely signify that the categorization of tourism sector and market adopted is too broad?

To answer the first question, the test of appropriateness of the theoretical concept is whether they can analyse the actual market structures and predict the outcome of changes occurring in the industry or its market. It is viewed that three elements namely Constantibility (where established firms can engage in precise competition with existing firms), Monopolistic competition and Oligopoly are the different forms of market in which tourism supply condition can be studied. It is also viewed that it is possible to explain the condition of tourism supply sector in a particular theoretical competitive structure; however, it is more difficult to predict the outcome in a changing environment.

For example, in the case of transport sector, mainly oligopoly type of market structure is present in air, bus, coach and ferry sectors. Initially, there will be stable price, given the constraints which individual firm may increase or decrease the price, because of the volatile condition of the possible reaction by the firms/rivals. However, once deregulation starts, it will create a volatile condition of pricing which will lead to influx of smaller companies and greater competition in short-term. Though this kind of situation is possible in bus and coach service sector, it is not likely to happen in airline sector. Thus, the predictive power of conventional theory is questionable.

In answering the above questions, it is observed that analysing within the conventional framework tends to compartmental market into clearly defined competitive structure, rarely acknowledging that submarket may be subject to different conditions. According to the mainstream economists, various segments should be treated as separate markets. However, this may not be possible where there is an interrelationship between the differing competitive segments within a single sector.

For example, the largest firm in the transport sector does react to the behaviour of the smaller or new rivals. However, a further subdivision in the tourism market to meet the traditional analytical requirements may not be appropriate.

It is evident from the above discussion that tourism sector mainly operates in a dynamic business environment which is based on the change in taste and preference of the tourist as well as the regulatory framework under which tourism activity operates. Since the business environment always fluctuates, an effective and responsive marketing strategy is necessary for both the public and private sectors to make tourism possible to remain focused as well as competitive in the global marketing scenario.

The scope to conceptualize and develop a proper framework of a tourism supply model in tourism is limited because of its complex nature of tourism products. This problem can be solved with the help of study of TSC. Therefore, it is said that researchers in tourism have placed more emphasis on consumption of tourism services (demand aspects) in comparison to the production of tourism goods and the complexities in decision-making process (supply aspects). Major aspect of tourism which is overlooked is the study of discretionary spending which specifically operates in tourism business. It is also seen that the retailing of tourism goods and services is highly competitive in most countries because of different regulatory frameworks that exist in different countries in relation to transport, accommodation and attraction by different regulatory bodies of different countries. Because of the fierce competition, the multinationals and large corporations are exerting more pressures on the existing tourism suppliers to gain financial leverage and exercise greater control over them through increased concentrations of their activities and integration in tourism sector. Apart from these, tourism sector has always faced the problem of re-examining their traditional methods of production due to reduction in the margin of profits as well as competition from the new entrants who are now using new technologies (use of internet) to improve business process and business performances. These supply-related issues should be taken care of seriously so that tourism sector can grow at a faster rate with improved communication between the clients and the produces as well as efficient and effective business performances may be ensured in future.

MODEL QUESTIONS

1. Define supply.
2. Explain law of supply with suitable examples.
3. Analyse various issues involved in tourism supply.
4. Write a note on elements of tourism supply.
5. Explain various determinants of tourism supply and explain types of business organizations involved in tourism-related activities.
6. What do you mean by TSC? Critically examine various supply chain models that exist in tourism-related business.
7. Discuss different elements involved in tourism supply chain business.
8. Write a note on various benefits of tourism supply chain business.
9. What are the components of tourism supply chain management?
10. Identify key supply chain management issues involved in tourism business.

Student Activities

1. With an increase growth in mobile technology, identify how travel services are adapting to suit the needs and/or demands of the traveller recently.
2. List out different travel portals available in your country and mention different travel services provided by them in your state/Country.

Suggested Readings

Banks, J. H. (2002). *Introduction to transportation engineering*. New York, NY: McGraw-Hill.

Beamon, B. M. (1999). Measuring supply chain performance. *International Journal of Operations & Production Management, 19*, 275–292.

Black, A. (1995). *Urban mass transportation planning*. New York, NY: McGraw-Hill.

Bull, A. (1991). *The economics of travel and tourism*. Melbourne: Pitman.

Chopra, S., & Peter, M. (2001). *Supply chain management: Strategy, planning and operations.* Upper Saddle River, NJ: Prentice-Hall, Inc.

Frechting, C. D. (1996). *Practical tourism forecasting.* Oxford: Butterworth–Heinemann.

Ganeshan, R., & Harrison, T. P. (1995). *An introduction to supply chain management.* Retrieved from http://mason.wm.edu/faculty/ganeshan_r/documents/intro_supply_chain.pdf

Holloway, J. C. (2001). *The business of tourism* (6th ed.). London: Pearson Education.

Kaukal, M., Ho¨pken, W., & Werthner, H. (2000). An approach to enable interoperability in electronic tourism markets. *Proceedings of the 8th European Conference on Information System (ECIS 2000),* pp. 1104–1111.

Lambert, D. M., James, R. S., & Lisa, M. E. (1998). *Fundamentals of logistics management.* Boston, MA: Irwin/McGraw-Hill.

Lapide, L. (2000, 15 April). What about measuring supply chain performance? In *Achieving supply chain excellence through technology* (Vol. 2). San Francisco, CA: Montgomery Research. Retrieved from http://lapide.ASCET.com

Leiper, N. (2004). *Tourism management* (3rd ed.). Frenchs Forest, NSW: Pearson.

Mentzer, J. T., DeWitt, W., Keebler, J. S., Min, S., Nix, N. W., Smith, C. D., & Zacharia, Z. G. (2001). Defining supply chain management. *Journal of Business Logistics, 22*(2), 1–25.

Mill, R. C., & Morrison, A. M. (1985). *The tourism system: An introductory text.* Englewood Cliffs, NJ: Prentice-Hall.

OntarioBuys. (2006). *Performance measurement: A report by the hospital supply chain metrics working group* (pp. 1–30). French Forest, NSW: Hospitality Press.

Pearce, D. G., Tan, R., & Schott, C. (2007). Distribution channels in international markets: A comparative analysis of the distribution of New Zealand tourism in Australia, Great Britain and the USA. *Current Issues in Tourism, 10*(1), 33–60.

Schiefelbusch, M., Jain, A., Schäfer, T., & Müller, D. (2007). Transport and tourism: Roadmap to integrated planning developing and accessing integrated travel chains. *Journal of Transport Geography, 15*(2), 94–103.

Schwartz, K., Tapper, R., & Font, X. (2008). A sustainable supply chain management framework for tour operator. *Journal of Sustainable Tourism, 16*(3), 298–314.

Simchi-Levi, D., Kaminsky, P., & Simchi-Levi, E. (2000). *Designing and managing the supply chain.* Boston, MA: Irwin McGraw-Hill.

Sinclair, Thea M., & Stabler, M. (1992). *The economics of tourism.* London and New York: Rutledge.

Stuart, P., Pearce, D., & Weaver, A. (2005). Tourism distribution channels in peripheral regions: the case of Southland, New Zealand. *Tourism Geographies, 7*(3), 235–256.

Swarbrooke, J., & Horner, S. (2007). *Consumer behavior in tourism* (2nd ed.). Boston, MA: Elsevier/Butterworth–Heinemann.

Ujma, D. (2001). Distribution channels for tourism: Theory and issues. In D. Buhalis & E. Laws (eds), *Tourism distribution channels: Practices, issues and transformations* (pp. 33–52). London: Continuum International Publishing Group.

UNWTO. (1975). *Distribution channels.* Madrid, Spain: World Tourism Organization. www.world-tourism.org.

Uysal, M., & Jurowski, C. (1994). Testing the push and pull factors. *Annals of Tourism Research, 21*(4), 844–846.

Wahab, S., & Pigram, J. J. (Eds.). (1997). *Tourism development and growth: The challenges of sustainability.* London: Routledge.

Williams, A., & Shaw, G. (1994). *Critical issues in tourism.* Oxford: Blackwell.

Yilmaz, Y., & Bitici, U. S. (2006). Performance measurement in tourism: A value chain model. *International Journal of Contemporary Hospitality Management, 18*(4), 341–349.

Zhang, Y., Song, H., & Huang, G. Q. (2009). Tourism supply chain management: A new research agenda. *Tourism Management, 30*(3), 345–358.

6 The Tourism Industry

LEARNING OBJECTIVES

After going through this chapter, the reader will be able to understand the following:

- ❏ The overview of tourism industry and its components
- ❏ Attractions and their types, and destination as an attraction
- ❏ Issues and challenges involved in managing visitor attraction
- ❏ Overview of accommodation industry, and types and characteristics of accommodation services
- ❏ The importance of transportation to tourism industry including its forms
- ❏ Water transport facilities including their history and development
- ❏ Surface transport: history, types and importance
- ❏ Air transport: history, overview and importance

CHAPTER OVERVIEW

Chapter 6 mainly deals with the overview of tourism industry including its components such as transportation, accommodation and attractions. This chapter elaborates attraction, its types, issues and challenges involved in managing tourist attraction. The overview of accommodation industry and its characteristics are discussed in detail. The chapter also discusses different forms of transport such as water transport, surface transport and air transport, and their significance in tourism business.

6.1. Overview of Tourism Industry

Tourism industry may be defined as 'the composite of both public and private organizations that are involved in the development, production and marketing of products and services to serve the needs of the tourists'. The tourism industry is gaining importance at the global level in terms of both income and employment generation. Tourism industry consists of various sectors grouped together through demand complementarities rather than through supply of homogeneous goods and services. A substantial number of disciplines have made contributions to the subject matter of tourism such as anthropology, ecology, environmental studies, geography, economics, political science, psychology, sociology and management. In tourism business, major themes are cultural, economic, social and environmental, travel patterns and modes between origin and destination, relationship of tourism with economic development, and tourist motivation and behaviour.

In terms of both expenditure and generation of foreign exchange earnings, tourism is considered to be one of the fastest growing industries in the world since the Second World War. Travel and tourism industry has been considered as one of the greatest enterprises of the 21st century of the world. In the present scenario, the world economy will be driven by three main sectors popularly known as 3 Ts. These are travel and tourism, telecommunications, and technology (information technology).

While understanding tourism business we should be aware that a large number of tourists and their expenditures have a great impact not only on the income, employment, balance of payment and government revenue of the destination but also on the culture and environment of the destination area. The tourist expenditure in the destination may be used for the welfare of the tourists as well as the residents of the destination itself. A decrease in demand of the destination can result in a fall in the living standard and rise in unemployment, and vice versa.

Tourism provides employment in both organized and unorganized sectors for highly skilled and unskilled manpower, and gradually helps in reducing the gap between the rich and the poor. The tourism sector has immense potential to help in the global fight against poverty. It can contribute significantly to rural development, agricultural transformation, community enrichment and social empowerment, particularly of women.

Components of Tourism Industry

The industry encompasses a panoply of businesses—airlines, tour operator, travel agents and hotels are representatives of the major sectors. However, there are a multitude of other businesses such as construction, engineering and entertainment, which, though not totally geared towards tourism, contribute and benefit this massive industry. It is this factor which makes it extremely difficult to estimate the true value and size of the travel and tourism industry.

Components of tourism industry include transportation, accommodation, attractions, food service, travel distributors, tourism promoters and land managing agencies. Each of these major components (Exhibit 6.1) plays vital roles in making the tourism industry a unified effort:

- **Direct providers** are those who are involved directly in the successful tourism operation.
- **Support service providers** are those who assist the direct service providers for successful tourism operation.
- **Developmental providers** are those who are working directly or indirectly for the development of tourism as well as tourist destinations of different countries.

6.2. Attractions

An attraction is an offer for the tourist at the destination as a major reason for visiting. It is a central component for the tourism trips, the serving resident community and the visitors on holiday away from home. Attractions are the fundamental elements of any tourist itinerary and in

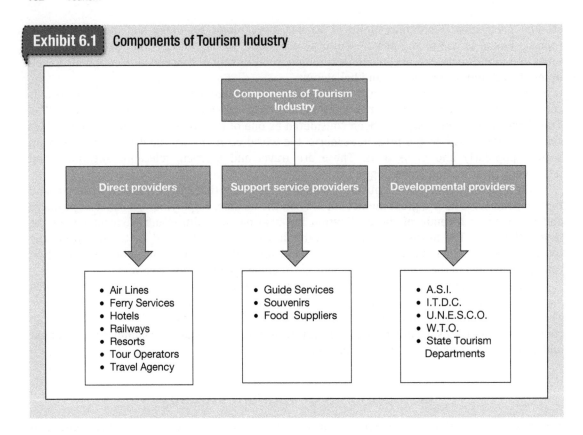

Exhibit 6.1   Components of Tourism Industry

many cases they may be the main reason for the visit. It comprises several varieties of built environment and natural environment including cultural resources, festivals, events and so on.

Attractions constitute one of the central components of tourism along with transport and accommodation which provide both enjoyment and experience. They are the reason people travel to a particular destination. Attractions form the supply side of tourism business. They provide the pull and bring people into an area. For a healthy tourism sector, a successful attraction industry is essential so that tourists have sufficient scope to undertake visits and spend during their tour.

- **Boniface and Cooper (2009)** defined attraction as '... raison d'être for tourism; they generate the visit, give rise to excursion circuits and create an industry of their own'.
- According to **Pearce (1991)**, 'a tourist attraction is a named sight with a specific human or natural feature which is the focus of visitor and management attention'.
- **Swarbrooke (2002)** differentiated attraction from destination as 'attractions are generally single units, individual sites or very small, easily delimited geographical areas based on a single key feature. Destinations on the other hand are larger areas that include a number of individual attractions together with the support services required by tourists'.
- **Gunn (1972)** identified three zones in relation to the spatial or physical layout of an attraction:
  - The core attraction which contains the central nucleus.

- o   The zone of closure surrounds the nucleus and contains the ancillary services associated with the attraction such as shops and car parking.
  - o   The inviolate belt is an area which protects the core products from the commercialized areas of the zone of closure.
- **McConnell (1976)** identified three elements of tourism attraction:
  - o   **A tourist:** A consumer with certain needs and searching for an experience.
  - o   **A sight:** The visitor attraction.
  - o   **A marker:** Forms of information about the attraction that stimulate decision-making and motivation to visit.
- **Middleton et al. (2009)** described that 'visitor attractions are resources that have been formally designated as permanent sites for the enjoyment, entertainment and education of the visiting public'.
- **Wanhill (2008)** mentioned that visitor attraction 'is a sight that is a focus of recreational activity by tourists and excursionists and may also be used by the host population of a destination'.
  - o   Interpretation may be used to create the visitor experience, enriching it and adding value to the visitor's perception

Types of Visitor Attractions

Visitor attractions can be classified on the basis of different features. Broadly, it can be classified into two types, namely **natural attractions and man-made attractions**. Natural attractions are created by nature, which include mountains, beaches, forests, deserts and so on. Man-made attractions, on the other hand, include historical building, theme parks, museums and art galleries, gardens, leisure parks and so on. Man-made attractions can further be classified into two types:

1. **Purpose-built attractions:** These are attractions mainly built for a particular purpose. These include theme parks, zoo, water park, museums, art gallery and so on.
2. **Built attractions:** These are attractions whose original purpose was not related to tourism. These include temples, churches, cathedrals, palaces and so on.

According to Middleton et al. (2009), attractions may be classified as follows:

- **Ancient monuments:** Great Wall of China, Pyramids in Egypt, Stonehenge in England and so on
- **Historic buildings:** Cassel, palaces, havelis, cathedrals, churches and so on
- **Designated natural areas, gardens and parks:** National parks, county parks, gardens, managed beaches and so on
- **Theme parks:** Walt Disney, Universal Studios of Singapore, Rock Garden of Chandigarh and so on
- **Wildlife attractions:** Zoo, game park, safari, aquaria and so on
- **Museums:**
  - o   *Subject specific:* Natural history museums, science museums, rail museums and so on
  - o   *Site specific:* Forbidden City in Beijing, Ironbridge Gorge in England
  - o   *Area based:* National, regional and local museums, and so on

- **Art galleries:** Jehangir Art Gallery in Mumbai, CIMA Gallery in Kolkata, Guggenheim in Spain and so on
- **Industrial archaeology sites:** Mining, textiles, railways and so on
- **Themed retail sites:** These are the centres located in historical building or in purpose-built sites
- **Amusements and leisure parks:** Examples of these parks are Nikko Park, EsselWorld, Aquatica and so on. According to English Tourism Council, visitor attractions can be classified into:
  - Cathedrals and churches
  - Country parks
  - Farms
  - Gardens
  - Historical houses and castles
  - Other historic properties
  - Leisure and theme parks
  - Museums and art galleries
  - Steam railways
  - Visitors centres
  - Wildlife attractions and zoos

Destination as an Attraction

There are elements within the destination environment which determine consumer choice—an influence perspective buyer's motivation. These include:

- Natural attractions
- Built attractions
- Cultural attractions
- Social attractions

These varieties of attraction can further be reclassified into following on the basis of pull factor of the destinations:

- **Natural attractions:** Natural attractions are basically the gift of the nature. These include pristine beaches, landscape, snow-clad mountains, climate, water bodies, flora and fauna and so on. Examples of popular natural attractions in India include major hill stations in different states such as Kashmir, Himachal Pradesh, Uttarakhand, Sikkim, Arunachal Pradesh and Meghalaya, and beaches in Puri, Chennai, Goa, Kovalam and so on. Some international destinations including Alps of Switzerland, Niagara Falls in the United States of America, Mediterranean region for pleasant climate and so on are some of the examples of natural attractions.
- **Built attractions:** These are man-made attractions. These types of attractions are mainly constructed for commercial purpose and have great appeal because of the variety of services and excellent planning. Built attraction needs facility construction in the existing tourism area. These categories of attractions include resort, amusement park or theme park, zoo, aquarium, sports stadium and so on. For example, Brindavan Gardens in Bangalore, Rock Garden in Chandigarh, EsselWorld and Water Kingdom in Mumbai, in India; Sentosa Island and Universal Studios in Singapore; Ocean Park in Hong Kong; and Walt Disney World in the United States of America.
- **Historical attraction:** These are attractions which are related with historical significance. These include havelis, forts and castles of old civilizations, monuments and places of historical importance. The main purpose of visiting these kinds of destinations includes

education, knowledge about the past, entertainment and so on. Some important historical attractions in India include Red Fort, Agra Fort, Taj Mahal, Cellular Jail and so on.

- **Cultural attraction:** These are attractions which mainly showcase people having different cultures and traditions. These include customs and traditions, fairs, festivals, food habits, and their lifestyles which may be considered as a tourist product. While showing these attractions, the sentiments of the host community should be taken care of and host culture should be respected for maintaining authenticity. Tribal tourism in Odisha, Northeastern states and Andaman and Nicobar, and so on are some of the best examples of cultural attraction.
- **Religious attractions:** The main purposes of visiting this attraction are pilgrimage, ritual, offering and so on. This is one of the oldest motivational factors to visit a destination. Some popular religious attractions include *Char Dham* yatra and popular Buddhist sites in India. Hajj yatra to Mecca and Medina, Vatican City of Rome and so on are some of the important religious destinations of the world.
- **Visiting friends and relatives:** This is one of the popular travel motivators as well as attractions in India. People travel to maintain social and personal relationship, and rejuvenate their social relations. Family get-together, marriage ceremony and celebrating festivals are some of the best examples in this regard.
- **Business-related attractions:** The main purpose of this type of attraction is to serve dual purpose. These are attending business meetings, exhibitions, launching new products, marketing and promotion, and so on, along with visiting cities and nearby tourist destinations. This type of attraction is mainly confined to the metro cities, resort areas or convention centres and so on.
- **Government attractions:** These attractions are mainly confined to the national capitals, the government headquarters and so on. Some examples in this regard are Rashtrapati Bhawan (Raisina Hills, New Delhi), Parliament House, New Delhi; White House, Washington D.C.; and Buckingham Palace, London and so on.
- **Medical attractions:** The main purpose of visiting this type of attractions is related with medical treatment. Health tourism, especially ayurveda, spa, herbal body massage and so on are some of the best examples in this regard. Places of tourist interest include Kerala, Tamil Nadu, Ananda spa in Uttarakhand, Patanjali Yog Peeth and so on.
- **Special events attractions:** There are a variety of temporary attractions which are created for a short period of time and sometimes at a regular interval. These are special organized festivals and mega events including tribal exhibitions, handloom exhibitions, international book fairs, Olympic Games, Commonwealth Games, World Cup cricket, football and so on.

Factors Responsible for Success of Visitor Attractions

Understanding the visitor experience is a key concept for visitor attraction management. The attraction market is very competitive and volatile. So the innovative concept which creates a unique experience is important for the successful development of attraction. For visitor attraction, creating the right appeal and ambiance is very important. Neglecting any element of visitor attraction whether it is high entry fees, poor toilet facilities and so on has the potential to harm the overall experience of the attraction.

According to Page and Connell (2009), for a successful visitor attraction following factors should be taken into consideration:

- Professional management skills and the operator's available resources
- Product offering or the type of attractions
- Market demand for the product
- Accessibility from the major routes and centres of tourist and resident population
- Appropriate opening times
- Provision of facilities and amenities at the destination including parking, visitor centre, signboard, shops, tourist guides, toilets and so on
- Provision of facilities for disabled persons
- Proximity to nearby amenities such as local accommodation, food and services
- Value for money
- Expectation, mood, behaviour and attitude of visitors
- Quality of service available at the destination such as staff appearance, attitude, competencies and so on

Issues in Managing Visitor Attraction

There are several important issues that need to be addressed while managing visitor attraction. Since the attraction faces a number of threats from both internal and external environments, so it is imperative to address these issues for managing attractions. These issues are discussed further.

Planning of Visitor Attraction

Planning is the crucial issue for management of visitor attractions. Some important factors such as identifying objectives, duration of planning, funding sources and implementation are needed for effective planning of visitor attraction. Proper planning is needed due to the following reasons:

- To increase tourist flow
- To generate gross revenue
- To have more asset value
- To generate more profit
- To increase the length of stay at the destination
- To have greater growth and confidence
- To increase entry fee to generate more revenue

Managing Environmental Impacts

The environmental impact on tourist attraction is a basic issue which needs to be addressed while managing a visitor attraction. It is rightly said, 'Tourism protects the environment and tourism also destroys the environment'. While developing an attraction, some of the primary environmental issues such as natural catastrophe, deforestation, poor water supply, inadequate sanitation and sewage facilities, poor housing planning and urbanization, and some of the secondary environmental issues such as pollution, waste disposal and congestion are becoming crucial issues which need to be addressed properly while managing attractions.

Managing Seasonality Issues

In many destinations, seasonality is a significant issue affecting the demand for tourism. Attractions in cities suffer less from seasonality than those located in remote areas. Some destinations such as sea beaches, hill stations, desert safaris, wildlife and so on are prone to affect by the seasonality factors.

Golulding (2008) has identified main operational effects of seasonality for visitor attraction including:

- Recruitment cost and difficulties
- Staffing issues
- Training and development cost
- Commitment of seasonal staff
- Loss of trained staff at the end of season
- Utilization of capacity
- Peak season overutilization and the consequent impact
- Opportunity cost of underutilization
- Peaks and troughs in cash flow and revenue generation
- Potential to deter capital investment due to the risk of long-term payback

Managing Visitors' Numbers

The most significant factor that affects visitors' numbers both positively and negatively is the weather which has a little control by the destination developers.

The major management issues related to managing visitors' numbers in a destination include increasing visitors' numbers, decreasing visitors' numbers, maintaining the present level and changing its composition of visitor's profile.

Visitors' numbers at the destination may be recorded in the form of calculating entry tickets, car parking receipts, manual or mechanical counts and so on. However, the above system of counting visitors can be difficult where entry is free or there are multiple entry points to the destination. The management of carrying capacity to the destination is an important issue while determining the visitors' numbers to the destination.

Managing Innovations and Change

Both innovation and change play a crucial role to manage the product life cycle. The visitors' numbers may decline due to the lack of innovation, change and expand the components of the attractions. In this regard, the manager should always introduce innovation, diversification or change in the process of various stages of life cycle to maintain sustainability.

Managing Economic Impacts

Tourism acts as an export industry by bringing in new revenues from external sources. Tourist expenditure increases the economic activity in the host community in various ways both direct and indirect. The two most visible economic impacts in destination are creation of new jobs and income. According to Shone and Parry (2004), creating new visitor attractions is best viewed as one option for stimulating or regenerating a local economy rather than a panacea.

Challenges for Managing Visitor Attractions

It is always necessary to cope up with the future challenges faced by the visitor attractions. The major challenges faced by the visitor attractions may be categorized into following headings (Page, 2006):

- **Product development and innovation:** Development of the right kind of product is a key factor for management of attraction in a competitive environment. To survive in a competitive market, destination should develop innovative and different products, and keep up to date with competitors. Successful attraction must identify new concept, techniques and business process to attract maximum number of visitors. So investment should be made on attraction for long-term purpose for regeneration of profit.
- **Marketing and promotion:** Marketing and promotion are the key challenges in managing visitor attraction for attracting potential customers and retaining actual customers. Attractions should invest more money on public relation, advertisement, promotional campaign, and developing new marketing tools and techniques for promoting attractions. In this context, attractions should develop excellent media relations and use cost-effective marketing tool through research.
- **Revenue generation and funding:** The most important challenges of managing a visitor attraction are to generate revenue and attract funding from various sources to manage the attraction. Revenue can be generated in the attraction by investing money on providing hospitality establishment such as café, restaurants and fast-food counters. For funding purpose, attraction may invite various corporate bodies and motivate them to invest in the destination as a part of corporate social responsibility (CSR). Basic amenities such as safe drinking water, toilet facilities and beautifications at the attraction may be developed by the corporate bodies as a part of CSR activity.
- **Education and training:** Education and training are the keys to the success of any attraction for its management and development in the changing business scenario. Organizations involved in the attraction management should recruit, retain and reward good staff. Training and development are necessary for the conservation and preservation of cultural attractions, artefacts and resources for its better use. Recruiting and training volunteers during managing special events will provide benefits to the attractions.
- **Community and public sector intervention:** Generally, the private sector is shy in making investment in tourism-related attractions because of its long-term return. Hence, the role of the public sector is imperative in this regard to attract the private sector by giving them different benefits in the form of providing tax concessions, tax rebate, interest subsidy and so on.

  Community participation is an essential element for success in cultural industry in the destination. Off-season visits by the local resident are important to the market for attractions. Local community may be involved in the preservation of local culture and may be motivated for participating in the decision-making process of destination planning and development.

6.3. Accommodation

In travel and tourism industry, the accommodation or lodging sector is one of the dominant industries. There is no other sector in the tourism industry more internal in nature than the accommodation industry. Accommodation provides the base by which tourists can engage in the process of staying at a destination. Besides revenue generation, this industry also creates millions of jobs directly and supports a huge number of indirect jobs internationally. Accommodation is the focal point for the hosting of visitors and guests in the destination. Tourists need accommodation for rest, sleep, storing of luggage and so on while they are undertaking tourist activity. This sector requires a capital-intensive infrastructure and commercial venture which tourists utilize. This is also a labour-intensive industry which is having potentials of employing huge number of people for proving service. It has the potential to generate additional revenue from food and beverage services.

The accommodation sector is one of the most tangible elements in the traveller's experience. According to Medlik and Ingram (2000),

> Hotels play an important role in most countries in providing facilities for the transaction of business, for meeting and conferences, for recreation and entertainment … In many areas hotels are important attractions for visitors who brings to them spending power and who tend to spend at a higher rate than when they do when they are at home.

According to them, accommodation product comprises the following:

- The location of the establishment
- The facilities it provides
- The service it offers
- Its image
- Price to the customer

History of Accommodation Industry

Various lodging facilities offered throughout the history were developed in response to the needs of the customers. Due to the changes of social and business needs, the style of lodging facility also changes.

The earliest form of accommodation was empty huts placed at caravan stops to shelter travellers and traders. Then for pilgrims, the religious places like temples were also provided for accommodation and refreshment. The credit goes to Romans who provided post stations as a lodging facility on the highways, especially for the use of messengers and privileged travellers. In the Middle Ages, religious groups developed inns on the road sides for providing food and lodging. In the 15th century, inns were used for profit-making in Europe. In England, inns were often named after the powerful family and on whose land they were visible.

Modern Hotels

The first full-fledged hotel was built in Covent Garden, London, in 1774. In New York, City Hotel was opened in 1794. The first complete hotel with French cuisine that was opened in the early 19th century was the hotel Tremont in Boston. Tremont was the first hotel to have a lobby, indoor plumbing and individual rooms that the guest may lock. Many famous hotels that opened in the second half of the 19th century were Palace in San Francisco, Savoy in London and so on.

Thereafter, the Grand Luxe hotel was started in the early 1900s. During that era, the Plaza was built in New York, what till today is known as the best single-site location in the world. During that period, some of the best known hotels were established in Paris, London and Madrid such as Ritz-Carltons and Waldorf Astoria in New York. After the Second World War, some reputed hotel chains came into existence such as Hilton, Hyatt Regency, Holiday Inn, Marriott and Sheraton.

Hotels

The word *hotel* is derived from the French *hôtel* (coming from *hôte* meaning *host*), which referred to a French version of a townhouse or any other building seeing frequent visitors, rather than a place offering accommodation.

A hotel is a home away from home. It is an establishment that provides paid lodging on a short-term basis.

Inns

Feifer (1985) defines inn as:

> The inn was built around a courtyard, where animals could be lodged. Inside the main hall, the floors were strewn with rushes, and there were long communal tables with benches: only the most luxurious inns had wall hangings. A single brazier provided warmth, and there was dim lighting and a want of ventilation ... Not even the virtuous spent the night alone; however guest slept a dozen to a room, and two or sometimes four to a bed.

Motels

Motels are often chalet type where the motorist can park, and avail lodging and refreshment for a short period of time. Food services are provided centrally and normally offer limited variety of food. It forms an increasingly important segment of the accommodation industry. The various types of motels are roadside motels, resort properties, suburb perimeter motels and city motels. Various services provided by a motel include the following:

- Parking
- Restaurant facilities
- Public catering
- Recreation facilities
- Accommodation
- Car maintenance and refuelling facilities
- Other related services

Budget Hotels

A budget hotel is also known as an economy hotel that provides clean, reasonably sized and furnished room. These hotels meet the basic needs of the guests by providing comfortable and clean room for a comfortable stay. Guests normally stay in this type of hotel for attending seminar and conference or on project-related works mainly for about a week or more.

Resort Hotels

They are also termed as health resort or beach hill resort and so on depending on their position and location. They cater to a person who wants to relax and enjoy themselves at hill station. Most resorts work to full capacity during peak season. Sales and revenue fluctuate from season to season.

These leisure hotels are mainly for vacationers who want to relax and enjoy with their family. The occupancy varies as per season. The atmosphere is more relaxed. These are spread out in vast areas. City dwellers and others having interest for vacation and exotic location prefer resort hotel. Resort hotels are mainly situated far from the main city and in the area of natural attractions such as sea beaches, hill stations, dessert area and beautiful landscape. Many resort hotels focus on providing major soft and hard adventure-based recreational activities such as fishing, golf, trekking, rock climbing, rappelling, paragliding and skiing.

Condominium Hotels

Condominium hotels or condotels are the hotels with apartments (condominium) instead of basic rooms. These are sold by the hotel developers who have title to the physical real estate. The individuals then contract back to the developer or to a third part to operate the hotel. The developer or management company receives a fee for managing and renting the units. These generally attract families because of their large sizes.

Camp Grounds

Camping is a popular form of overnight accommodation. Sometimes these are owned by the hotels. Recreational vehicles are generally provided at the camp ground. Camp ground and recreational vehicles are found in forest, deserts and so on.

Time Sharing

This is a specialized form of condominium ownership. This may also be called interval or deeded ownership when the purchaser takes title to the property. This concept is to divide ownership and use of a property among several investors. There are two basic types of time sharing: the interval or deeded ownership system or the right to use system. In time share, buyers share the cost of maintenance, taxes associated with this and in return they revived the following benefits:

- A guaranteed place to stay in a desirable vacation area for several years in future.
- Shared cost: This may be lower than renting hotel rooms over the period of years.
- A low initial investment compared to the monthly rent and down payment for availing accommodation.
- A chance to exchange time share units who own units in other places. Sometimes share properties own property in the destination and they allow members to exchange their vacation with other.

Pensions

These are accommodation facilities owned and operated by a family that usually lives in that building. These are mainly popular in Europe. In Germany, a pension is referred to as a *gasthaus*. Usually pensions and gasthaus offer a continental breakfast.

Paradors

They are generally old castles, convents or monasteries that have been converted into hotels by the government and also operated by the government. The concept of paradors is popular in Spain.

Youth Hostels

The concept of youth hostel was first started in Germany in 1919. The main idea is to provide low-cost overnight lodging to the travellers throughout Europe. Initially, the plan was directed to provide service to the students. Hence, the name was given as youth hostel. Today there are thousands of youth hostels throughout the world under the umbrella of International Youth Hostel Federation with head office in Washington D.C. These hostels are often associated with non-profit organizations such as Young Men's Christian Association (YMCA) and World Young Women Christian Association (YWCA). Youth hostels provide only basic bedroom (mostly dormitory type) with commonly shared bathroom. Most youth hostels offer communal living room with self-cooking kitchen, self-servicing dining area and sometime recreational facilities.

Bed and Breakfast (B&B) Hotels

The concept of B&B was first started in England. It is a kind of homestay where accommodation is provided in the form of a guest house in a private home. The concept of B&B is very popular all over the world who wants to enjoy the hospitality in the form of a familiar environment in private home. In this form of accommodation, the house owners let out their extra rooms to tourists during peak season as a supplement of hotel accommodation. The minimum facilities in this form of B&B include comfortable room and English breakfast.

Dharamshala

This type of supplementary accommodation is mainly available at different pilgrimage destinations. In this form of accommodation, only simple rooms are provided at a cheaper rate and sometimes with simple meals on demand.

Types of Accommodation

Burkart and Medlik classified holiday accommodation into four categories:

1. **Service accommodation:** This includes hotels, pensions, guest and boarding houses and so on.
2. **Self-catering accommodation:** This includes camping, caravans, rented flats and houses.

3. **Homes of friends and relatives:** In this type of accommodation no payment is made.
4. **Other accommodation:** This includes house boats, youth hostels and so on.

Type of Accommodation by OECD

According to the Organisation for Economic Co-operation and Development (OECD), there are 13 types of accommodations in addition to other categories of supplementary accommodations. These include:

1. Hotels
2. Commercial hotels
3. Airport hotels
4. Conference centres
5. Economy hotels
6. Suite hotels
7. Residential hotels
8. Casino hotels
9. Resort hotels
10. Motels
11. Inns
12. B&B
13. Paradors

Characteristics of Tourist Accommodation

The characteristics of tourist accommodation are as follows:

- Seasonality is considered to be one of the most important characteristics of tourist accommodation. Here, the demand is more in the peak season and vice versa.
- Occupancy level of tourist accommodation should be high. Accommodation wants to sell its room to maximize its room revenue just to get rid of the perishable nature of the product which cannot be sold or stored at a later stage.
- The appeal and accessibility of hotel are determined by location. For example, luxury hotels are located in a prime location with great access to attractions and facilities.
- Star categorizations of hotel often denote the quality of the establishment. This may be statutory or voluntary.
- In accommodation sector since fixed costs are high, the manager/owner wants to always optimize the occupancy level to cover its costs.
- Accommodation sector is subject to be regulated by different laws including health and safety legislations, food safety regulations, environmental regulations, and other necessary licenses required for its successful operations.
- Because of its nature of service requirements, skilled and trained staffs are required in different operational departments.

6.4. Transportation

Transport is one of the fundamental components of the tourism industry. It acts as a link between origin and destination. Tourism is being elsewhere, and the major components of any tourist activity involve transportation. In some cases the mode of transportation may be an attraction. Transport facilitates mobility of tourists from their place of origin to their destination and back.

Transport system is highly productive and large-scale economies appear at an initial point in production. Different forms of transport have been associated with the growth and development of tourism. Technological developments in transport have led to the expansion of international and domestic tourism.

The mode of transport is integral to the overall experience of tourism like scenic railway journey or cruising. The success of transport system depends on safe, comfortable, affordable and efficient transport network which helps in enjoying the vacation period to their maximum potential. The movement of people, especially in large volumes, requires specialized managerial skills and understanding its logistic operation. The main features for transporting tourist are managing the supply of transport to meet its demand and to operate in an efficient timely and convenient manner.

The main elements involved in the interrelation between transport and tourism (Page, 2003) are as follows:

- The tourist
- The relationship between transport and the tourist experience
- The effects of transport problems on the travellers' perceptions
- The tourist's requirement for safe, reliable and efficient mode of transport

Key Features of Successful Tourist Transport

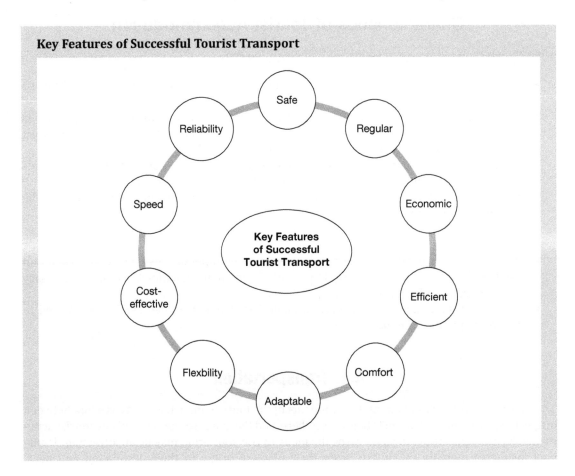

Forms of Transport

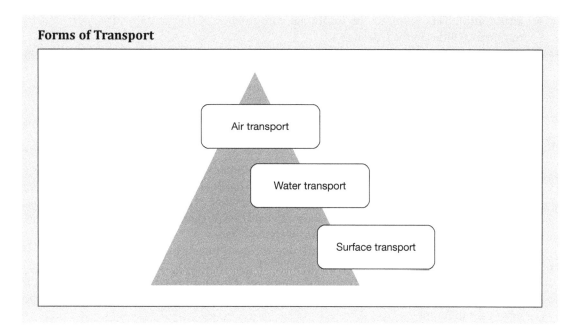

Selection of Mode of Transportation

Why people select a particular transportation mode over other is a subject matter of discussion. Many theories have been discussed in this regard. Mill and Morrison (1992) mentioned that following major factors are responsible for the selection of transportation mode:

- Availability of modes of transport
- Frequency
- Cost/Price of transport
- Speed/Time
- Comfort/Luxury

Some other factors which are responsible for choosing a mode of transportation are:

- Safety
- Convenience
- Ground services
- Terminal facility and location
- Status and prestige
- Departure and arrival times

According to 'Sheth Travelers', a travel mode is selected based upon the following five dimensions:

1. **Functional:** It simply means the performance for a specific purpose. Examples include departure and arrival times, safety records, the directness of routes, and the absence of stops and transfers.
2. **Aesthetic/Emotional:** This includes inner value, style, interior and exterior decorations, comfort, luxury, and safety.
3. **Social/Organizational:** This refers to stereotypes that various modes have such as cruises and bus tours have been stereotypes for senior people.

4. **Situational:** This refers to the locational convenience of the mode of transport and its terminal facilities to the traveller.
5. **Curiosity utilities of the alternative modes:** It refers to the traveller's tendency to try something new and different.

Characteristics of Transportation-Demand Side

The demand for passenger transportation is characterized by the following:

- **Demand is instantaneous:** In transportation, the demand is always fluctuating. There is a great uncertainty to what the demand will be on a particular day, time and season. Though past trend must be used but it cannot be fully dependable. If demand is greater than supply, then travellers become unhappy. And, on the contrary, if supply is more than the demand, the customers may find alternate means of transportation.
- **Overcapacity of demand:** This results due to instantaneous demand and variability of demand.
- **Presence of more than one type of segment of demand for transportation:** Simply it can be either business demand or pleasure demand. The motivations, frequencies and the prices are different.
- **Travellers can substitute one mode of transportation for the other:** People use train instead of bus and vice versa.
- **Competitions exist within one mode between carriers:** Prices and the speed of the journey are the same among competing carriers and competition may be in prestige, comfort and convenience.
- **Some transportation offer more than one type of service:** Airlines are providing economy, business and first class, and trains are also providing different classes of journey.
- **Demand is also affected by the relationship between the price charged and the income level of the traveller:** Pleasure travel is income elastic.
- The demand for travel is sometimes felt more not because of people's desire to travel but is felt by the demand for non-priced items. Sometimes the frequency of departure, conditions of the equipment, service of the employees, etc., often more important than the price.

Characteristics of Transportation-Supply Side

The supply of passenger transportation is characterized by the following:

- Transportation industry is a capital-intensive industry. Equipment and terminal cost need huge amount of investment.
- **Transportation costs are indivisible:** A tourist coach cannot put in 'half a coach' on the road if the coach is only half full. Many of the costs of transportation are fixed. This puts a great deal of pressure on management to fill seats.
- **Transportation costs are sunk cost with few alternatives:** The use for transportation is for same purpose.
- **Though the demand is instantaneous but supply is not:** Supply needs time to adjust with it, while demand can shift very fast.

- **The incremental costs of operation are small:** This cost is the cost of adding one more unit.
- **Supply of transport is perishable in nature:** It cannot be stored for future use.
- **Transportation service must be available on a continuous basis:** It is expected to be reliable on long-term continuous basis. People expect same level of service always, whether it is day or night, summer or winter.
- **In transport business, there is always a problem of labour:** Whether in operation or maintenance, the service is offered 24 hours a day.

Conclusion

The tourism industry has been considered as one of the fastest growing industries in the 21st century. The phenomena of tourism and travel industry can be studied from different perspectives depending on its nature, scope and development. This chapter highlights various components of tourism industry including the interlink of tourism with other industry. This chapter will provide a comprehensive understanding of tourism industry from both macro and micro levels. The importance of 3 As, namely, attraction, accommodation and accessibility (various modes of transport) are also discussed in detail with their needs and importance in this chapter. Some of the important issues, roles and future prospects involved in airlines industry, water transport and surface transport are also discussed in this chapter.

MODEL QUESTIONS

1. Why do studies of tourism industry require interdisciplinary approach?
2. What are the various types of water transport offered on a commercial basis?
3. Explain the role of the government in promoting commercial passenger transport.
4. How did the Second World War promote the growth of airlines industry?
5. Write a note on freedom of air.
6. What are the primary problems presently faced by international airlines? How does International Air Transport Association (IATA) fit into this situation?
7. Explain in detail various classifications of commercial accommodations.
8. Name the various alternative forms of accommodation industry.
9. Discuss the advantages and disadvantages of various ownership criteria of hotel.
10. Explain different forms of visitor attractions with suitable examples.

Student Activities

1. Visit any five/four star hotel and make project report on general features, services and facilities of that hotel.
2. You are advised to visit any natural or man-made attractions and list out their uniqueness and characteristics.

Suggested Readings

Boniface, B., & Cooper, C. (2009). *Worldwide destinations: The geography of travel and tourism.* Oxford: Butterworth Heinemann.

Goulding, P. (2008). Managing temporal variation in visitor attractions. In A. Fyall, B. Garrod, A. Leask, & S. Wanhill (eds), *Managing visitor attractions: New directions* (pp.197–216). Oxford: Butterworth-Heinemann.

Gunn, C. A. (1972). *Vocations cape: Designing tourist regions.* Austin, TX: University of Texas.

MacCannell, D. (1976). *The tourist: A new theory of the leisure class.* London: Macmillan.

Medlik, S., & Ingram, H. (2000). *The business of hotels* (4th ed.). Oxford: Butterworth-Heinemenn.

Middleton, Victor T. C., Fyall A., Morgan, M., & Ranchhod A. (2009). *Marketing in travel & tourism.* Routledge.

Page, S. J. (2006). *Transport and tourism: Global perspectives.* Harlow: Prentice Hall.

Pearce, P. (1991). Analyzing tourist attractions. *Journal of Tourism Studies, 2*(1), 46–55.

Shone & Parry. (2004). *Successful event management: A practical handbook.* London: Thomson.

Wanhill, S. (2008). Interpreting the development of the visitor attraction product. In A. Fyall, B. Garrod, A. Leask, and S. Wanhill. *Managing visitor attractions: New directions* (2nd ed.). Oxford: Butterworth Heinemann.

Travel Formalities

After going through this chapter, the reader will:

❏ Have a basic understanding on frontier formalities.

❏ Understand the definition of passport, its types, how to obtain a passport and so on in the Indian context.

❏ Gain knowledge about visa, types of visa, issuing of visa, transit without visa, visa on arrival and so on.

❏ Acquire knowledge about health regulations, issue of health certificates and so on during international travel.

❏ Understand the requirements of tax, customs and currency while undertaking international travel.

❏ Have a basic knowledge on the need and importance of travel insurance and various clauses included in different types of insurance for undertaking international travel.

CHAPTER OVERVIEW

Chapter 7 mainly deals with different frontier formalities such as passport, visa, health regulations, and customs and currency required for undertaking international travel. Different types of passport, requirements to obtain a passport, visa, types of visa, including visa on arrival and so on, for the Indian context are discussed in this chapter. Various health regulations including the need and importance of travel insurance for undertaking international travel are also discussed in this chapter.

7.1. Introduction

A passenger is a person, other than a member of the crew rostered to operate a particular flight, who is carried or who is to be carried on an aircraft, with the consent of the carrier.

Besides having a ticket, a passenger going on an international journey must possess the following three important documents, along with any other documents that may be required by the country of departure/transit/visit/destination: passport, visa and healthcare certificate.

It is the legal responsibility of the passenger to fulfil all the government requirements/adhere to the governmental regulations in connection with his/her travel.

However, if the onus of correct and complete documentation is left on the passenger alone, then there is every possibility that the airline may have passengers with incomplete documents and the consequences to the airline could be disastrous. Non-fulfilment of government formalities will entail the following:

- Offloading at the origin resulting in empty seat, which will lead to loss of revenue.
- Repatriation of the passenger from the destination—most likely at the cost of the airline.
- Loss of passenger goodwill because the passenger may blame the airline for inadequate briefing.
- Loss of goodwill of the government authorities and they will have to check/recheck passengers' documents resulting in delay in processing the formalities.
- Reflection of inefficiency on part of the airline.

So the passengers must ensure that all bookings made directly or through travel agents must fulfil the governmental requirements related to their journey before their visit.

7.2. Passport

A passport is an official document of identity issued by a competent authority to nationals of the issuing country and sometimes to an alien resident (stateless persons). It is basically a document to pass through a port. It is an identification card which shows a person's nationality and country of residence, and in some cases also of stateless persons (alien residents).

To be more precise,

A passport is a wallet size (Purse/pocket) document issued by the competent authority on behalf of the head of the state under his pardon ship. It signifies a person's nationality and place of domicile or the place from where the person is originally belonging to.

In other words, 'a passport is an official document issued by a government identifying an individual, granting him/her permission to travel abroad and requesting the other government to protect him/her'.

Every Indian who is willing to travel to other countries from India is required to hold a valid passport and travel documents. Under the Passport Act 1967, the Government of India may issue different types of passports and travel documents.

Both for embarkation and disembarkation, a passenger must hold valid passport to travel a country or countries.

Types of Passport

There are different types of passports. These include:

- **General/Normal passport:** Most countries issue a normal passport. It is dark blue in colour. It is issued to any ordinary citizen of India.

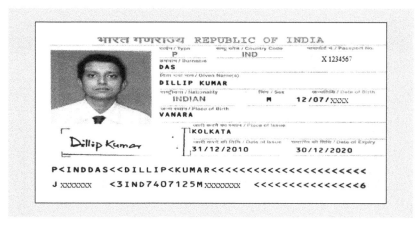

Disclaimer: The above image is for representation purpose only.

- **Alien's passport:** These types of passport are issued to the alien resident of the issuing country. An alien is classified as a person living in the country where he is not actually a citizen. They are popularly known as stateless person. However, aliens (non-residents) would travel on a passport of their citizenship.
- **Kinderausweis passport:** Instead of issuing passport to the children, they are issued identity card which is popularly known as kinderausweis passport. However, not all the countries accept/issue this type of passport.
- **Official or service or special passport:** This type of passport is issued to the government officials or other persons who are on official mission and the type of passport should be mentioned by the authority. This is white/grey in colour.
- **Joint passport/Family passport:** Persons travelling together may hold joint passport which may be used to cover either of the following.
  - Husband or wife with or without children
  - Holder of a passport and a child (under certain age not necessarily related)
  - Two or more children. For travelling alone, such passports may only be used by the person whose name is written first. For example, a wife is not allowed if the husband name is written first, or a younger child is not allowed if the elder is listed first.
- **Diplomatic passport or consular passport:** This type of passport is red in colour. This is issued to diplomats, consularies and other officials on missions, entitling the bearer to diplomatic or consular status under international laws and customs.
- **Laissez-passer/UN passport:** International Red Cross passport issued by United Nations and International Red Cross Society for military purpose at the time of war and crisis. It is also known as Nansen passport.
- **CDC passport:** CDC is generally issued to those seamen who have to join on duty or go off duty. It is issued by the directorate general of shipping.
- **Pilgrim passport:** Issued by the Haj committee for Haj, Ummah and Lirat programme.
- **Military I-cards:** These are issued to defiance personnel.

A passport must be checked for the following:

- Identity of the holder
- Validity
- Endorsement for countries being visited
- Visa and its validity

Source: https://www.immihelp.com/nri/indianpassport/sample-indian-passport.html
Disclaimer: The above images are for representation purpose only.

Requirements to Obtain a Passport

The following documents are required to obtain a passport:

1. Six passport size photographs
2. Income tax certificates (if applicable)
3. Educational certificates
4. Ration card/electricity bill/telephone bill
5. Passport fees (for 10 years/20 years) as prescribed by the government
6. Clearance certificate from the local police stations
7. Proof of date of birth certificate
8. Photo identity card
9. Salary certificate
10. No objection certificate from the government/organization where you are working
11. Driving licence
12. Aadhaar card
13. Marriage certificate (applied in the case of female married candidates)

How to Obtain a Passport

Acquiring a passport is a fundamental right of a legal citizen. A legal citizen is a person who does not have any sort of liabilities on the country, rather the country is dependent on him.

Person excluded from the category of legal citizen are as follows:

- Any person against whom any civil or criminal allegation is pending in the court of law.
- Any person against whom a case is pending in the police station.
- Any person who is too old/disable whom the competent authority finds as a burden on the foreign country is also denied of a passport.

Entry Restrictions

The following do not require a passport to enter into India:

- Holders of identity emergency certificates (along with visa).
- Laissez-passer issued by United Nations.
- Military I-card with movement order issued by British service personnel.
- Seaman Book (travelling on duty) issued by any country except if seamen are of Chinese origin.

The Government of India refuses admission to Afghan nationals even if they hold a valid visa for India at the time of disembarkation in India and also the authority will not force them to enter India, if the passengers' tickets or passport shows any evidence of transit or boarding in Pakistan during their journey from Afghanistan to India.

It is the carrier who has to carry him back. They are not allowed to leave the airport.

PASSPORT APPLICATION FORM
Government of India, Ministry of External Affairs

Please read the Passport Instruction Booklet carefully before filling the form. Furnishing of incorrect information/ suppression of information would lead to rejection of application and would attract penal provisions as prescribed under the Passports Act, 1967. Please produce your original documents at the time of submission of the form. All fields marked with (*) are mandatory to fill.

Service Required

Applying for *

Type of Application *   ○ Normal   ○ Tatkaal

Type of Passport Booklet *   ○ 36 Pages   ○ 60 Pages

Applicant Details

Applicant's Given Name (Given Name means First Name followed by middle Name (if any)) *

Surname

Gender *

Are you known by any other names(aliases)? *   ○ Yes   ○ No

Have you ever changed your name ? *   ○ Yes   ○ No

Date of Birth (DD/MM/YYYY) *

Place Of Birth

Is your Place of Birth out of India? *   ○ Yes   ○ No

Village or Town or City *

Marital Status *   Citizenship of India by *

PAN (If available)   Voter ID (If available)

Employment Type *

Is either of your parent (in case of minor)/ spouse, a government servant? *

Educational Qualification *   Are you eligible for Non-ECR category? *

Visible Distinguishing Mark

Aadhaar Number

I, the holder of above mentioned Aadhaar Number, hereby give my consent to Passport Seva to obtain my Aadhaar Number, Name and Fingerprint/Iris for authentication with UIDAI. I have no objection using my identity and biometric information for validation with Aadhaar (CIDR) database only for the purpose of authentication.
I agree ☐ Yes   ☐ No

Family Details (Father/Mother/Legal Guardian details; at least one is mandatory.) *

Father's Given Name (Given Name means First Name followed by Middle Name (if any))

Surname

Legal Guardian's Given Name (if applicable)

Page 1 of 2

Surname

Mother's Given Name (Given Name means First Name followed by Middle Name (If any))

Surname

Present Residential Address Details (where applicant presently resides)

Is your present address out of India? *   ○Yes   ○No

Do you have a Permanent Address? *   ○Yes   ○No

Emergency Contact Details *

Name and Address *

Mobile Number*   Telephone Number

E-mail ID

Identity Certificate /Passport Details

Have you ever held/hold any Identity Certificate? *   ○ Yes ○ No

(Identity Certificate(IC) is normally issued to Tibetan/other stateless people residing in India)

Details of Previous/Current Diplomatic/Official Passport*

○ Details Available   ○ Details Not Available/Never Held Diplomatic/Official Passport

Have you ever applied for passport, but not issued? *   ○ Yes ○ No

Other Details

1) Have you ever been charged with criminal proceedings or any arrest warrant/ summon pending before a court of India? *   ○Yes ○No

2) Have you at any time during the period of 5 years immediately preceding the date of this application been convicted by a court in India for any criminal offence and sentenced to imprisonment for two years or more? *   ○Yes ○No

3) Have you ever been refused or denied passport? *   ○Yes ○No

4) Has your Passport ever been impounded or Revoked? *   ○Yes ○No

5) Have you ever applied for/ been granted political asylum to/ by any foreign country? *   ○Yes ○No

6) Have you ever returned to India on Emergency Certificate (EC) or were ever deported or repatriated? *   ○Yes ○No

Self Declaration
I owe allegiance to the sovereignty , unity & integrity of India, and have not voluntarily acquired citizenship or travel document of any other country. I have not lost, surrendered or been deprived of the the citizenship of India and I affirm that the information given by me in this form and the enclosures is true and I solely responsible for its accuracy, and I am liable to be penalized or prosecuted if found otherwise. I am aware that under the Passport Act, 1967 it is a criminal offence to furnish any false information or to suppress any material information with a view to obtaining passport or travel document.

☐ I Agree

Place *   Date (DD/MM/YYYY) *

NOTE :
Applicants are required to submit the proof of address of the present address only, irrespective of the date from which he/she has been residing at the given address. However, he/she is required to mention all the places of stay during previous one year (from the date of application filling) in the Passport application form.

VALIDATE & SAVE

Page 2 of 2

Source: https://portal2.passportindia.gov.in/AppOnlineProject/secure/mainFormOptions

7.3. Visa

A visa is nothing but an endorsement on the passport itself by the competent authority (consulate general or ambassador general) to allow a valid passport holder of a country to enter a foreign country.

To be more precise, visa is a permission to enter a foreign land. However, the custom authority reserves the right to deny entry to the country if it finds someone unsuitable even if he or she has a valid passport.

Categories of visa as per entry restrictions:

- Single entry: One-time entry and exit
- Double entry: Entry–exit and entry–exit
- Multi entry: Entry–exit, entry–exit, entry–exit, …, ∞

Types of Visa (As per Purpose)

The types of visa in the Indian context include the following:

Transit visa

- *Eligibility:* A transit visa is granted for the sole purpose of enabling the visa holder to travel through India to reach the ultimate destination. In this case, change of purpose is not allowed.
- *Validity:* Transit visa is granted by Indian Mission abroad for a maximum period of 15 days from the date of issue. It is valid for direct transit only for a maximum period of 3 days. For staying more than 3 days in India, one requires an appropriate visa.

Tourist visa

- *Eligibility:* The purpose of people who are travelling on tourist visa to India should be touristic only other than non-business purpose. The following persons are not eligible for a tourist visa:
  - Persons of Indian origin
  - Spouse and children of a person of Indian origin
  - Spouse and dependent family members of a foreign national coming to India on a long-term visa such as employment, business, research and students.

The main purpose of issuing tourist visa is for recreation, sightseeing, casual visit to meet VFR and so on. It is issued to those who do not possess any house in India as well as do not involve in any occupation in India.

- *Validity:* This type of visa is issued by Consulate General abroad for a maximum period of 6 months (180 days). However, citizens from the United States of America can obtain tourist visa maximum up to 5 years or 10 years depending on a bilateral agreement. This visa validity begins on the first day of issuance. Extensions of stay are not granted on tourist visa.
- *Restrictions:* If any foreign nation applies for a tourist visa frequently within one month of his/her expiry of previous visa, then the consulate office/embassy will thoroughly look into this matter and if necessary will refer to the matter to Ministry of Home Affairs for clearance for granting him/her fresh tourist visa.

Business visa

A business visa is issued to those persons who would like to travel India on business-related issues such as making sales or establishing contacts on behalf of the company outside of India. The business visa applicant must receive the visa prior to applying for accompanying spouse and dependent family members.

- *Eligibility:* Business visa is granted to the following foreign nationals:
  - Foreign nationals visiting India to establish an industry/business or to explore possibilities to set up industry/business venture in India.
  - Persons coming to India to sell or purchase industrial/commercial products or consumer durables.

- o Foreign nationals coming to India for recruitment of manpower.
- o Foreign nationals who are partners in business function as directors in the company.
- o Foreign nationals coming to India for consultations regarding exhibitions, participation in exhibitions, trade fairs and so on.
- o Foreign buyers, who visit to transact business with suppliers in India and also to evaluate or monitor quality, give specifications, place orders and so on relating to goods and services produced in India.
- o Foreign experts/specialists on a visit or short-term duration in connection with ongoing projects with the objectives of monitoring the progress work, conducting meetings with Indian customers and to provide high-quality technical guidance.
- o Foreign nationals coming to India for a pre-sale activity.
- o Foreign trainees of multinational companies. Corporate houses arriving for in-house training to the regional hubs inside India.
- o Foreign students sponsored by Association Internationale des Étudiants En Sciences Économiques et Commerciales (AIESEC) for internship on projects-based work in industries/companies.
- o Senior executives of firms, experts, tour operators, travel agents and so on visiting in connection with work related to projects of national importance, including those undertaken by the public sector undertakings, and conducting business tourists of foreigners or business relating to it.
- *Conditions:* Business visa is issued subject to the following conditions:
  - o The applicants should have sound financial conditions and proper expertise in the field of international business.
  - o The applicants should not involve in money lending or petty trading or full-time employment in India involving payment of salary in India and so on.
  - o The applicant must have to fulfil the requirements of paying tax liabilities.
  - o The grant of business visa is subject to any instructions issued by the Government of India on the basis of reciprocity with other foreign countries from time to time.
  - o The business visa must be issued from the country of origin, or from the country of domicile of the foreigner, provided the period of permanent residence of the applicant in that particular country is more than 2 years.
- *Validity:* Business visa is valid for 1 year or more with multiple entry facility; however, citizen from the United States of America can get business visa for 5 years or 10 years with multiple entry visa. The period of stay in India for each visit is limited to 6 months. A multiple entry business visa valid up to 10 years may be available to foreign businessmen who have set up or intend to set up joint ventures in India. The duration of visa is valid from the date of issue but not the date of entry into India.
- *Extension of business visa:* In case the business visa is initially issued for a period of less than 5 years, it can be extended up to a maximum period of 5 years subject to the following conditions:
  - o The gross turnover from the business activity should be more than 1 crore per annum which will be achieved within 2 years of business activity.
  - o The first extension of business visa shall be granted by Ministry of Home Affairs.
  - o The second extension may be granted by the state government/union territory (UT) administration/Foreigners Regional Registration Offices (FRROs)/Foreigner Registration Offices (FROs) on year-to-year basis subject to the good conduct of the person.
  - o In case the extension of visa is denied, the foreigner shall leave India forthwith on expiry of the period of validity of the visa.

Student visa

Student visa or study visa is given to bona fide students on a multiple entry basis to pursue courses/study at various recognized institutions of India.

- *Validity:* It is a multiple entry visa. This type of visa is valid up to the period of study as approved by the educational institute of India. Visa duration starts from on the day of issuance and not on the day of entry into India.

Provisional visa

In cases such as pending admission test result or other requirements, a provisional visa may be issued on the basis of provisional admission certificate letter issued by the institution. This visa is valid for 3 months. If admission is not given within this period, then the student has to leave India. It is noted here that extension of provisional visa is not allowed.

Employment visa

- *Eligibility:* In India, an employment visa is issued to the following:
  o An employee or paid intern of an Indian company.
  o Person travelling to India for volunteer work with an NGO.

In case there will be special case, there will be a special endorsement on e-visa 'to work with NGO' where the name and the place of work will be given.

If the spouse or dependent family member is travelling along with the applicant, then the spouse will apply for entry visa instead of tourist visa. The duration of this visa depends on the terms of appointment.

For getting employment visa, the following types of foreign nationals are eligible:

- o Foreign nationals coming to India as consultants or contacts for whom the Indian company pays a fixed remuneration (this may not be in the form of a monthly salary).
- o Foreign artists engaged in regular performances for the duration of employment contract given by hotels, clubs or other related organizations.
- o Foreign nationals who are coming to India to take up employment as coaches of national/state level teams or reputed sports clubs.
- o Foreign sportsmen who are given a contract for a specified period by the Indian clubs/ organizations.
- o Self-employed foreign nationals coming to India for providing engineering, medical, accounting, legal or such other highly skilled services in their capacity as independent consultants, provided that the provision of such services by foreign nationals is permitted under laws.
- o Foreign language teachers/lectures.
- o Foreign specialist chefs.
- o Foreign engineers/technicians coming to India for installation and commissioning of equipment/machines/tools in terms of the contract for supply of such equipment/ machines/tools.
- o Foreign nationals deputed for providing technical support/services and transferring know-how/services for which the Indian companies pay fees/royalties to the foreign company.
- o Senior management personnel and/or specialist employed by foreign firms who are relocated to India to work on specific projects/management assignment.

- o Foreign nationals visiting India for execution of a project/contract (irrespective of the duration of visit).
- o Foreign nationals who are coming to India on short visits to a customer location to repair any plan or machinery as part of warranty or annual maintenance contracts.
- o Foreign nationals who are visiting to India for imparting training for the personnel of the Indian company.
- *Conditions:* In India, an employment visa is issued subject to the fulfilment of the following conditions:
  - o The applicant should be a highly skilled and/or qualified professional being engaged or appointed by a company or organization or industry or undertakings in India on a contract or an employment basis at a senior level, skilled position such as technical expert, senior executive and in a managerial position
  - o There should not be a qualified Indian available to do the job that the visa holder would be performing.
  - o The employment visa cannot be granted for ordinary, routine or secretarial/clerical jobs.
  - o The employment must either be in a company/firm/organization registered in India or in a foreign company/firm/organization engaged for the execution of some projects in India.
  - o The employee's salary must not exceed US $25,000 per year. However, this does not apply to the following:
    - Ethnic cook
    - Language teachers (other than English teachers)/translators
    - Staff working for concerned embassy/high commission in India.
  - o The foreign nationals must comply all legal requirements like payments of tax liabilities.
  - o The documents relating to the proposed employment should be thoroughly checked to decide the category of visa that may be issued to the foreigner.
  - o The name of the sponsoring employer/organization shall clearly be stipulated in the visa sticker.
  - o A foreign company/organization that do not yet have any project office/subsidiary/joint venture/branch office in India can sponsor a foreign national/employee of a foreign company for an employment visa. However, if the Indian company/organization has awarded a contract for the execution of a project to a foreign company that does not have any base in India, such foreign company can sponsor the employee for an employment visa.
  - o The Indian company/organization engaging a foreign national for executing projects/contracts would be responsible for the conduct of the foreign nationals during their stay in India and also for the departure of such foreign nationals upon expire of the visa.
- *Validity:* Initially, the consulate office/embassy may grant a visa up to 1 year maximum, irrespective of the duration of contract. Further extensions up to 5 years may be obtained from Ministry of Home Affairs/FRRO in the concerned state in India.

The duration of visa starts from the day of issuance, but not on the day of entry into India.

- – A foreign technician will get an employment visa for a maximum period of 5 years or the duration of the assignments whichever comes earlier is applicable with multiple entry facility.

- A highly skilled foreign national like professionals can avail employment visa up to a maximum period of 3 years or the duration of assignments whichever comes earlier is applicable with multiple entry facility.
- Others can avail an employment visa with a maximum period of 2 years or the terms of assignments whichever comes earlier is applicable with multiple entry facility.
  - *Registration of foreigners with FRRO:* Foreigners who have obtained the visa for a period of 180 days and less do not require registration. An employment visa which is valid for more than 180 days, require to register themselves in the FRROFRO within 14 days of their arrival.

For those whose registration is required, FRRO/FRO may issue a residential permit for the validity of the visa period. However in case of any change in residential address, one has to immediately inform in writing to the concerned FRRO/FRO.

  - *Extension of employment visa:* The employment visa can be extended by the state government/UT administration/FRROs/FROs beyond the initial visa period, up to a total period of 5 years from the date of issue of the initial employment visa on the annual basis, subject to good conduct and production of necessary documents in support of continued employment, filling of income tax return and no adverse security inputs about the foreigner.

Medical visa

One can get medical visa to seek medical treatment only in the case of reputed/recognized specialized hospital/treatment centres in India. Two persons who are blood relatives of the patients are allowed to accompany during his/her treatment under separate medical visa. The validity of the visa will be same as that of the medical visa of the patient.

The primary concern for consideration of treatment includes following serious ailments:

- Neurosurgery
- Ophthalmic disorder
- Heart-related problems
- Renal disorder
- Organ transplantation
- Congenital disorder
- Gene therapy
- Radio therapy
- Plastic surgery
- Joint replacement and so on

- *Validity:* The duration of the visa is valid up to 1 year of the treatment, whichever comes earlier is applicable. The entry restriction is limited to a maximum of three during a year. The duration of visa starts on the day of issuance and not on the day of entry into India.

Diplomatic visa

This type of visa is normally processed by Indian Embassy/consulates. However, UK diplomats/officials/service passport holders visiting India on a private visa will submit a regular visa application through Cox & Kings Global services which normally process the visa.

Consulate hours are between 9.30 AM and 12.30 PM on all working days. There is no visa fee as well as no service charges while issuing a diplomatic visa. For processing a diplomatic visa one has to take the passport along with the visa stamped after four working days. If it is not ready within the stipulated four days due to administrative delay, then the person will be intimated over phone or mail.

E-tourist visa

The countries that are getting the facility of availing e-tourist visa while visiting India on touristic purpose include Andorra, Anguilla, Antigua and Barbuda, Argentina, Armenia, Aruba, Australia, Bahamas, Barbados, Belgium, Belize, Bolivia, Brazil, Cambodia, Canada, Cayman Islands, Chile, China, SAR Hong Kong, China SAR Macau, Colombia, Cook Islands, Costa Rica, Cuba, Djibouti, Dominica, Dominican Republic, East Timor, Ecuador, El Salvador, Estonia, Fiji, Finland, France, Georgia, Germany, Grenada, Guatemala, Guyana, Haiti, Honduras, Hungary, Indonesia, Ireland, Israel, Jamaica, Japan, Jordan, Kenya, Kiribati, Laos, Latvia, Liechtenstein, Lithuania, Luxembourg, Malta, Malaysia, Marshall Islands, Mauritius, Mexico, Micronesia, Monaco, Mongolia, Montenegro, Montserrat, Mozambique, Myanmar, Nauru, Netherlands, New Zealand, Nicaragua, Niue, Norway, Oman, Palau, Palestine, Panama, Papua New Guinea, Paraguay, Peru, Philippines, Poland, Portugal, Republic of Korea, Republic of Macedonia, Russia, Saint Christopher and Nevis, Saint Lucia, Saint Vincent & the Grenadines, Samoa, Seychelles, Seine, United Kingdom, Singapore, Slovenia, Solomon Islands, Spain, Sri Lanka, Sweden, Taiwan, Tanzania, Thailand, Tonga, Turks & Caicos, Tuvalu, UAE, Ukraine, United Kingdom, USA, Uruguay, Vanuatu, Vatican City-Holy See, Venezuela and Vietnam.

- *Eligibility:* International travellers whose sole objective of visiting India is recreation, sightseeing, casual visit to meet friends or relatives, short duration medical treatment or casual business visit.
- Passport should have at least 6 months validity *from the date of arrival in India.* The passport should have at least two blank pages for stamping by the immigration officer.
    - International travellers should have return ticket or onward journey ticket with sufficient money to spend during his/her stay in India.
    - International travellers having Pakistani passport or Pakistani origin may apply for regular visa at Indian Mission.
    - Not available to diplomatic/official passport holders.
    - Not available to individuals endorsed on parent's/spouse's passport, that is, each individual should have a separate passport.
    - Not available to international travel document holders.
- *Documents required for E-tourist visa:*
    - Scanned first page of passport
    - Format—PDF
    - Size—minimum 10 KB and maximum 300 KB
    - The digital photograph which needs to be uploaded along with the visa application should meet the following requirements:
        - Application form which is available in the website in JPEG format.
        - The height and width of the photo must be equal.
        - Photo should present full face, front view and eyes open.
        - Centre head within frame and present full head from top of hair to bottom of chin.
        - Background should be plain light coloured or white background.
        - No shadows on the face or on the background.
        - Without borders.

Visa on arrival

This is a new type of visa issued by Indian Mission abroad for tourists visiting India. The validity for it is 30 days. It would be valid only for single entry and is available only in international airports at Bangalore, Chennai, Cochin, Delhi, Goa, Hyderabad, Kolkata, Mumbai and Trivandrum. This visa can neither be extended nor converted to any other kind of visa during the stay in India except in certain exceptional circumstances. Indian tourist visa on arrival is issued to the following countries: Australia, Brazil, Cambodia, Cook Islands, Djibouti, Fiji, Finland, Germany, Indonesia, Israel, Japan, Jordan, Kenya, Kiribati, Laos, Luxemburg, Marshall Islands, Mauritius, Mexico, Micronesia, Myanmar, Nauru, New Zealand, Niue, Norway, Oman, Palau, Palestine, Papua New Guinea, Philippines, Republic of Korea, Russia, Samoa, Singapore, Solomon Islands, Thailand, Tonga, Tuvalu, UAE, Ukraine, USA, Vanuatu, Vietnam.

The citizens of the above-mentioned countries may get the visa in advance of their arrival to India.

- *Eligibility:* The following conditions need to be fulfilled before issue of the tourist visa on arrival:
    - The sole objective of visit to India by the international traverses should be recreation, sightseeing, casual visit to meet friends or relatives, including short duration medical treatment or casual business visit.
    - Passport should have at least 6 months validity *from the date of arrival in India.*
    - International travellers should have return ticket or onward journey ticket, with sufficient money to spend during his/her stay in India.
    - International travellers having Pakistani passport or Pakistani origin may please apply for regular visa at Indian Mission.
    - Not available to diplomatic/official passport holders.
- *How it works:*
    - Apply online (upload your photo as well as passport pages)
    - Payment of visa fee should be made online (using credit card/debit card/internet banking)
    - Receive your expected time of arrival online (this message will be sent to the concerned mail ID of the application holder).
    - Then fly to India (printed Electronic Travel Authorization Arrival [ETA] is required to carry with the passenger at the time of travel).
- **Instruction for tourist visa on arrival:**
    - Applications should be applied online 4 days in advance for the above countries with a window of 30 days. For example, if the applicant chooses the arrival date as 4 December, then the applicant has to apply online on 1 December for this type of visa.
    - Recent front photograph with white background and photo page of passport containing personal details such as name, date of birth, nationality and expiry date to be updated properly, falling which the application may be rejected.
    - For processing this visa application, required payment should be made 4 days before the expected date of travel.
    - Visa fee once submitted is non-refundable.
    - At the time of arrival, applicant should carry a copy of ETA with him/her.
    - Applicant's biometric test is compulsory by the immigration authority at the time of arrival in India.
    - Visa validity is 30 days from the date of arrival in India.
    - Electronic Travel Authorization is valid for 9 international airports which are named above.

- o   This type of visa service is available in addition to other existing visa service.
- o   This type of visa is allowed for a maximum of two times in a calendar year.
- o   Tourist visa on arrival once issued cannot be extended, converted and is not valid for restricted/protected and cantonment area inside India.
- o   Visa application status can be tracked online and assistance for getting this visa support can be send to indiatvoa@gov.in.
- *Documents required for applying tourist visa on arrivals:*
  - o   Scanned first page of passport.
  - o   Format: PDF available for filling up the form in the sites.
  - o   Size: Minimum 10 kB and Maximum 300 kB
  - o   The digital photograph which needs to be uploaded along with the visa application should meet the following requirements:
    - –   Application form which is available in the website with JPEG format size.
    - –   The height and width of the photo must be equal.
    - –   Photo should present full face, front view and eyes open.
    - –   Centre head within frame and present full head from top of hair to bottom of chin.
    - –   Background should be plain light coloured or white background.
    - –   No shadows on the face or on the background.
    - –   Without borders.

Collective visa

Facility for providing collective visa to group not less than 4 and not more than 40 in numbers, and sponsored by a recognized travel agency by the Government of India under the condition of arrival and departure should be made in the original group. For travelling inside India in separate groups, individual travel certificate must be obtained from the immigration authority.

Sports visa

It is just like collective visa. But the difference is that the arrival and departure in sports visa may not be in the same group.

Visa to mountaineers

It is a kind of visa where the validity is up to the period of expedition of the mountaineers who are participating in the events.

Visa to foreign technicians

It is issued to foreign technicians who are coming to India on an assignment in which the validity is up to the period of expedition.

Transit without visa (TWOV)

This is an exclusive facility given to exclusive persons in exclusive cases, that is, in the case of emergencies or in the case of special considerations. In this case, passengers are allowed to stay for a definite period of time in a pass by country to catch the next alternative flights.

- In the case of India, it is given to those who have conform onward or return tickets and continue their journey within 72 hours provided they should have possession of all travel-related documents.

Obtaining a Health Certificate

Health certificate is generally available from different vaccination centres and doctors in most of the countries and issued by the competent authority who administered the vaccinations.

Checking of Health Certificates

Prior to travel to different countries, it is necessary to enquire carefully the health regulations of

- The country of destination
- The country of departure
- The transit destinations/stations

Different Diseases for Which Health Certificates Are Issued

Mostly in international travels, the following diseases are considered to be important:

- **HIV (in extreme cases):** This is the most recent type of health regulations introduced in international air transport. Although this is not adopted by most of the countries, very few countries in the world are now making it mandatory, as a precautionary measure, for the passengers to go for this health check who want to enter into their countries.
- **Cholera:** There are some countries in which cholera disease is common. So to get rid of that WHO provides vaccinations for these cholera-prone areas. Once the vaccination is given to the person, the validity will be in effect after 6 days for 6 months with effect from the date of vaccination. However, the old certificate must be shown during the first 6 days after re-vaccination.
- **Yellow fever:** Like cholera, some endemic yellow fever zones are there for which yellow fever vaccination is provided. The validity of yellow fever vaccination is from 10 days to 10 years with effect from the date of vaccination. However, the old certificate must be shown during the first 10 days after re-vaccination.

On the next page is shown the format of international certificate of vaccination against yellow fever which is mandatory to obtain before visiting to endemic yellow fever zones of the world:

7.5. Tax, Customs and Currency

Tax

These are some of the most important frontier formalities while undertaking international travel to different countries. Travel Information Manual (TIM) provides information on tax, customs and currencies of different countries alphabetically.

TIM gives information on tax aspects under the following:

- Tax collected from passengers on purchase of tickets
- Type and amount of tax
- Conditions of applications or to whom it applies

- Place of payment
- Exemptions and so on

Specimen copy of yellow fever certificate

INTERNATIONAL HEALTH REGULATIONS

WORLD HEALTH ORGANIZATION
ORGANIZATION MONDIALE DE LA SANTE

INTERNATIONAL CERTIFICATE
OF VACCINATION

CERTIFICAT INTERNATIONAUX
DE VACCINATION

Issued to
Delivers...................................

Passport No.
or
Travel Document No.......................................

Numero du Passport
ou
de is piece jusyificative..

PUBLIC HEALTH INSTITUTE
(GOVERNMENT OF KARNATAKA)
SHESHADRI ROAD, BANGALURU-560 001.
INDIA

Disclaimer: The above image is for representation purpose only.

Therefore, it is always necessary to advice passengers/clients if they are expected to pay departure tax, so that they can reserve some local currency for payments. Some important types of tax normally paid by the passengers during air travel include:

- Inland air travel tax (IATT)
- Passenger service fare (PSF)
- Insurance charges and so on

Customs

Popularly known as custom duty is one type of tax that normally the country imposes as custom duty to protect local manufactures. It is generally levied on imported goods. As a result of this custom duty, the cost of the goods increases which discourages the passenger to go for imported product and thereby increases the demand for local product. This custom duty provides huge revenue for the government.

In some cases, different countries give concessions for travellers which are applied to items including cigarettes, tobacco products; alcoholic beverages, perfumes and so on; things which are generally used for personal purposes are exempted from paying custom duty. Personal effect normally means all the items which travellers normally wear or require for personal use during their travel. These normally include jewellery and cosmetics, a camera and films, a pair of binoculars, portable typewriters, clothing, footwear and toiletries.

The products which may be imported, exported or duty free are included in TIM under the following headings:

- Free import allowance
- Free export allowance
- List of prohibited import/export items
- Information on the transport of animals (pets only)

Currency

Currency regulations are given for import and export of currency based on normal travelling and hotel expenses. For regulations regarding current payments and capital payments, one should consult the nationalized bank or foreign exchange dealers of the country for regular updates including the limits. In this regard, the travel agents are considered to be the best person to give proper updated advice regarding the carrying of funds while travelling overseas. The following are the forms of carrying funds:

- Cash
- Travellers' cheques
- Bank drafts
- Telegraphic transfer
- Credit cards and so on

7.6. Travel Insurance

Travel insurance is an important formality which has to be completed before travelling abroad. All travellers who travel abroad must carry travel insurance with them. Although it is not compulsory but still for security and safety purpose it is always advisable to have travel insurance during their overseas travel. Insurance is a means of 'spreading the risk' whereby all premiums paid are used to pay out to recover the losses. The premium is paid so that the insurance company takes the risk instead of the travellers.

The insurance companies generally offer comprehensive travel insurance for travellers to cover the most likely contingencies that may occur. The following clauses are usually included in most policies:

- **Loss of deposits:** This type of policy is made to cover cancellation price to the journey due to unexpected circumstances. The declaration included by the passenger on the proposal is a clause which states that the passenger knows of no reason why they may be forced to cancel.
- **Delay in travel:** This policy includes a payment if a passenger is delayed due to some unforeseen circumstances. The main intension is to cover any unexpected expenses that may occur and normally per day amount is paid with a maximum of claim.

- **Medical and related expenses:** This policy normally covers medical, surgical, hospital and other medical related expenses incurred overseas as a result of bodily injury, illness and disease to relieve pain. Related expenses such as travel and accommodation expenses are covered for another person to escort the client or patient home or in the event of death, to cover the cost of returning the body or ashes home. Careful attention needs to be paid to the exclusion because most of the policies do not cover pre-existing illness, while in some cases few policies cover that also, provided that a doctor certificate of fitness to travel is given.
- **Interruption and curtailment:** This type of policy is mainly designed to cover financial loss due to interruption and curtailment of travel during the trip. Interruption occurs when a passenger has to discontinue travel for a time before continuing travel at a later date. The main cause of interruptions includes illness of passenger before travel, strike, hijack and so on.
  - Curtailment of travel occurs when a traveller is forced to return home through circumstances which are beyond the control. In this case, once the traveller returns home, the insurance company has no further responsibility to the client; therefore, if the client wishes to go back and continue travelling, this will be at his or her expenses. Most of the policies do not include the clause of interruption and curtailment. Claims under this clause can be considerable; especially when the client has prepaid a major holiday where no refund is available once the travel is commenced.
- **Return travel:** This policy normally covers the cost for a traveller to return back to his destination overseas to complete his original travel arrangements, provided this should occur within the specified dates of the original travel arrangement and subject to a variety of conditions as stated in the policy.
- **Personal accident:** Most policies will pay a lump sum amount in the event of accidental death or permanent total disablement through accident.
- **Luggage, personal effects and money:** This type of policy is mainly designed to either replace the items or to cover the cost of replacing the items which have been lost, stolen or damaged. A point to be noted here is that sometimes the insurance companies deduct the amount for general wear and tear.
- **Personal liability:** This policy is mainly designed to cover the passenger in the event that he or she may be sued for causing bodily injury or someone else's property. There is normally an exclusion if damage occurs when the ensured is driving a motor vehicle.

Conclusion

Frontier formalities or travel formalities are nothing but the information about the formalities or procedures to be accomplished in order to travel abroad. In simple language, it is a procedure to be followed by each passenger to prove that the passenger has accomplished the formalities for travel for that/those particular country/countries in which the passenger intends to visit.

In the case of tourism, certain formalities are needed to be furnished by the tourists before they can leave their country or enter into another country. This is in the interest of the tourist as well as the country being visited. These formalities are normally in the form of official documents and endorsements which need to be produced well in advance before the competent authority for a hassle free travel. Frontier formalities vary from country to country and even from region to region. However, for a better understanding about the travel formalities, TIM is the only official document available for getting updated and authentic information about passport, visa, health regulation, customs and currency of almost all countries in the world.

MODEL QUESTIONS

1. What do you understand by frontier formalities?
2. How do you define passport? What are the requirements to obtain a passport?
3. What is a visa? Name the different types of visas that are issued as per purpose.
4. Write a note on collective visa.
5. What is TWOV?
6. Write a note on entry restrictions.
7. Explain the need and importance of travel insurance and its types in international travel business.
8. Write an explanatory note on health regulations.
9. Analyse the importance of customs and currency in international travel business.
10. Briefly explain the merits and demerits of visa on arrival in international travel business.

Student Activities

1. Prepare assignment to find out different cholera-prone areas and endemic yellow fever zones of the world with the help of TIM.
2. Find out different countries enlisted for visa on arrival for their own countries.

Suggested Readings

IATA. (1997, March). *Travel information manual* (a joint publication of 14 IATA member airlines). Amsterdam, the Netherlands: Author.

Law Publishers. (1980). *The Passport Act, 1967* with Passport (Entry into India) Act, 1920 and Passport Rules. Allahabad: Author.

Roday, S., Biwal, A., & Joshi, V. (2009). *Tourism operations and management*. New Delhi: Oxford University Press.

Sharma, P. S. (2004). *Tourism education—Theories and practices*. New Delhi: Kanishka Publications.

Suggested Websites

Ministry of External affairs, Government of India: http://www.mea.gov.in
Ministry of Finance, Government of India: https://www.finmin.nic.in/
World Health Organization: http://www.who.int/
https://www.immihelp.com/nri/indianpassport/sample-indian-passport.html
https://www.who.int/ihr/IVC200_06_26.pdf

Impacts of Tourism

LEARNING OBJECTIVES

After going through this chapter, the reader will:

- ❏ Have a basic understanding on various impacts of tourism.
- ❏ Understand the concept of various types of impacts that arise due to tourism development.
- ❏ Gain knowledge about economic impact, its benefit and cost.
- ❏ Acquire knowledge about environmental impacts, their types and controlling measures.
- ❏ Understand the aspects of sociocultural impacts, their applications and mitigation measures.
- ❏ Understand the concept of carrying capacity, its types, measurements and limitations.

CHAPTER OVERVIEW

Chapter 8 discusses various types of impacts arising out of tourism activities. Different impacts such as economic, sociocultural and environmental are described in detail. Both positive and negative aspects of those impacts are analysed here with the help of various models. Different methods of mitigating various negative impacts of tourism are discussed here. The concept of tourism carrying capacity including its elements, types and measurements is also discussed in this chapter.

8.1. Introduction to Tourism Impact

Tourism is a multidimensional complex phenomenon. Its effects are also multidimensional and spread to almost all the sectors of tourism industry. The effects are on both the sides, that is, the positive and negative sides. Tourism almost spreads its wings to all the segments of human civilization, be it society or economy or environment.

Tourism, both international and domestic, brings about a mixture of people from diverse social and cultural backgrounds, and also a considerable spatial redistribution of spending power which has a significant impact on the economy of the destination area. Early works on the impact of tourism upon destinations were primarily focused on economic aspects only. This was not only because such impacts are more readily quantifiable and measurable, but also there was a pervading climate of optimism that these studies would show that tourism was of net economic benefit to host destinations. In many cases, this was indeed true. Yet, tourism by its very nature is attracted to unique and fragile environments and societies, and it became apparent that in some cases, the economic benefits of tourism may be offset by adverse and previously unmeasured environmental and social consequences.

Tourism impacts mean 'all those important activities undertaken by the tourism phenomenon to conserve, preserve or deteriorate the actual set-up of the society, economy, culture or environment'.

The growth of mass communication and education plays a significant role in the development of modern tourism industry. Advancement in technology and changes in tourism market have affected the economy and at the same time provoked the social and environmental issues.

As tourism grows and the number of tourist increases, the positive as well as negative impact arises. The development of tourism normally causes change. This change is not really tangible and occurs gradually. In some cases, tourism has been developed at the expense of the host community, where the economic gain has been given a higher priority than the development and integrity of the local people. Some of those changes are beneficial, others are not. The changes are considered as good or bad depending upon the interest group the individual is associated with. Whether such changes due to tourism development are good or bad can be determined by effectively evaluating the tourism impact.

Impacts are considered to be the major elements of tourist activity and their effect on the tourist destination. These effects can be both positive and negative for the destination. These effects often coexist, causing beneficial and undesirable impacts simultaneously, making it difficult for policymakers to plan and manage the destination. The shift to service-oriented economy from the developed to the developing countries that started mainly from the second half of the 20th century mostly ties to an increase in the development of tourism.

Initially, tourism studies were mainly focused on the economic benefits derived from tourism. Since tourism was rather a new field of study, early works were mainly concerned with the economic development of tourism. Even today economic gain is given higher priority than the other impacts that arise due to tourism development.

One of the major problems that tourism planners are facing while assessing the impacts of tourism is the establishment of an appropriate base line to measure the existing and future changes induced by tourism. The complex interactions of tourism with the physical environment make it difficult to measure impacts with accuracy. Impacts may be large scale and tangible or small scale and intangible.

Cost-benefit analysis is essential while measuring both the positive and negative impacts of tourism at the destination. One has to calculate the cost and benefits of economic, social, cultural and environmental aspects. On the **benefit side**, tourism development provides employment and revenue to support local community; development of infrastructure of tourism often benefits the community. Regular contact of visitors and local residents may broaden cultural and educational horizons. The other social benefits for the local community may arise in the form of improvement in the quality of life and standard of living.

On the contrary on the **cost side**, tourism development in underdeveloped regions may lead to life-threatening environmental problems. Other examples including law and order problems, drug addiction, losing ethnicity of endogenous culture, health-related issues and so on are discussed under the cost side of tourism development.

The Desirability of Impacts

Impact is often used as a pejorative term and is often assumed to be negative. However, residents of destination areas often want tourists to visit their places; they seek tourism development and advertisements to attract tourists. They want this because it will lead to better lifestyles. They want jobs, higher incomes, increased tax revenue and better opportunities for their children. Of course, the benefits may be largely economic and sometimes illusory, and there may be adverse consequences, often of an environmental or sociocultural nature, associated with acquiring the benefits. Thus, trade-offs are likely to be involved. Are the benefits worth the costs? Most of the tourism professionals pointed out that it is not possible to maximize the benefits and, at the same time, minimize the costs, as many tourism professionals continue to suggest.

The Context of Impacts

The impact of tourism can be viewed as arising from the type(s) of tourism involved, the characteristics of communities in which tourism is taking place and the nature of resident–visitor encounters. Furthermore, investigators of tourism cycles suggested that impact on a destination area is likely to change with time as the nature of tourists, the community and resident–visitor interactions also change (Butler, 1980). Furthermore, many changes associated with tourism may be cumulative as a number of small enterprises are developed in sequence in close proximity, each having a minor impact when viewed alone. However, together they may have far-reaching consequences. Cumulative impact assessment is a challenging topic which is beginning to attract the attention of those charged with conducting and evaluating impact assessment, although it has yet to receive much recognition in the tourism literature (Shoemaker, 1994). While environmental impact assessments (EIAs) for specific tourism developments such as resorts and marinas have an important place, it should be recognized that tourists are mobile and their impacts are not confined to the bounds of such establishments, for example, having implications for transportation termini through which access is provided and attractions which are visited (Butler, 1993). Thus, in addition to impact assessment, monitoring of change and mitigation strategies may be required to reduce the magnitude of environmental consequences (Nelson et al., 1993).

While much of the work has documented the impact of tourism, often under economic and sociocultural headings, few tourism professionals have taken the trouble to document adequately the types of tourism, the community characteristics or the nature of host–guest encounters which give rise to these impacts. In fact, it would be worthwhile to review the tourism impact literature in an attempt to establish more precisely the context in which authors have documented specific impacts. Failure to provide such information or to take note of it adequately has resulted in the following:

- **Communication failures:** Due to differing evaluations of impacts.
- **Contradictory findings:** If literatures are inconsistent.
- **Limited policy relevance:** If it fails to specify adequately the context in which impact occurs, meaning that the impact literature provides limited guidance to decision-makers.
- **Cultural brokers:** As the literature on cultural brokers is emerging slowly and an extensive literature on interpretation exists, very little of this deals explicitly with the role of cultural brokers in influencing the impact of tourism in destination areas.

- **Salinity:** It refers to the importance of impacts usually according to the views of residents of destination areas and usually ascertained through public opinion surveys. The interpretation of survey results is often facile.
- **Aggregated and disaggregated measures:** As different types of impacts are measured in different ways. For example, the economic impact of tourism may be recorded in currency units of employment, environmental impacts may be assessed through concept like species diversity, and social impacts are assessed through surveys whose result may be presented according to the proportion of respondents agreeing or disagreeing with particular propositions.

Thus, from the above discussions, it is suggested that the existing literature of impact has a number of deficiencies and these are required to

- Verify the tourist typologies which exist, most of which have not been based upon detailed empirical investigations (Murphy, 1985).
- Develop classifications of destination area communities.
- Examine the nature of resident–visitor interactions including the extent to which they are medicated by culture brokers.
- Place the recording and monitoring of impact in the context of all the above.
- Assess the utility of the widely discussed related planning and management concepts.

If such steps were taken, the quality of impact analysis and their comparability would be greatly improved and the body of knowledge might be cumulative rather than a series of case studies.

Potter's Framework of Tourism Impacts

Potter has given a general framework for the assessment of tourism impact on environmental, sociocultural and economic issues. This framework is useful for planning and managing destination. The various steps involved in Potter's tourism impact framework (after Potter, 1978; Pearce, 1989; Page, 1995) are given below:

Step 1	Examine the context of tourism development
Step 2	Forecast the future for area/place if development does/does not proceed
Step 3	Examine the nature of tourism development
Step 4	Forecast future if development proceeds/examine what happens when development occurred
Step 5	Identify the qualitative and quantitative differences between step 2 and step 4
Step 6	Suggest amelioration/mitigation measures to reduce the adverse impacts
Step 7	Analyse the impacts and compare the alternatives
Step 8	Present the results
Step 9	Make a decision

- It is also given to those holding a Seaman Book provided they travel on duty to join a ship in an Indian harbour and also holding a letter of guarantee of the shipping company (7 days).
- It is also given to merchant seaman travelling on duty and arriving by a ship in an Indian harbour to leave for repatriation by air.

The following conditions must be checked while issuing visa:

- Identity
- Validity

- Types of visa
- Endorsement

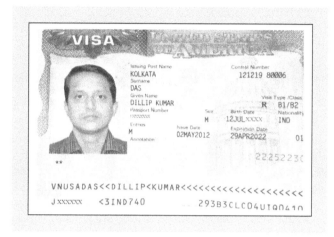

Specimen copy of a visa

Disclaimer: The above image is for representation purpose only.

7.4. Health Regulations

Health Certificate Issued by World Health Organization (WHO)

This is another formality that needs to be completed prior to travelling to any country. Before travelling it is necessary to check whether vaccination have been given to the person to protect the traveller's health while travelling. Travellers visiting from an infected area are required to prove that they have been vaccinated against infected diseases. In this regard, the WHO issues an international certificate on vaccination for this purpose. Health certificate is in the form of a booklet and its size is the same as a passport.

If a passenger reaches in a country, but failed to prove that he/she had taken necessary vaccinations, the following things can happen to him/her

- Refused to enter to that country
- Put under medical surveillance

- Put into quarantine
- Vaccinated on the spot

So to avoid any inconvenience caused by this, the passenger should always carry the medical certificate along with the passport for proper documentation.

8.2. Types of Impact

The types of impacts of tourism can be basically divided into three types:

1. Economic impact
2. Environmental impact
3. Sociocultural impact

Economic Impacts

Introduction

Tourism is the largest growing industry in the world, so it is natural to discuss and understand the economic impact of tourism at all levels—regional, national and local. Evaluating the impact of tourism provides information necessary for the formulation of tourism development policies. These policies determine the type of infrastructure and superstructure a country needs to invest in to encourage the most appropriate kind of tourism production. Nevertheless, the analysis of economic effects of tourism is vital to the analysis of global economics. Tourism is the most productive industrial sector in the world and accounts for 12 per cent of its GNP. It is also the sector that creates maximum employment with over 100 million employees.

The influence of tourism extends to several fields of economic activity. These are as follows:

- Employment
- Human resource
- Development
- Foreign trade
- Balance of payments

Some of the positive economic impacts like job generation, foreign exchange earnings and development of infrastructure by the government as well as industry highlighted the benefits for a variety of reasons and stressed upon the multiple benefits and positive economic impacts as they happen in such a way that these benefits will be experienced/consumed/felt without any leakages in the economy.

Economic Benefits of Tourism

According to the UNWTO, following are the major economic benefits of tourism:

- **Export earning:** International tourism being the world's largest export earners, for many countries, it is important as far as the balance of payments is concerned.
- **Employment:** Tourism employs about 100 million people in the world. It is considered as a job creator with multiplier effects. Job creation in tourism is growing one and half time faster than any other industrial sector.
- **Rural opportunities:** By creating jobs in underdeveloped regions, tourism helps us to equalize economic opportunities throughout the countries and provide incentives against migration of cities.
- **Infrastructure investment:** It stimulates investment and new infrastructural development which improve the living conditions in the regions where the projects are undertaken.

Tourism development projects include airport roads, civic systems restoration of monuments and so on.

- **Tax revenue:** Tourism industry provides huge tax revenue to the government through the tax levied on accommodations, restaurants, various forms of fees and so on.
- **Gross domestic products:** International and domestic tourism together generate up to 10 per cent of the world's GDP and a considerably higher share in many small and developing nations.

Types of Economic Analysis

According to Daniel J. Stynes (1997), 'an economic impact analysis of tourism activities normally focuses on changes in sales, income, and employment in a region resulting from tourism activities'.

There are a number of methods which have been used for analysing the economic impacts of tourism. The major among them are discussed further.

Visitors' Survey or Input–Output Method

The impact of travel and tourism on the economy of an area or state is best described through input–output analysis. The visitors' survey or input–output models is directly linked with surveying tourism spending; various equations are used to determine how the tourist spending affects jobs and so on. There are three key inputs to have an economic impact estimate:

1. No. of tourists (including this type-NV)
2. Average spending per tourists (AST)
3. Multipliers (M)

So, Economic Impact = NV × AST × M

This can be further simplified as:

- Dividing visitors/tourists into different segments based on spending patterns.
- Measuring spending category-wise (such as accommodation, shopping and travel).
- Allocating tourist spending into receiving economic sector.

Satellite Account Method

The satellite account method has been adopted and encouraged by UNWTO to measure tourism role in national economies. Satellite accounts are primarily used to provide an overall aggregate estimate of the accounting approach that uses existing accounting data and incorporates tourism in the accepted system of accounts.

This method, though accepted in many countries, is still considered in a formative stage, as information which is necessary to extract tourism activities from the national economic account is most of the time not complete. Many efforts in this direction of satellite accounting initially focused on visitors' trip spending while others added capital expenditure and selected durable goods purchased (river boats) to the tourism accounts.

One should always keep in mind that satellite accounts generally take into account the direct effects of tourists' spending and not the indirect or induced effects that are induced from the economic activity of tourism.

The purpose of Tourism Satellite Account is to analyse in detail all the aspects of demand for goods and services associated with the activities of visitors; to observe the operational interface with the supply of such goods and services within the economy; and to describe how this supply interacts with other economic activities.

Types of Economic Analysis

- **Economic impact analysis:** *What is the contribution of tourism activity to the economy of the region?*
  - ○ An economic impact analysis traces the flow of spending associated with tourism activity in a region to identify the changes in sales, tax revenues, income and jobs due to tourism activity. The principal methods here are visitor spending surveys, analysis of secondary data from government economic statistics, economic base models, input–output models and multipliers (Frechtling, 1994a).
- **Fiscal impact analysis:** *Will government revenues from tourism activity, taxes, direct fees and other sources cover the added costs for infrastructure and government services?*
  - ○ Fiscal impact analysis identifies the changes in demands for government utilities and services resulting from some action, and estimates the revenues and costs to local government to provide these services (Burchell & Listokin, 1978).
- **Financial analysis:** *Can we make a profit from this activity?*
  - ○ A financial analysis determines whether a business will generate sufficient revenues to cover its costs and make a reasonable profit. It generally includes a short-term analysis of the availability and costs of start-up capital as well as longer-range analysis of debt services, operating costs and revenues.
- **Demand analysis:** *How does the number and types of tourists change due to the change of price, promotion, quality and quantity of services, competitions and so on?*
  - ○ A demand analysis estimates the number and types of visitors to an area via a use estimation, forecasting or demand model. The number of visitors or sales is generally predicted based on judgement, historic trends or using a model that captures how visits or spending varies with key demand determinants such as, population size, distance to markets, income levels, and measures of quality and competition (Walsh, 1986; Johnson & Thomas, 1992).
- **Cost-benefit analysis:** *Which alternative policy will generate the highest net benefit to society over time?*
  - ○ It estimates the relative economic efficiency of alternative policies by comparing benefits and costs over time. Cost-benefit analysis identifies the most efficient policies from the perspective of societal welfare, including both monetary and non-monetary values. It makes use of a wide variety of methods for estimating values of non-market goods and services such as the travel cost method and contingent valuation method (Stokey & Zeckhauser, 1978; Sudgen & Williams, 1978).
- **Feasibility study:** *Can this policy or project be undertaken?*
  - ○ A feasibility study determines the feasibility of undertaking a given action to include political, physical, social and economic feasibilities. The economic aspects of a feasibility study typically involve a financial analysis to determine financial feasibility and a market demand analysis to determine market feasibility. The feasibility study focuses largely on the benefits and costs to the individual business or organization, while cost-benefit analysis looks at benefits and costs to society more generally (Warnell, 1986).
- **Environmental impact assessment:** *What are the impacts of an action on the surrounding environment?*
  - ○ An EIA determines the impacts of a proposed action on the environment, including changes in social, cultural, economic, biological, physical and ecological systems. Economic impact assessment methods are often used along with corresponding measures and models for assessing social, cultural and environmental impacts. Methods range from simple checklists to elaborate simulation models (Williams, 1994).

Source: Staines, *Economic impacts of tourism.*

Economic Impacts of Tourism	
Benefits	**Costs**
1. Financial	**1. Financial**
• Foreign exchange earnings • GNP • State Taxes • Income: For businesses for individuals	Leakages: Imports and repatriation of profits Opportunity costs Inflation Higher land prices
2. Employment	**2. Employment**
• Creates jobs	Often part-time Low paid Low skilled Seasonal For women May take employees from other sectors
3. Development	**3. Development**
• Broadens economic base • Inter-sectoral linkages can occur • Multiplier effects • Encourage entrepreneurial activity • Infrastructural provision • Improvement of social services • Promotes regional development in underdeveloped areas	Danger of dependency and neo-colonialism with foreign/non-local ownership

Sources: Mathieson and Wall (1982), Lea (1998), Pearce (1989), Ryan (1991), and Burns and Holden (1995).

Environmental Impact

Environment refers to the physical environment which consists of natural and built components. The natural environment is what exists from nature—climate and weather, water features, topography and soils, flora and fauna, and so on. Built environment is the man-made physical features, mainly all types of buildings and other structures. However, it must be understood that in comprehensive environmental analysis, sociocultural and economic factors are included, and in fact, it is often difficult and desirable to try to separate the socio-economic and physical components of the environment.

Relation between Tourism and Environment

The relation between tourism and environment is a much close one. Many features of environment are attractions for tourists. Tourist facilities and infrastructure comprise one aspect of the built environment, and tourism development and tourist use of an area generate environmental impacts. It is essential that this relationship be understood in order to properly plan, develop and manage tourism.

Importance of Environment in Tourism

The environment is recognized as one of the major resources for tourism. Since tourism depends ultimately on the environment, it is a main source of attraction by itself or is the context in which tourism activity is undertaken. It was the Manila declaration of World Tourism Organization, adopted in 1980, which emphasizes the importance of both natural and cultural resources in developing tourism, the need to conserve these resources for the benefit of tourism as well as residents of the tourism areas. The joint declaration of WTO and United Nations Environment Programme (UNEP), which formalized inter-agency coordination on tourism and environment in 1982, states:

> The protection, enhancement and improvement of the various components of man's environment are among the fundamental conditions for the harmonious development of tourism. Similarly, rational management of tourism may contribute to a large extent to protecting and developing the physical environment and the cultural heritage, as well to improving the quality of life.

There has been much concern justifiably expressed in recent years about the undesirable environmental impacts from unplanned to uncontrolled tourism development, as well as the environmental impacts of all types of developments. Tourism is only one of the several types of development and in some areas, cannot be easily separated from general development patterns. There is particularly a close relationship between outdoor recreation and tourism.

Considerable research has been accomplished during the past 30 years on the environmental impacts of development, including some research specifically on the impacts of tourism development. So it is now possible to systematically evaluate these impacts and recommend ways to mitigate them, either through 'preventive' measures to environmental planning and engineering or remedial measures of solving mistakes already made. However, this is still a relatively new field of study and there is a need for continuing research, especially on the environmental impact of various types of tourism development in tropical environment, and specific types of ecologically sensitive and vulnerable areas such as small islands, reefs and deserts oases. Research is particularly needed on the environmental impact of tourism in South Asian countries because this is relatively a new type of development here.

There are two types of related environmental concerns in developing tourism. One is the environmental impacts generated by the tourism development itself, and the other is maintenance and, where necessary, improvement of the overall environmental quality of the tourism area. Although related and overlapping, it is more systematic to evaluate them separately in the tourism areas.

Types of Environmental Impact

The environment in which tourism takes place is important to the quality of tourist experience. Both the natural environment in the form of land, water, plants and animals, and the man-made environment, which includes buildings and streets, form the foundation of tourism industry. In the absence of an attractive environment, tourism rarely succeeds, because this is one of the vital elements which tourists look for in a destination.

Tourism can have two different types of impact on the environment where it takes place:

- Tourism and environment can exist together in **harmony** when tourism benefits the environment in some way.
- Tourism and environment can exist together in **conflict** when tourism damages the environment in some way.

Tourism can generate both positive and negative environmental or no appreciable impacts, depending on how well its development is planned and controlled. The most commonly accepted types of impacts are outlined further.

The various types of negative or undesirable environmental impacts which can be generated by tourism development if it is not carefully planned, developed and controlled, include those listed below. Not all these impacts would likely take place in one area because the types of impacts often depend on the kind of tourism development and the environmental characteristics of the tourism area. The scale of tourism development in relation to the scale of the environment greatly influences the extent of environmental impact.

- **Water pollution:** If a proper sewage disposal system has not been installed for a hotel, resort or other tourist facilities, there may be pollution in groundwater from the sewage; or if a sewage outfall has been constructed into a nearby river or coastal water areas but the sewage has not been properly treated, the effluent will pollute that water area. This is not an uncommon situation in beach resort areas where the hotels have constructed an outfall into the adjacent water area which may be used by tourists for swimming.
- **Air pollution:** Tourism is considered as a 'clean industry' but air pollution from tourism development can result from excessive use of internal combustion vehicles of cars and buses used by and for tourists in particular area, especially at major tourist attraction sites, which are only accessible by road. Often compounding this problem is improperly maintained exhaust systems of vehicles. Also, pollution in the form of dust and dirt in the air may be generated from open, de-vegetated area if the tourism development is not properly planned and developed.
- **Noise pollution:** Noise generated by a concentration of tourists, tourist vehicles, sometimes by certain types of tourist attractions such as amusement parks, or car or motor cycle race tracks, may reach uncomfortable and irritating levels, and very loud noise can result in ear damage and psychological stress.
- **Visual pollution:** Poorly designed or inappropriately designed hotels and tourist facilities buildings, badly planned layout of tourist facilities, inappropriate or inadequate landscaping, excessive use of large and ugly advertising signs, and poor maintenance of buildings and landscaping can result in an unattractive environment for both tourists and residents.
- **Overcrowding and congestion:** Overcrowding of tourists, especially at popular tourist destinations, and vehicular congestion resulting from tourism generate environmental problems and also lead to resentment on the part of the residents of an area.
- **Land use problem:** If not planned well and developed according to good planning principles, tourism development may appropriate land which is more valuable for other types of land use such as agriculture, residential, park and recreation, or should remain under strict conservation control; may take the form of 'ribbon' commercial development which is inefficient to serve with infrastructure, generates traffic congestion and is not aesthetic, constructed too near beaches or other attraction features thus detracting from that features; and may cause other land use problems.
- **Ecological disruption:** Several types of ecological problems can result from uncontrolled tourism development and tourist use, such as overuse of fragile natural environment by tourists leading to ecological damage, for example, killing or stunting the growth of vegetation in a park/conservation area by many tourists tramping through it; collecting

rare types of seashells, coral, turtle shells or other such items by tourists (or by local persons for sale to tourists) which depletes certain species; breaking and killing of coral by boats and boat anchors and divers (coral requires decades for regeneration); undue filling of mangrove swamps—which are important habitats for sea life and also help control the circulation of water—for development; building of groins, piers and similar structures into the coastal waters which may change beach formation processes and lead to beach erosion; disruption of animal habits and activities by photographing and feeding them; and other types of ecological problems through uncontrolled tourism development and tourist use.

- **Environmental hazards:** Poor sitting and engineering of tourist facilities, as of any type of development, can generate landsides, floods, sedimentation of rivers and coastal areas resulting from removal of vegetation, disruption of natural drainage channels and so on.
- **Damage to historic and archaeological sites:** Overuse or misuse of environmentally fragile archaeological and historic sites can lead to damage of these features through excessive wear, vibration, vandalism, graffiti writing and so on.
- **Improper waste disposal:** Littering of debris on the land scrape is a common problem in tourism areas because of the large number of people using the area and the kind of activities they engage in. Improper disposal of solid waste from resorts and hotels can generate both litter and environmental health problems causing different diseases and pollutions, as well as make the place unattractive and unhygienic.

Positive Environmental Impact

Tourism, if well planned and controlled, can also help maintain and improve the environment in various ways, such as:

- **Conservation of important natural areas:** Tourism can help justify and pay for conservation of tourism parks, outdoor recreation and conservation areas (as attraction for tourists) which otherwise might be improperly developed or allowed to ecologically deteriorate. This can be an important benefit in South Asian countries which have limited resources for nature conservation.
- **Conservation of archaeological and historic sites:** Tourism provides the incentives and helps pay for the conservation of archaeological and historic sites (as attraction for tourists) which might otherwise be allowed to generate or disappear. This can also be an important benefit in South Asian countries which possess many requiring attention.
- **Improvement of environmental quality:** Tourism can provide the incentive for 'cleaning up' the overall environment through control of air, water and noise pollution, littering and other environmental problems, and for improving environmental aesthetics through landscaping problems, appropriate building design and better maintenance, and so on.
- **Enhancement of the environment:** Although a more subjective benefit, development of well-designed tourist facilities may enhance a natural or urban landscape which is otherwise dull and uninteresting.
- **Improvement of infrastructure:** An economic as well as environmental benefit, local infrastructure of airports, roads, water and sewage systems, telecommunications and so on, is often improved through development of tourism which uses and helps pay for these improvements.

Environmental Impact Assessment and Checklist

EIA is becoming a widely used method for evaluating possible environmental consequences of all forms of development and is potentially a valuable tool for translating sustainable principles into working practice. In particular, EIA provides a framework for informing decision-making process that surrounds development, and a wide number of industries are routinely required to undertake EIAs, and produce written environmental impact statements. The four key principles of EIA are as follows:

1. Assessment should identify the nature of the proposed and induced activities that are likely to be generated by the project.
2. Assessment should identify the elements of environment that will be significantly affected.
3. Assessment will evaluate the nature and extent of initial impacts and those that are likely to be generated via secondary effects.
4. Assessments will propose management strategies to control impacts and ensure maximum benefits from the project.

The impacts mainly depend on the value and judgement of the observer who is calculating the impact. The methodologies of environmental impact analysis are diverse and may embrace the use of key impacts checklists (each factor is evaluated in terms of possible type and extent of impacts).

- Air pollution
- Surface water pollution including rivers and streams, lakes, ponds and coastal waters
- Groundwater pollution
- Pollution of domestic water supply
- Noise pollution, generally and at peak periods
- Solid wastewater disposal problems
- Water drainage and flooding
- Ecological disruption and damage including both land and water areas, and plant and animal habitats
- Land use and circulation problems within the project area
- Land use and circulation problems created in nearby areas by the project
- Pedestrian and vehicular congestion, generally and at peak periods
- Landscape aesthetic problems
- Electric and telecommunication problems
- Environmental and health problems such as malaria and cholera
- Damage to historic, archaeological and cultural sites
- Damage to important and attractive environmental features, like large trees
- Generation of erosion and landslide problems
- Likelihood of damage from environmental hazards such as earthquakes, volcanic eruptions, hurricanes and so on

Environmental Impact Control Measures

Some of the implementation techniques to mitigate negative environmental impacts from tourism and maintain overall environmental qualities of tourism area are as follows:

1. Installation of water supply and sewage treatment and disposal systems for hotels and other tourists facilities which meet local standards if they are sufficiently high level, or WHO standards if local requirements are not adequate; the most appropriate type of system and treatment will be determined by the local situation.
2. Construction of adequate drainage systems to prevent flooding during rainy periods and standing water which may cause health problem.
3. Development of proper sanitary disposal of solid waste generated by hotels and other tourist facilities; the most appropriate type of solid waste collection and disposal collection and disposal system also will be determined by the local situation.
4. Avoidance of overdevelopment of tourist facilities, overuse of tourist attraction features and congestion generally through application of regional environment planning policies, strategies and zoning, as explained earlier, and development of adequate transportation systems and efficient organization of tourist movements.
5. Provision of open space and parks, and generous use of suitable landscaping in resorts, at tourist attraction features, in urban areas and along shorelines, roads and walkways.

Environmental Impacts of Tourism	
Benefits	**Costs**
1. Conservation of natural areas and wildlife	1. Energy cost of transport
2. Environmental appreciation	2. Loss of aesthetic value
3. Rehabilitation and often also transformation of old buildings and sites into new facilities	3. Noise
4. Introduction of planning and management	4. Air pollution
	5. Water pollution and the generation of waste
	6. Disruption of animal breeding patterns and habits
	7. Impacts on vegetation through the collections of flowers and bulbs
	8. Destruction of beaches, dunes, coral national parks and wilderness areas through trampling and/or the use of vehicles
	9. Change of landscape—permanent environmental restructuring
	10. Seasonal effects on population densities and structures

Sources: Mathieson and Wall (1982), Lea (1998), Pearce (1989), Ryan (1991), and Burns and Holden (1995).

Sociocultural Impact

Cultural impacts of tourism refer to the change in arts, artefacts, customs, rituals and architecture of a place. Culture, cultural attractions, experiencing culture, marketing culture and so on are certain terms that are frequently used in relation to tourism. Of late, attention is paid to what bearing tourism has on the culture of the host communities. Hence, it is no more a question of culture being used as a tourist attraction but also an issue of tourism impact on culture. Similarly, there are contradictory views in relation to methods and models of presenting the culture to the tourists. Travel experiences vary according to the verities of human kind and their geographical distribution.

Although culture is the only one that determines the overall attractiveness of tourism region, it is a very rich and diverse one. The elements of a society's culture are a complex reflection of a way its people live, work and play.

Cultural tourism covers all aspects of travel whereby people learn about each other's way of life and thought. Tourism is thus an important means of promoting cultural relations and international cooperation. Conversely, the development of cultural factors within a nation is a means of enhancing resources to attract visitors. In many countries, tourism can be linked with a 'cultural relation' policy. It is used to promote not only knowledge and understanding but also a favourable image of the nation among foreigners in the travel market.

The channels through which a country presents itself to tourist can be considered as cultural factors. These are entertainment, food, drink, hospitality, architecture, manufactured and handcrafted products of a country, and all other characteristics of a national\natural way of life.

Successful tourism is not simply a matter of having better transportation and hotels but of adding a particular flavour in keeping with traditional way of life and projecting a favourable image of the benefits to the tourists of such goods and services. A nation's cultural attraction must be presented intelligently and creatively. In this age of uniformity, the products of one nation are almost indistinguishable from those of another. There is a great need for encouraging cultural diversity. Improved technique of architectural design and artistic presentation can be used to create an expression of originality in every part of the world.

Valence Smith (1992) defines cultural tourism as 'including the picturesque or local color, a vistage of the vanishing lifestyle that lies within human memory with its old style houses, homespun fabrics, traditional transport and technology and handicraft'.

Cultural tourism, on the other hand, defines situations where the role of culture is contextual, where it shapes the tourist experience, without a focus on its uniqueness. It emphasizes artefacts rather than concrete cultural activities of the people.

According to James Clifford (1986), 'culture is a coherent body that lives and dies. Culture is enduring, traditional and structural (rather than contingent, Synergetic, historical). Culture is the process of ordering not disruption. It changes and develops like a living Organism. It does not normally survive abrupt alternations'.

The science of anthropology defines culture as an integrated system of meanings by which the nature of reality is established and maintained by people. In other words, culture is what a society wishes to be in order to cope with life.

The social impacts of tourism development are complex in nature and very difficult to assess. Most of the social impacts are also economic in character. These relate to the creation of new jobs and the influx of new income in the area. Although such jobs are analysed in terms of economic benefits, their social implications cannot be overlooked. Although social impacts can be quantified, many of these studies on social impacts measure perceived impacts.

Sociocultural Elements Contributing Attractiveness in a Tourism Region

Socio-cultural impact refers to changes to the residents' day-to-day life experiences, as well as to their values, lifestyle, intellectual and aesthetic needs. Various sociocultural elements include the following:

1. **Music:** All forms are included.
2. **Dance:** The costumes, music, settings and skills of the dancers are what differentiate the dances of various nations.
3. **Fine arts:** This includes architecture (including landscape architecture), painting, sculpture and graphic arts.
4. **Language:** Many people become tourists in another country because the culture embodied in its language appeals to them.
5. **Literature:** This includes books, magazines and newspapers, or the lack of them in some countries, which may reflect the restriction of the political system.
6. **Education:** The general level of education of a country often shows how developed the country is. Its historic university buildings are often a tourist attraction in their own right.
7. **Science:** The state of a country's science is generally reflected in its scientific displays and museums.
8. **Handicrafts:** These are considered cultural only if local people in the country, where they are sold, make them.
9. **Agriculture, business and industry:** These are all reflections of how a country has developed and what its economic base is.
10. **Government:** The method of the government is sometimes a reflection of its culture, and many government buildings are popular tourist attractions that many people visit to learn about the country's governmental culture.
11. **History:** The history of a country can often be absorbed through visits to its museums and historic preservation areas.
12. **Religion:** Many people travel for religious motivations and also the desire to see how a religion is practiced in a foreign culture or to visit the centre of that religion.
13. **Gastronomy:** Food and drinks are a reflection of a country's cultural heritage. Unfortunately, too many tourists never seek out, or wish to try, a foreign country's food specialty.
14. **Traditions:** It may be in the form of greeting, handshaking or bowing or folding hand together (*namaste* in India).

McIntosh and Goeldner (1984, pp. 140–141) listed the following possible negative social/cultural effects on a host society:

- Introduction of undesirable activities such as gambling, prostitution, drunkenness and other excesses.
- The so-called 'demonstration effects' of local people wanting the same luxurious and imported goods as those indulged in by tourists.
- Racial tension, particularly where there are very obvious racial differences between tourists and their hosts.
- Development of a servile attitude on the part of tourist business employees.
- Standardization of employee roles like the international waiter—same type of individual in every country.
- Loss of cultural pride, if the visitor views the culture as a quaint custom or as entertainment.
- Too rapid change in local ways of life due to being overwhelmed by too many tourists.
- Disproportionate numbers of workers in low-paid, menial jobs, a characteristic of hotel and restaurant employment.

Aspects of Sociocultural Impact

There are three aspects of the sociocultural effects of tourism.

1. **On the destination:** How well a destination is able to assimilate given number of visitors.
2. **On the way of life:** The impact that visitors have on people's values and the way of life.
3. **On the arts:** The influence of the visitors on the art, music, dance, painting, sculptures, theatre, architecture, handicrafts and so on.

These three types of impacts have the following positive effects:

- A number of visitors boost the local economy. They create wealth, generate jobs, produce improvements in the local infrastructure, trigger a range of new facilities and services, and stimulate other types of investment.
- Tourism creates more contact with the outside world, fosters a process of internationalization, stimulates two-way flows of information, promotes cultural exchange, leads to the import of more goods and services, and generally acts to develop the whole field of trade and communications.
- It creates an audience and patronage for the local arts—particularly for music, dance, theatre and handicrafts. It also has a significant indirect on all other artistic expressions—including literature, painting and architecture.

Types of Sociocultural Impact

Socio-cultural impact refers to the effects society and culture have on the host communities of direct and indirect relations with tourist and of interactions with tourism industry. Members of the host society are drawn to the tourist culture because of the emphasis on pleasure and seemingly endless supply of money, which many represent a modern way of life (Smith, 1982). Younger members of the host society are most susceptible to the demonstration effect (Murphy, 1985), abandonment of traditional enterprises (e.g., agriculture) to join the labour force catering to tourists, adoption of tourist dress and language, change in societal values and roles, and migration from rural areas to tourist destinations. It is not unusual for young members of a society to earn more money from tourists by pandering and prostitution than their parents, who are engaged in producing culturally reinforcing handicrafts, which may be sold to tourists at unbelievably low prices. In addition to the decline in moral values, the demonstration effect can result in the loss of artistic skills, as young members of the host society reject the low-paying, long-apprenticeship periods required to learn traditional skills. The demonstration effect is also observable when members of the host society try to fully assimilate themselves into the tourist culture.

It should not be assumed that all demonstration effect impacts are inherently bad. Rural economies may not be able to support an increasing population, and tourism may offer employment opportunities that were not previously available in the local community. Changing societal roles may give more decision-making power to women and younger members of the society who, prior to tourism development, held subservient and depend positions within the household. Herein lies one of the problems in analysing the sociocultural impact of tourism. Who determines whether changes are detrimental or beneficial? If the interpreter of change assumes that any modification to the traditional culture is unacceptable, then the demonstration effect will be seen as negative sociocultural impact. However, if one assumes that cultural change is inevitable and it is accompanied by other opportunities related to tourism development, then the demonstration effect need not always be something to avoid.

Marginal Man

Associated with the demonstration effect is the phenomenon known as the marginal man. When members of a host society attempt to fully assimilate them into the tourist culture, they reject some or all of the values of the host society. This rejection constitutes a removal from one culture, with the expectation of acceptance by another. However, because the tourist culture is often based on excessive play behaviour made possible by large amount of money, full assimilation is not probable. Tourists always have the option of returning to the ordinary life to build the financial resources needed for another round of tourist experience. The marginal man does not have this option as he has rejected his ordinary life. When it dawns on the marginal man that he cannot continue his pursuit of pleasure, he finds that it is impossible to assimilate back into the original culture. Not only did he reject his original culture, but it in turn rejects him. Marginal refers then to a person who is living on the outside boundaries of both the host and tourist culture, with full assimilation into either one impossible. The marginal man has not adopted a set of norms and standards acceptable to either culture or both groups consider his behaviour deviant, further separating the marginal man from either culture. One of the only options left to the marginal man is to physically move to another place and attempt the process of assimilation into a new culture.

Cultural Shock

Culture shock can be defined as the anxiety, which results from losing the physical and psychological markets of one's home environment. It is one of the few sociocultural impacts of tourism which affects tourists. Most of the literature on tourism's impact centres around the effects of tourism on host societies. This phenomenon is understandable since tourists choose where and what they want to visit, while members of the host society are often unable to choose if they even want tourists. However, culture shock is one of the identified sociocultural impacts that affect both tourist and guests.

Cultural shock manifests itself in different ways. For the tourists, it appears when they adjust to different language, lifestyles, dress and other aspects of behaviour acceptable in the destination but different from the home environment. The extent of culture shock is a function of cultural distance. The greater the difference in the culture of the tourist's home environment and what he or she encounters at the destination, the greater the cultural distance and hence cultural shock. Culture shock for host societies is also related to cultural difference, but in this case it refers more to the difference between the prevailing tourist culture and the host culture than to any specific culture existing within a particular market. Tourists can and do insulate themselves against culture shock by travelling in groups or purchasing a package tour. Travelling within the 'environmental bubble' of a package tour allows an exotic culture to be observed without having to be experienced. Enclave developments exclusively for tourists also erect a protective culture shock barrier. Unfortunately for host societies, enclaves or travel within an 'environmental bubble' only serves to widen the gap between tourist and host cultures, thereby increasing culture shock for hosts. Host societies are reduced to the level of objects which can collect on film or in the mind as souvenirs of the trip. The methods used to eliminate or reduce culture shock for tourists in turn increase the extent of culture shock for host societies.

Cultural Commoditization

The natural beauty of an area attracts tourists; facilities are constructed to meet their needs. Cultures also exert a strong draw, especially if they are considered exotic or differ markedly from the tourist's home environment. Because of the attractive potential of culture, attempts are made to package them for sale. This packaging is often referred to as cultural commoditization. Dances or rituals with religious or culturally reinforcing properties for a host culture, may not be viewed with the same sense of importance by tourists, but they are nonetheless sought after cultural experiences. Some rituals may take days to perform, too long to maintain a heightened arousal level for most tourists. However, the dances or costumes used in the ritual may seem exotic expressions worthy of purchase.

Cultural commoditization also occurs when members of host society mass-produce handicrafts to sell to tourists, bypassing the traditional methods of manufacture, or when they offer bodies as photo opportunities to tourists at a price. If economic forces prevail, strong traditions are ignored and eventually lost as they become modified products for sale. Further modification of traditions occurs as marketing concepts of target markets and product positioning replace the fundamental reasons for the existence of the traditions.

Greenwood (1989) argues that cultural commoditization occurs whenever local cultures are used as part of the pull component for destination promotion. It is more profound when local cultures are not compensated for the attraction embodied in them, but can also occur if tourists paying for the privilege of viewing somehow alter the meaning of the activities presented.

Relocation and Displacement

People move freely within their country in pursuit of employment opportunities or in search of a better quality of life. In other societies, free relocation is not commonly practised or accepted. The economic forces of tourism development can result in population shifts. New tourism developments can provide employment opportunities for local people as well as immigrants to the area. New immigrants to an area can bring in new cultural values. Cultural changes not only arise from mixing cultures with different values, but also through legislative or policy shifts. In democratic societies where all residents of a community express their opinion by voting, immigration can shift the balance of power, resulting in changing norms and standards supported by legislations. Displacement occurs whenever people move from the area because a tourism industry develops. People on fixed incomes may not be able to afford the higher property taxes, which accompany an increase in assessed value. Other local long-term residents may not like what the area has become and seek a different living environment. Forced displacement also occurs when the governments exercise their authoritative power, in some countries called the rights of eminent domain, to force people off land designated for tourism development. Displacement causes culture change, since cultures are built on the traditions of a group of people. When people move, their traditions move with them. New people moving into an area bring their traditions, resulting in wholesale cultural change. Any sociocultural impact of displacement or relocation is often difficult to quantify since these events may occur gradually over time. If a sociocultural assessment occurs after significant relocation or displacement that has already occurred, it may not be possible to reconstruct the culture that existed in the area prior to tourism development; hence, there is no base to measure change.

Dependency

When tourism supplants traditional economic enterprises or creates a strong, new economic system, it results in dependency relationships. This is most likely in developing countries, which do not have the capital or expertise to develop their own tourism industry. Instead, they rely on businesses from the developed world to bring tourists into the area, build facilities and manage the industry. The result is high leakage, as tourist money does not stay in the local area for responding and income generation, but is returned to the headquarters of multinational firms, which operate tourist facilities and provide transportation services. Mathieson and Wall (1982) refer to this dependency as neo-colonialism. Dependency relationships can contribute to cultural commoditization as entrepreneurs from the developed world decide what tourists want and repackage cultures for presentation and sale to tourists. Because of the loss of traditional enterprises, local residents accept tourism as the only means of employment and income. At the extreme, neo-colonialism provides very few additional economic gains from tourism, and developing countries find themselves being viewed as pleasure colonies for the elite of the developed world.

Crime

One of the few quantifiable sociocultural impacts is the type and magnitude of crime associated with tourism. Crime statistics are routinely maintained, allowing for an analysis of change over time. Tourism contributes to crime increase in a couple of ways. First, as the level of development increases, there is a corresponding increase in people attracted to the area for employment. As local populations increase, the potential for criminal activity increases. In this case, tourism should not be viewed as the cause of crime any more than an increase in any other industrial activity which contributes to population growth causes increase in crime. Second, tourists are often an easy prey for criminal activity. The majority of crimes against tourists are robbery, larceny and burglary. Tourists are generally concentrated in an area (e.g., hotels) which makes them easy to locate. They are often free spenders, which reinforces the income differential existing between them and local residents. They are also less likely to return for any legal trials if the crime is not major (e.g., loss of jewellery) and losses are covered by insurance. Resorts and hotels attempt to reduce the incidence of criminal activity by instituting security programmes for guests which may include increasing the number of security personnel on the premises, offering safe storage for valuables, use of surveillance cameras in high crime areas, or publishing recommendations for areas to avoid during certain periods of the day. Some destinations also have victim-compensation programmes, including covering expenses associated with a return visit for testifying during any subsequent court case.

One of the reasons frequently mentioned for increase in criminal activity directed at tourists is the perceived gap between the wealth of visitors and residents. If only a small portion of the host population economically benefits from tourism, negative attitudes about tourism and tourist wealth are common. When local inhabitants are not allowed to enter tourist facilities, this increases the level of resentment against the privileged class (Dogan, 1989).

Prostitution

Prostitution is not included in the above crime category, although it is illegal in many countries. In other areas, it can be considered part of the attraction package. Prostitution is legal in the state of Nevada, and when one of the more well-known brothels was unable to maintain its mortgage payment, ownership reverted to the mortgager, in this case to the US government. The tourist culture, based on non-ordinary life and pursuit of pleasure, supports the types of activities not normally pursued in one's home environment; prostitution may be one of those activities. Since local standards differ in their acceptance of prostitution, there is no evidence based on statistical data of tourism's role in increasing prostitutions. However, tourism is conducive to perpetuating and supporting activities outside the bounds of ordinary life. It is generally assumed that the nature of tourism contributes to prostitution (Jud & Krause, 1976). Even when tourism may not be the cause of prostitution and other illicit activities such as drug trafficking and smuggling, host communities may still perceive that it is the reason for the increase in these activities (Belisle & Hoy, 1980). Certain tourism activities, like casino gambling, may be more susceptible to this criticism than others (Pizam & Pokela, 1985).

Others

The use of stimulants, mind-expanding hallucinogenic and other sense altering drugs have been around probably as long as prostitution. Because travel provides physical and psychological escape, drug use is viewed as contributing to the enhancement of psychological escape. Hashish use in India, although illegal, is accepted as part of daily life for many people and is commonly made available to tourists. Tourism's contribution to increasing drug use by local residents has not been thoroughly studied, but its influence can be viewed as one of the manifestations of the demonstration effect.

Religious value changes have also been addressed as a product of a strong tourist culture. The powerful influence of the tourist culture manifested in the demonstration effect has the potential to overthrow strong moral conduct values inherent in different religions. Religious experiences, important to tourists on a pilgrimage, can also be affected by increasing levels of tourism. The presence of non-believers mixing with serious religious pilgrims at a holy site can reduce the spiritual experience for true believers. Inappropriate behaviour (e.g., photography of holy shrines), based on ignorance rather than malice, can degrade the quality of the religious experience for pilgrims who may only be able to make the pilgrimage once in their life.

Language changes are also noted as a consequence of tourism. Loss of native languages occurs when host societies adopt the language of their visitors, usually as a result of the tourist's inability to communicate in the language of their hosts. Societies with a language difficult to learn or one that is regionally limited are most at risk. Language changes also occur from the importation of slang or phrases that are not translatable into the native tongue. Language changes may be an indicator of acculturation and can be used to study the effects of tourist contact with local societies.

Social structures frequently redefine themselves after tourism becomes a significant economic force. Young people may decide to forego traditional skills training, opting for jobs, including illicit occupations, in the tourism industry. In patriarchal societies with clearly defined roles, women working outside the home may upset traditional family member's roles (Kousis, 1989). While some may feel that this eventually leads to economic emancipation for women in societies which place little value on their intellectual abilities, there is nonetheless a change occurring whose long-term consequences are debatable.

Sociocultural Benefits

Not all sociocultural impacts are detrimental to host societies. The process of development provides opportunities for an improved quality of life. Increased employment opportunities, possibly allowing for multiple income households, enhance purchasing power and the acquisition of goods previously considered cost prohibitive. Increasing levels of tourism can also result in improvements of basic social services (e.g., medical and security). Determining what constitutes beneficial change is based on subjective value judgements. Acquisition of material goods may be viewed as a move to secularization and away from spiritually reinforcing traditional values. Alternately, it can be viewed as an improvement in living standards and quality of life. What constitutes sociocultural benefits and costs remains a controversial topic. In spite of this difficulty, some non-quantifiable sociocultural benefits are assumed to be associated with tourism development.

Peace and Understanding

Cultural differences between groups of people result primarily from the formation of complex social relationships, which develop in relative isolation from each other. Misunderstanding between social groups can be reduced by sharing and learning from each other what is important to each group's value system. Tourism provides an opportunity for this sharing and learning to take place.

Dann (1988) describes some of the classic arguments against tourism, including tourism as a form of imperialism, capitalist exploitation, and promoter of master/servant relationships. He counters each argument against tourism with equally compelling evidence supporting tourism as a means of promoting understanding and exchange (social and economic). Although no substantial evidence exists to support the statement that tourism is a force for peace, it is clear that peace is not attainable without tourism. People-to-people interaction is necessary for understanding and discovering common grounds, and tourism provides the stage for social exchange to occur. Where tourism involves more than a cursory interaction between hosts and guests, there is some evidence to indicate that it has beneficial consequences.

Cultural Pride

The process of hosting guests implies a sharing of resources, both environmental and social. If cater to the needs and desires of a host society, the type of tourism created will project a sense of place. Although developing a sense of place and a local tourism industry at the same time may not be an easy task, the rewards are substantial. Not only does the community benefit from an active tourism industry, but the community takes pride in what it has been able to accomplish is enhanced. Instead of leaving town during the height of the tourist season, local residents exhibit pride in showcasing their community for visitors. Similar to the feeling of hosting friends in one's house, community pride is exhibited in the type of development created, and extends into the quality of service delivered to visitors. In the absence of any strong sense of place, tourism can easily overwhelm a community and result in some of the negative social impacts discussed above. Cultural pride and preservation may reinforce for one group of people in one particular situation, and viewed as cultural commoditization by another group in a similar situation.

Benefits/Positive Impacts

- Increased family income visibly raised the standard of living in the community.
- Expanded social contact with fellow employers and tourists produced unexpanded awareness of outside world among women workers.
- New skills and salaries gave women workers a sense of increased self-growth and accomplishment.
- Family roles were changing for the better as assumed more of households and child-rearing chores.

Exhibit 8.1	Sociocultural Impacts of Tourism

Cultural Impacts Cost	Benefits
1. Disappearance, degradation or commoditization leading to a loss of authenticity of • Art and music • Handicrafts • Dance • Ceremonies • Architecture • Dress • Food	1. Renaissance and/or retention of Art Handicrafts Dance Ceremonies
	2. Restoration of monuments

Social Impact Cost	Benefits
1. Local resentment resulting from 'the demonstration effect'.	1. Tourists gain through relaxation and recreation, a change of environment and social contact with others.
2. Moral Problems: • Crime • Prostitution • Gambling • Decline of traditional beliefs and religion.	2. Locals gain through: Impetus to modernization Women given a level of independence People break out of traditional restrictive roles
3. Health problems	
4. Strain on local hospitality become intolerable	
5. Employment in tourism can be dehumanizing	
6. Adverse effects on family and community life	
7. Neocolonialism	
8. Unbalanced population structures	

Sources: Mathieson and Wall (1982), Pearce (1989) and Ryan (1991).

- Husbands were beginning to develop respect for their wives as competent individuals were able to hold good jobs.
- Increased income and an expanded worldview could result in more opportunity for higher education of the workers' children.

Social Impact and Consumer Behaviour

From social point of view, tourist expenditure can have both positive and negative effects on a community. When business is good, the additional revenue generated by visitors raises the general level of income in the community, which in turn raises the standard of living of the resident. On the observer side, when residents begin to emulate the lifestyle of outsiders, their own value and consumption behaviour may change, shifting from the conservative consumption patterns towards the instant gratification of wants and desires.

Residents of rural communities quickly observe that their own locally produced consumer goods are often inferior to imported goods. As a result, residents began to save less and borrow more in order to support altered consumption hobbits.

Social Impact and Sociological Cycle

From a sociological point of view a tourist destination development follows five basic stages, which are as follows:

1. Discovery stage
2. Developmental stage
3. Conflict stage
4. Confrontation stage
5. Decline stage

The discovery stage is characterized by low volume of visitors and hence, residents are not exposed to any of the effects of development. Residents welcome tourism development enthusiastically in the development stage, because of its visible contribution to the local economy. Benefits are possible in terms of improved infrastructure and higher income levels generated directly by tourism or tourism-related jobs. However, development also encourages crime, as visitors become visible prey for perpetrators and juvenile mischief-makers.

Local residents first appear in the conflict stage, which is reflected in hostile attitudes towards visitors. This hostility usually results from competition over resources—water, energy, land use, recreational facilities, beachfront property and so on. More problems arise when residents are excluded from such facilities.

Problems are further accentuated in the confrontation stage, which result in organized opposition to new development, land use right and fights over the use of scares resources.

The decline stage is usually signalled by hostile activities such as forms of sabotage, rampant crime, lack of safety and outflow of capital. A progressive erosion of community goodwill attends the last three stages: once goodwill and community supports are gone, the consequences are difficult, if not impossible to reverse.

It is necessary that these social phases be understood in order to prevent or at least deter the erosion, social planning is one of the viable means to do so effectively. Research on social consequences of tourism on the community is the first step. The information generated by research should lead to an action plan to circumvent possible unfavourable social impact and to reinforce tourism's positive contributions.

Second, it should be mandatory that the community be involved in actual planning and development process. Residents should be made to feel that they have a stake in the success of the destination.

Social planning is necessary at all levels of development for mature as well as new tourism destinations. Mature destinations are more susceptible to social deterioration when destinations become saturated, markets dissipate and new investments are not forthcoming. Planning efforts at this point must be focused on halting the erosion process although the measures taken may not always be successful.

A social plan, therefore, must be given as much weight as an economical or an environmental plan in tourism development to fight against lower employee morale, reduced productivity, poor service absenteeism and delay or strike resulting from tourism activity.

Sociocultural Impact Model

As mentioned, it is difficult to determine what constitutes a sociocultural benefit or cost. When a benefit crosses the line and becomes a cost, it may be a function of an individual's perception or may relate to stages in the development process. The magnitude and types of sociocultural impacts depend on the intensity and speed with which tourism development occurs. Doxey (1976) identifies four stages in the development process which help determine when social impacts are most likely to occur. The first stage he terms euphoria, which occurs during the discovery or initial tourism development phase for a destination. Each succeeding stage is characterized by increasing levels of facility development.

Doxey's Index of Irritation

One of the simplest but most widely used frameworks for describing the effects of tourist on a host society is Doxey's (1976) so-called index of irritation. This represents the changing attitudes of the host population to tourism in terms of a linear sequence of increasing irritation as the number of tourists grow. In this perspective host society, tourist destinations pass through stages of euphoria, apathy, irritation, antagonism and loss in the face of tourism development.

Levels of Host Irritation

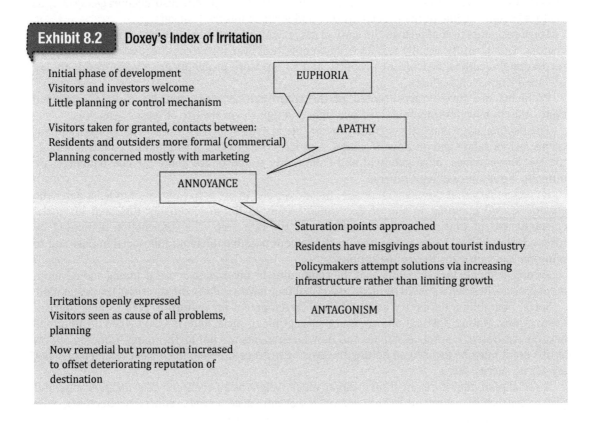

Exhibit 8.2 **Doxey's Index of Irritation**

Initial phase of development
Visitors and investors welcome
Little planning or control mechanism

EUPHORIA

Visitors taken for granted, contacts between:
Residents and outsiders more formal (commercial)
Planning concerned mostly with marketing

APATHY

ANNOYANCE

Saturation points approached

Residents have misgivings about tourist industry

Policymakers attempt solutions via increasing infrastructure rather than limiting growth

Irritations openly expressed
Visitors seen as cause of all problems, planning

Now remedial but promotion increased to offset deteriorating reputation of destination

ANTAGONISM

Euphoria

In the euphoric stage, local residents support tourism development, and are willing and eager to share their community with visitors. New employment opportunities, increased income and escalating property values are often cited as positive benefits. Rapid development is frequently associated with higher levels of euphoria. Development opponents are few in number and generally dismissed as part of radical fringe element.

The euphoria stage is most likely to occur when local economies have been in a dormant stage for a period of time and tourism brings new opportunities for growth and expansion. They also occur when existing industry leaves unemployment results, and tourism is viewed as a replacement industry. Local support for the tourism industry is based on economic projections that ignore or downplay social costs. Most likely, few local residents have had any experience with an economic tourism boom and are unaware of the potential negative consequences.

Apathy

Eventually, the growth which fuelled rapid tourism development begins to slow. Land values and business expansion, although continuing their upward rise, are no longer increasing at the same rate as during the tourism boom period. The level of tourism reaches a point where the novelty of arriving visitors gives way to the acceptance of tourism as part of the community's economic base. The social structure of the area most likely changes with new migrants arriving in search of jobs, and family roles change as different members (e.g., youths) find employment within the industry. The promise of economic 'good times' which pervaded the euphoria stage is now viewed as accruing to only a limited number of residents, with the rest not realizing or believing the potential.

Irritation

If the level of tourism activity continues to expand, either through increases in arrivals or season extension, a stage of irritation may occur. Most likely, tourism development has been unplanned and has spread into environmentally sensitive areas. Locals must now share with outsiders what used to be their own recreation areas. Concurrently, prices of staple goods (e.g., food) rise at a much faster rate than local incomes. Income growth realized in earlier stages vanishes as inflation takes back earlier gains. If the environment or the attractiveness of the local area is drastically modified through development, visitor numbers may decrease, resulting in an overabundance of facilities and eventually economic decline. During the irritation stage, the social and environmental impacts of unplanned tourism development begin to receive attention. Local residents perceive a loss of 'place' and blame tourism for it.

Antagonism

As a sense of loss of 'place' becomes more profound, residents blame tourists for the changes rather than the unplanned and uncontrolled developments. Most likely, the type of tourist that arrived when the area was in the euphoria stage has been replaced with an entirely new type of visitor that is less interested in local customs and traditions, and more drawn to specific physical attractions. Local residents manifest their antagonism through the passive aggressive types of behaviour they exhibit towards tourists, for example, through angry letters to the local newspaper editor complaining about different types of tourist behaviour. They may come up with names for tourists which have a derogatory connation understood only by the locals. Passive aggressive behaviour may shift to overtly aggressive actions, as when automobiles with out-of-state licence plates are chosen as objects for criminal activity.

Antagonistic activity can occur in any area, but it is more apparent where a wide gap between the lifestyle of the tourists and locals exists. In developing countries, it may occur after local residents realize that the tourism industry does not offer the type of jobs desired. If development is of an enclave, 'environmental bubble' nature, very little social exchange between locals and tourists occurs, in contrast to the first tourists who arrived when the area was necessary and desired. The stage of antagonism can occur whenever either group, or most likely both, is perceived as a commodity to be exploited rather than as a guest or host.

The different stages discussed above are graphically represented in Figure 8.1. In the figure X- axis measures the tourist arrivals and Y-axis measures the level of social impact. It is evident from the figure that even though tourist arrivals increase from point A to point B, social impacts decrease; this is the stage of euphoria. The dashed horizontal line AD depicts social impact levels which existed prior to tourism development. With the euphoric feeling that accompanies rapid growth and development, the aggregate perceived level of social impacts experiences a decline. As tourists continue to arrive and facility development increases, the nature of host/guest interaction begins to change. Eventually euphoria gives way to apathy, and the level of social impacts begins to move upward (point B). The types of social impacts may be entirely different from those that existed prior to tourism development. Discontent with the type of development or the level of tourism that the area now experiences begins to pervade the social consciousness. Even though it is not entirely possible to compare the different types of social impacts of pre-and post-tourism development, certain indicators show that the level of impacts increases. Eventually, a point C is

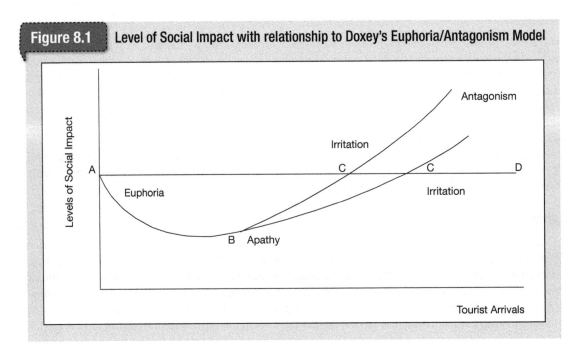

Figure 8.1   Level of Social Impact with relationship to Doxey's Euphoria/Antagonism Model

reached where apathy gives way to irritation. If a social carrying capacity for tourism could be determined, it would be somewhere between point B and C, or where the level of social impacts is less than that existing before tourism growth and development. Anything beyond point C results in an even greater level of social impacts than before development, and if put in economic terms, would be beyond the point of diminishing returns. If tourism continues to expand, irritation changes to antagonism. At this point, it is too late to turn back the level of tourism development and recapture the sense of 'place' that previously existed.

The process outlined by Doxey is no fait accompli. It can be directed, but to do so requires the active involvement of community residents and business. Methods of coping behaviour or sociocultural impact mitigation strategies must be adopted.

Sociocultural Impact Mitigation

The time taken to proceed through each of Doxey's stages depends on various factors, including the types of development, number of tourists, preferred tourists activities, and extent of development planning. There is no set social carrying capacity for any area, as various techniques can forestall the advent of the irritation stage and at least hold the line on the level of perceived sociocultural impacts. In Figure 8.1, the curve ABC depicts the stage where additional tourist arrivals can be accommodated without reaching the irritation stage as quickly.

Numerous methods can be employed to deal with the onset of the irritation stage. A brief overview of some of these is listed below. Most are revisited in subsequent chapters of this text when they become integral components of other concepts that are related to the development process.

- Inform residents of the advantages and costs of tourism development. Too often, residents are not familiar with the concept of economic multipliers. Explaining how tourism expenditures are distributed throughout the local economy should be one of the primary objectives of a resident education programme. Information on some of the consequences of increased levels of tourism should also be addressed in order to avoid surprises.
- Plan tourism based on goals and priorities identified by local resident. Obviously, this is much easier to recommend than to implement. There are many ways to obtain public inputs including public meetings, opinion polls, studies of perceptions and attitudes, and referenda. The main idea is to allow local people to feel a part of the development planning process. Development plans proceed more smoothly when local residents sense that they have ownership of the resources used for tourism development.
- Involve both public and private sectors in the development process with the intent of maintaining the integrity and quality of local natural resources. Many local residents find that the same resources, which attract them to the area, attract tourists. Crowding and congestion can seriously affect local residents' perceptions of the benefits of tourism development. If the resources are used wisely and their integrity is maintained, most residents do not oppose or begrudge visitor's use of the resources.
- Provide opportunities for minority groups or negative peoples to become involved in the tourism industry. Tourism development benefits from diversity. Minority or native people have a unique sociocultural resource, which, if developed properly, adds to the local attraction package.

- Utilize local capital, expertise and labour whenever possible. Local ownership of tourism industry is an important ingredient for obtaining support. It may not be always possible to utilize local capital, as in small rural communities or developing countries it is not always readily available. Similarly, local expertise may not exist for the type of management positions required. Whenever these resources are found in short supply, development must proceed at a slow pace to allow for local capital accumulation and expertise to be acquired before the next phase of growth begins. Rapid growth and development tend to exclude local investment and participation in the industry, leading to a feeling of alienation.
- Provide opportunities for community participation in local events and festivals. One of the advantages gained from festivals and events is community pride. Inviting visitors to participate in the events that reinforce community identity and values is the basis on which strong host recognition can be built.
- Deal with present problems before proceeding with increased tourism development. Once negative sociocultural impacts are recognized, the community must deal directly with resolving those problems. Further development at this time will only create new problems and exacerbate present ones.
- If thematic development is chosen, it should reflect the area's historical, lifestyle or geographic setting. Disney-type themes are suited to created attractions. Communities are living attraction and should project development themes that have relevance to local residents. Fantasy theme parks may be wonderful places to visit but they do not make acceptable places to live. Well-planned 'sacrifice areas' for major contrived attractions are necessary in order to manage some of the sociocultural impacts.
- Promotional programmes should reflect images supported by and subject to the endorsement of local residents. Again, this involves a concerted effort to involve local residents in the tourism industry. The extent of involvement will determine the point at which apathy changes to irritation.

Even when the above methods become part of the strategic planning process for tourism development, there will still be debates over what constitutes a benefit and cost, and how important each one is. There will be forces pushing for increased levels of development at the same time that other groups claim too much development has already occurred. Ultimately, the final decision about acceptable levels of development finds its way into the political arena. Political decisions can be simply a power struggle between different interest groups, or they can proceed based on a defined process which includes collecting factual data to guide the decision. The limits of acceptable change strategy, first discussed in the preceding chapter, combine data with politics to achieve this goal. With slight modifications, the strategy can incorporate sociocultural elements into the development process.

8.3. Concept of Tourism Carrying Capacity

Concept

Tourism carrying capacity is the optimum tolerance level of a destination without degrading the quality of environmental composition, reducing the quality of economy, culture and society, and also without decreasing the visitor experience in a given set of time. The concept of carrying capacity emerged in the 1980s to analyse the negative impacts of tourism. Earlier the concept of carrying capacity was mostly used in the field of civil engineering which meant 'determining the maximum capacity which a building, an infrastructure or a facility could sustain as regards the number of its user'. In civil engineering, the concept was used by engineers, architects and building planners for constructing structures and popularly referred to as physical carrying capacity.

Definitions of Carrying Capacity

- According to Wall and Mathieson (2006), 'carrying capacity is the maximum number of people who can use a site without an unacceptable alteration in the physical environment and an unacceptable decline in the quality of the experience gained by the visitors'.
- According to World Tourism Organization (1993, p. 18), 'carrying capacity is the level of visitor use an area can accommodate with high levels of satisfaction of visitors and few impacts on resources'.
- McIntyre (1993, p. 23) defines carrying capacity as, 'the maximum use of any site without causing negative effects on the resources, reducing visitor satisfaction, or exerting adverse impact upon the society, economy and culture of the area'.

It can be defined as, 'the limits in which nature can respond to the demands of the creatures up to their satisfaction level'. In tourism, carrying capacity is defined as, 'how much tourism is permissible for positive gains and the point at which what was a gainful activity turns into a negative one'.

Tourism carrying capacity determines the optimum use of destination without degrading its environment, resources, community, economy and culture.

Carrying capacity basically depends on the following:

- Biophysical (ecological)
- Sociocultural (which basically relates to the impact on host population and culture)
- Facility (which relates to the visitor experience)

Types of Carrying Capacity

Tourism carrying capacity is broadly classified into four types. They are:

1. **Physical carrying capacity:** It refers to the physical space and the number of people that can be accommodated by the available infrastructure in a given set of time. It measures the number of tourists that may be accommodated in a destination. Physical carrying capacity is a numerical measure and is useful for facility-oriented urban and suburban recreation. It is measured in two dimensions.
   a. **Per space unit,** that is expressed in terms of number of persons per square hectare of land and
   b. **Per facility unit,** that is expressed in terms of number of beds in a hotel, number of cars parked, campers in a campground and so on.
2. **Perceptual carrying capacity:** It refers to the number of tourists who can be accommodated in the destination without affecting the comfort level and quality of the destination.

In other words, it measures the number of people that may be accommodated before the visitor's experience is damaged.

According to Lankford and Howard (1994, 38), if local communities felt that the increasing number of visitors impaired on their access to and use of preferred outdoor recreation areas, their attitudes towards tourism development irreversibly and progressively becomes more negative. They also recommended that

> Local governments and tourism promoters should play particular attention to the finding that if people feel they have access to the planning/public review process and that their concerns are being considered, they would support tourism. Extensive efforts should be made to identify ways to involve the local residents in the continuing planning and design of their community.

3. **Economic carrying capacity:** It refers to the overall economic benefits by the tourism development in a destination without disturbing the economy or in other words it measures the number of tourists that may be welcomed to a location before the economy of the area is adversely affected.

   According to Borg (1992), there are twin effects of tourism development in an urban area. These are:

   1. As the market expands, competition among tourist's destinations gets increasing more intensely. The localities which do not possess adequate civic infrastructure also join the race and by doing so, they enter into vicious cycle.
   2. Tourism development may trigger a process known as 'crowding out'. The mechanism tends to expel the less lucrative urban functions and replace them with tourist's activities.

4. **Ecological carrying capacity:** It refers to the number of people that may be accommodated to a destination before damage occurs to the environment. Or in other words it determines the conservation importance of flora and fauna, water quality, soil erosion and so on in the destination. The ecological carrying capacity implies on the following:
   - The ecological systems are maintained before the damage occurs.
   - Acceptable levels of air, water and noise pollution.
   - Conservation of wildlife and natural vegetation of both land and marine environments.

   According to UNWTO, tourism carrying consists of the following elements:
   - Physical
   - Ecological
   - Cultural
   - Tourist satisfaction index
   - Resident's social tolerance

   Carrying Capacity can vary with the following:
   - Season
   - Overtime (duration of stay)
   - Tourist behavioural patterns (cultural)
   - Facility design and management
   - Dynamic characteristic of the environment
   - Dynamic characteristics of the host community
   - Types of destination environments

Measurement of Carrying Capacity

Tourism carrying capacity can be measured by the following determinants:

- **Limits of tangible resources in a destination:** In any destination, there may be some resources which can be completely destroyed due to overuse. There are some resources which cannot be replenished such as water and land in an island. Tangible resource limit can be overcome on capital and technology uses. There are three types of resources which can be overcome. These are:
    - Those tangible resources are perceived as obstacle that can be overcome.
    - Those resources which cannot be overcome with present capital and technological inputs.
    - Those tangible resources which will be destroyed if not protected.
- **Tolerance by the host population:** Attitudes and perceptions of the host population are important while planning and policy consideration for development. Participation of local communities is essential in tourism policy decision-making process. Dogan (1989) analysed the reactions of the local population to adjust themselves to the new conditions. According to him, if the impacts are deemed to be positive, the reaction is acceptance to change, alternatively, if the impacts are deemed to be negative, the reactions take the form of resistance.
- **Visitor's satisfaction:** Satisfaction is a dynamic factor which may change with the other factors. However if the attitudes and perceptions of the tourists are negative, it can affect the growth of tourism. Sometimes reluctance of the tourists to give frank opinions, problems regarding the determination of levels and causes of satisfaction are more difficult to measure than residence response. Collection and analysis of visitor's feedback can be the important tools for measuring visitor's satisfaction.
- **Capacity linked to costs and benefit analysis:** Cost-benefit analysis needs to be carried out to determine destination's capacity. Three aspects of capacity linked to cost-benefit analysis are as follows:
    - The first aspect is the opportunity costs of the investments. Analysis should be done to know whether the investments are beneficial and feasible.
    - The second aspect is to understand in what extent the costs have to be tolerated for the economic growth.
    - The third aspect is to find out an optimum balance between all costs and benefits.
- **Capacity in a systems approach:** Role of capacity in a systems approach highlights the assessment of costs and benefits through prediction, analysis of impacts and to find out goals for planning and management. To determine the role of capacity, four key requirements have to be discussed in systems approach. These are: explicit goals, determination of the planned system, search for optimization, and considering future costs and benefits while determining current desirable levels of use.
- **Excessive rate of growth:** Carrying capacity in a destination can be affected by rapid and excessive rate of tourism growth. Due to appropriate policy and inadequate system to make changes in the policy may be limiting factors. As Dekadt (1979, p. 17) stated, 'the term carrying capacity applies not only to the maximum number of tourists or tourist accommodation which seem desirable at a given time, but also to the maximum rates of growth above which the growth process itself would be unduly destructive'. Excessive rate of growth may cause overstrain of physical resources and cultural shock in a traditional society.

Limitations of Carrying Capacity

Though the concept of carrying capacity is an important tool for planning and development of a tourist destination, it has some limitations. These are:

- The definition of carrying capacity provides little direction for practical implementation. It is an evaluative criterion and if the criterion is imprecise, it becomes difficult to implement.
- Carrying capacity may be considered as a scientific concept, but it is often criticized as a mere management tool and inherently it is subjective.
- Though the objectives of the management mostly relate to 'condition', carrying capacity focuses on the use of levels or number of visitors.
- Because the perception of tourists and local residents to the saturation level may be different; the analysis of carrying capacity is difficult. The original level of environmental damage may exceed tourist's perception.
- 'Seasonality' is one of the most important characteristics of a tourism destination. It is also an important reflection of carrying capacity. During the peak season the saturation level of any destination is often reached and not in off season. So the impact of carrying capacity varies. Therefore, the specific techniques should be adopted to reduce the peak season demand and maintain tourist flow throughout the year.

Conclusion

Tourism development, be it local, regional, national or international level, can cause both positive and negative impacts on the destination. These impacts may be broadly classified into three types: economic, Sociocultural and environmental. In order to achieve sustainable tourism development, various stakeholders of tourism industry, tourism operators and destination planners must come forward to take appropriate action to minimize the negative impacts and maximize the positive impacts. Since the key to achieve an acceptable balance between the positive and negative impacts of tourism is only possible by adopting the principles of the sustainable development approach, ecological, environmental and sociocultural sustainability should be carried out properly in order to achieve sustainable tourism development.

MODEL QUESTIONS

1. What do you understand by tourism impact?
2. Analyse how do different types of impacts arise due to tourist activities in a destination.
3. Critically examine the economic impact of tourism.
4. Write a note on the economic benefits of tourism according to UNWTO.
5. Explain different methods of calculating economic impacts of tourism.
6. Evaluate the interrelationship between tourism and development.
7. Briefly explain how various types of environmental impacts arise due to tourism development.

8. Write in detail about the environmental impact checklists and control measures.
9. What do you mean by sociocultural impact? What are the sociocultural elements that contribute to the attractiveness of a tourism region?
10. What do you understand by carrying capacity? Explain various types of tourism carrying capacity with suitable examples.

Student Activities

1. Visit a popular tourism destination of your choice and find out various economic and environmental impacts arising due to mass tourist movement.
2. Visit any rural tourism destination of your state and mention the sociocultural impacts on the local community.

Suggested Readings

Adams, K. (1990). Cultural commoditization in Tana Toraja, Indonesia. *Cultural Survival Quarterly, 14*(1), 31–34.

Blake, A., & Sinclair, M. T. (2003). Tourism crisis management: US responses to September 11. *Annals of Tourism Research, 30*(4), 813–832.

Budowski, G. (1977). Tourism and conservation: Conflicts, coexistence and symbiosis. *PARKS, 1*, 3–6.

Bull, A. (1995). *The economics of travel and tourism* (2nd ed.). Melbourne: Longman.

Burchell, R.W., & Listokin, D. (1978). *The fiscal impact handbook.* New Brunswick, NJ: Center for Urban Policy Research.

Burns, P., & Holden, A. (1995). Tourism: A new prospective. New Jersey: Prentice Hall.

Butler, R. W. (1974). The social implications of tourist developments. *Annals of Tourism Research, 2*(2), 100–111.

———. (1993). Tourism: An evolutionary perspective. In J.G. Nelson, R.W. Butler and G. Wall (eds), *Tourism and sustainable development: Monitoring, planning, managing* (pp. 27–44). Waterloo, Ontario: University of Waterloo (Department of Geography Publication 37).

Clifford, James. (1986). On ethnographic allegory. In James Clifford and George Marcus (eds), *Writing culture* (pp. 98–121). Barkley, CA: University of California Press.

Cohen, E. (1979). Rethinking the sociology of tourism. *Annals of Tourism Research, 6*(1), 18–35.

Connell, J., & Page, S. J. (2005). Evaluating the economy and spatial effects of an event: The case of the world medical and health gains. *Tourism Geographies, 7*(1), 63–85.

Craven, J. (1990). *Introduction to economics* (2nd ed.). Oxford: Blackwell.

Daniel, J. Stynes (1997). Economic impact of tourism. *A handbook for tourism professionals.* Urbana: University of Illinois, Tourism Research Laboratory.

De Kadt, E. (ed.) (1979). *Tourism: Passport to development?* New York: Oxford University Press.

Din, K. (1988). Social and cultural impacts of tourism. *Annals of Tourism Research, 15*(4), 563–566.

Dwyer, L., Forsyth, P., & Spurr, R. (2004). Evaluating tourism's economic effects: New and old approaches. *Tourism Management, 25*(3), 307–317.

Fletcher, J., & Snee, H. (1989). Tourism in South Pacific Island. In C. Cooper (Ed.), *Progress in tourism, recreation and hospitality management* (Vol. 1, pp. 114–124). London: Belhaven.

Frechtling, Douglas C. (1994). Assessing the economic impacts of travel and tourism – Introduction to travel economic impact estimation. In J.R. Brent Ritchie and Charles R. Goeldsner (eds), *Travel, tourism and hospitality research* (2nd ed.). New York: John Wiley and Sons Inc.

Gee, C. Y., Choy, D. J. L., & Makens, J. C. (1984). *The travel industry* (pp. 110–115). York, NY: Van Nostrand Reinhold (a division of International Thomson Publishing Inc.).

Greenwood, D. (1889). Culture by the pound. In V. L Smith (ed.), *Host and guest: The anthropology of tourism* (2nd ed., pp. 177–185). Philadelphia, PA: University of Pennsylvania Press.

Holloway, J. C., & Robinson, C. (1995). *Marketing for tourism*. Harlow: Longman.

International Union of Official Travel Organization (IUOTO). (1976). *The impact of international tourism on the economic development of developing countries*. Geneva: World Tourism Organization.

Jafri, J. (1989). Tourism as a factor of change: An English language literature review. In J. Bystrzanowski (Ed.), *Tourism as a factor of change: A socio cultural study* (pp. 17–60). Vienna: European Coordination Centre for Research and Documentation in Social Science.

Johnson, P., & Thomas, B. (eds). (1992). *Choice and demand in tourism*. London: Mansell.

Kausis, M. (1989). Tourism and the family in a rural Cretan community. *Annals of Tourism Research, 16*(3), 318–332.

Lankford, S. V. (1994). Attitudes and perceptions toward tourism and rural regional development. *Journal of Travel Research, 31*(3), 35–43.

Lankford, S. V., & Howard, D. R. (1994). Developing a tourism impact attitude scale. *Annals of Tourism Research, 21*, 121–139.

Lea, J. (1998). *Tourism and development in the third world*. London: Routledge.

Leiper, N. (2008). Why the tourism industry is misleading as a generic expression: The case for the plural variations, tourism industries. *Tourism Management, 29*(2), 237–251.

Mathieson, A., & Wall, G. (1982). *Tourism, economic, physical and social impacts*, Essex, London: Longman Group Limited.

Murphy, P. E. (1985). *Tourism: A community approach*. New York: Methuen.

Nelson, J. G., Butler, R. W., & Wall, G. (eds). (1993). *Tourism and sustainable development: Monitoring, planning, managing*. Waterloo, Ontario: University of Waterloo (Department of Geography Publication 37).

Oppermann, M., & Chon, K. (1997). *Tourism in developing countries*. London: International Thomson Business Press.

Pearce, D. G. (1989). *Tourist development*. London: Longman.

Pearce, P. (1989). Social impacts of tourism. *The social, cultural and environmental impacts of tourism*. Sydney: New South Wales Tourism Commission.

Pizam, A. (1978). Tourism's impacts: The social cost to destination communities as perceived by its residents. *Journal of Travel Research, 16*(4), 8–12.

Pizam, Abraham, & Pokela, Julianne. (1985). The perceived impacts of casino gambling on a community. *Annals of Tourism Research, 12*, 2, 147–165.

Ryan, C. (1991). *Recreational tourism: A social science perspective*. London: Routledge.

Shoemaker. (1994). Segmenting the US travel market according to the benefits realized. *Journal of Travel Research, 32*, 8.

Smith, V. (1992). *The anthropology of tourism*. Madrid: Endymion.

Smith, V. L. (Ed.). (1977a). *Hosts and guests: The anthropology of tourism*. Philadelphia: University of Pennsylvania Press.

——— (1977b). The anthropology of tourism: A science-industry evaluation. *Annals of Tourism Research, 7*(1), 13–33.

Stringer, P. (1981). Hosts and guests: The bed and breakfast phenomenon. *Annals of Tourism Research, 8*(3), 357–376.

Stynes, D. J., & Propst, D. B. (1992). A system for estimating local economic impacts of recreation and tourism. In S. Reiling (ed), *Measuring tourism impacts at the community level* Maine Agricultural Experiment Station Miscellaneous Report No. 374). Orono, ME.

Sugden, Robert, & Williams, Alan. (1978). *The principles of practical cost–benefit analysis*. Oxford: Oxford University Press.

Van der Borg, Jan. (1992). *Tourism and urban development*. Amsterdam: Thesis Publishers.

Waggle, D., & Fish, M. (1999). International tourism cross elasticity. *Annals of Tourism Research, 26*(1), 191–194.

Wall, G., & Ali, M. (1977). The impact of tourism in Trinidad and Tobago. *Annals of Tourism Research, 4*(4), 43–49.

Wall, G., & Mathieson, A. (2006). *Tourism: changes, impacts, and opportunities* (2nd ed.). New York: Pearson Prentice Hall.

Walsh, R. G. (1986). *Recreation economic decisions: Comparing benefits and costs*. State College, PA: Venture Publishing Co.

Warnell, Gary. (1986). Feasibility analysis in tourism. Extension bulletin E-1992. East Lansing, MI: Michigan State University Cooperative Extension Service.

Williams, Peter W. (1994). Frameworks for assessing tourism's environmental impacts. In J.R. Brent Ritchie and Charles R. Goeldner (eds), *Travel, tourism and hospitality research* (2nd ed.). New York: John Wiley and Sons Inc.

Witt, S. (1991). Tourism in Cyprus: Balancing the benefits and costs. *Tourism Management, 12*(1), 37–46.

WTO. (1983). Risks of saturation of tourist carrying capacity overload in holiday destinations. Report of the secretary-general on the execution of the general programme of work for the period 1982–1983, New Delhi

Young, G. (1973). *Tourism: Blessings of blight?* Harmondsworth, England: Penguin.

Tourist Transportation

After going through this chapter, the reader will be able to understand:

❑ **The importance of transportation in tourism business**
❑ **Different forms of tourist transport**
❑ **The growth and advantage of road transport**
❑ **The airlines industry and its role in travel business**
❑ **The domination of the automobile in travel industry**
❑ **The contribution and role of rail and motor coach travel**
❑ **The nature and importance of cruise industry**

CHAPTER OVERVIEW

Chapter 9 mainly deals with the importance of transportation in tourism business. Different forms of transport such as road transportation, air transportation, rail transportation and water transportation are discussed in detail in this chapter. Transportation in international context is also elaborated here with suitable examples.

9.1. Introduction

Transport is an important part of the tertiary sector and is the lifeline of a country. It plays an important role in connecting cities with remote areas. Development in transport facilities has played an important role in the diversification of communication and modernization. The main forms of transport in India are public transport and private transport. Buses, trains, metro rail, hired cars and auto rickshaws come within the category of public transport. A network of railways connects villages to cities, towns and metropolitan hubs. Thus, transport in India is a very well-developed sector (Figure 9.1).

Following are the urgent transportation problems:

- Congestion
- Safety and security
- Environmental damage
- Seasonality

The factors that affect the mode selection decisions are as follows:

- *Major factors*
  - Availability
  - Frequency
  - Cost/Price
- *Other factors*
  - Safety
  - Convenience
  - Ground services

- Speed/Time
- Comfort/Luxury

- Terminal facilities and location
- Status and prestige
- Departure and arrival times

Travellers choose a travel mode based upon five dimensions:

1. **Functional:** Departure and arrival times, safety records, direct routes, absence of stops and so on
2. **Aesthetic/Emotional:** Style, interior/exterior decorations, comfort, luxury and safety
3. **Social/Organizational:** Stereotypes (bus and cruise may be unsuitable for old people, good for young people)

Figure 9.1   **Operating Sectors of the Tourism Industry**

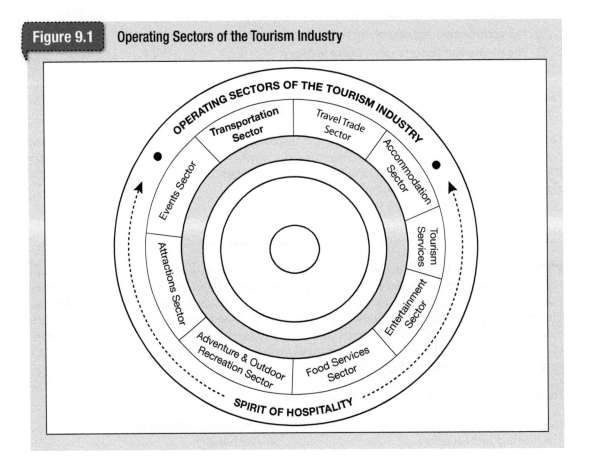

4. **Situational utilities:** Location convenience of the mode and its terminal facilities to the traveller
5. **Curiosity utility:** Travellers' tendency to try something because it is new and different

9.2. Types of Tourist Transportation

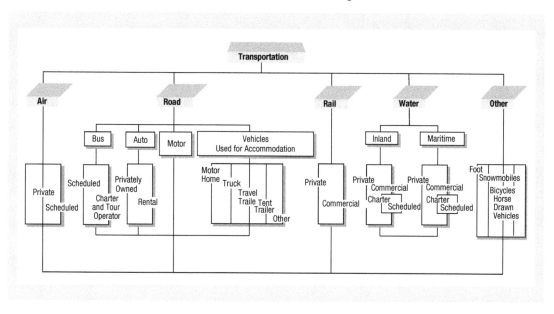

Airlines Industry

- World airlines industry carries over 2.2 billion passengers per year.
- Low-cost carriers (LCCs) are growing.
- Some typical characteristics of LCCs are:
  - One passenger class.
  - One type of airplane to reduce fleet maintenance costs.
  - Using secondary airports.
  - Quick airport turnarounds.
  - Point-to-point service.
  - Employees working in multiple roles.
  - Internet booking.
  - No frills, just low fares.

Rail Industry

The characteristics of rail industry are:

- Efficient
- Economical

- High-speed trains provide an alternative to air travel

Motor Coach Industry

The characteristics of motor coach industry are:

- Intercity bus passengers tend to be lower income non-business travellers who are very price sensitive.
- Intercity bus service is becoming less important due to increased auto ownership and aggressive airline pricing.
- Bus travel is characterized by:
  - More travel to and from rural areas and small towns than other modes of transportation.
  - Lower average ticket revenues than other modes.
- Intercity bus industry is a small-business industry with a great deal of flexibility.
  - Many bus companies focus primarily or exclusively on charter, tour or commuter operations.

Road Transport

Road transport is considered to be one of the most cost-effective and preferred modes of transport, for both freights and passengers. Because of its level of penetration into populated areas, it is vital for the economic development and social integration of the country. Road transport is a decisive infrastructure for the economic development of a country. It influences the pace, structure and pattern of development.

Some of the important benefits of road transport are easy availability, adaptability to individual needs and cost savings. Other benefits are:

- It provides the Arterial Network to facilitate trade, transport, social integration and economic development.
- It facilitates specialization, extension of markets and exploitation of economies of scale.

Advantages

- Flexibility
- Reliability
- Speed and door-to-door service

Growth in Road Length (In India)

India has one of the largest road networks of over 46.99 lakh km. It comprises national highways, expressways, state highways, major district roads, other district roads and village roads with the following length distribution:

National Highways/Expressway	96,214 km
State highways	1,47,800 km
Other roads	44,55,000 km
Total	46,99,014 km

Udaipur–Chittorgarh Section of NH-76
Source: Annual Report of Ministry of Transport and Highways

The national highways have further been classified depending on the carriageway width of the highway. Generally, a single lane has a width of 3.75 m and 3.5 m per lane in the case of multilane national highways.

Authorities responsible for different categories of roads are given in the table below:

Category of Roads	Authorities Responsible
National highways	Central Government (through Ministry of Road Transport and Highways–The National Highways Authority of India [NHAI])
State highways and major highways	State governments (Public Works Departments)
Rural roads and urban roads	Rural engineering organizations, local authorities such as panchayats and municipalities

Expressways

1. National Expressway 1(India) or Ahmedabad–Vadodara Expressway
2. Delhi–Gurgaon Expressway
3. Mumbai–Pune Expressway
4. Noida–Greater Noida Expressway
5. Delhi–Noida Direct Flyway
6. Jaipur–Kishangarh Expressway
7. Durgapur Expressway
8. Kolkata–Dumdum Expressway
9. Panipat Elevated Expressway

Ahmedabad–Vadodara Expressway

Source: Annual Report of Ministry of Transport and Highwayas

State Highways

The state highways usually are roads which link important cities, towns and district headquarters within the state and connect them with national highways or highways of the neighbouring states.

These highways provide connections to industries/places from key areas in the state, making them more accessible.

Border Road

These roads are:

- Constructed along or near the international border.
- Maintained by the Border Roads Organisation.
- Mainly used by the armed forces (Central Reserve Police Force (CRPF), Border Security Force (BSF) and Army). For example, Srinagar–Leh–Kargil.

Other Roads

- Village roads (link villages of a state)
- Kuccha roads

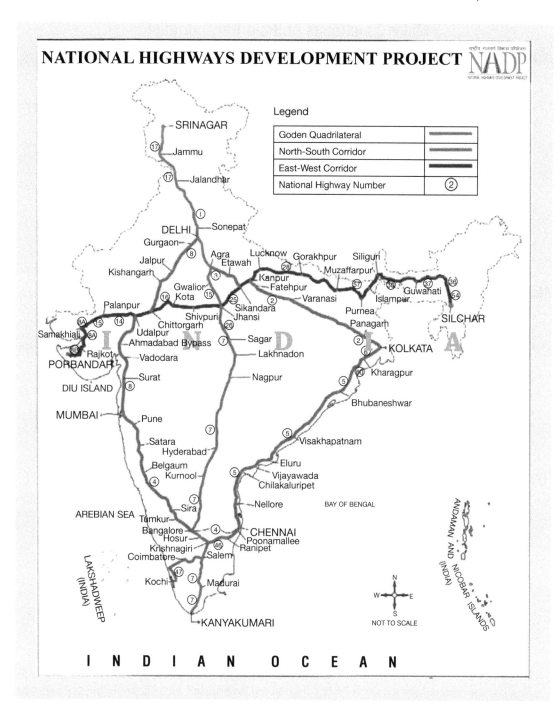

Source: National Highway Development Project, India
Disclaimer: This figure is not to scale. It does not represent any authentic national or international boundaries and is used for illustrative purposes only.

Major Constraints of Road Transportation

- Land acquisition
- Environment and forest clearances
- Clearances of railways for railway overbridges designs
- Shift of utilities (electric lines, water pipelines, sewer lines and telecommunication lines)
- Law and order problems
- Poor performance by some contractors

Acts/Rules

- Motor Vehicles Act, 1988
- Central Motor Vehicles Rules, 1989
- Road Transport Corporations Act, 1950
- Carriers Act, 1865 (to be replaced by the new Carriage by Road Act, 2007)

Motor Vehicles Acts in India

- First enactment relating to motor vehicle in India: Indian Motor Vehicles Act, 1914
- Replaced by Motor Vehicles Act, 1939
- In January 1984, a working group was constituted to review all the provisions of Motor Vehicles Act, 1939
- Motor Vehicles Act, 1988
- Central Motor Vehicles Rules, 1989
- Road Transport Corporations Act, 1950
- Carriage by Road Act, 2007 repealed to Carriers Act, 1865
- Carriage by Road Rules, 2011

Types of Motor Vehicle

1. **Contract Carriage:** According to Section 2 in The Motor Vehicles Act, 1988 of India, 'contract carriage' means a motor vehicle which carries a passenger or passengers for hire or reward and is engaged under a contract, whether expressed or implied, for the use of such vehicle as a whole for the carriage of passengers mentioned therein and entered into by a person with a holder of a permit in relation to such vehicle or any person authorised by him in this behalf on a fixed or an agreed rate or sum.
   a. On a time basis, whether or not with reference to any route or distance or
   b. From one point to another, and in either case, without stopping to pick up or set down passengers not included in the contract anywhere during the journey, and includes:
      i. A maxi cab; and
      ii. A motor cab notwithstanding that separate fares are charged for its passengers.
2. **Goods Carriage:** According to Section 2 in The Motor Vehicles Act, 1988 of India, 'Goods carriage' means any motor vehicle constructed or adapted for use solely for the carriage of goods, or any motor vehicle not so constructed or adapted when used for the carriage of goods.
3. **Motor Cab:** Motor cab means any motor vehicle constructed or adapted to carry not more than six passengers excluding the driver for hire or reward.

4. **Motor Car:** Motor car means any motor vehicle other than transport vehicle, omnibus, road roller, tractor, motorcycle or invalid carriage.
5. **Maxi Cab:** Maxi cab means any motor vehicle constructed or adapted to carry more than 6 passengers, but not more than 12 passengers excluding the driver for hire or reward.
6. **Motor Vehicle:**
   a. Motor vehicle means any mechanically propelled vehicle adapted for use upon road whether the power of propulsion is transmitted there from an external or internal source.
   b. It does not include a vehicle running upon fixed rails or a vehicle of a special type adapted for use only in a factory or a vehicle having less than four wheels fitted with engine capacity of not exceeding 35 cm^3.
   c. **Omnibus:** Omnibus means any motor vehicle constructed or adapted to carry more than six persons excluding the driver.
   d. **Stage Carriage:** Stage carriage means a motor vehicle constructed or adapted to carry more than six passengers excluding the driver for hire or reward at separate fares paid by or for individual passengers, either for the whole journey or for stages of the journey.
   e. **Tourist Vehicle:** According to Section 2 in The Motor Vehicles Act, 1988, of India, 'tourist vehicle' means a contract carriage, constructed or adapted and equipped and maintained in accordance with such specifications as may be prescribed in this behalf.

National Permit

'National permit' means a permit granted by the appropriate authority to goods carriages to operate throughout the territory of India or in such contiguous states not being less than four in number, including the state in which the permit is issued as may be specified in such permit in accordance with the choice indicated in the application.

According to Sub-section 12 of Section 88 of the Motor Vehicle Act of India, 1988,

(a) No national permit shall be issued:
   (i) To an individual owner so as to exceed five national permits in its own name.
   (ii) To a company so as to exceed ten valid national permits in its own name.
(b) The restriction under clause (a) regarding the number of permits to be issued shall not apply to the State transport undertakings.
(c) In computing the number of permits for the purposes of clause (a), the number of permits held by an applicant in the name of any other person and the permits held by any company of which such applicant is a director shall also be taken into account.

Regional Transport Authority

The state government shall, by notification in the official gazette, constitute for the state, a State Transport Authority (STA) to exercise and discharge the powers and functions specified in subsection (3), and shall constitute Regional Transport Authorities (RTAs) to exercise and discharge throughout the region as may be specified in the notification, in respect of each RTA.

The aims and objectives of the public authority are:

1. Implementation of provisions of the Motor Vehicles Act, 1988, and the rules framed thereunder.
2. Registration of motor vehicles.
3. Collection of taxes and fees for motor vehicles.

4. Help State Transport Department to formulate policy.
5. Help transport ministry in fixation and regulation of tariff on goods and passengers' transport.
6. Facilitation of passenger services to the travelling public.
7. Control of traffic accident offences.
8. Issue of driving licences and registration certificate.
9. Impart driving training to educated unemployed youths with a view of creating opportunities for self-employment.
10. Check over interstate vehicles.
11. Road safety and awareness measures.
12. Traffic survey on behalf of ministry.
13. Use of CNG/LPG as auto fuel.
14. Pollution control measure.
15. Grant of permits to stage carriages, interstate vehicles and goods vehicles.
16. Legislative measures on road transport.

Regional Transport Office

Regional Transport Office or as commonly known as RTO is a licensing, registration, taxation authority of a particular region. It is empowered to cancel the valid fitness certificate of vehicle if it is caught in mechanically unfit and unroadworthy condition.

The RTO official has the power to issue memo for the breach of provisions of Motor Vehicles Act and rules. These memos generally consist of description of the offence, seal and signature of the issuing authority. The document is impounded only for minor offences.

Each RTO, while issuing licence plates, has its own code which is broken down into states or UT, and their districts. For example, if Port Blair issues a licence, its code is AN-01. 'AN' is the code for Andaman and Nicobar Islands and 01 is the code for Port Blair in the Andaman district.

Guidelines for Recognition as an Approved Tourist Transport Operator (in India)

1. The aims and objectives of the scheme for recognition of Tourist Transport Operator are to encourage quality standard and service in this category so as to promote tourism in India. This is a voluntary scheme open to all bona fide Tourist Transport Operators to bring them in the organized sector.
2. **Definition:** A Tourist Transport Operator Organization is one which provides tourist transports such as cars, coaches and boats to tourists for transfers, sightseeing, journey to tourist places and so on.
3. Applications for recognition shall be addressed to the Additional Director General, Transport Bhawan, No. 1, Parliament Street, New Delhi 110 001.
4. The recognition as an approved Tourist Transport Operator shall be granted by the Ministry of Tourism, Government of India, New Delhi initially, for 5 years, based on the inspection report/recommendations of a committee comprising of concerned Regional Director and a member of International Travel & Tourism Academy (ITTA).
5. Applications for **renewal/extension** shall be addressed to the regional director of the concerned region as per the following addresses:
   a. The Regional Director (East), India Tourism, 'Embassy', 4, Shakespeare Sarani, Kolkata–700 071, West Bengal.
   b. The Regional Director (West), India Tourism, 123, M. Karve Road, Opp. Church Gate, Mumbai–400 020, Maharashtra.
   c. The Regional Director (North), India Tourism, 88–Janpath, New Delhi–110 001.

 d. The Regional Director (South), India Tourism, 154, Anna Salai, Chennai–600 002, Tamil Nadu.

 e. The Regional Director (North–East), India Tourism, Amarawati Path, (Opposite Dispur Post Office), Christian Basti, G. S. Road, Guwahati–781 006, Assam.

6. The renewal/extension thereafter shall be granted for 5 years after inspection is conducted by a committee comprising of concerned regional director and a member of ITTA, on an application made by the Tourist Transport Operator along with the requisite fee/documents.

7. Documents received from applicants after scrutiny in all respects will be acknowledged by the regional director concerned. The inspection for renewal shall be conducted by the inspection team within a period of 2 months from the receipt of complete application, failing which it will be deemed as renewed.

8. The following conditions must be fulfilled by the Tourist Transport Operator for grant of recognition by the Ministry of Tourism:

 a. The application for grant of recognition shall be in the prescribed form and submitted in duplicate.

 b. The applicant should have been in the tourist transport hire business for a minimum period of 1 year at the time of application.

 c. The Tourist Transport Operator has operated in the above period a minimum number of four tourist vehicles with proper tourist permits issued by the concerned STA/RTA for tourist vehicles. Out of these four tourist vehicles, at least two must be cars. The Tourist vehicles and the related documents should be in the name of the company.

 d. The applicant has adequate knowledge of handling the tourist transport vehicles for transferring tourists from the airport, railway stations and so on, and for sightseeing of tourists, both foreign and domestic. The drivers should have working knowledge of English and Hindi/local languages.

 e. The drivers of the tourist vehicles have proper uniform and adequate knowledge of taking the tourist for sightseeing.

 f. The applicant should have proper parking space for the vehicles.

 g. The Tourist Transport Operator is registered with the appropriate authority for carrying on the business of operating tourist transport vehicles.

 h. The minimum office space should be 200 sq. ft. Besides this, the office may be located in neat and clean surroundings and equipped with telephone, fax, computers and so on. There should be sufficient space for reception and easy access to the toilet facilities.

 i. The turnover by the firm from tourist transport business should be a minimum of ₹5 lakhs duly supported by a certificate issued by chartered accountant.

  A. For ex-defence personnel, the condition of being in the business of tourist transport vehicles for 1 year is relaxable to 6 months and having four vehicles is relaxable to two tourist vehicles provided the candidate is sponsored by the Director General of Resettlement, Ministry of Defence, New Delhi. However, the ex-defence personnel who apply under this scheme must themselves operate the tourist transport business and should not be hired man of other financiers.

  B. The condition of being in operation for 1 year for recognition as an approved tourist transport operator can be relaxed to six months and number of tourist vehicles to three in the case of those applicants who have their business at the centres identified and declared for the purpose by the Ministry of Tourism from time to time. A current list of such centres can be made available on request.

9. The Tourist Transport Operator is required to pay a non-refundable fee of ₹3,000 while applying for the recognition for Head Office and each Branch Office. The same fee is payable at the time of renewal of Head Office as well as Branch Offices. The fee will be made payable to the Pay & Accounts Officer, Ministry of Tourism in the form of a bank draft.
10. The applicant should be income tax assessee and should submit copy of acknowledgement certificate as proof of having filed income tax return for current assessment year.
11. The decision of the Government of India in the matter of recognition shall be final. The Government of India may in their discretion refuse to recognize any firm or withdraw/withhold at any time recognition already granted without approval of the competent authority. Before such a decision is taken, necessary show cause notice would invariably be issued and the reply is considered on merit. This will be done after careful consideration and generally as a last resort; circumstances in which withdrawal is resorted would also be indicated.
12. Tourist Transport Operator granted recognition shall be entitled to such incentives and concessions as may be granted by the government from time to time and shall abide by the terms and conditions of recognition as prescribed form time to time.

Road Transportation Terms and Definitions

1. **Roads**
   a. **Track:** A path on the land much trodden by persons and animals.
   b. **Cart track:** A land for use by carts.
   c. **Road:** A way on land with a right of way for the public.
   d. **Urban road:** A road within the limits of the area of municipality, military cantonment, port or railway authority.
   e. **Project road:** A road within the limits of the area of a development project of a public authority for the exploitation of resources such as forest, irrigation, electricity, coal, sugarcane and steel.
2. **Highway Classes by Function**
   a. **Expressways:** Expressways offer superior highway facility with higher specifications. They provide more lanes, better surface, divided carriageway, controlled access grade separations at crossroads and fencing, and so on. Expressways permit only fast-moving vehicles and are meant to carry through traffic. The Expressways may be owned by the Central Government or state government depending on whether the route is a national highway or a state road.
   b. **National highways:** The arterial roads of the country for interstate movements of goods and passengers. They traverse the length and width of the country connecting the national and state capitals, major ports and rail junctions, and link up with border roads and foreign highways.
   c. **State highways:** The arterial roads in a state for inter-district movements. They traverse the length and width of a state connecting the state capital, district headquarters and important towns and cities, and link up with the national highways and adjacent state highways.
   d. **District roads:** The branch roads of the state and national highways to serve as the main roads for intra-district movements. They traverse the length and breadth of a district to connect the area of production and marketing in the district to one another and to the national highways.
   e. **Village roads:** These roads serve as the feeder roads as well as the roads for inter-village movements. They pass through rural areas connecting the village to one another and to the nearest road of higher category, namely district roads, state highways, national highways and so on.

3. **Highway Classes by Width**
   a. **Below standard s lane:** Surfaced roads having clear carriageway width of below 3.75 m.
   b. **Standard:** Single surfaced roads having clear carriageway width between 3.75 m and below 7.0 m lane.
   c. **Standard double lane:** Surfaced roads having clear carriageway width between 7.0 m and below 10.5 m.
   d. **Standard multilane:** Surfaced roads having clear carriageway width of 10.5 m and above.
4. **Road Surface**
   a. **Bitumen or tar macadam:** A type of construction in which the fragments of coarse aggregate are bound together by bitumen applied either premix or by grouting method.
   b. **Bitumen concrete surfacing:** A type of construction in which coarse and fine mineral aggregates are mixed with bitumen and laid to the desired thickness.
   c. **Black top surface:** The surface of roads made with bitumen as a binder.
   d. **Brick paving:** A paving composed of bricks laid in regular courses.
   e. **Cement bound macadam:** A surface in which a matrix of a cement sand mixture is interposed between two layers of road metal spread on the road, and the whole mass is watered and consolidated so that the matter works into the interstices of the road metal to produce a compact mass.
   f. **Cement concrete:** A surface obtained by placing and consolidating cement concrete to required thickness.
   g. **Earth road:** A road with the carriageway composed of natural soil.
   h. **Gravel road:** A road with the carriageway composed of a consolidated layer of gravel.
   i. **Water bound macadam:** A type of surfacing in which stone fragments are first interlocked by rolling and then bound with smaller stone gravel and so on which are enforced into the intersection by brimming, watering and rolling.
   j. **Motorable:**
      A. **For plain areas:** Surfaced or unsurfaced road of minimum 3.0 m carriageway width is motorable.
      B. **For hilly areas:** Surfaced or unsurfaced road of minimum 3.0 m carriageway width having no horizontal curve of radii less than 14 m and grade not steeper than 7 per cent is motorable. A bridle path is non-motorable.

Rail Transport

In the last 15–20 years, the railway industry worldwide has experienced big challenges and changes. In Latin America, Canada, Sub-Saharan Africa, Australia, New Zealand and the United Kingdom, the private sector participation in the railway industry has increased substantially. Virtually all rail freight activities on the American continent are now carried out by the private sector though most urban and long-distance passenger trains remain publicly owned and operated.

In Central and Eastern Europe, and Central Asia, the change has been of ownership and the ending of political unions of the Union of Soviet Socialist Republics (USSR), Yugoslavia and Czechoslovakia led to the emergence of over 20 newly independent national railway companies, some of which (Russia, Kazakhstan and Ukraine) may be counted individually as some of the world's largest railway businesses.

In the world, China has led to the highest average rail traffic densities in the world. The network enhancement programme that has been adopted by the government started since the 19th century, with multiple objectives of increasing capacity, extending the network to more remote areas and enhancing service quality.

Railways of the World

Trans-Asian Railway

The Trans-Asian Railway or TAR is a project undertaken by UNESCAP, the United Nations Economic and Social Commission for Asia and the Pacific to create an integrated freight railway network across Asia and Europe. The project was initiated for providing a continuous rail link between Singapore and Istanbul, Turkey. This will again connect with Europe and Africa. The Trans-Asian Railway network now comprises 117,500 km of railway lines serving 28 member countries. Trans-Asian Railway aims to serve cultural exchanges and trade within Asia and between Asia and Europe.

The Agreement for Trans-Asian Railway Network was signed on 10 November 2006, by 17 Asian nations as part of a United Nations Economic and Social Commission for Asia and the Pacific (UNESCAP) effort to build a transcontinental railway network between Europe and Asia. With reference to the historical Silk trade routes, the plan has sometimes been called the Iron Silk Road.

The Northern Corridor of TAR links Europe and the Pacific, via Germany, Poland, Belarus, Russia, Kazakhstan, Mongolia, China and the Koreas. The Southern Corridor connects Europe to Southeast Asia including Turkey, Iran, Pakistan, India, Bangladesh, Myanmar, and Thailand, Malaysia and Singapore. The TAR is trying to reduce transport gaps between India and Myanmar, between Myanmar and Thailand, between Thailand and Cambodia, between Cambodia and Vietnam and between Thailand and Yunnan.

The North–South Corridor links Northern Europe to the Persian Gulf. The main route starts in Helsinki, Finland, and continues through Russia to the Caspian Sea, where it divides into three routes, like, a western route through Azerbaijan, Armenia, and western Iran; a central route across the Caspian Sea to Iran via ferry; and an eastern route through Kazakhstan, Uzbekistan and Turkmenistan to eastern Iran.

Northern East West Freight Corridor

The N.E.W. Corridor or Northern East West Freight Corridor is a project organized by the International Union of Railways (UIC) for connecting with east coast of the USA to East Asia by train and ship. There are two main routes. Both routes start from east coast ports of North America then across the Atlantic Ocean to the port of Narvik, from there by rail through Sweden to Finland and Russia.

From Russia there are two routes: either via the Trans-Siberian Railway to Vostochny Port, or though Kazakhstan to Ürümqi in China. From Ürümqi the route goes to Lanzhou and the port city Lianyungang.

Japan–Korea Undersea Tunnel

The Japan–Korea Undersea Tunnel is a proposed project to connect the two countries Japan and the South Korea through an undersea tunnel crossing the Korea Strait using the strait islands of Iki and Tsushima. This is the shortest straight-line distance of approximately 128 km via undersea tunnel. The tunnel could potentially connect Kyushu to Busan, South Korea's second-largest city, via the Japanese islands of Iki and Tsushima.

Others:

- Transcontinental Railroad
- African Union of Railways
- Scandinavian Railways (Sweden, Norway, Finland, Denmark)

Amtrak

The National Railroad Passenger Corporation, Amtrak, is a corporation striving to deliver a high-quality, safe, on-time rail passenger service that exceeds customer expectations. Learn all about Amtrak here from every angle.

The **National Railroad Passenger Corporation**, doing business as **Amtrak**, is a government-owned corporation that was organized on 1 May 1971 to provide intercity passenger train service in the United States of America. It is headquartered at Union Station in Washington DC.

Facts and services

As the nation's intercity passenger rail operator, Amtrak connects America in safer, greener and healthier ways. With 21,000 route miles in 46 states, the District of Columbia and three Canadian provinces, Amtrak operates more than 300 trains each day at a speed up to 150 mph to more than 500 destinations. Amtrak is also the operator of choice for state-supported corridor services in 15 states and for 4 commuter rail agencies.

The **National Railroad Passenger Corporation**, doing business as **Amtrak** is operated and managed as a for-profit corporation and began operations on 1 May 1971, to provide intercity passenger train service in the United States of America. 'Amtrak' is a portmanteau of the words 'America' and 'track'. It is headquartered at Union Station in Washington, D.C.

The Rail Passenger Service Act of 1970, which established Amtrak, specifically states that 'the Corporation will not be an agency or establishment of the United States Government'. Common stock was issued in 1971 to railroads that contributed capital and equipment. Amtrak employs more than 20,000 people. It operates passenger service on 21,200 miles (34,000 km) of track primarily owned by freight railroads. Amtrak operates more than 300 trains each day at speed up to 150 mph (240 km/h) connecting more than 500 destinations in 46 states and three Canadian provinces. In fiscal year 2012, Amtrak served a record of 31.2 million passengers and had $2.02 billion in revenue.

Types of Equipment in Amtrak

1. **Amfleet:** Coach cars used for short runs. Amfleet Turboliner is used for longer hauls.
2. **Heritage coach cars:** Deluxe trains for overnight travel.
3. **Metroliner:** Operate between Washington, D.C. and New York.
4. **Superliner:** Operate in the western US—among the most modern and luxurious trains in the world (sightseeing lounges, full-service dining cars and so on).

Accommodations (First Class and Coach)

First Class:

1. **Roomette (one bed):** A small comfortable private room with a seat, single bed, toilet and washbasin.
2. **Bedroom accommodation:**
   a. Economy (accommodates two adults without private bedrooms)
   b. Standard (two berths, a toilet and a washbasin)
   c. Family (three berths and five seats)
   d. Deluxe (located on the upper level with bathroom)
   e. Handicapped (disabled travellers; special facilities for wheelchair)
   f. Suite (two adjoining rooms with four beds)

Coach:

- **Seating:**
  - — Reserved coach
  - — Unreserved coach
  - — Custom class

- **Sleeping:**
  - — Single slumber coach
  - — Double coach
  - — Economy bedroom
  - — Family bedroom

BritRail

BritRail is a trademarked name of the Association of Train Operating Companies (ATOC) of Britain. BritRail was created as an initiative by the many private railway companies of ATOC in order to entice international travellers to visit Britain and explore its countryside by train.

- The British rail network allows access to fascinating destinations in England, Scotland and Wales but remember Brit Rail's products are not available for purchase in Britain.
- High-speed intercity network links throughout the country.

Brit Rail Pass (Subject to Change)

- Use pass within a year of the issue date.
- Choose from more than 16,000 trains daily; 1,800 of them are intercity express.
- Unlimited travel for 7, 14 and 21 days or 1 month.
- Senior citizen passes for 65 or older.
- For Britain to Ireland—sea pass (one or two-way journey) served by British Rail's ship routes.
- BritRail packages include:
  - o Rail and hotel accommodation
  - o Rail travel with car rental

Features

- Unlimited travel on the national rail network of Britain from morning until night within the specified regional territory.
- The pass will contain two extra coupons valid on the Heathrow Express, Stansted Express or Gatwick Express. Coupons need not be used on same express.
- Available in both first and standard classes.
- These passes are not available to buy in the United Kingdom or available to the residents of the United Kingdom—they are designed specifically for international guests to the United Kingdom.
- Some trains in Great Britain do not have first class accommodations.

Eligibility

- BritRail passes are designed for sale overseas by tour operators and travel agencies to persons having their permanent residence outside the United Kingdom.

Types

- BritRail guest passes
- BritRail England passes
- BritRail England guest passes
- BritRail London plus pass
- BritRail Scottish freedom pass
- Brit Rail Central Scotland

Eurail

Europe is the home of some of the most efficient rail networks in the world. The atmosphere, on board of most trains, tends to be relaxed and the speed is perfect for sightseeing, making this the ideal way to explore the landscape.

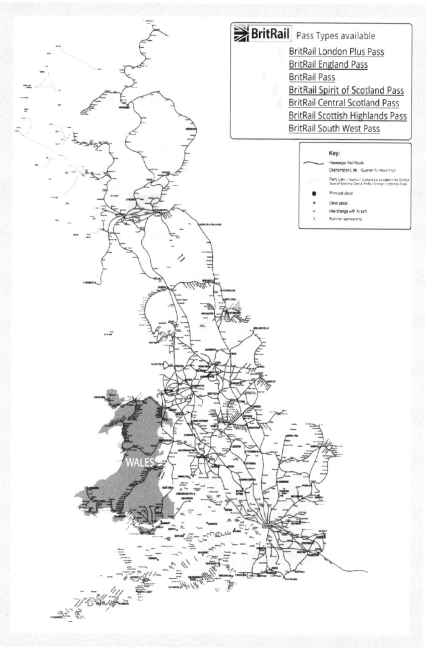

Source: www.eurail.com
Disclaimer: The above images is for representation purpose only.

Eurail Passes

The features of Eurail pass are as follows:

- Eurail pass is a single ticket valid for unlimited travel within a specified time.
- This is valid for many boats & bus ticket.
- Valid Passport is required to purchase Eurail pass.
- Eurail pass is valid for 15, 21 days, 1, 2, 3 months.
- Half ticket or 50% discount is applicable for the age group of 4–12 years.
- Eurail youth pass is applicable for the age group of 12–26 years in second class only.
- Eurail pass has to be used within six months from the date of issuance.

For choosing suitable rail pass, tourist must consider following points:

- How many people are travelling together? (for two or more, there are discounts)
- Which countries would you like to know?
- How many rail days are you planning to use?
- The passenger's age (travellers between 12 and 25 years of age can save money with youth discounts; there are also children and senior discounts)

Eurail High-Speed Trains

Eurostar: This famous train takes passengers under the sea through the famous Channel Tunnel, establishing connections between London/Paris, and London/Brussels.

Thalys: This is one of the most famous TGV, known as 'the red train'. It links the main cities in European Northwest: Paris, Brussels, Amsterdam, Koln, Dusseldorf and others.

AVE: It is the high-speed train that operates in Spain, connecting Madrid/Seville, Madrid/Cordoba, and Cordoba/Seville.

ICE: This comfortable and quick premier train links all major cities in Germany, Austria and Netherlands.

Overnight trains: There is an option of travelling at night with the comfort of a hotel, and wake up ready and recomposed. These offer a range of destinations, including the main European cities.

Swiss scenic trains: It gives the chance to admire the most beautiful sceneries in Switzerland.

Eurail

Railways of following countries are included in Eurail:

1. Austrian Federal Railway–OCBB
2. Belgian National Railroads–SNCB
3. Czechoslovak State Railways–CSR
4. Danish State Railways–DSR
5. Finnish State Railways—VR
6. French National Railroads—SNCF
7. German Federal Railroads—DB
8. German Rail–DR
9. Hungarian State Railways–MÁV

10.   Italian State Railways–FS
11.   Luxembourg National Railroads–CFL
12.   Norwegian State Railways–NSB
13.   Portuguese Railways–CP
14.   Romanian Railways–CFR
15.   Spanish State Railways—RENFE
16.   Swedish State Railways–SI
17.   Swiss federal railways–SBB
18.   Yugoslav Railways–JZ
19.   Netherland Railways—NS

Japanese Rail

Rail transport in Japan is a major means of passenger transport, especially for mass and high-speed travel between major cities and metropolitan areas. Japan railways companies were born in 1987, when Japanese National Railways was privatized, and then divided into six regional companies and Japan Freight Railway Company.

Although Japan Rail was split into six companies, fares and regulations are standard for all companies and every region of Japan, except Okinawa which is covered by the railway network, spanning approximately 12,400 miles.

Source: http://shipshop.pk/top-10-fastest-trains-in-the-world/
Disclaimer: The above image is for representation purpose only.

Shinkansen

- Shinkansen is a high-speed rail system that serves as the core of Japan's rail transportation network. Each line has its own name (Tokaido, Tōhoku and so on), and each type of train is identified by a name (Nozomi, Hikari and so on).

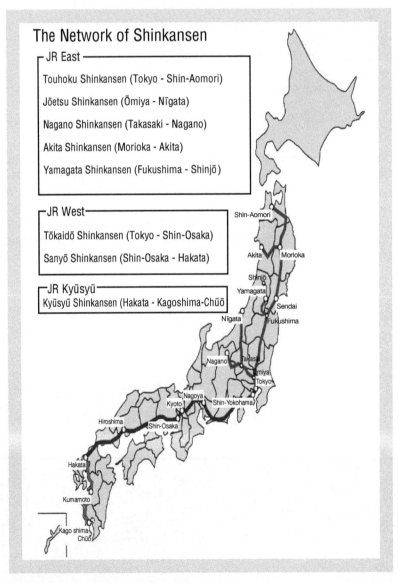

Source: http://www.j-journeys.com/essential/transportation/shinkansen.html
Disclaimer: The above images is for representation purpose only.

- In almost 40 years since it opened, the Shinkansen network has carried over 6 billion passengers without a single major accident. The Shinkansen network boasts not only high speed up to 300 km/hr, but also high frequency.

Japan Rail Pass

Following are the features of Japan rail pass:

- The Japan Rail pass is a discount ticket allowing unlimited rail travel throughout Japan over a 7, 14 or 21 consecutive day period.
- It is available in either an ordinary (coach class) or green (first class) version. Because Japan Railways has 12,400 miles of track, it is possible to travel almost anywhere in the country by train.
- Japan Rail pass cannot be purchased inside Japan. You must purchase an exchange order from an authorized sales office.
- Two types of passes that are available are as follows:
  - Green passes: These are entitled for superior class (most comfortable accommodation).
  - Ordinary passes: These are for standard coach.
- Japan Rail pass is also used for unlimited travel in buses and ferries.

Tibetan Rail

The features of Tibetan rail are as follows:

- China has rewritten the world's history of railway construction with its completion of the world's highest railway, the Qinghai–Tibet Railway, on the Roof of the World.

Source: https://www.lonelyplanet.com/china/travel-tips-and-articles/railway-to-heaven-a-trip-on-the-qinghai-tibet-train/40625c8c-8a11-5710-a052-1479d2768c34
Disclaimer: The above image is for representation purpose only.

- Qinghai–Tibet Railway is the world's highest railway that extends 1,956 km from Xining to Lhasa.
- Some 960 km of its tracks are located 4,000 m above sea level and the highest point is 5,072 m.
- On 1 July 2006, a train ran from Qinghai–Tibet Plateau (located in western China and called as the Roof of the World) to Lhasa, namely the snow-capped holy city, which announced to the whole world that Qinghai–Tibet Railway, that is, the longest plateau railway with highest altitude in the world is open to traffic.
- With an average height above sea level up to 4,000 m, Qinghai–Tibet Plateau is called 'The Roof of the World' and 'The Third Pole', and it is always considered as the 'Forbidden Zone of Life'.
- Qinghai–Tibet Railway stretches 1,956 km from Xining, capital of Qinghai Province, to Lhasa, capital of Tibet Autonomous Region across the Kunlun and Tanggula mountain ranges.
- About 550 km of the tracks run on frozen earth, the longest in any of the world's plateau railways.
- Tanggula railway station, 5,068 m above sea level, is the highest railway station in the world.
- Fenghuoshan Tunnel, 4,905 m above sea level, is the world's most elevated tunnel on frozen earth.
- Kunlun Mountain Tunnel, running 1,686 m, is the world's longest plateau tunnel built on frozen earth.
- Upon its completion, the maximum train speed is designed to reach 100 km/hr in the frozen earth areas and 120 km/hr on non-frozen earth.

Indian Railway

Indian Railways (IR) is one of the world's largest rail networks with 63,273 route km of route length. The size of the network—gauge-wise and zone-wise is as follows:

Gauge	Route (km)
Broad gauge (1,676 mm)	51,082
Metre gauge (1,000 mm)	9,442
Narrow gauge (762 mm and 610 mm)	2,749
Total	**63,273**

Zones/Headquarters	Route (km)	Zones/Headquarters	Route (km)
Central, Mumbai	3,849	North Western, Jaipur	5,275
Eastern, Kolkata	2,414	Southern, Chennai	5,169
East Central, Hajipur	3,465	South Central, Secunderabad	5,734
East Coast, Bhubaneswar	2,568	South Eastern, Kolkata	2,639
Northern, New Delhi	6,859	South East Central, Bilaspur	2,440

North Central, Allahabad	3,078	South Western, Hubli	3,106
North Eastern, Gorakhpur	3,447	Western, Mumbai	6,509
Northeast Frontier, Maligaon, Guwahati	3,757	West Central, Jabalpur	2,965

The facts of Indian railways are as follows:

- When Lord Dalhousie was the Viceroy of India, in 1950, the East Indian Railway Company and the Great Indian Peninsular Railway Company, established in England had started the initial construction of railway tracks.
- IR has 127,768 bridges, out of which 637 are important, 10,453 are major and 1,16,678 are minor bridges. In 2010–2011, 1,208 bridges including 29 distressed bridges were rehabilitated/rebuilt.
- First toilet facilities started in 1891 in first class bogies.
- First toilet facilities started in 1909 in second class bogies.
- On 3 February 1925, first electric train started from Bombay VT to Kurla.
- National Rail Museum was set up on 1 February 1977.
- First Rajdhani Express started on 1 March 1969 from New Delhi to Howrah.
- Shatabdi Express started on 1989.
- Fastest train in India: Shatabdi Express (New Delhi–Bhopal)—140 km/hr.

Types of Rail Tour in India

- Palace on Wheels
- Deccan Odyssey
- Heritage on Wheels
- Royal Orient
- Buddhist Special Train
- Fairy Queen
- Hill Trains

- North India by Rail
- South India by Rail
- Golden Triangle by train
- Central India by train
- West and South India by train
- Hindu Pilgrimage tour
- Bharat Darshan

Indrail Pass

To explore the splendour of multifaceted India, Indrail passes provide excellent value and enhances the charm of holidays from abroad. Indrail passes offer visitors on a budget, the facility to travel as they like, over the entire IR system, without any route restriction within the period of validity of the ticket. These passes can only be purchased by foreign nationals and non-resident Indians (NRIs) on payment of US dollars, pound sterling and other convertible foreign currencies.

The pass holder is not required to pay any reservation fee, superfast charges or surcharge for the journey.

These passes have been made more attractive for transit and short-stay visitors. The passes are now also available for half day, two days and four days for the facility of visitors arriving by international flights and visiting only one or two connecting destinations. Indrail passes are sold through general sales agents (GSA) abroad, Indian Airlines and Air India's overseas outlets at Oman, Australia, Malaysia, the United Kingdom, Germany, Finland, United Arab Emirates (UAE), Bangladesh, South Africa, Kuwait, Bahrain, Thailand, Myanmar, Singapore, Nepal and Sri Lanka.

In India, Indrail passes are available for sale in **tourist bureaus** at major railway stations.

Certain recognized **travel agents** are also authorized to sell these passes in Delhi, Mumbai, Calcutta and Chennai.

Useful Information about Indrail Pass

1. The Indrail pass is only an authorization to travel subject to the availability of accommodation on the journey train. For confirmed reservation, booking can be made 90 days in advance.
2. Indrail passes are issued to three different categories: First A/C, First class AC 2 tier and AC chair car, and second class.
3. Time as indicated under the heading 'time' in the brochure is given in hours, Indian Standard Time.
4. The Indrail pass is sold to only foreign nationals and Indians residing abroad with valid passport. It is non-transferable and the tourist must show his/her passport whenever asked for.
5. Payment at railway booking offices is accepted only in Forex in US dollar/pound/traveller's cheque at travel/tour agencies in any foreign currency in cash, traveler's cheque/credit cards.
6. The pass entitles the holder to travel within a period of validity by all trains throughout India.
7. A tourist holding an Indrail pass is exempted from paying reservation or sleeper surcharge or charges for travelling by superfast trains.
8. Children between 5 and 12 years of age are charged half fare. Those below 5 years can travel free with their parents.
9. Free baggage allowance: 70 kg in first class AC, 50 kg in AC 2 tier and AC 3 tier, 35 kg in second class.
10. For any assistance in the railway station, the stationmaster or the chief reservation supervisor may be contacted.
11. Accommodations in retiring rooms are available at most railway stations.
12. Refreshment rooms, waiting rooms and left luggage rooms are available at most railway stations.
13. Request can also be made to the Government of India and state government tourist offices for sightseeing purposes.
14. GSA are authorized to sell Indrail passes in respective countries.

Note: An exclusive Central space control international tourist bureau function at New Delhi railway station with telex facilities to cater to reservation arrangements for foreigner tourists.

Palace on Wheels The destinations covered by the Palace on Wheels are: Delhi–Jaipur–Jaisalmer–Jodhpur–Sawai Madhopur–Chittorgarh–Udaipur–Bharatpur–Agra–Delhi. The routes covered by the Palace on Wheels are shown in the route map on the next page.

Palace on Wheels is a royal experience, a journey that is much more than a luxury train ride. Palace on Wheels epitomizes the rich Indian heritage and journeys through one of the most exotic regions in the world—Dazzling Delhi, Amazing Agra, and especially Royal Rajasthan. Pamper yourself with unlimited royalty. Where else can you relax in comfort and witness exotic India passing by. Welcome aboard the royal journey called **Palace on Wheels**.

Source: https://www.thepalaceonwheels.org/

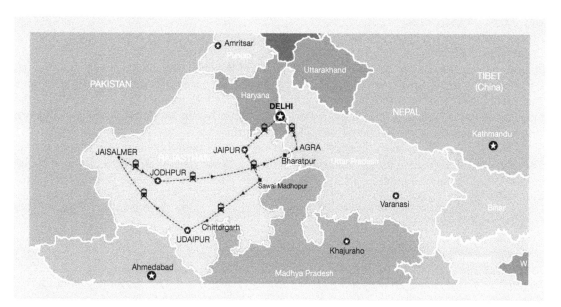

Source: https://www.rajasthantrip.com/palace-on-wheels.html

Itinerary

Duration: 7 Nights/8 Days
Destinations covered: Delhi–Jaipur–Jaisalmer–Jodhpur–Sawai Madhopur–Chittorgarh–Udaipur–Bharatpur–Agra–Delhi

The **itinerary of Palace on Wheels** includes 7 Nights/8 Days of an unforgettable lifetime journey, covering some of the most fascinating tourist destinations of India. The train takes you to colourful cities, magnificent forts and palaces, wildlife sanctuaries of Rajasthan and last but not least to the Taj Mahal at Agra. The train starts its fabulous journey from Delhi Cantonment railway station every Wednesday (September–April).

Day 01, Wednesday, Delhi

On arrival at Delhi Cantonment railway station, the guests are accorded a warm and traditional welcome, and you start the momentous journey on the Palace on Wheels. The train departs at 5:45 PM for Jaipur. Enjoy a delicious on-board dinner at 8 PM. Overnight will be onboard the train.

Day 2, Thursday, Jaipur

Arrival: 2:00 AM

Departure: 7:30 PM

On your arrival at Jaipur—the pink city of India—you are greeted by colourfully decorated elephants and a *shehnai* recitation. Enjoy a half-day sightseeing tour of Jaipur. You will visit the Hawa Mahal—the palace of winds—followed by the visit to magnificent Amber Fort. Enjoy an elephant ride at the Fort. Thereafter, you can enjoy shopping for Jaipur's famous jewellery, handicrafts, carpets, blue pottery and textiles.

After lunch at the famous **Rambagh Palace Hotel**, visit **Jantar Mantar** (the largest observatory built by Maharaja Sawai Jai Singh) and the City Palace. Return back to the Palace on Wheels around 6:30 PM and start for Jaisalmer. Enjoy on-board dinner on the train.

Day 03, Friday, Jaisalmer

Arrival: 8:15 AM

Departure: 11:00 PM

Famous as 'the Golden City of India', Jaisalmer is one of the most popular tourist destinations in Rajasthan. The city is famous for its Golden Fort and beautiful *havelis* (mansions). Visit the famous Patwon ki Haveli, Nathmalji ki Haveli and Salim Singh ki Haveli. Thereafter, shop at Rajasthali—the only emporium of Rajasthan government offering fine pattu shawls, mirror work and embroidered articles, wooden boxes, trinkets, silver jewellery and curios.

After on-board lunch, enjoy an exciting camel ride on the sand dunes of Sam. Dinner on the sand dunes under the moonlit sky is another highlight of your visit. Thereafter, enjoy a colourful cultural programme at a hotel in Jaisalmer. Later, return back to the Palace on Wheels to start for Jodhpur.

Day 04, Saturday, Jodhpur

Arrival: 7:00 AM

Departure: 3:30 PM

In the morning, the **Palace on Wheels** arrives in Jodhpur—the second largest city of Rajasthan fortified by a high stonewall with seven gates and several fortresses. Visit the famous Mehrangarh Fort, Moti Mahal, Sheesh Mahal, Phool Mahal, Sileh Khana and Daulat Khana. Then, enjoy your lunch at the majestic Umaid Bhawan Palace. Return to the Palace on Wheels and start for Sawai Madhopur.

Day 05, Sunday, Sawai Madhopur

Arrival: 4:00 AM

Departure: 10:30 AM

Sawai Madhopur is famous for its proximity to the **Ranthambore National Park**—one of the most famous **national parks** and tiger reserves of India. Enjoy a jeep safari to explore the flora and fauna of the park. Enjoy tracking tigers, chital, deer, monkeys and a wide variety of exotic and colourful birds. Also visit the 10th-century Ranthambore Fort. Thereafter you return to the Palace on Wheels and start for Chittorgarh.

Day 05, Sunday, Chittorgarh

Arrival: 4:00 PM

Chittorgarh—the legendary city of Rajasthan—is famous as the city of bravery and romance. The 7th-century Chittorgarh Fort, has witnessed many wars fought over to protect the dignity and respect of the beautiful land. Other attractions worth visiting the Fort include Vijay Stambh (tower of victory) and the Kirti Stambh (tower of fame). Overnight stay onboard the train.

Day 06, Monday, Udaipur

Departure: 8:00 PM from Chittorgarh

In the morning, a luxury coach takes you to Udaipur, famous as the city of lakes. Enjoy a memorable tour of the palaces, forts and temples at Udaipur. Visit the two most beautiful landmarks of Udaipur—the Jag Niwas (Lake Palace) and the Jagmandir, which appear to rise from the blue waters of Lake Pichola. Enjoy lunch at the **Lake Palace Hotel**. The luxury coach then takes you back to the **Palace on Wheels at Chittorgarh**. Board the train at Chittorgarh and start for Bharatpur.

Day 07, Tuesday, Bharatpur

Arrival: 6:30 AM

Departure: 11:45 AM

The Palace on Wheels arrives at Bharatpur early in the morning. After breakfast, visit the world famous Bharatpur Bird Sanctuary also known as Keoladeo Ghana National Park. Enjoy spotting numerous colourful varieties of birds including the Siberian cranes—the migratory birds coming to the Park from Siberia 5,000 km away during winters.

Day 07, Tuesday, Agra

Arrival: 2:30 PM

Departure: 11:00 PM

On the way to Agra, visit Fatehpur Sikri—the 16th-century historical town, built by the Mughal Emperor Akbar. See the Buland Darwaza—the largest gateway in the world, the Jama Masjid and the Tomb of Salim Chisti, a famous Sufi saint of India.

On arrival at Agra, enjoy lunch at a hotel. Thereafter, visit the magnificent Red Fort also known as the Agra Fort. After visiting the Fort, visit the world famous Taj Mahal—the most amazing and beautiful historical monument in the world. The Taj Mahal was built by the Mughal Emperor Shah Jahan, as a symbol of love, in the memory of his beloved wife Mumtaz Mahal. Enjoy on-board dinner on the train and start for Delhi.

Day 08, Wednesday, Delhi

Arrival: 6:00 AM

The Palace on Wheels arrives at Delhi Cantonment railway station early in the morning. Enjoy your on-board breakfast and leave the train with sweet memories of the past week. And here comes your unforgettable journey to its conclusion.

Coaches

The **Palace on Wheels** has a total of 14 fully air-conditioned deluxe coaches or saloons, two restaurants cum kitchen cars, one bar cum lounge and four service cars. One of its own kinds in the world, the coaches of the Palace on Wheels are decorated like a beautiful palace. All of them have lavish interiors with beautiful paintings and comfortable furniture, providing you the comforts and splendour of a real palace.

All the coaches of the **Palace on Wheels** are well equipped with all modern amenities to enhance the pleasure of your journey. Each coach has four twin-bedded cabins attached to it. The on-board facilities available in the **coaches of the Palace on Wheels** include the bath and shower facility, H/C water supply, attached toilets, channel music, intercom, interesting games for children and wall-to-wall carpeting. The satellite phone service makes it sure that you communicate anywhere in the world from the train. In addition, there is a friendly and smiling attendant or '*Khidmatgar*' on each coach, to cater to all your travelling requirements.

The coaches of the **Palace on Wheels** derive their names from the erstwhile princely states of Rajasthan, namely Jaipur, Jodhpur, Jaisalmer, Bikaner, Alwar, Udaipur, Bundi, Kota, Jhalawar, Dungarpur, Dholpur, Bharatpur, Sirohi, and Kishangarh. Each coach is decorated in accordance with the culture and characteristics of the respective places.

The two restaurants cum kitchen cars—the *Maharaja* and the *Maharani*–on the Palace on Wheels offer traditional Indian, Rajasthani, continental and Chinese cuisines. The separate lounge attached at the end of each coach provides passengers a relaxing ambience and exotic views of the great Indian countryside.

Facilities

The **Palace on Wheels** is one of the most luxurious trains in the world. The on-board facilities available on the Palace on Wheels are unrivalled and difficult to be found in any other trains all over the world. Completely royal in nature, the facilities on the Palace on Wheels are comparable to the best of the 5-star hotel facilities. Traveling in the royal comforts of the Palace on Wheels would surely be a unique and rewarding experience for you.

The on-board facilities on the **Palace on Wheels** can be divided into the following categories.

- **Accommodations:** The **Palace on Wheels** boasts 14 fully air-conditioned deluxe coaches or saloons. All the coaches are well appointed and beautifully decorated with traditional paintings. Each coach has four cabins attached to it. The facilities available in coaches of the Palace on Wheels include bath and shower, H/C water supply, attached modern toilets, channel music, intercom, satellite phones, wall-to-wall carpeting and many more.
- **Dining:** The **Palace on Wheels** has two well-maintained restaurants cum kitchen cars—the Maharaja and the Maharani—offering delicious and mouth-watering traditional Rajasthani, Indian, continental and Chinese cuisines.
- **Lounge:** A separate beautiful lounge car is attached to the **Palace on Wheels**, providing peaceful ambience to passengers to relax. In lounge, the tourists get an opportunity to interact with each other. The lounge also offers a good collection of books to choose from. The lounge is also equipped with a colour television and a CD player. The lounge also provides you an enchanting view of the great Indian countryside during the daytime. In addition, you can enjoy reading the famous newspapers and journals in the lounge, available at your disposal.
- **The Bar:** The **Palace on Wheels** has a 24-hour well-maintained bar to take care of your drinking pleasures. The well-stocked bar offers a wide variety of scotches, wines and cocktails of Indian and international brands.
- **The Bazaar:** The **Palace on Wheels** also boasts a beautiful gift shop called 'the bazaar'. Tourists can purchase exotic handicrafts and gift items from the bazaar.

  The other major facilities available on the Palace on Wheels include beauty salons, luggage collection, mineral water and laundry services (on request). The on-board mailbox facility is also available for posting your mails. In addition, an attendant or 'Khidmatgar' is always there at your service, to cater to all your travel needs.

Many facilities such as internet, ATM facility and e-commerce are being planned for the **Palace on Wheels**, to take care of the very modern requirements of the valued guests of the Palace on Wheels.

Schedule

The luxurious Palace on Wheels starts its royal journey on every Wednesday from Delhi Cantonment railway station during the cooler months of September–April. Due to hot weather, and the time required for renovation and maintenance of its coaches, the train does not operate from May to July.

Cultural Attraction

The Palace on Wheels is a train of its own kind in the world. The on-board facilities available to guests are absolutely incomparable and difficult to be found on any other train in the world. In addition to royal comforts the Palace on Wheels offers, guests can also enjoy a variety of on-board cultural programmes on the train, and on arrival and stay at every destination. These especially designed programmes are organized for enhancing the pleasure of your 7 nights/8 days journey on the Place on Wheels.

Guests are accorded a warm reception on their arrival at Delhi and Jaipur. At Jaipur, a shehnai recitation and a herd of colourfully decorated elephants greet them. Many colourful dance and music programmes are organized during your travel in the lounge car of the Palace on Wheels. Guests of the Palace on Wheels can enjoy the finest regional dance and music performances by talented artists at every destination of the train. Live performances of Rajasthani folk dances (such as Ghoomar, Chari Dance, Fire Dance, Terah Taali, Kachchhi Ghodhi, Kalbelia and Agni Nritya), and colourful and exciting puppet shows.

Air Transport

Open Sky Policy

'Open skies' means unrestricted access by any carrier into the sovereign territory of a country without any written agreement specifying capacity, ports of call or schedule of services.

Therefore, theoretically, when the skies are open, any foreign airline can land any aircraft at any airport with no restrictions on frequency and seat capacity.

However, in the interest of better discipline and regulation, open skies policy translates as bilateral treaties to determine the aviation relations between two countries. Almost 99 per cent of the members of the International Civil Aviation Organisation (ICAO) have such agreements, specifying regularity of operations, basis of ownership, type and certification of aircraft, and so on.

Indian aviation cleared major air pockets in the early 1990s when more private airlines began their operations, besides the national carrier. Air services in India were liberalized in 1994. In India, traffic rights are exchanged between the two sovereign countries under bilateral air services agreements on the basis of reciprocity keeping in view the requirements of tourism, travel and trade. In addition to the capacity granted in the bilateral agreements, foreign airlines are also permitted to operate extra section flights to take care of seasonal spurts in traffic.

A near open sky regime has been concluded with the member states of SAARC, allowing its designated airlines seven flights/week to six metro cities (Delhi, Mumbai, Kolkata, Chennai, Hyderabad and Bangalore) in addition to unlimited capacity to 18 points of tourist interest in India. There is no restriction on the number of airlines which can operate to each other's territory.

India has also declared open sky policy for cargo flights, under which foreign airlines are allowed to operate any number of all-cargo flights to/from any destination in India.

Freedom of Air According to ICAO

- **First freedom of the air:** the right or privilege, in respect of scheduled international air services, granted by one State to another State or States to fly across its territory without landing.
- **Second freedom of the air:** the right or privilege, in respect of scheduled international air services, granted by one State to another State or States to land in its territory for non-traffic purposes.
- **Third freedom of the air:** the right or privilege, in respect of scheduled international air services, granted by one State to another State to put down, in the territory of the first State, traffic coming from the home State of the carrier.
- **Fourth freedom of the air:** the right or privilege, in respect of scheduled international air services, granted by one State to another State to take on, in the territory of the first State, traffic destined for the home State of the carrier.
- **Fifth freedom of the air:** the right or privilege, in respect of scheduled international air services, granted by one State to another State to put down and to take on, in the territory of the first State, traffic coming from or destined to a third State.

    ICAO characterizes all 'freedoms' beyond the Fifth as 'so-called' because only the first five 'freedoms' have been officially recognized as such by international treaty.
- **Sixth freedom of the air:** the right or privilege, in respect of scheduled international air services, of transporting, via the home State of the carrier, traffic moving between two other States. The so-called Sixth Freedom of the Air, unlike the first five freedoms, is not incorporated as such into any widely recognized air service agreements such as the 'Five Freedoms Agreement'.
- **Seventh freedom of the air:** the right or privilege, in respect of scheduled international air services, granted by one State to another State, of transporting traffic between the territory of the granting State and any third State with no requirement to include on such operation any point in the territory of the recipient State, that is, the service need not connect to or be an extension of any service to/from the home State of the carrier.
- **Eighth freedom of the air:** the right or privilege, in respect of scheduled international air services, of transporting cabotage traffic between two points in the territory of the granting State on a service which originates or terminates in the home country of the foreign carrier or (in connection with the so-called Seventh Freedom of the Air) outside the territory of the granting State (also known as a Eighth Freedom Right or 'consecutive cabotage').
- **Ninth freedom of the air:** the right or privilege of transporting cabotage traffic of the granting State on a service performed entirely within the territory of the granting State (also known as a Ninth Freedom Right or 'standalone' cabotage).

Source: https://www.icao.int/pages/freedomsair.aspx

Water Transport

Water transport is the oldest mode of transport in the world. Initially, in the prehistoric period around 4000 BC, small boats were used mainly by the fishermen. The earliest forms of boats were used by the people who were living near the water bodies and were made from hollowed tree trunks. In the later period, when sophisticated tools and kits were developed, people were able to build good quality boats. For example, the Egyptians invented a primitive kind of boats. Similar types of boats were also made from the skins of animals stretched over a wicker frame known as coracles.

Till the 19th century, water transportation was the only mode of transportation in most of the overseas countries. Early in the 19th century, first steamships were designed. First steamship for overseas transportation came into existence in 1819 when the full rigged ship fitted with engines and side paddle wheels started from Savannah, Georgia to Liverpool, England. The Cunard Steamship Company was formed in 1838 with regular service on the North Atlantic from Liverpool to Halifax and then to Boston. After First World War, the steamship luxury liners had flourished and from that time ship travel has been common for exploration, commerce, passenger transportation and leisure tour. During that time, other reputed companies such as Peninsular and Oriental Steam Navigation Company (P&O) cruise, and Royal Mail Steam Packet companies started their operations. At the end of the 19th century, Britishers dominated the service of Transatlantic steamship and they have named these as 'liners'. After the First World War, steamship services expanded from Europe to Latin America, South America and Australia for carrying tourists, emigrants and cargo. After the Second World War, large luxury liners started their operations by mainly carrying the long haul holidaymakers. Some of those liners were even accommodating more than 1,000 passengers and provide facilities such as indoor games, swimming pools, shops, casino, cinema halls and library. Some reputed cruise liners including SS Queen Mary II, Queen Elizabeth 2, United States and so on were popular during that period.

Water transport can be broadly divided into two groups—inland water transport and shipping. Shipping can again be divided into two categories—coastal shipping and overseas shipping.

Inland Water Transportation

The features of inland water transportation are as follows:

- Inland water transport includes natural modes like navigable rivers and artificial modes like canals. The Inland waterways have played an important role in the Indian transport system since ancient times.
- However, in recent times, the importance of this mode of transport has declined considerably with the expansion of road and rail transport.
- In addition, diversion of river water for irrigation has also reduced the importance of inland water transport.
- The decline is also due to the deforestation of hill ranges leading to erosion, accumulation of silt in rivers and failure to modernize the fleet to suit local conditions.
- Development of inland water transport in the regions where it enjoys natural advantage.
- Modernization of vessels and country crafts to suit local conditions.
- Improvement in the productivity of assets. The Inland Waterways Authority has been set up, which is a big step forward and should help in the accelerated development of inland water transport.

Coastal Shipping

Coastal shipping holds a great promise more so because it is the most energy-efficient and cheapest mode of transport for carriage of bulky goods such as iron, steel, iron ore, coal and timber over long distances.

The main factors affecting the growth of coastal shipping adversely have been 'High transportation costs especially for movement other than those between a pair of water front locations, port delays, poor turnaround time of coastal ships on account of overage vessels, lack of mechanical handling, facilities etc.'

Overseas Shipping

Because of the importance of overseas shipping in international trade, considerable attention has to be paid to increase the shipping tonnage in the planning period. Following points may be considered for that:

1. Modernization of fleet on the basis of improved ship designed and fuel efficiency in engines.
2. Replacement of overaged fleet on a selective basis.
3. Drivers' fixation of fleet by acquisition of cellular container ships and specialized product carriers.
4. Addition to fleet on a selective basis, keeping in view the long-term objective of achieving self-sufficiency in tanker fleet.

Shipping

- Bulk goods carried by coastal shipping were low-freight commodities such as coal, cement and salt. As the railway freights for these commodities were less, the railways were a preferred mode of dispatch. The government should plan to divert some traffic from the railways to coastal shipping.
- Another broad objective should be to build a fleet of tankers to meet the increasing wet cargo requirements.

Ships and Watercraft

1. **Bulk carrier:** These are cargo ships used to transport bulk cargo items such as ore, rice and grain. It can be recognized by the large box-like hatches on its deck, designed to slide outboard for loading. A bulk carrier could be either dry or wet.

Source: https://en.wikipedia.org/wiki/Bulk_carrier
Disclaimer: The above image is for representation purpose only.

2. **Container ship:** These are cargo ships that carry their entire load in truck-size containers, in a technique called containerization. Informally known as 'box boats', they carry the majority of the world's dry cargo. Most container ships are propelled by diesel engines. They generally have a large accommodation block at the stern, directly above the engine room.

Source: https://pxhere.com/en/photo/820915/Colombo.Express.wmt.jpg
Disclaimer: The above image is for representation purpose only.

3. **Tanker:** These are cargo ships for the transport of fluids such as crude oil, petroleum products, LPG and chemicals, vegetable oils, wine and other food. The tanker sector comprises one-third of the world tonnage.

Source: https://www.marineinsight.com/types-of-ships/top-3-biggest-ships-in-the-world/
Disclaimer: The above image is for representation purpose only.

4. **Reefer ship:** These are cargo ships typically used to transport perishable commodities which require temperature-controlled transportation, mostly fruits, meat, fish, vegetables, dairy products and other foodstuffs.

Source: https://www.marineinsight.com/refrigeration-air-conditioning/how-perishable-food-products-are-transported-using-reefer-ship/
Disclaimer: The above image is for representation purpose only.

5. **Roll-on/roll-off (RORO) ship:** These are cargo ships designed to carry wheeled cargo such as automobiles, trailers or railway carriages. RORO (or ro/ro) vessels have built-in ramps which allow the cargo to efficiently 'roll on' and 'roll off' the vessel when in port. While smaller ferries that operate across rivers and other short distances still often have built-in ramps, the term RORO is generally reserved for larger ocean-going vessels.

Source: http://www.nykroro.com/
Disclaimer: The above image is for representation purpose only.

6. **Coastal trading vessel:** These are also known as coasters; are shallow-hulled ships used for trade between locations on the same island or continent. Their shallow hulls mean that they can get through reefs where sea-going ships usually cannot.

Source: https://pxhere.com/en/photo/820915/Handelsschiff_%2801%29_2006-09-21.JPG
Disclaimer: The above image is for representation purpose only.

7. **Ferry:** These are a form of transport, usually a boat or ship, but not limited to these, carrying passengers and sometimes their vehicles, and are also called a waterbus or water taxi. Ferries are also used to transport freight. Most ferries operate on regular, frequent and return services. Ferries form a part of the public transport systems of many waterside cities and islands.

Source: Ferry at Sunderban, India (photo taken by the author).
Disclaimer: The above image is for representation purpose only.

8. **Cable layer:** This is a deep-sea vessel designed and used to lay underwater cables for tele-communications, electricity and so on.

Source: https://pxhere.com/en/photo/820915/Colombo.Express.wmt.jpg

9. **Tugboat:** This is a boat used to move by towing or pushing other vessels in harbours, over the open sea or through rivers and canals. They are also used to tow barges, disabled ships and so on.

10. **Dredger:** It is a ship used to excavate in shallow seas or fresh water areas with the purpose of gathering up bottom sediments and disposing them off at a different location.

Source: http://hutagroup.com/english/equipment1.php?id=18-Huta

11. **Barge:** This is a flat-bottomed boat, built mainly for river and canal transport of heavy goods. Most barges are not self-propelled and need to be moved by tugboat's towing or towboats pushing them.

Source: https://pxhere.com/en/photo/820915/b6/CrushedStoneBarge.jpg

12. **Cruise ship:** These are passenger ships used for pleasure voyages, where the voyage itself and the ship's amenities are considered an essential part of the experience. Cruising has become a major product of the tourism industry.

Source: https://www.starcruises.com/us/en/ships/gemini (reproduced with Permission).

Cruise Tourism

Cruise tourism is becoming an increasingly popular 'leisure choice' throughout the world. Once upon a time, cruises were considered the choice of the rich, the aged and the natural choice for honeymooners, but is nowadays getting importance in the mass leisure market.

Cruise market trends indicate a qualitative as well as quantitative consolidation in the industry and represent one of the fastest growing sectors worldwide. It is gaining greater significance in the global sector. Cruise liners have equally high requirements from the ports of call, principal expectations being proximity of access to major markets, quality, availability of port infrastructure and services, competitive cost of port services, capacity of the port to accommodate and process high volumes of passengers efficiently and the quality of the destination in terms of shore-based attractions available.

International ports have dedicated cruise terminals designed to satisfy the cruise liners and the cruise tourists. Ports constitute the core infrastructure requirement of the cruise sector. If a country wishes to integrate her position in this market, ports would have to meet internationally accepted standards of port infrastructure, passenger services, linkages, other conveniences and amenities. Internationally, cruise terminals are similar in facilities and services offered to tourists at airports.

Cruise terminals represent the entry point of the cruise tourists into various tourism locations and offer important opportunity to market the country's brand, its culture, heritage, cuisine and other offerings.

Cruise tourism development would be impossible without all strategies being preceded by an integrated and sustained development of the identified cruise ports. Singapore and Dubai are good examples for proving that developing quality cruise terminals are essential for stimulating the growth in cruise tourism.

Theme Cruise

These are built by offering new itineraries or by adding specialized products as a theme. For example, Disney Cruise, Carnival Cruise (has the Paradise ship exclusively for non-smokers) and cruises dedicated to wine tasting and other exotic themes.

Adventure Cruise

Expedition cruises have a modest, though not insignificant, demand. Most companies that operate in this market do not belong to the big groups. There are also other liners such as the Swan Hellenic and Orient Lines with a strong educational element. There is an incredible diversity of cruise vacations available, most of them are custom designed to suit different interests and personal preferences. Examples are adventure tour to Amazon, Antarctica and so on.

Ocean Voyage

An ocean voyage is a one-way passage from one point to another over a major body of water. Some voyages have intermediate ports of call while others do not. Transatlantic or transpacific crossings are the most common ocean voyages. The ships most used for ocean voyages are cruise ships, yacht-style ships and freighters.

Standard Cruise

An open water cruise may be one-way or round trip with several ports of call. These cruises are traditionally vessel-oriented trips in which the ship and all the amenities it provides are the main focus of the voyage. The ship is selected based on accommodations, recreation, entertainment and service.

River/Canal Cruise

River and canal cruises are closely linked to the culture and heritage of the country being toured. Along the journey, the waterway's villages, town and cities offer particular appeal to scenery buffs for those who enjoy ever-changing landscape. Travellers choosing river and canal cruises are interested in and attracted to the destinations as well as the cruising experience. The ships most used for river and canal cruises are yacht-style ships, river ships, barges and private yachts.

Destination/Expedition Cruise

Destination and expedition cruises are selected same as river cruises, based on the destination to be visited. Travellers are attracted by the unique, remote or exotic ports of call. These cruises offer the stimulation of exploring new destinations.

Luxury Cruise

These cruises have newer and larger cruise ships with lots of amenities including lavish showrooms, extensive spa facilities, expansive children's programmes, televisions and in-room movies in all cabins, double/queen beds, and so on. These constitute the ultimate cruise experience, taking service to a different level. These cruises offer high-style luxury and carry few passengers. Accommodations are often more spacious with a very high percentage of ocean-view staterooms and suites.

Luxury cruises cater to the mature, experienced tourists and less suitable for young children or the first choice for families. Most popular luxury cruises are Cunard Cruises, Oceania Cruises, Crystal Cruises, Silver Star Cruises and so on.

Activities in Cruise

While providing entertainment on journey, cruises offer a variety of activities that are as follows:

- Karaoke contests
- Game shows
- Night club
- Wine tasting classes
- Cooking demonstrations
- Casino
- Ice carving instruction
- Jewellery seminars
- Ethnic dance
- Tournaments such as ping-pong, floating golf green, billiards, shuffleboard, ring toss, and basketball and volleyball tournaments
- Library
- Dance floors, wine bars, night clubs/lounges for pub-goers and so on

Accommodation in Cruise

Cruise accommodation is targeted for different categories of people and their preferences. These vary from cruise to cruise; however, most common and standard types are as follows:

1. **Superior ocean view staterooms:** These offer a gorgeous view often with a mini bar and private balcony among their amenities. With an area of 188 sq. ft. and balcony 50 sq. ft., these staterooms consist of two twin beds, private balcony, sitting area and a private bathroom.
2. **Ocean view staterooms:** These offer all of the amenities of a star hotel added to a magnificent view of the ocean. Generally covering an area of 180 sq. ft., these staterooms have two twin beds, sitting area with sofa, vanity area and a private bathroom.
3. **Deluxe ocean view staterooms:** These offer an ocean view with mini bar and private balcony among their amenities. Measuring 173 sq. ft. with 47 sq. ft. balcony, they consist of two twin beds, private balcony, some offer Pullman beds, sitting area with sofa, and a private bathroom.
4. **Royal family suites:** These have a whirlpool bathtub, entertainment centre, a separate living area with refrigerator and wet bar, and complimentary concierge service, which includes access to a private lounge as well as personalized service to help make reservations or other arrangements. These large rooms measure 1,188 sq. ft., with a balcony of 170 sq. ft. Most royal suites have a separate bedroom with a king-size bed and some even have a baby grand piano.
5. **Grand suites:** These come with a private balcony, sitting area, bathtub, a mini bar and complimentary concierge service with an area of 381 sq. ft., 95 sq. ft. balcony.

6. **Junior suites:** These offer a private balcony, sitting area, refrigerator and bathtub. With an area of 277 sq. ft., 69 sq. ft. balcony, these suites, also called superior ocean view suite, have two twin beds, private balcony and private bathroom.

River and Canal Cruise

Cruise ships take coastal routes because the rivers and canals cannot accommodate large cruise ships, whereas all of the destination's charm can hardly be explored within the constraint of a one-day stop at a port of call. However, it would be possible to enable interested passengers to explore the charms of the destination through specially designed river ships and cruise barges. As a niche of cruising, river and canal voyages are an increasingly popular option, particularly for tourists who want to see more of the heartland.

River/canal cruise ships are essentially smaller versions of cruise ships, and generally carrying less. The river/canal barges are even smaller, carrying between 6 and 50 passengers. The entertainment on board is also much simpler. River cruise ships do not provide a range of experiences as happens aboard a large ship.

Conclusion

Transportation is the backbone of tourism industry. Tourism is an international phenomenon where the choice of a destination depends on individual's preferences, costs, and time and accessibility factors. Therefore, the role of transportation is vital. Since the success of any tourist destination mostly depends on the development of transport facilities and is proved that people in general prefer speed and convenience over costs, transportation is considered to be an important facilitator of tourism business. From the above discussion, transportation is considered as the key element that matches the gap between tourism demand and supply. The current transportation industry has witnessed a radical shift in the regulatory framework of tourism due to technological advancement, economic growth, people's inclination for travel and so on. As a result of these changes, the inflow of tourist from origin to destination has increased considerably. However, the present transport industry is facing several challenges including safety and security, competition, legal issues and environmental issues. In spite of these, the transport industry will continue to play a vital role in shaping the tourism industry in future. Further, if the collection of statistics including revenue generation, operational information, safety measures, development of new tourism markets and so on are maintained properly, the future of transportation industry will achieve a great height. This will further lead to an increase in the employment generation, profit maximization, revenue generation, increased tourist flow, infrastructure development and overall growth of other related industries.

MODEL QUESTIONS

1. Why are modes, networks and flows important in understanding the relationship between transport and tourism?
2. What are the key factors that influence the demand for transport?

3. Briefly explain the importance of international railway system with special reference to Eurail.
4. Explain the importance of air transport in global tourist flow.
5. Examine the importance of low-cost carrier in tourism business.
6. Write a note on freedom of air.
7. Analyse the importance of luxury trains for promotion of international tourism in India with special reference to Palace on Wheels.
8. Briefly explain various issues and challenges of promoting cruise tourism in a country.
9. Write a note on Indrail pass.
10. Examine different constraints involved in constructing road transport for tourism development in a region.

Student Activities

1. Prepare an assignment to find out different types of luxury cruises and their areas of operation worldwide.
2. Find out different luxury trains operating in the world and write their uniqueness.

Suggested Readings

Banks, J. H. (2002). *Introduction to transportation engineering.* New York, NY: McGraw-Hill.

Bell, P., & Cloke, P. (1990). *Deregulation and transport: Market forces in the modern world.* London: Fulton.

Bhaumik, P. K. (2002). Regulating the domestic air travel in India: An umpire's game. *Omega, 30*(1), 33–44.

Black, A. (1995). *Urban mass transportation planning.* New York, NY: McGraw-Hill .

Button, K., & Gillingwater, K. (Eds.). (1983). *Future transport policy.* London: Routledge.

Button, K. J., & Stough, R. (2000). *Air transport networks: Theory and policy implications.* Cheltenham: Edward Elgar.

Button, K. J., Haynes, K., & Stough, R. (1998). *Flying into the future: Air transport policy in the European Union.* Cheltenham: Edward Elgar.

Cooper, C., Fletcher, J., Fyall, A., Gilbert, D., Wanhill, S., & Shepherd, R. (1998). *Tourism principles and practice* (2nd ed.). London: Longman.

Copeland, D., & McKenney, J. (1988). Airline reservation systems: Lessons from history. *Management Information Systems Quarterly, 12,* 535–570.

Debbage, K. (2000). Air transportation and international tourism: The regulatory and infrastructural constraints of aviation bilaterals and airport landing slots. In M. Robinson, N. Evans, P. Long, R. Sharpley & J. Swarbrooke (Eds.), *Management, marketing and the political economy of travel and tourism* (pp. 67–83). Sunderland: Business Education Publishers.

Doganis, R. (2001). *Airline business in the 21st century.* London: Routledge.

Gee, C. Y., Makens, J. C., & Choy, D. J. L. (1997). *The travel industry.* New York, NY: Van Nostrand Reinhold (a division of International Thomson Publishing Inc.).

Hall, C. M. (1998). *Introduction to tourism: Development, dimensions and issues* (3rd ed.). South Melbourne: Addison–Wesley Longman.

——— (2003). *Introduction to tourism: Dimensions, and Issues* (4th ed.). French Forest, NSW: Hospitality Press.

Hanlon, P. (1999). *Global airlines: Competition in a transnational industry.* Oxford: Butterworth–Heinemann

Inskeep, E. (1991). *Tourism planning: An integrated and sustainable development approach.* New York, NY: Van Nostrand Reinhold.

Cooper, C., Fletcher, J., Fyall, A., Gilbert, D., Wanhill, S., & Shepherd, R. (1998). *Tourism principles and practice* (2nd ed., pp. 423–446). London: Longman.

Mill, R., & Morrison, A. (1998). *The tourism system: An introductory text* (3rd ed.). Dubuque, IA: Kendell/Hunt Publishing Co.

Negi, J. (2008). *International tourism and travel: Concepts and principles*. New Delhi: S. Chand and Company Ltd.

Page, S. J. (1999). *Transport and tourism*. Harlow: Addison–Wesley Longman.

Pender, L. J. (2001). *Travel trade and transport: An introduction*. London: Continuum.

Prideaux, B. (2000). The role of the transport system in destination development. *Tourism Management, 21*(1), 53–63.

Pustay, M. W. (1993). Towards a global airline industry: Prospects and impediments. *Logistics and Transportation Review, 23*(1), 103–128.

Ryan, C. (1991). *Tourism, terrorism and violence: The risks of wider world travel* (*Conflict Studies Series No. 244*). London: Research Institute for the Study of Conflict and Terrorism.

Seth, P. N. (2006). *Successful tourism management: Tourism practices* (Vol. 2). New Delhi: Sterling Publisher Pvt Ltd.

Sharpley, R., Sharpley, J., & Adams, J. (1996). Travel advice or trade embargo? The impacts and implications of official travel advice. *Tourism Management, 17*(1): 1–7.

Singh, R. (2008). *Tourism and transport management: Practice and procedures*. New Delhi: Kaniska Publishers.

Sönmez, S., & Graefe, A. (1998). Determining future travel behaviour from past travel experience and perceptions of risk and safety. *Journal of Travel Research, 37*(2), 172–177.

Telfer, D. J. (2002). The evolution of tourism and development theory. In R. Sharpley & D. J. Telfer (Eds.), *Tourism and development: Concepts and issues* (pp. 35–78). Clevedon: Channel View Publications.

Telfer, D., & Sharpley, R. (Eds.). (2002). *Tourism and development: Concepts and issues* (pp. 231–262). Clevedon: Channel View Publications.

Tribe, J. (1999). *The economics of leisure and tourism*. Oxford: Butterworth–Heinemann.

Urry, J. (1990). *The tourist gaze: Leisure and travel in contemporary societies*. London: SAGE Publications.

Walker, J. R., & Walker, T. (2011). *Tourism concepts and practices*. New Delhi: Pearson Education, Prentice Hall.

Wheatcroft, S. (1994). *Aviation and tourism policies: Balancing the benefits*. London: Routledge.

10   Tourism Organizations

After going through this chapter, the reader will be able to:

❏   Understand the meaning, concept and importance of tourism organization
❏   Understand the overview of tourism organizations and their types
❏   Understand the magnitude of world tourism in terms of vast number of organizations that cater to the needs of their diverse members
❏   Identify various types and functions of tourism organizations including their aims and objectives for the promotion and development of tourism at different levels
❏   Understand the structure and operation of different national and regional trade-related organizations

CHAPTER OVERVIEW

Chapter 10 mainly deals with the understanding of various tourism organizations at various levels—regional, national and international, including their objectives, roles, membership criteria and functions for growth, planning, promotion and development of tourism. The growth and development of any field including tourism depends mainly on the manner in which it associates with other related organizations. These organizations provide a solid platform where issues, ideas, problems and future challenges are discussed at length for mutual cooperation, growth and bonding. Tourism being a multidisciplinary approach, the need for combined efforts of various organizations at various levels holds a great significance for strengthening tourism worldwide.

10.1. Introduction

An organization is a social unit of people that is structured and managed to meet the needs or to pursue collective goals. Organization consists of individuals whose basic role is the achievement of the objectives for which it has been set up. Almost all organizations have a specific management structure that determines relationships between the different activities and the members, and subdivides and assigns roles, responsibilities and authority to carry out different tasks and duties. Organizations are like open systems—they affect and are affected by their environment. In a common parlance, an organization can be a company, business, club, etc., which is formed for a particular purpose.

Understanding Tourism Organizations

Nowadays, tourism is one of the largest and fastest growing industries in the world and certainly a remarkable phenomenon having social, economic, cultural and environmental implications. A multifaceted industry like tourism deserves to be operated by an active involvement of a multitude of players, out of which 'tourism organizations' comprise a prominent group. With the rapid expansion of tourism across the globe, numerous tourism organizations have emerged in both the public and private sectors, and also at different levels—international, national, regional, state or local. Organizations such as UNWTO, Pacific Asia Travel Association (PATA) and World Tourism and Travel Council (WTTC) operating at the international level; governmental ministries/departments/divisions of tourism; various associations of travel agencies and tour operators; and tourism clubs are all examples of tourism organizations. Tourism organizations mainly consist of international, national, regional and local organizations which help to develop and manage tourism worldwide. This chapter discusses the importance, role and functions of some selected tourism organizations.

Tourism organizations may be viewed on the basis of the following factors:

- Function
- Ownership criteria
- Geographical location
- Motive
- Industry

The classifications of tourism organizations on the basis of above purposes may be understood with the help of following table:

Factors Responsible for Types of Organization	National	Regional	International
Function	TAAI, IATO	FHRAI	IATA, ICAO, UNWTO, WTTC
Ownership	ITDC, ANTO	PATA	ICAO, IATA
Geographical location	ASTA, BTA	PATA	UNWTO, WWF
Motive	TFCI, ASI	ADB, APEC	UNDP, UNESCO, ICCA.
Industry	TAAI	ASEAN	WTTC

Notes: ADB: Asian Development Bank; APEC: Asia-Pacific Economic Cooperation; ASTA: American Society of Travel Agents; BTA: Bermuda Tourism Authority; FHRAI: The Federation of Hotel & Restaurant Associations of India; IATO: Indian Association of Tour Operators; ICCA: International Congress and Convention Association; TAAI: Travel Agents Association of India; TFCI: Tourism Finance Corporation of India; UNDP: United Nations Development Programme; WWF: World Wildlife Fund.

Types of Tourism Organizations

Tourism organizations are primarily concerned with the development and promotion of tourism at various levels. However, some organizations may not concern themselves primarily with tourism but may involve indirectly with tourism industry such as airlines, travel agents, tour operators and hoteliers. Tourism organization may be an association or other organized group that promotes both domestic and international tourism. It can be in the form of a governmental institution that determines state policy on tourism. Tourism organization may also be in the form of a multinational association for the purpose of facilitating tourist traffic worldwide.

On the basis of the above discussions, tourism organizations may be classified into following types:

- International tourism organizations such as UNWTO, IATA and WTTC.
- Regional–international tourism organizations such as PATA and Action Group on Erosion, Technology and Concentration (ETC).
- Developmental tourism organizations such as UNESCO and tourism development corporations.
- National tourism organizations like tourism departments.

It is important to study about these organizations because in-depth study of these organizations will not only help in identifying better career path but also help in getting an idea about where to apply in the case of tourism investment and how to finance different projects? For example, if we see organizations such as TAAI, IATO, FHRAI and WTTC, they are engaged not only to safeguard the interest of its members (travel agencies and tour operators) but also work closely with different organizations to promote and develop tourism at various levels. Similarly, international organizations such as ICAO, IATA and UNWTO are working in coordination with each other for the growth and development of airlines and tourism industries worldwide at both governmental and non-governmental levels. Specialized agencies organizations such as TFCI, Industrial Finance Corporation of India (IFCI) and ADB are mainly established for finance-related issues involved in tourism and tourism-related business at different levels. Regional organizations such as PATA and Universal Federation of Travel Agents Association (UFTAA) are also involved in marketing and promotion of tourist products in their respective areas for the development and growth of tourism on regional basis. So it is evident from the above discussion that tourism being a multidimensional and multifaceted industry needs a comprehensive effort from different segments of the industry as well as different forms of organization. Without a combined effort, tourism activities may not be fruitful as well as may not be economically viable for different industries and different countries. So, a sustainable development approach followed by a combined effort by different organizations such as airlines, hotels, travel agencies, tour operators, hotels, conference and convention industries will always be helpful for the growth and development of tourism in national, regional and international levels.

Factors Influencing Types of Organizations in Tourism

There are several factors which can influence the formation of different types of tourism organizations in a country, region or at international level. These factors include **economic** and **political factors, and the presence of social system** of that country or region. The character of an organization in a particular country or region is also influenced because of the importance of tourism in the national economy. In a country where tourism is given due importance in comparison to the other industry or conversely where tourism is well developed and the economic importance is substantial, it is likely that tourism organization in that country is well developed and the government is actively concerned. These types of organizations are now coming up in a big way and are more popular in countries such as Italy, Spain and France.

Countries where government is run centrally, the types of organizations are mainly dominated by the government. However, countries where the presence of federal structure of government prevails, tourism industry is decentralized, which is characterized by the minimum government interference. In those countries, tourism organizations are formed by one or more cooperative bodies at the national level and a high degree of decentralization is given to the individual states or regions in different matters related to different tourism issues. Countries such as Austria, Switzerland and Great Britain are some of the best examples in this regard.

Presence of social system, political considerations and so on can also influence the formation of organization in different countries. Sometimes factors such as culture, traditions, value system, belief and social influence compel the state/region/country to form different organizations for the benefit of their industries, communities as well as for their government. In the case of tourism industry, countries where tourism is newly developed, government should come forward to play a crucial role in planning, developing and promoting tourism; and in those countries where tourism has already developed in the form of governmental, semi-governmental and private organizations, and so on, government should come forward to assist the underdeveloped and recently developing countries in providing financial support, expertise, technical know-how and so on. In this way, these developed countries can play an effective role in the promotion and sustainable development of tourism worldwide. For example, countries such as France, the United Kingdom, the United States of America, Switzerland, China and so on, which have already developed may come forward to help the developing and underdeveloped countries to promote and market tourism in their region by providing various avenues in the form of technical expertise, marketing tourist destinations, development of infrastructure, improving transport services and so on.

10.2. Role, Objectives and Functions of Tourism Organizations

International Civil Aviation Organization

International Civil Aviation Organization	
Logo	INTERNATIONAL CIVIL AVIATION ORGANIZATION *A United Nations Specialized Agency*
Headquarter	Montreal
Regional offices	Paris, Dakar, Bangkok, Cairo, Lima and Mexico City
Year of establishment	1944
Websites	www.icao.int

Introduction

ICAO is a specialized agency which provides a global forum for civil aviation at the governmental level. Its vision is to provide safe, secure and sustainable development of civil aviation through cooperation among its member nations. In November 1944, 54 nations attended the Chicago Convention and agreed that international civil aviation may be developed in a safe and orderly manner, and that international air transport service may be established on the basis of equality of opportunity, and operated smoothly and economically.

In October 1947, ICAO became a specialized agency of the United Nations. The headquarter of ICAO is located in Montreal, Canada. There is a close association between ICAO and IATA which is the world organization of the scheduled airlines.

Aims and Objectives of ICAO

The aims and objectives of ICAO are as follows:

- Ensure the safe and orderly growth of ICAO throughout the world.
- Encourage the art of aircraft design and operation for peaceful purposes.
- Encourage the development of airways, airports and air navigation facilities for international civil aviation.
- Meet the needs of the people in the world for safe, regular, efficient and economic air transport.
- Prevent economic waste caused by unreasonable competitions.
- Ensure that the rights of contracting states are fully respected and that every contracting state has a fair opportunity to operate international airlines.
- Avoid discrimination between contracting states.
- Promote safety of flight in international air navigation.
- Promote, generally, the development of all aspects of international civil aeronautics.

Technical As Well As Commercial Functions of ICAO

ICAO performs both commercial and technical subjects on an intergovernmental level. Major technical and commercial functions of ICAO include:

- **Flying over territory:** ICAO will look into the matter relating to flying over territory. This function is performed in relation to bilateral agreements (freedom of air) among its members.
- **Nationality of aircraft:** Under this function, ICAO will designate the national carrier of each country so that it will be easier for its member countries to identify the national and international carriers, and accordingly service will be provided to its member countries as per norms. For example, in the case of India, Air India is designated as the national/international carrier which can operate its flight all over the world.
- **Documentation:** Under this function, ICAO will help its member countries to fulfil all the documentation procedures such as issue of licence to the pilots, and designations of national and international carriers by its member countries.

- **International standards:** ICAO will maintain international standards in terms of flight operations, maintenance of flights, safety and security issues, and so on.
- **Statistics and finance:** Under this function, ICAO will collect, analyse and disseminate the statistical information among its member countries for the provision of statistical information related to flight operation, revenue generations and so on. ICAO will also provide financial assistance to its member countries as or when required as well as assist financially during the time of aircraft purchase and technology transfer.
- **Technical assistance:** ICAO will help the member countries by providing technical assistance pertaining to aircraft design, airways and air navigation facilities. It will also provide technical assistance during crew training, provision of construction of airports, airways and air navigation services on a governmental level as and when demanded by the member nations.

Organizational Structure of ICAO

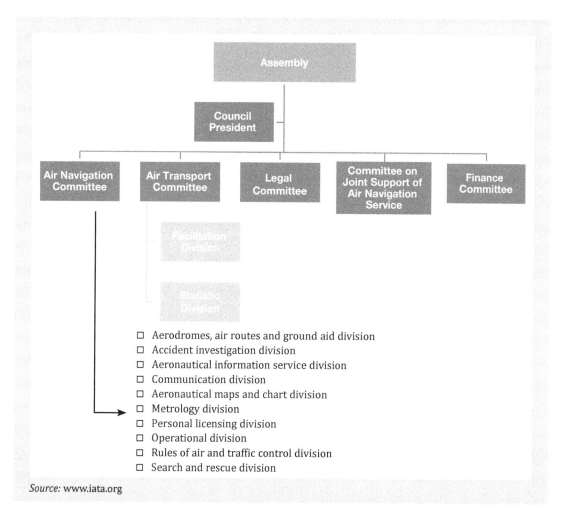

☐ Aerodromes, air routes and ground aid division
☐ Accident investigation division
☐ Aeronautical information service division
☐ Communication division
☐ Aeronautical maps and chart division
☐ Metrology division
☐ Personal licensing division
☐ Operational division
☐ Rules of air and traffic control division
☐ Search and rescue division

Source: www.iata.org

United Nations World Tourism Organization

United Nations World Tourism Organization	
Logo	
Headquarter	Madrid (Spain)
Year of establishment	2 January 1975
Website	http://www.unwto.org

The World Tourism Organization is an intergovernmental technical body dealing with all aspects of tourism and started its legal existence on 2 January 1975. The previous name of WTO was International Union of Official Travel Organization (IUOTO) which was established in 1925 with headquarter at Hague. In December 2006, WTO was renamed as United Nations World Tourism Organization (UNWTO). The rapid expansion of travel had created a need for a world body which can deal with tourism problems at the international level. The headquarter of UNWTO is located at Madrid (Spain). UNWTO is considered as one of the apex bodies dealing with tourism at the international level.

UNWTO's membership includes **156 countries, 6 associate members and over 400 affiliate members as on 2014,** representing the private sector, educational institutions, tourism associations and local tourism authorities. UNWTO is regularly involved in publishing different tourism-related information including tourism statistics, world tourism forecasts, tourism carrying capacity, sustainable development and so on.

As a pioneer of international tourism organization, UNWTO promotes tourism as a major catalyst for the **economic growth, inclusive development** and **environmental sustainability** throughout the world. It also offers leadership and support to various sectors in providing knowledge and helps in framing working tourism policies internationally.

UNWTO helps in implementing the **Global Code of Ethics for Tourism** to maximize tourism's socio-economic contribution while minimizing its possible negative impacts, and is committed to promoting tourism as an instrument in achieving the **United Nations Millennium Development Goals (MDGs)**, geared towards eliminating poverty and fostering sustainable development.

Aims of UNWTO

The aims of UNWTO are as follows:

- The fundamental aim of the organization is the promotion and development of tourism to contribute in economic development, international understanding, peace, prosperity, and universal respect for and observation of human rights and freedoms for all without distinction of race, sex, language or religion.
- The organization will pay particular attention in the field of tourism to the interest of the developing countries.

- The organization will establish and maintain effective collaboration with the appropriate organs of the United Nations and its specialized agencies. The organization is acting as a participating and executing agency of the United Nations Development Program (UNDP).

Missions of UNWTO

UNWTO plays a central and decisive role in the following:

- Promote the development of responsible, sustainable and universally accessible tourism, paying particular attention to the interest of developing countries.
- Organize and encourage the implementations of Global Code of Ethics for Tourism to ensure that member countries, tourist destinations and business entrepreneurs maximize the positive economic and sociocultural effects of tourism, and fully reap its benefits while minimizing its negative environmental and social impacts.
- UNWTO is committed to MDGs which includes the following:
  o Eradicate the extreme hunger and poverty
  o Achieve universal primary education
  o Promote gender equality and women empowerment
  o Reduce child mortality
  o Improve mental health
  o Combat HIV/acquired immunodeficiency syndrome (AIDS), malaria and other diseases.
  o Ensure environmental sustainability
  o Develop a global partnership for development

UNWTO Work Programme

UNWTO work programme covers six main areas of tourism-related activities and services. These are as follows:

- **Statistics and market research:** Under this programme, the UNWTO Statistics and particularly the Tourism Satellite Account Programme are committed to developing tourism measurement for furthering knowledge of the sector, monitoring progress, evaluating impact, promoting results-focused management, and highlighting strategic issues for policy objectives. This programme works towards advancing the methodological frameworks for measuring tourism and expanding its analytical potential, designing practical guidance for their implementation in countries, supporting statistical strength in countries through capacity building, and compiling and disseminating tourism statistics of countries all over the world.
- **Education and training:** The main mission of UNWTO under this programme is to enable its member countries to devise and implement education and training policies, plans and tools that fully harness the employment potential of their tourism sector and effectively enhance their competitiveness and sustainability.
- **Environment and planning:** Under this programme, UNWTO will support the tourism sector for better management and development of environment, and plan to adopt the principle of sustainability which is the main motto of UNWTO mandate. The goal of this programme is to promote tourism development that supports biodiversity conservation, social welfare and economic security in the host countries and communities.

- **Quality of tourism services:** The main objective of this programme is to provide quality tourism services to the tourist. Since travel facilitation of tourist travel is closely interlinked with tourism development, it can be a tool to foster increased demand, and generate economic development, job creation and international understanding, so providing quality service is essential to achieve the main motto of the UNWTO.
- **Technical cooperation:** The missions carried out under this programme are carried out at the request of countries or groups of countries to identify, evaluate and describe their specific technical assistance needs, and provide policy advice on the problems they are faced with. These missions are usually fielded for a short duration and result in further project proposals for funding and, in some cases, in direct UNWTO recommendations to members which they can implement themselves.
- **Communication and documentations:** The major aim of this work programme is to promote and facilitate access to tourism information for UNWTO members and other institutional partners through appropriate mechanisms and effective information support services in three main areas.

UNWTO Membership Criteria

Following are the three categories of membership criteria operating within UNWTO:

- **Full members:** These include all sovereign states. Those countries that are independent come directly under full member category. For example, India is a full member of UNWTO.
- **Associate members:** They are the territories or group of territories not responsible for their international relation but whose relationship is approved by the state assuming responsibilities by their external relations. Currently there are six associate members who are representing UNWTO. These include: Flemish Community, Puerto Rico, Aruba, Hong Kong, Macau and Madeira.
- **Affiliate member:** They include both intergovernmental and non-governmental bodies concerned with specialized interest in tourism. Currently there are some 400 affiliate members representing the private sector, educational institutions, tourism associations and local tourism authorities, non-governmental entities with specialized interests in tourism, and commercial and non-commercial bodies and associations with activities related to the aims of UNWTO or falling within its competence. These include travel agents, tour operators, tourist transport operators, foreign exchange bureaus, travel insurance companies, hotels and so on.

Activities of UNWTO

The activities of UNWTO can be described as follows:

- UNWTO will perform the role of clearing house (collecting, analysing and disseminating information) for all available information on international and domestic tourism including:
  - Statistical data regarding tourist arrivals.
  - Legislation, regulation and special events, and its systematic collection, analysis and dissemination.
- Making travel easier by reducing frontier formalities and removing barriers to the free movement of tourists.

- Organizing and convening international conferences, seminars, round tables and technical meetings.
- Preparing draft international agreements on tourism.
- Examining vocational training programme, especially in developing countries.
- Research activities for tourism market for the purpose of marketing and promotion as well as destination development.
- Reviewing tourism trends, developments and market fluctuations over the changes in the world economy and social conditions due to tourism activities.
- Setting standard for education.
- Accreditation programme for tourism education.
- Improvig quality tourism by creating safety, security, technical standards and providing access for travellers with disability.
- Forming of regional representatives.
- Implementing regional projects.

The permanent activities of UNWTO include the collection and update of available information on training needs, specific activities including participation in technical cooperation projects for vocational training and so on.

Organs through Which UNWTO Functions

The organs through which UNWTO functions are as follows:

- **General Assembly:** This is the supreme organ and sovereign body of UNWTO. It is composed of delegates representing full members, associate members and representatives of affiliate members. General Assembly meets in every 2 years. It consists of six regional commissions. These are Africa, America, Europe, Middle East, Pacific and East Asia, and South Asia.
- **Executive Council:** It consists of full members elected by the Assembly at the ratio of one member for every five full members of UNWTO for achieving fair and equitable geographical distribution. The Executive Council takes all necessary measures in consultation with the Secretary General for the implementation of decisions and recommendations of the Assembly.
- **The secretariat:** The secretariat is headed by Secretary General who is the legal representative of UNWTO. He/she supervises the required full-time staff at UNWTO's Madrid headquarter. These officials are responsible for implementing UNWTO's work programme and serving the needs of its members. The Secretary General is responsible for carrying out the general policy and work programme of the organization in accordance with the directions of General Assembly and Executive Council.

Themes of World Tourism Day over the Years

World Tourism Day (WTD) is generally observed annually on 27 September every year. The main purpose is to increase awareness among the international community about the importance of tourism and its social, cultural, political and economic values. The event seeks to address global challenges outlined in the United Nations MDGs and to highlight the contribution of the tourism sector for achieving these goals.

Establishment of WTD

The concept of celebrating the 'World Tourism Day' was initiated in the third session (Torremolinos, Spain, September 1979), where the UNWTO General Assembly decided to celebrate the 'World Tourism Day', with effect from 1980. This date was chosen to coincide with an important milestone in the world of tourism: the anniversary of the adoption of the UNWTO Statute on 27 September 1970.

WTD Themes and Official Celebrations

WTD is celebrated by events around the themes decided by the UNWTO General Assembly on the recommendation of the UNWTO Executive Council. While UNWTO invites people of all ages and backgrounds to hold and take part in celebrations in their respective country or holiday destination, official WTD celebrations take place in a UNWTO member state, on the basis of geographic rotation. Given below are the various themes which were undertaken by UNWTO, including the host countries, which are selected on the basis of geographical location on a continuous basis by the Executive Council for its observations.

- **1980:** Tourism's Contribution to the Preservation of Cultural Heritage and to Peace and Mutual Understanding
- **1981:** Tourism and the Quality of Life
- **1982:** Pride in Travel: Good Guests and Good Hosts
- **1983:** Travel and Holidays Are a Right but Also a Responsibility for All
- **1984:** Tourism for International Understanding, Peace and Cooperation
- **1985:** Youth Tourism: Cultural and Historical Heritage for Peace and Friendship
- **1986:** Tourism: A Vital Force for World Peace
- **1987:** Tourism for Development
- **1988:** Tourism: Education for All
- **1989:** The Free Movement of Tourists Creates One World
- **1990:** Tourism: An Unrecognized Industry, a Service to be Released (The Hague Declaration on Tourism)
- **1991:** Communication, Information and Education: Powerlines of Tourism Development
- **1992:** Tourism: A Factor of Growing Social and Economic Solidarity and of Encounter between People
- **1993:** Tourism Development and Environmental Protection: Towards a Lasting Harmony
- **1994:** Quality Staff, Quality Tourism
- **1995:** WTO: Serving World Tourism for 20 Years
- **1996:** Tourism: A Factor of Tolerance and Peace
- **1997:** Tourism: A Leading Activity of the 21st Century for Job Creation and Environmental Protection
- **1998:** Public–Private Sector Partnership: the Key to Tourism Development and Promotion (Host: Mexico)
- **1999:** Tourism: Preserving World Heritage for the New Millennium (Host: Chile)
- **2000:** Technology and Nature: Two Challenges for Tourism at the Dawn of the 21st Century (Host: Germany)
- **2001:** Tourism: A Toll for Peace and Dialogue among Civilizations (Host: Iran)
- **2002:** Ecotourism: the Key to Sustainable Development (Host: Costa Rica)

- **2003:** Tourism: A Driving Force for Poverty Alleviation, Job Creation and Social Harmony (Host: Algeria)
- **2004:** Sport and Tourism: Two Living Forces for Mutual Understanding, Culture and the Development of Societies (Host: Malaysia)
- **2005:** Travel and Transport: From Imaginary of Jules Verne to the Reality of the 21st Century (Host: Qatar)
- **2006:** Tourism Enriches (Host: Portugal)
- **2007:** Tourism Opens Doors for Women (Host: Sri Lanka)
- **2008:** Tourism: Responding to the Challenge of Climate Change (Host: India)
- **2009:** Tourism—Celebrating Diversity (Host: Africa)
- **2010:** Tourism and Biodiversity (Host: China)
- **2011:** Tourism Linking Cultures (Host: Egypt)
- **2012:** Tourism and Sustainable Energy: Powering Sustainable Development (Gran Canarias)
- **2013:** Tourism and Water: Protecting our Common Future (Maldives)
- **2014:** Tourism and Community Development (Guadalajara, Mexico)
- **2015:** 1 Billion tourists, 1 billion opportunities (Burkina Faso, Africa)
- **2016:** Tourism for All —Promoting Universal Accessibility (Thailand)

International Air Transport Association

International Air Transport Association	
Logo	
Headquarter	Montreal
Regional offices	Paris, Dakar, Bangkok, Cairo, Lima and Mexico City
Year of establishment	Initially 1919 (International Air Traffic Association), then founded in 1945
Websites	www.iata.org

Introduction

After the Second World War, under the leadership of Franklin D. Roosevelt, the then president of the United States of America, one international convention was organized at Chicago from 1 November to 7 December 1944. The convention contributed the formation of two permanent bodies named as ICAO and IATA. The IATA was founded in Cuba, Havana, in 1945 by the airlines of different countries to meet the problems created by the rapid expansion of civil air services after the Second World War. The previous name of IATA was International Air Traffic Association which was founded in the year 1919 with headquarter at Hague with the swift expansion of air transport.

IATA is the world organization of scheduled airlines. Being an international scheduled airlines industry, its membership carries the bulk of international air traffic under the flag of over 117 nations with 265 members. IATA major purpose is to assure that all airline traffic anywhere in the world moves with the greatest possible speed, convenience and efficiency despite the differences between languages, currencies, law and measurement.

Nature of Organization

The nature of organization of IATA includes the following:

- Non-governmental
- Voluntary
- Non-exclusive

- Non-political
- Democratic
- Non-profit making

Membership Criteria

The membership criteria of IATA are open automatically to the approved carrier of a sovereign state. This implies that each country has to designate its own national and international carrier first. After that these carriers will automatically be eligible for the membership of IATA. Membership of IATA is open to airlines operating for scheduled and non-scheduled air services which are maintained by an IATA Operational Safety Audit (IOSA) registration formed by IATA. IATA members include the world's leading passengers and cargo airlines. The membership criteria of IATA can be categorized under three headings:

- **Active members:** Active members are the most powerful members of IATA. As a democratic organization, these members are having highest voting rights. Active members include all international airlines including both passenger and cargo. They participate in mostly all activities of IATA. For example, Air India is an active member of IATA.
- **Active trade associate members:** These are another type of members who have their voting rights as of active members, but the only difference is that like active members, these members do not have their rights to participate in the international fare calculation and tariff standardization while formulating the international fare construction and tariff fixation.
- **Associate members:** Associate members are all domestic airlines/carriers designated by the respective countries. For example, domestic airlines such as SpiceJet, Indigo and Jet Airways are some of the associate members of IATA.

Benefits of IATA Membership

All the different types of members are benefited in several ways. IATA provides a powerful, unified and experienced voice that supports and promotes the interests of its members. These members get different types of benefit through:

- International recognition and lobbying by the member nations.
- Targeting key industry priorities as per situation/environment.

- Driving industry change trough cooperation among members.
- Reducing costs in international air travel and cargo operation.
- Communication campaigns.
- Training and other services, and so on.

Functions of Basic Trade Associate Members of IATA

The Basic trade association activities of IATA can be categorized under six headings:

1. **Technical Function:**
   a. Technical assistance ──────► Airport
   b. Crew training ──────► Aircraft
   c. Communication (Global Ticket Network)
2. **Medical Function:**
   a. Global inoculations
   b. Specification of medicine as per region
   c. Standardize first-aid technique
   d. Maintain hygienic condition in food
3. **Legal Function:**
   a. Controlling unethical practice
   b. Curbing unusual competition
   c. Simplification of fare formula
   d. Legal authority for members in front of the global community
   e. Settlements of accounts
4. **Security Function:**
   a. Restricted article (inflammable items, alcoholic goods and so on)
   b. Technical specification (licensing of pilot, issue of fit certificates to airlines)
   c. Security during war (during war time, provide extra security to passenger flights and cargo flights of different countries)
   d. Effort mobilization against hijacking
5. **Procedural Function:**
   a. Fare calculation standardization
   b. Ticket format
   c. NUC (Neutral unit of currency/Construction—a single currency which may be accepted by all members to accept as common medium of exchange. E.g., US dollar)
   d. Air pricing
   e. Standardization of services
   f. Baggage check and rules
6. **Administrative Function:**
   a. Interacting with ICAO and other organizations
   b. Interacting with United Nations
   c. Interacting with world community
   d. Supervision of functions and implementations
   e. Agency Investigation Panel function (AIP-9)

IATA Organizational Structure

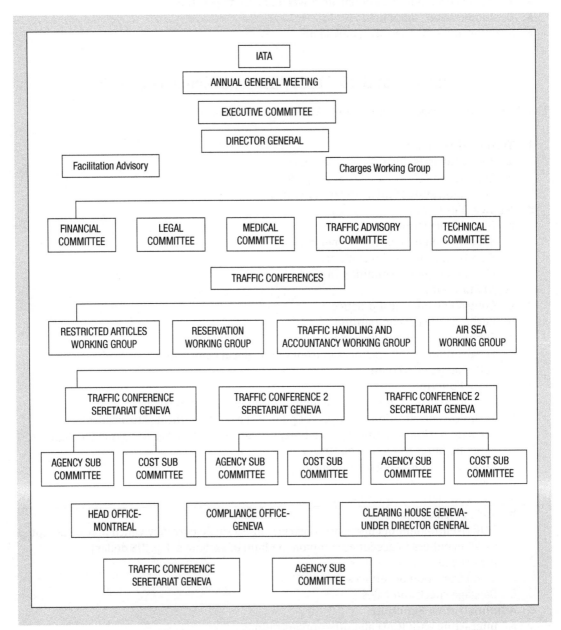

Regarding Organization

The above organizational chart indicates that IATA conducts the Annual General Meeting (AGM) every year. From AGM, they form the Executive Committee. The Executive Committee is headed by the Director General. It can be broadly divided into two broad groups, namely the Facilitating

Working Group and the Charges Working Group. Under the Facilitating Working Group', the major committees who perform various duties are as follows:

- **Finance Committee** who looks after the financial issues
- **Legal Committee** who looks after the legal matters that arise during its operations and
- **Medical Committee** who looks after the medical-related issues such as global inoculations and first-aid techniques

Under the Charges Working Group, the major committees who discharge their duties are as follows:

- **Traffic Advisory Committee** who looks into the matters related to traffic handling like traffic conferences (TC): TC1, TC2 and TC3.
- **Technical Committee** who looks into the matters such as providing technical support to aircraft, airways, air navigations and airports.

Regarding IATA Traffic Conference, IATA has altogether three traffic conferences: TC1, TC2 and TC3. There are four working groups operating under traffic conference, namely the Restricted Area Working Group, the Reservation Working Group, the Traffic Handling Working Group and the Air Sea Working Group. Under each working group, there are two subcommittees who discharge their duties as per the instructions of the working groups. IATA's headquarter is in Montreal, Canada. IATA clearing house and its secretariat are located at Geneva.

Pacific Asia Travel Association

Pacific Asia Travel Association	
Logo	**PATA**® Pacific Asia Travel Association
Headquarter	San Francisco
Divisional offices	Sydney (Pacific), Singapore (Asia), Monaco (Europe) and San Francisco (America).
Year of establishment	1951
Websites	www.pata.org

Introduction

PATA was founded in 1951 in Honolulu (Hawaii Island) and became functional in 1952. At the time of its inception, there were 44 members in PATA. It was developed with an objective of marketing tourism products in the Asia-Pacific region. In 1953, PATA's headquarter was moved from Hawaii to San Francisco. Considered as the state of 'money and influence', San Francisco was home to an influential group of individuals who served on the PATA board and committees during the 1950s and the 1960s. The 1960s also witnessed PATA's first move towards promoting education and training, helping to set up the School of Tourism Industry Management at the University of Hawaii—the first such institution to be established in the region. In 1978, the first ever PATA Travel Mart in Manila was organized.

In the mid-1980s, there was a change in the nature and scope of travel and tourism industry, particularly in this region. Mainly the larger members are relatively self-sufficient in the promotion of tourism product. For this purpose, in 1989, the board of PATA approved the creation of a task force to find out the necessary adjustments to these changes. In April 1990, in the Annual Conference in Vancouver, the report of the task force, *Direction 2000*, was approved. The task force defined a new vision for PATA to be the leader of, and authority on, Pacific Asia Travel and Tourism with the mission to contribute to the growth, value and quality of travel and tourism to and within the Asia-Pacific region on behalf of its members. Currently, PATA comprises 95 government, state and city tourism bodies, 29 international airlines, airports and cruise lines, 63 educational institutions, and hundreds of travel industry companies in Asia–Pacific and beyond.

PATA is a non-profit travel association. The headquarter of PATA is in San Francisco. The divisional offices of PATA are located in Sydney (Pacific), Singapore (Asia), Monaco (Europe) and San Francisco (America).

Memberships

The memberships of PATA are diversified. These include:

- Governmental
- Non-governmental
- National tourist organizations
- Airlines
- Travel agencies
- Tour operators
- Hoteliers
- Allied destinations and so on

Activities of PATA

The primary activities of PATA on behalf of its members and chapters include the following:

- Directing services such as training, branding, insightful research and innovative events to its member organizations and chapters
- Promoting members, products and services
- Supporting the development of member's destinations, products and services
- Market research and information services
- Provision of leadership on industry issues
- Promoting PATA itself

Other Activities of PATA

- PATA develops some products and services that have broader communicational values and which can contribute to the cost of those strategic programmes that by their nature will not generate sufficient revenue to pay for themselves.
- PATA involves in scientific nature of marketing from segmentation to focusing on individual, which aims at supporting members' efforts in marketing and selling their products and services.

- PATA develops the capacity for leadership and authority for technological innovation.
- PATA provides information and practical assistance in the field of tourism.
- PATA solves the problems related to human resource through education and training, and human resource management programmes.
- PATA helps for the development and marketing of upcoming destinations.
- PATA acts as a facilitator in the conservation of the natural environment and the cultural heritage of member countries.
- The advisory council and intelligence centre of PATA plays a crucial role in the identification and development of positions on important issues for the industry and for PATA.
- PATA organizes Annual Travel Mart and deals with various issues on:
  - Tourism Research Forum
  - Heritage Conference
  - Adventure Tourism Conference
  - Seminar on various themes such as human resource, open skies policy.
  - Identifying with new trends
  - Hub City Forum Series
  - Responsible Tourism Conference
  - PATA Annual Summit
  - PATA Travel Mart

PATA Chapters

PATA chapters are established throughout the world to assist in the fulfilment of the objectives of the association. They are the local community organizations of the travel industry professionals who join a cooperative endeavour—within the framework of PATA—to develop travel and tourism to, from and within the Pacific area. Currently here are altogether 40 chapters around the world which are making valuable contributions to the entire travel communities.

The above chapters arrange meetings, seminars, conferences and travel marts for tourism in the Asia-Pacific region. PATA promotion is made through *Pacific Area Destination Handbook*, Pacific Travel News, hotel directory and travel guide. PATA's India chapter is one of the area chapters, dealing with the promotion of India as a destination.

American Society of Travel Agents

American Society of Travel Agents	
Logo	
Headquarter:	Alexandria, Virginia, USA
Year of establishment	1931
Websites	www.asta.org

Introduction

The world's largest professional travel trade association, ASTA was founded on 20 April 1931 in New York City as the American Steamship and Tourist Agents Association. ASTA changed its name to the American Society of Travel Agents in 1944. In 1931, more than 60 agents joined an association that promised to protect and promote the mutual interests of its members, maintain a dignified code of ethics, combat unfair competition, stimulate the public's desire to travel and promote the use of ASTA members' services. The headquarter of ASTA is located in New York City, USA.

The mission of ASTA and its affiliated organizations is to facilitate the business of selling travel through effective representation, shared knowledge and the enhancement of professionalism. ASTA seeks a retail travel marketplace that is profitable and growing, and a rewarding place to work, invest and do business. ASTA and its affiliates now comprise the world's largest and most influential travel trade association with members in 140 countries. The main aim of ASTA is the promotion and advancement of the interest of the travel agency and to promote ethical practices in tourism industry. The ASTA's aim is to safeguard the travellers against fraud, misrepresentation and unethical practices.

Membership

ASTA has eight membership categories, which are as follows:

1. Travel agent members
2. Premium
3. International travel agency company
4. International travel professional
5. Travel school
6. Allied company (product, service and information suppliers to travel agencies)
7. Allied associate
8. Honorary

Services

ASTA offers the following services:

- Provides educational training through ASTA travel courses and seminars for business and trade
- Assists all agencies in travel-related matters
- Sponsors conferences on tourism-related issues
- Publishes newsletter and monthly magazines for providing information
- Co-operates with other agencies, including governments and states
- Invests in travel-related research
- Discusses the matter related to fare construction and travel destination with airlines

ASTA organizes world congress annually which includes workshops, seminars, business meetings, social events and so forth on various tourism-related issues. It provides an important forum for launching important programmes for travel agents.

Indian Association of Tour Operator

Indian Association of Tour Operator	
Logo	
Headquarter	New Delhi
Year of establishment	1982
Website	www.iato.in

Introduction

IATO was founded in the year 1981 with its headquarter in New Delhi. It is a joint forum of tour operators to promote and develop tourism in India. The main purpose for establishing IATO was to promote international understanding and goodwill.

Membership

The membership of IATO is open to organizations of good professional reputations that have been connected with the tourism industry for at least 1 year. IATO offers various categories of membership. The membership of the association shall be composed of (a) active members, (b) associate members, (c) allied members and (d) honorary members.

The Executive Committee may at any time create different classes of members, provide entrance fees and subscriptions, and define their respective rights and privileges. The Executive Committee shall have power to dispense with the payment of the entrance fee/membership fee, if they deem it fit. The decision of the Executive Committee will be final in all cases.

Active Members

A firm or company having an established place of business in India and recognized by the Department of Tourism as tour operator/travel agent for a minimum period of 2 years, and its major substantial part of activity of promotion of tourism and foreign exchange earnings in a year is minimum ₹2,000,000 shall be eligible for membership as an active member of the association, provided that an application is made and accepted by the Executive Committee. However, only one office of a firm or company shall be admitted as an active member of the association.

Associate Members

Any other office including overseas offices of an active or allied member shall be eligible for associate membership of the association. The minimum turnover of the company/firm should be ₹10 lakh. They shall have no right to vote in the proceedings of the association.

Allied Members

Any firm or company, which is regularly engaged or associated with tourism and travel industry such as carrier companies, hoteliers, restaurants, excursion agents, transport contractors, forwarding and clearing agents, shipping companies, state tourist corporations/organizations, hotel marketing representatives/agencies, trade publications, and any overseas firm/company/corporation/organization shall be eligible for the membership as an allied member. The minimum turnover of the company/firm should be ₹10 lakh. The allied members shall have the right to participate in the activities of the association except to vote. The allied members will be represented in the Executive Committee by the nomination of office bearers of various national trade associations who reciprocate membership to IATO executive members on their association.

Any international firm or company who is engaged or associated with tourism and travel industry shall be eligible for the membership as allied members of the association. The members shall have the right to participate in the activities of the association, except to vote.

Honorary Members

The Executive Committee may invite persons who are Hall of Fame Awardees and distinguished society members, and/or who have distinguished themselves by the services provided to the tourism and travel industry in the national or international field to become honorary members of the association. Such members will be invited to the association by the unanimous vote of all the members of the Executive Committee.

Aims of IATO

The main aims of IATO are as follows:

- To promote national integration, international welfare and goodwill
- To promote, encourage and assist in the development of tourism throughout the country
- To communicate with government departments, public bodies and chamber of commerce for the interest of travel trade, and to nominate members to act on them
- To set up and maintain high ethical standards in the tourism industry
- To promote and encourage friendly feelings among the travel agents and tour operators
- To protect the interest of the members from malpractices of foreign tour operators
- To promote equal opportunities for all visitors in India without distinction of race, sex, religion and nationality
- To conduct seminars, meetings, discussions, workshops and so on
- To help students in the field of tourism in the form of providing scholarship for higher education and research

- To provide information and publish IATO newsletter regularly, popularly known as 'IATO Imprint' for the benefits of its members
- To get affiliation with similar organizations operating in other countries
- To provide regular reports about the achievements by the members of the association and to do all such things that are necessary for its members
- To undertake promotional tour abroad in collaboration with Air India and Department of Tourism, Government of India.

Travel Agents Association of India

Travel Agents Association of India	
Logo	
Headquarter	Mumbai
Year of establishment	1951
Websites	http://travelagentsofindia.com/

Introduction

TAAI is a professional coordinating body consisting of various travel and tourism industry. It is recognized as the main representing body of the travel industry in India. TAAI is a professional and regulating body dealing with travel and tourism industry in India. It was established in the year 1951 with its headquarter in Mumbai. At the time of its inception, 12 leading travel agents of India started an association with a view to regulate the travel industry in an organized manner with sound business principles.

Purpose

The main purpose of TAAI includes the following:

- To protect the interest of those engaged in the travel industry
- To promote its orderly growth and development
- To safeguard the interest of the travelling public from exploitation by unscrupulous and unreliable operators

Nature of Organization

TAAI is

- Non-political
- Non-commercial
- Non-profit making

Membership

The membership categories of TAAI include the following:

- **Active members:** Any firm or company having an established place of business in India and is a travel agent approved by IATA shall be eligible for membership as an active member of the association, provided that an application is made and accepted by the Managing Committee.
- **Branch Associates:** Any active member having a branch in India that is approved by IATA as an accredited agent, shall be eligible to be a branch associate.
- **Allied associates:** Any firm or company who is regularly engaged or associated with the travel and tourism industry, and having their place of business in India such as carrier companies, hoteliers, caterers, excursion agents, forwarding and clearing agents, tour operators, guide organizations, computer reservation system or central reservation system companies, press and media, GSA's and travel-related services, other than airline ticket services, shall be eligible to be an allied associate. The applicant must have recognition from the Department of Tourism, Government of India for those tour operators applying for allied membership.
- **Allied branch associates:** Any allied associate having a branch in India shall be eligible to be an allied branch associate.
- **Overseas associates:** Any firm or company having an established place of business not in India, and is a travel agent approved by its country's National Travel Agents Association shall be eligible for membership as overseas associate of this association. The applicant must be an IATA agent and a member of the respective National Travel Agents Association.
- **Overseas branch associates:** Any overseas associate having a branch office in the same country or another country shall be eligible to be an overseas branch associate.
- **Government associates:** Any tourist department of any Central Government or state government or foreign government shall be eligible for the membership as government associate.

Aims of TAAI

The main aims of TAAI include the following:

- To safeguard the interest of the travelling public
- To maintain high ethical standards in travel and trade industry
- To develop tourism industry through improving the travel agency business and service for tourists
- To promote mutual cooperation among TAAI members
- To contribute to the sound progress and the growth of the industry

Activities of TAAI

The major activities of TAAI are as follows:

- It helps to promote, maintain and stimulate the growth of travel and tourism in the country.
- It directs the controlling and regulating authorities related with the problems faced by the industry and discusses with them the means of survival and betterment of its members.
- It maintains close contact with world bodies and represents matters affecting the travel and tourism industry in India.
- It collects and disseminates useful information on travel and tourism among members for their guidance.
- It educates members for meeting future challenges through seminars, conferences and so on.
- It helps to develop better understanding among different segments of travel industry.

Federation of Hotel & Restaurant Association of India

Federation of Hotel & Restaurant Association of India		
Logo	FH&RA INDIA	The Federation of Hotel & Restaurant Associations of India 011-40780780
Headquarter	New Delhi	
Regional offices	Kolkata, Mumbai, Chennai and New Delhi	
Year of establishment	1954	
Website	www.fhrai.com	

Introduction

FHRAI was formed in 1955 and later on incorporated as a company under Indian Companies Act, 1956. This apex body was formed by four regional hospitality associations functioning in the country, namely

- Hotel and Restaurant Association of Eastern India with regional office in Kolkata
- Hotel and Restaurant Association of North India with regional office in New Delhi
- Hotel and Restaurant association of Western India with regional office in Mumbai
- South India Hotel and Restaurant Association with regional office in Chennai

FHRAI protects the interest of the hospitality industry in India. It provides a link between the hospitality industry, political leadership, academics, international associations and other stakeholders. The business of the federation is managed by the Executive Committee comprising 24 members, 6 from each region. The federation secretariat is functioning from New Delhi with Secretary General, Joint Secretary, Deputy Secretary and other staffs. The federation is a member of International Hotel Association.

The other aim of the federation includes increase in foreign exchange and increase in employment opportunities. The federation acts as eyes and ears of the government in the hotel and restaurant sectors. It reminds the government about the problems faced by the industry and takes necessary measures to remove operational bottleneck. It helps the government in decision-making process relating to the hospitality industry.

Objectives of FHRAI

The main objectives of FHRAI include the following:

- To unite four regional associations as a representative of national organization.
- To create a national fraternity of the hotel and restaurant establishments located all over India.
- To advice and inform members about national and international matters of the hospitality industry.
- To consider and take decision on all questions of interest of the hospitality industry.
- To act as an information centre, and disseminate statistical and other information concerning the hotel and restaurant industries, and advice the members on matters important to them.
- To promote and market hospitality industry in India, especially hotel and restaurant in the national and international markets.
- To coordinate and liaison with ministry and department of tourism and other concerned departments/agencies of the Central and state governments to achieve the accelerated growth of the hotel and restaurant industries by securing suitable incentives for its industry and consider all questions connected with hotel and restaurant industries as far as possible to secure grievance of the industry.
- To convene national and international conferences related with hospitality industry.
- To publish and circulate books, literature and hotel directory on a regular basis.

Membership

The membership criteria of FHRAI can be categorized under the following headings:

- **The FHRAI hotel membership:** This membership is offered to the hotels which have at least 10 lettable rooms and a restaurant.
- **The FHRAI restaurant membership:** It offers membership to the restaurants which are operational and have a minimum of 25 covers or capacity to seat.
- **The FHRAI associate member:** This type of membership is offered to the companies and firms who are associated with the hospitality industry.

Activities of FHRAI

The main activities of FHRAI include the following:

- It disseminates information among its members.
- It conducts research on hotel and restaurant industries, and informs its members about the recent trends.

- It conducts professional development programmes for the hotel professionals to improve their knowledge and skill.
- It gives training to the human resources of hotel and restaurant industries.
- It organizes seminars, conferences and conventions to exchange ideas on a regular basis.

Tourism Finance Corporation of India Limited

	Tourism Finance Corporation of India Limited
Logo	Tourism Finance Corporation of India Ltd. *helping tourism grow*
Headquarter	New Delhi
Year of establishment	1989
Websites	www.tfciltd.com

Introduction

Based on the recommendations of the National Committee on Tourism and subsequent decision by the Government of India, IFCI along with other banks and financial institutions had taken the initiative to form TFCI.

TFCI was incorporated as a public limited company on 27 January 1989. It became operational from 1 February 1989. The registered office of TFCI is situated in IFCI Towers, New Delhi. It was established to cater to the needs of the tourism and tourism-related projects in India.

Resources of TFCI

The authorized share capital of TFCI is ₹100 crore, out of which the initial paid up share capital was 50 crore. This amount was subscribed by:

- IFCI
- Industrial Development Bank of India
- Industrial Credit and Investment Corporation of India
- Life Insurance Corporation of India
- State Bank of India
- Unit Trust of India
- General Insurance Corporation of India
- Canara Bank
- Bank of India

TFCI also issues bonds which will be guaranteed by the Government of India in mobilizing resources.

Objectives of TFCI

TFCI provides financial assistance to enterprises for setting up and developing tourism, tourism-related activities, facilities, services which inter alia includes hotels, restaurants, holiday resorts, amusement parks and complexes for entertainment, education and sports, safari parks, ropeways, cultural centres, convention centres, transport, travel and tour operating agencies, sports facilities and tourists emporia.

Besides those, TFCI will also be coordinating and formulating guidelines and policies related to the financing of such projects. TFCI have a developmental role within the overall policies of the government.

Activities of TFCI

TFCI gives all forms of financial assistances for new projects including expansion, diversification, and modernization of projects in tourism and tourism-related industry. The other activities are as follows:

- Engaging in tourist flow survey
- Providing facilities and services for tourists
- Preparing tourism master plan
- Planning for amusement and nature parks
- Undertaking environmental carrying capacity studies

TFCI provides services and financial assistance to both the public and private sectors. Financial assistance is provided in the form of:

- Rupee loans
- Foreign currency loans
- Underwriting public issue shares/debentures and direct subscription of such securities
- Guarantee for deferred payments and credits raised in India and abroad
- Equipment finance
- Equipment's lease
- Assistance under suppliers credit
- Merchant banking and advisory service
- Refinance assistance to state level institutions and banks

India Tourism Development Corporation

India Tourism Development Corporation

Logo

Headquarter	New Delhi, India
Regional offices	Ashok Group Hotels, Duty Free, Travel Solutions, Advertising Solutions, Engineering Consultancy, Education and Training, Event Management, and Art Gallery
Founded in	**October 1966**
Websites	www.theashokgroup.com

Introduction

ITDC is a public sector organization which was established in the year 1966. It was formed as an implementing wing of Department of Tourism, Government of India. As a public sector organization, ITDC is expected to function on a commercial basis. ITDC also has some social responsibilities. The main purpose of establishing ITDC is to promote India as a tourist destination.

Background

There was a decline in tourist flow to India from 139,804 in 1961 to 134,036 in 1962. As a result, the government had set up an ad hoc committee on tourism in March 1963, under the chairmanship of L. K. Jha. The committee recommended that the public sector should assume a comprehensive role for promoting tourism in India. On the recommendation of the L. K. Jha Committee, in 1965, the government established three separate corporations, namely

- Hotel Corporation of India Limited
- ITDC Limited
- India Tourism Transport Undertaking Limited

The functions of those corporations were to manage hotels, tourist publicity and provide transportation facility to the tourists. Later on it was observed that there was a lack of coordination among these three organizations. In order to improve coordination and smooth functioning of these corporations, government had merged these corporations into single public sector undertaking body in October 1966 which is popularly known as ITDC Limited.

Objectives of ITDC

The objectives of ITDC are as follows:

- To construct, take over and manage existing hotels and market hotels, beach resorts, travellers' lodges/restaurants
- To provide transport, entertainment, shopping and conventional services
- To produce and distribute tourist publicity material
- To render consultancy cum managerial services in India and abroad

- To carry on the business as Full Fledged Money Changers (FFMC), restricted money changers and so on
- To provide innovative, dependable and value for money solutions to the needs of tourism development and engineering industry, including providing consultancy and project implementation

Functions of ITDC

Since ITDC is a corporation that oversees many functions related to the hospitality sector, in its multifunctional role, ITDC aims at running all its units efficiently and productively, and with improved margins of profit. It has the following functions:

- As the mainstay of the hospitality industry in India, ITDC plays a pivotal role in the creation and advancement of tourist infrastructure in India.
- ITDC is a corporation under the Ministry of Tourism, Government of India and carries a large number of employees in its different sections at various levels of calibre and status. ITDC aims at achieving high levels of productivity from its personnel through superior education, stimulus and human resource development practices.
- ITDC plays a vital role in getting together the government of each different state and its corresponding Tourism Development Corporation in planning and implementing new tourism-related projects, promotion of these projects, and training of required personnel. It is through the impetus created by ITDC that new tourism projects across the country are being developed.
- A successful organization needs to have the correct ratio of man and work. ITDC works towards rationalizing the size of the human resources so that the organization is trim and competent.
- Shareholders who have put their trust in the organization should be adequately compensated by creating value for them.
- Customers who are the backbone of any business venture should be provided with more than their money's worth so that they are satisfied and return for more.
- Construction of new hotels and other hospitality-related units, management of the existing ones and takeover of those hotels, motels, resorts, lodges and restaurants that are not doing well but have potential is one of the primary functions of the corporation.
- All other activities that are related to tourist facilities and interests such as transportation, entertainment, shopping, and facilities for conventions and meetings come in the purview of the functions of the corporation.
- Publicity matter related to tourism is envisioned, designed, produced and distributed by the corporation.
- ITDC also takes up consultancy and management of tourism-related projects in the country and overseas.
- Official money-changing facility for tourists. FFMC and restricted money changers are also the functions of the Corporation.
- Keeping tourism as the centre of the focus, the Corporation provides innovative and viable answers to problems related to the tourism and engineering industries that include the whole gamut; visualization, planning, strategy and implementation of project or consultancy as need to be.

- ITDC runs hotels and restaurants all over the country and also provides transportation for tourists. It is also involved in the production of publicity material related to tourism, entertainment of tourists, managing duty free shops and money changing facilities for tourists. The Ashok Institute of Hospitality & Tourism Management under the ITDC is one of the top hotel management institutes in the country. Other new ventures include engineering-related consultancy services and so on.

Current Properties

Presently, ITDC has a network of 8 Ashok Group of Hotels, 6 Joint Venture Hotels, 2 restaurants (including 1 airport restaurant), 12 transport units, 1 tourist service station, 37 duty-free shops at international as well as domestic customs airports, 1 tax-free outlet and 2 sound and light shows.

Besides, ITDC is also managing a hotel at Bharatpur and a restaurant at Kosi on behalf of the Department of Tourism. In addition, it is also managing catering services at Western Court, Vigyan Bhawan, Hyderabad House and National Media Press Centre at Shastri Bhawan, New Delhi.

Joint Venture Companies of ITDC

ITDC works in tandem with State Tourism Development Corporations or State Tourism Departments in joint ventures that run properties that have now gained popularity and acclaim.

Name of the Joint Venture Company	Name of the Hotel Property
Ranchi Ashok Bihar Hotel Corporation Ltd	Hotel Ranchi Ashok, Ranchi
Utkal Ashok Hotel Corporation Ltd	Hotel Nilachal Ashok, Puri
Donyi Polo Ashok Hotel Corporation Ltd	Hotel Donyi Polo Ashok, Itanagar
Assam Ashok Hotel Corporation Ltd	Hotel Brahmaputra Ashok, Guwahati
MP Ashok Hotel Corporation Ltd	Hotel lake View Ashok, Bhopal
Pondicherry Ashok Hotel Corporation Ltd	Hotel Pondicherry Ashok, Pondicherry
Punjab Ashok Hotel Company Ltd	Hotel Anandpur Ashok, Anandpur (project stage)

Source: www.theashokgroup.com

List of ITDC Hotels

- **The Ashok:** The Ashok, Delhi, the flagship hotel of ITDC, symbolizes and sets the tone for the brand 'Ashok' under which most of the activities of the Corporation are carried out. The Ashok is a grand hotel built in the late 60s in the distinctive environs of the Capital's Diplomatic Enclave. The architecture reminiscent of Mughal monuments that dot the city and the imposing facades live up to the image of tradition and heritage which is synonymous with the Ashok brand.
- **Samrat:** Just behind The Ashok in Delhi is Samrat, another well-planned and beautifully laid-out hotel. The hotel's manicured gardens, open courtyards, and the marble and stone edifice

surrounding an elegant atrium keep the hotel a notch apart from other run-of-the-mill hotels that are found in plenty in Delhi.

- **Janpath:** In the centre of the city, a stone's throw away from Connaught Place, Hotel Janpath on Janpath in New Delhi is a hotel of the ITDC that has the most convenient location and is immensely favoured because of it.

- **Lalitha Mahal Palace:** The royal abode of the Maharaja of Mysore, this heritage palace has been converted into a hotel and run by ITDC. Located on the outskirts of the city of Mysore, the palace with its domes and turrets amid sprawling grounds and terraced gardens is a sight to behold, and it provides a taste of regal luxury.

- **Bharatpur Ashok:** Located in the Keoladeo National Park, a wildlife and bird reserve which is a haven for hundreds of native bird varieties and migrant birds that visit the sanctuary every year from thousands of miles across the globe in winter for a better clime. The hotel is an ideal watering hole for bird watchers and nature lovers.

- **Jaipur Ashok:** The Jaipur Ashok, located in the Pink City is a small elegant Rajasthan Haveli with heritage architecture with turrets and balconies, built with the pink trademark stone of Jaipur. Surrounded by landscaped gardens, the hotel is favoured by foreigners who love to come to enjoy the traditions and heritage of Rajasthan.

- **Kalinga Ashok:** Located in Bhubaneswar, the ancient city of Odisha, Hotel Kalinga Ashok is a congenial combination of time-honoured, courteousness and modern lifestyle. Visitors can enjoy the real Odisha experience including traditional handicrafts, handloom weaves and the local cuisine.

- **Jammu Ashok:** At the foot of the Himalayas just outside the Kashmir Valley in Jammu, the winter capital of the Jammu and Kashmir state is Hotel Jammu Ashok, a modern hotel with all amenities for tourists to Kashmir and for pilgrims to the Vaishno Devi Shrine.

- **Patliputra Ashok:** Named after the ancient name of the city of Patna, Patliputra, Hotel Patliputra Ashok is popular among pilgrims on the Buddhist circuit, Rajgir, Gaya, Bodh Gaya and Vaishali, and also offers low-tariff rooms for visitors who are stopping over for a few hours in the day in Patna.

- **Lake View Ashok:** Overlooking the lake from the Shamla Hills in Bhopal, Hotel Lake View Ashok presents a pretty picture. The newly constructed four-floored building stands amidst beautifully landscaped gardens, and taking advantage of the location on the slope of the hill, the hotel has two floors above the level of the lobby and two floors below.

- **Brahmaputra Ashok:** Located in Guwahati, Assam, Brahmaputra Ashok is one of the most prominent hotels in the Northeast and caters to visitors to the business city of Guwahati and Kaziranga Wildlife Sanctuary famous for the mighty one-horned rhino. The modern hotel offering all the latest facilities and comforts is constructed in north-eastern style and furnished using local bamboo and cane furnishing.

- **Donyi Polo Ashok:** Located in Itanagar, the capital of Arunachal Pradesh, Donyi Polo Ashok offers modern amenities and local decor to the visitors of the beautiful state of the rising sun.

- **Pondicherry Ashok:** Hotel Pondicherry Ashok is a popular 3-star beach resort on the east coast of India. Pondicherry is a beautiful place with white and sunny beaches, and peaceful green forests. The hotel offers modern amenities and a peaceful holiday break.

- **Nilanchal Ashok:** Located close to the sparkling white sands of the beaches of Puri, near the famous temple of Lord Jagannath, the hotel provides all creature comfort to the visitors to the pilgrim city.

- **Ranchi Ashok:** Located in Ranchi, the capital of Chhattisgarh state, Hotel Ranchi Ashok offers all modern amenities to the visitors to Ranchi and the Chota Nagpur plateau.

Transportation

Transportation facilities available are as follows:

- **Taxi service at airport:** ITDC operates travel counters at Indira Gandhi International Airport Domestic and International Terminals. The counters are located in the arrival halls of both terminals. Other services: Car rentals, air tickets and hotel booking.
- **Car rentals:** Ashok Travels and Tours, a division of ITDC, offers cars, luxury limousines and coaches, local sightseeing, and trips to nearby cities for business or pleasure.
- **Air ticketing:** Ashok Travels and Tours, a division of ITDC, is IATA-approved travel agent that offers economical domestic and international air ticketing facilities for all airlines.
- **Money changing:** Ashok Travels and Tours, a division of ITDC, operates an FFMC operation dealing in all main legal tenders of the world such as Euros, US dollars, pound sterling and Australian dollars in keeping with the regulations and rules of the Reserve Bank of India. This facility is available at airports at Delhi, Mumbai, Chennai, Kolkata and Bangalore.

International Hotel & Restaurant Association (IHRA)

International Hotel & Restaurant Association	
Logo	 **ihra** INTERNATIONAL HOTEL & RESTAURANT ASSOCIATION
Headquarter	Lausanne, Switzerland
Regional offices	Global
Year of establishment	1947
Website	www.ih-ra.org

Introduction

It was officially founded in November 1947 in London as the International Hotels Association. In 1949, it was registered by the French Government and was headquartered in Paris, France, from 1949 to 2007. As of January 2008, the corporate headquarter is located in Lausanne, Switzerland. IHRA is the only business organization representing the hospitality industry worldwide. Its members are national hotel and restaurant associations throughout the world, and international and national hotel and restaurant chains representing some 50 brands. Officially recognized by the United Nations, IHRA monitors and lobbies all international agencies on behalf of this industry.

The IHRA is the only international trade association exclusively devoted to promoting and defending the interests of the hotel and restaurant industries worldwide. It is a non-profit organization and is officially recognized by the United Nations. IHRA monitors and lobbies all international agencies on behalf of the hospitality industry.

Members

Following are the members of the organization:

- International, national and regional hotel, and/or restaurant associations
- International and national hotel, and/or restaurant chains
- Owners, developers and investors
- Individual hotels and restaurants
- Institutions of the industry (hotel schools, educational centres and universities)
- Students/independent hoteliers and restaurateurs

Functions of IHRA

The functions of IHRA are as follows:

- Represents the collective industry interests before policymakers.
- Lobby for better recognition of the hospitality industry worldwide.
- Lobby against damaging or costly attempts to regulate the industry.
- Creates Global Councils around industry issues to debate positions and create solutions.
- Listens to its members to ensure that all issues are addressed.
- Plans a series of Informative Council and Board meetings, and an annual congress.
- Provides support where requested to lend weight to local and regional issues.

United Nations Educational, Scientific and Cultural Organization (UNESCO)

The United Nations Educational, Scientific and Cultural Organization	
Logo	
Headquarter	Paris, France
Year of establishment	1945
website	www.unesco.org

Introduction

UNESCO is a specialized agency of the United Nations and was established in 1945. Its purpose is to contribute to peace and security by promoting international collaboration through education, science and culture to further universal respect for justice, the rule of law, and human rights along with fundamental freedom proclaimed in the United Nations. It is the heir of the League of Nations' International Committee on Intellectual Cooperation.

UNESCO pursues its objectives through five major programmes:

- Education
- Natural sciences
- Social/human sciences
- Culture and
- Communication/information

Projects sponsored by UNESCO include literacy, technical and teacher–training programmes; international science programmes; the promotion of independent media and freedom of the press; regional and cultural history projects; the promotion of cultural diversity; translations of the world literature; international cooperation agreements to secure the world's cultural and natural heritage (World Heritage Sites); the preservation of human rights; and attempts to bridge the worldwide digital divide. It is also a member of the United Nations Development Group.

UNESCO's aim is 'to contribute to the building of peace, the eradication of poverty, sustainable development and intercultural dialogue through education, the sciences, culture, communication and information'. Following are some of the programmes and activities of this organization that are of direct relevance to decision-makers in tourism:

- UNESCO is responsible for the world famous Heritage Sites that include popular tourist destinations such as Taj Mahal in Agra, India and Red square in Moscow, Russia.
- UNESCO is carrying out several projects worldwide about cultural tourism.

As of 2016, there are 35 World Heritage Sites in India that are recognized by the UNESCO. Out of these 35 sites, 27 are cultural sites and the other 8 are natural sites. The cultural sites in India are marked by their brilliant craftsmanship on stone. Most of the temples of India which are inscribed on this list are built with stone, without any mortar, and with brilliant sculptures carved on it. These World Heritage Sites in India are considered to be of immense cultural and natural importance in the world.

10.3. List of Heritage Sites in India

S. No.	Name	Region	Image	Year of Declaration	Description
1.	Kaziranga Wildlife Sanctuary	Assam, India		1985	Kaziranga Wildlife Sanctuary is located in the south bank of Brahmaputra River, Assam, the Northeastern state of India. It was declared a World Heritage Site by UNESCO in 1985 for its unique natural environment. The park, covering an area of 42,996 hectares, is the home to the world's largest population of the one-horned rhinoceros. There are many other mammals and birds species in the sanctuary.

| 2. | **Manas Wildlife Sanctuary** | Assam, India |  | 1985 | Manas Wildlife Sanctuary is located in Assam, India. It covers an area of 50,000 hectares in the plains of the Manas River. It was declared as a World Heritage Site by UNESCO in 1985 for its unique natural environment. The sanctuary is the habitat to several species of plants; 55 mammal species, 36 reptile species, 3 amphibians and 350 species of birds; and endangered species including tiger, pygmy hog, clouded leopard, sloth bear, Indian rhinoceros and wild buffaloes. |
| 3. | **Mahabodhi Temple** | Bihar, India |  | 2002 | Mahabodhi Temple Complex at Bodh Gaya is spread over an area of 4.86 hectares and inscribed in the UNESCO World Heritage Site List as a unique property of cultural and archaeological importance. The first temple was built by Emperor Ashoka in the 3rd century BC (260 BC) around the Bodhi Tree (*Ficus religiosa*) where Siddhartha (Gautama Buddha) was enlightened in 531 BC at the age of 35, and then propagated his divine knowledge of Buddhism to the world. However, the temples seen now are dated between 5th and 6th centuries AD. The structures have been built with bricks. The main temple is 50 m in height and is built in an Indian architectural style. It is the oldest temple in the Indian subcontinent built during the 'Golden Age' of Indian culture credited to the Gupta period. |

4.	**Humayun's Tomb**	Delhi, India		1993	Humayun's Tomb, Delhi, was built in 1570 by the second Mughal Emperor Humayun's widow Biga Begum (Hajji Begum). It was inscribed as a UNESCO World Heritage Monument in 1993 for its cultural importance. Its Mughal architectural style has been applauded as the 'necropolis of the Mughal dynasty' for its double domed elevation provided with *chhatris*. Apart from the tomb of Humayun, it has 150 tombs of various members of the royal family.
5.	**Qutb Minar**	Delhi, India		1993	Qutb Minar and its monuments were built in the beginning of the 13th century and are located in Delhi. It is a red sandstone tower of 72.5 m height with a base of 14.32 m, reducing to 2.75 m diameter at the top. History records its construction, initially by Qutub ud-Din Aibak in 1192, its completion by Iltutmish (1211–1236) and again by Alauddin Khalji (1296–1316). For its unique representation of the Islamic architectural and artistic excellence, it was adorned under the UNESCO World Heritage List.
6.	**Red Fort Complex**	Delhi, India		2003	The Palace, Red Fort Complex (Lal Qila) was built in the 17th century by Shah Jahan, the fifth Mughal Emperor as part of his new capital city of Shahjahanabad. It is located in Delhi and represents the glory of the Mughal rule and Mughal architecture. It was built between 1639 and 1648, with an area of 215,168 sq. m and rising to a height of 23 m on the right bank of the Yamuna River. The palace includes the

Diwan-i-Aam (Hall of Public Audience), comprises a series of richly engraved marble palace pavilions, interconnected by water channels called the 'Nehr-i-Bihishit' (Stream of Paradise), the Diwan-i-Khas (Private Audience Hall), and the Moti Masjid (Pearl Mosque built by Mughal Emperor Aurangzeb).

| 7. | **Churches and Convents of Goa** | Goa, India | | 1986 | Churches and Convents of Goa are monuments that were built by the Portuguese colonial rulers of Goa between 16th and 18th centuries. They were inscribed by UNESCO under the World Heritage List in 1986 as a cultural property. The most significant of these monuments is the Basilica of Bom Jesus, which enshrines the tomb containing the relics of St. Francis Xavier. These monuments of Goa, known as the 'Rome of the Orient', were established by different Catholic priests. Other popular churches are the Saint Catherine's Chapel, the Church and Convent of Saint Francis of Assisi, the SéCatedral de Santa Catarina, the Theatine Igreja da Divina Providência (São Caetano) and Igreja de Santo Agostinho (Church of Saint Augustine). The monuments are built with laterites and walls plastered with limestone mortar mixed with broken shells. |
| 8. | **Champaner-Pavagadh Archaeological Park** | Gujarat, India | | 2004 | Champaner-Pavagadh Archaeological Park is situated in a hill fortress of an early Hindu capital, and remains of the 16th-century capital of the state of Gujarat. It was inscribed in UNESCO World |

				Heritage Site in 2004 as a cultural site. There is a concentration of largely unexcavated archaeological, historical and living cultural heritage properties cradled in an impressive landscape which includes prehistoric sites. The Kalika Mata Temple on top of the Pavagadh Hill is considered to be an important shrine, attracting large number of pilgrims throughout the year.
9.	**Group of Monuments at Hampi**	Karnataka, India		1986	The Group of Monuments at Hampi is situated on the banks of the river Tungabhadra in Karnataka. Hampi includes the ruins of Dravidian temples and palaces of Vijayanagara, which was the former capital of the powerful Vijayanagara Empire. Hampi, as an important Hindu religious centre, has the Virupaksha Temple and several other monuments, which are part of the cultural heritage site in the UNESCO World Heritage List.
10.	**Group of Monuments at Pattadakal**	Karnataka, India		1987	The Group of Monuments in Pattadakal include nine outstanding architectural Hindu temples, as well as a Jain sanctuary in northern Karnataka. These are a remarkable combination of temples built by the Chalukya Dynasty in the 6th–8th century. The temples represent a remarkable fusion of the architectural features of northern (*Nagara*) and southern (*dravida*) India. Pattadakal is considered a Hindu holy city and within the heritage complex there are eight temples dedicated to Shiva. This was included in UNESCO World Heritage List in 1987.

11.	**Buddhist Monuments at Sanchi**	Madhya Pradesh, India		1989

Buddhist Monuments at Sanchi is located around 45 km far from Bhopal, the capital of Madhya Pradesh. These are a group of Buddhist monuments and stupa dated between 200 BC and 100 BC during the rule of Mauryan Empire, especially the great Ashoka. These Buddhist sanctuaries were active Buddhist religious monuments, which flourished till the 12th century. It was inscribed as a World Heritage Site by UNESCO in 1989 for its unique cultural importance.

12.	**Rock Shelters of Bhimbetka,**	Madhya Pradesh, India		2003

Rock Shelters of Bhimbetka is located in the foothills of the Vindhya Range in Madhya Pradesh. The rock shelters, discovered only in 1957, comprise a group of 'five clusters of rock shelters' with paintings that are inferred to date from the 'Mesolithic period right through to the Historical period', with the 21 villages surrounding them reflecting the traditions displayed in the rock paintings. It was inscribed as a World Heritage Site by UNESCO in 2003 as a unique cultural property of the past.

13.	**Khajuraho Group of Monuments**	Madhya Pradesh, India		1986

Khajuraho Group of Monuments attributed to the Chandela dynasty of the 10th century is located in Madhya Pradesh. India. Out of the 85 temples built, only 22 temples have survived in an area of 6 sq. km. It was inscribed by UNESCO as a World Heritage Site, a cultural property in 1986 for its unique original artistic creation and proof of the Chandela culture that existed prior to the Muslim invasion of India in the early 12th century.

14.	**Ajanta Caves**	Maharashtra, India		1983	Ajanta Caves, listed under UNESCO World Heritage as a cultural heritage site, are Buddhist caves that were built in two phases. The first phase was from 2nd century BC. The second phase was made during the 5th and 6th centuries AD of the Gupta period. As a whole, there are 31 rock-cut cave monuments which are unique representations of the religious art of Buddhism.
15.	**Ellora Caves**	Maharashtra, India		1983	Ellora Caves are a cultural mix of religious arts of Buddhism, Hinduism and Jainism dating from 600 to 1000 AD. There are 34 monasteries and temples sculpted contiguously into rock walls of a high basalt cliff. They are a reflection of artistic creation of the ancient civilization of India. This cultural property has been inscribed under the UNESCO World Heritage list.
16.	**Elephanta Caves**	Maharashtra, India		1987	The Elephanta Caves are sculpted caves located on the Elephanta Island of the Arabian Sea in Mumbai Harbour, 10 km to the east of the city of Mumbai. The rock-cut architecture of the caves is dated between the 5th and 8th centuries. The island consists of two groups of caves—the first is a large group of five Hindu caves, and the second, a smaller group of two Buddhist caves. The Hindu caves contain rock-cut stone sculptures, dedicated to the god Shiva. The caves are made with solid basalt rock. The caves were designated in UNESCO World Heritage Site in 1987 to preserve the artwork.

17.	**Chhatrapati Shivaji Terminus (Victoria Terminus)**	Maharashtra, India		2004

The one of the busiest railway stations in India, Chhatrapati Shivaji Terminus, is a historic railway station in Mumbai, and headquarter of the Central Railways of India. The station was designed by Frederick William Stevens, a consulting architect in 1887–1888. It took 10 years to complete and was named 'Victoria Terminus' in the honour of the Queen and Empress Victoria. This famous architectural landmark in Gothic style was built as the headquarter of the Great Indian Peninsular Railway. In 1996, the station was renamed by the state government after the 17th century Maratha king Chhatrapati Shivaji. In 2004, the station was designated as a World Heritage Site by the UNESCO.

18.	**Sun Temple, Konârak**	Puri District, Odisha, India		1984

Konark Sun Temple is a 13th century built Temple (also known as the 'Black Pagoda'), at Konark, Odisha. It was built in the form of the chariot of the sun god, Surya (Arka), with 24 wheels, and is heavily decorated with symbolic stone carvings and led by a team of six horses. It was constructed with sandstone by King Narasimhadeva I of the Eastern Ganga Dynasty. The temple was inscribed in World Heritage List in 1984 as cultural property by UNESCO.

19.	**Keoladeo National Park**	Bharatpur, Rajasthan, India		1985

Keoladeo National Park in Bharatpur, Rajasthan, extends over an area of 2,783 hectares. It was declared a national park in 1982 and was inscribed in the UNESCO World Heritage List in 1985. It is famous for 364 species of migratory birds that come in large numbers from Afghanistan, Turkmenistan, China and Siberia.

20.	**Jantar Mantar, Jaipur**	Jaipur, Rajasthan, India		2010	The Jantar Mantar in Jaipur is a collection of architectural astronomical observatory, built by Maharaja Jai Singh II. He had constructed five such observatory at different locations. The Jaipur observatory is the largest and best preserved of these and has a set of some 20 main fixed instruments built in masonry. It has been designated as cultural property on the UNESCO World Heritage List as 'an expression of the astronomical skills and cosmological concepts of the court of a scholarly prince at the end of the Mughal period'.
21.	**Great Living Chola Temples**	Brihadisvara Temple, Gangaikonda Cholapuram, Tamil Nadu, India		1987	The Great Living Chola Temples were built by the kings of the Chola dynasty stretched over all of Tamil Nadu. This cultural heritage site includes three great temples of 11th and 12th centuries, namely the Brihadisvara Temple at Thanjavur, the Brihadisvara Temple at Gangaikonda Cholapuram and the Airavatesvara Temple at Darasuram. These temples are the brilliant achievements of the Chola dynasty in architecture, sculpture, painting and bronze casting. The site was inscribed under UNESCO World Heritage List in 1987 as cultural heritage.
		Airavatesvara Temple, Darasuram, Tamil Nadu, India		1987	
		Brihadisvara Temple, Thanjavur, Tamil Nadu, India		1987	
22.	**Group of Monuments at Mahabalipuram**	Mamallapuram, Tamil Nadu, India		1984	The Group of Monuments at Mamallapuram is situated about 58 km from Chennai, the capital of Tamil Nadu and was built by the Pallava kings in the 7th and 8th centuries. The temple town has approximately 400 monuments, including the largest open-air rock relief in the world. It was inscribed under the UNESCO World Heritage list in 1984 as a cultural heritage site.

23.	**Agra Fort**	Uttar Pradesh, India		1983	The Agra Fort (Red Fort of Agra), built in red sandstone, is located on the right bank of the Yamuna River, and covers a length of 2.5 km. This was built from the 16th century onwards till the early 18th century, starting with Emperor Akbar's reign (in the 16th century) to Aurangzeb (in the early part of the 18th century). The Fort includes the Khas Mahal, the Shish Mahal, Diwan-i-Khas, Diwan-i-Am, the Pearl Mosque and the Nagina Masjid. It is very close to the famous Taj Mahal, and represented Mughal affluence and power as the centrepiece of their empire. It was inscribed in the UNESCO World Heritage List in 1983.
24.	**Fatehpur Sikri**	Uttar Pradesh, India		1986	Fatehpur Sikri (the City of Victory) was built during the second half of the 16th century by the Mughal Emperor Akbar. It was the capital of the Empire. The construction was completed in 1573 in Mughal architectural style. It includes one of the largest mosques in India, the Jama Masjid, the Buland Darwaja, the Panch Mahal and the Tomb of Salim Chishti.
25.	**Taj Mahal**	Uttar Pradesh, India		1983	The great Taj Mahal, one of the Seven Wonders of the World, is a mausoleum. It was built by Emperor Shah Jahan in the memory of his third wife, Begum Mumtaj Mahal, who died in 1631. It was made with white marble in typical Mughal architecture style. This was built over 16 years between 1631 and 1648. It has an octagonal layout marked by four exclusive minarets at four corners with a pristine elevation of a central bulbous

dome below which the tombs are laid in an underground chamber glorifying the monument's graphic beauty. It was inscribed in the UNESCO World Heritage List in 1983 as a cultural monument.

26.	**Mountain Railways of India**	Darjeeling Himalayan Railway, West Bengal		1999
		Nilgiri Mountain Railway, Ooty, Tamil Nadu		1999
		Kalka–Shimla Railway, Himachal Pradesh. India		1999

The Mountain Railways of India represents a collective listing of the Darjeeling Himalayan Railway, the Nilgiri Mountain Railway and the Kalka–Shimla Railway under the UNESCO World Heritage Site. The World Heritage UNESCO recognition to those three Railways of India has been stated as for being 'outstanding examples of bold, ingenious engineering solutions for the problem of establishing an effective rail link through a rugged, mountainous terrain'. The Darjeeling Himalayan Railway was recognized first in 1999, the Nilgiri Mountain Railway followed suite as an extension to the site in 2005, and in 2008 the Kalka–Shimla Railway was further added as an extension; and the three together have been titled as Mountain Railways of India.

27.	**Nanda Devi and Valley of Flowers National Parks**	Chamoli District, Uttarakhand, India		1988

Nanda Devi and Valley of Flowers National Parks are situated in West Himalaya. Valley of Flowers National Park is well known for its alpine flowers and outstanding natural beauty. It is located in the Garhwal Himalayas of Chamoli District of Uttarakhand. This richly diverse area is also home to rare and endangered animals such as Asiatic black bear, snow leopard and blue sheep.

The beautiful landscape of the Valley of Flowers National Park complements the rugged mountain wilderness of Nanda Devi National Park. The park was established as a national park in 1982 and inscribed under the UNESCO World Heritage List in 1988 with extension in 2005. Together, they comprise the Nanda Devi Biosphere Reserve, which is on the UNESCO World Network of Biosphere Reserves since 2004.

| 28. | **Sundarbans National Park** | West Bengal | | 1987 |

The Sundarbans National Park, the largest estuarine mangrove forest in the world, is located in the Ganges river delta bordering the Bay of Bengal, West Bengal. It is in the world's largest delta of 80,000 km^2 formed from sediments deposited by the three great rivers, the Ganges, the Brahmaputra and the Meghna, which are flowing together in the Bengal Basin. It is a national park, tiger reserve, a biosphere reserve and a UNESCO World Heritage Site. The Sundarban as a whole includes 10,000 km^2 of land and water. Out of this, about 5,980 km^2 is in India and the balance is in Bangladesh. This region is densely covered by mangrove forests, and is one of the largest reserves for the Bengal tiger, variety of birds, reptiles and invertebrate species, including the salt-water crocodile. It was declared as the core area of Sunderban Tiger Reserve in 1973 and a wildlife sanctuary in 1977. In 1984, it was declared a National Park. It was inscribed on the UNESCO World Heritage List in 1987 as a natural property.

	Agasthyamalai		2012	Western Ghats, also known as the Sahyadri Mountains, is a mountain range along with the western side of India. This is one of the 10 'biodiversity hotspots' of the world. A total of 39 properties of national parks, wildlife sanctuaries and reserve forests were designated as World Heritage Sites. Out of these, 20 are in the state of Kerala, 10 in Karnataka, 5 in Tamil Nadu and 4 in Maharashtra.
	Periyar		2012	
	Anaimalai		2012	
29. **Western Ghats**	Nilgiri		2012	
	Talakaveri		2012	
	Kudremukh		2012	
	Chittorgarh		2013	Hill Forts of Rajasthan are a series of sites located on the Aravallis mountain range in Rajasthan. They represent a typology of Rajput hill architecture, a style characterized by its mountain peak settings, utilizing the defensive properties of the terrain. These hill forts in Rajasthan represent Rajput military strongholds across a vast range of geographical and cultural zones. Major hill forts of Rajasthan are: Chittorgarh Fort, Kumbhalgarh Fort, Ranthambore Fort, Amber Fort, Gagron Fort and Jaisalmer Fort.
	Kumbhalgarh		2013	
30. **Hill Forts of Rajasthan**	Ranthambhore		2013	
	Amber		2013	
	Jaisalmer		2013	

| 31. | Rani ki Vav (The Queen's Step well) | Patan, Gujarat, India | | 2014 | Rani ki Vav (The Queen's Stepwell) at Patan, Gujarat, is a famous stepwell. Rani Ki Vav is an 11th-century stepwell situated in the town of Patan in Gujarat, India, on the banks of the Saraswati River. The stepwell is said to have been constructed by Udayamati, the widowed Queen of Bhimdev I (AD 1022–1064), around 1050 AD in the memory of the king. Bhimdev I was the son of Mularaja, the founder of the Solanki dynasty of AnahilwadaPatan. The stepwell was later flooded by the nearby Saraswati river and silted over until the late 1980s, when it was excavated by archaeologists. When restored, the stepwell's magnificent carvings were found in pristine condition. |
| 32. | Great Himalayan National Park | Himachal Pradesh, India | | 2014 | Great Himalayan National Park at Kullu, Himachal Pradesh, is characterized by high alpine peaks, alpine meadows and riverine forests. This is the upper mountain glacial and snow melt water source origin of several rivers, and the catchments of water supplies that are vital to millions of downstream users. This protects the monsoon-affected forests and alpine meadows of the Himalayan front ranges. It is part of the Himalaya biodiversity hotspot and includes 25 forest types along with a rich assemblage of fauna species, several of which are threatened. This gives the site outstanding significance for biodiversity conservation. |

33.	**Archaeological Site of Nalanda Mahavihara**	Bihar, India		2016	Nalanda Archaeological Site in Bihar was a centre of learning and a Buddhist monastery from 3rd century BC to the 13th century AD. One can witness the remains of stupas, shrines and *viharas* if someone visit around in the campus of this manifestation of a glorious epoch. Nalanda vouched for the evolution of Buddhism as a religion and remained an abode of knowledge for 800 years. Known for its formalized Vedic learning, scholars from as far as Tibet, China, Korea and Central Asia used to attend this first residential university of the world during that period.
34.	**Khangchendzonga National Park (KNP)**	Sikkim, India		2016	KNP, named after mountain Khangchendzonga, the third highest peak in the world was notified in the year 1977 with an area of 1,784 sq. km. About 29 species of widely used medicinal plants are recorded from the area. It is also a source of a variety of natural attractive materials in the form of decorative. KNP includes the Kangchenjunga Peak, which is the 3rd highest peak in the world. The national park is famous for its fauna and flora, with snow leopard being occasionally sighted. There are few trekking routes in this national park which are mainly developed for the trekking enthusiasts.
35.	**Chandigarh Capitol Complex**	Chandigarh, India		2016	The Capitol Complex in Chandigarh is famous for hosting the Legislative Assembly for both the states of Haryana and Punjab, High

Court and the Secretariat. Located in Chandigarh, this Capitol Complex was built when Chandigarh was being developed as the capital of Punjab in 1950 after the partition of India. This is the architectural work of **Le Corbusier** who built many unique architectural wonder in different countries of the world. The famous Capital Complex of Chandigarh is recognized as a World Heritage Site as part of outstanding contribution to Modern Movement. This was part of Le Corbusier's work, which he did in 17 countries in the first half of the 20th century.

Disclaimer: The images used in this table are for representation purpose only.

Conclusion

For the development of any industry, organizations play a crucial role for its growth, planning, development and promotion at various levels, and tourism industry is no exception to it. For any industry or discipline to flourish, an organization is an essential prerequisite as it plays a crucial role for its proper planning, development and growth. It is evident from the above discussion that these national, regional and international organizations' role is to strengthen tourism by the way of combined efforts which is necessary for a multidimensional industry like tourism and is therefore of vital importance. Organizations help in getting certain conclusions by effective discussion at different levels at different forums. In tourism industry, some organizations are international in character, whereas some are regional. There are also some international organizations in tourism industry which are not directly connected to tourism industry specifically but are closely related fields such as airlines, hotels and travel agencies. The authors would like to conclude that in today's scenario almost all the countries have one or more tourism organizations. This is due to the rapid growth of economy followed by the increase in awareness about tourism, financial and sociocultural advantages, increase in environmental awareness and so on, which can be achieved through systematic effort by forming different tourism and tourism-related organizations. It is also felt that the formation of tourism organization has a considerable impact on the stages of tourism development of any country, region or internationally. So the authors viewed that the formation and need for tourism organizations is a complex process involving different forms of organizations which are influenced by a variety of factors.

MODEL QUESTIONS

1. Analyse the need and importance of different organizations involved in tourism business.
2. Explain in brief the role and functions of IATA in international air transportation.
3. Write a note on the nature of organization and membership criteria of IATA.
4. Critically examine the role and functions of UNWTO for the promotion and development of tourism worldwide.
5. State and explain the aims and objectives of UNWTO.
6. Discuss various work programmes of UNWTO and explain the organs through which UNWTO functions.
7. Critically examine the activities and functions of TAAI for the promotion and development of travel agency business in India.
8. What is ICAO? Discuss the aims, objectives and functions of ICAO.
9. Briefly explain the membership criteria and activities of IATO for improving tour operations in India.
10. Critically examine the role and functions of ITDC for tourism development in India.
11. What is PATA? Explain its work programme and activities to promote and market tourism in the Asia-Pacific region.

Student Activities

1. Identify different newly formed national tourist organizations present in your country. List out their main objectives and membership criteria.
2. Find out the official dignitaries (President, Secretary) of different national and international tourism organizations.

Suggested Readings

Bennet, M. (1997). Strategic alliance in the world airline industry. *Progress in Tourism and Hospitality Research*, *3*(3), 213–223.

Bhatia, A. K. (1982). *Tourism development: Principles and practices*. New Delhi: Sterling Publishers Private limited.

Coltman, M. (1989). *Introduction to travel and tourism: An international approach*. New York, NY: Van Nostrand Reinhold.

Gartner, W. C. (1996). *Tourism development: Principles, processes and policies*. New York, NY: Van Nostrand Reinhold.

Gee, C. Y., Makens, J. C., & Choy, D. J. L. (1997). *The travel industry*. New York, NY: Van Nostrand Reinhold (a division of International Thomson Publishing Inc).

Goeldner, R. C., & Ritchie, J. R. B. (2009). *Tourism: Principles, practices, philosophies*. New Jersey, NJ: John Wiley & Sons.

Inskeep, E. (1991). *Tourism planning: An integrated and sustainable development approach*. New York, NY: Van Nostrand Reinhold.

Lumsdon, L., & Page, S. J. (Eds.). (2004). *Tourism and transport: Issues and agenda for the new millennium*. Oxford: Elsevier.

McIntosh, R. W., & Goeldner, R. C. (1984). *Tourism: Principles, practices and philosophies*. New York, NY: Willy.

Mill, R. C., & Morrison, A. M. (1992). *The tourism system—An introductory test*. New Jersey, NJ: Prentice-Hall Inc.
Page, S. J., & Connell, J. (2009). *Tourism: A modern synthesis* (3rd ed.). UK: Cengage Learning EMEA.
Wahab, S. (1975). *Tourism management*. London: Tourism International Press.

Suggested Websites

www.pata.org
www.iata.org
www.iato.in
www.travelagentsofindia.com
www.icao.int
www.unwto.org
www.asta.org
www.unesco.org
www.ihra.com

11   Legal Aspects of Tourism

LEARNING OBJECTIVES

After studying this chapter, the reader will be able to understand the following:

- ❐ The need, importance and purposes of tourism legislations
- ❐ The application of consumer protection law in tourism
- ❐ The Passports Act
- ❐ The Tourism Bill of Right and Tourist Code
- ❐ The classification and star gradation of hotels in India
- ❐ The important statement of Manila Declaration in tourism
- ❐ The major findings of different tourism conventions, especially Warsaw Convention and Chicago Convention
- ❐ The major guidelines of the Global Code of Ethics for Tourism (GCET)
- ❐ The importance of Wild Life (Protection) Act, 1972

CHAPTER OVERVIEW

Chapter 11 discusses legal aspects and their application in tourism business. The need, importance and purposes of legislations are discussed in this chapter. This chapter mainly deals with understanding tourism law, code of conducts and different acts which are applicable to tourism industry. Various legal issues involved in tourism business, especially in the Indian context, are discussed in this chapter. Code of ethics for tourism, Wild Life (Protection) Act, Passports Act and so on are also described in this chapter.

11.1. Introduction

Presence of a logical and well-defined legal and regulatory framework for tourism with all stakeholders will always help to identify current gaps and constraints in legislation related to tourism planning, development, management and promotion. Formulation of a properly organized legal and regulatory framework will lead to the achievement of sustainable development and management of tourism including protection and conservation of natural and cultural resources, and facilitation of the involvement of private sector and local communities in tourism development activities. These laws and regulations will reflect the roles and responsibilities of all stakeholders, ensure the rights of international/local tourists, and ensure the rights and obligations of participating businesses, inbound and outbound tour operators and all other concerned players in the field of tourism. These legal and regulatory aspects will provide benefit to different players of tourism industry including the following:

- Government bodies (both at the national and the international levels)
- National tourism administrations
- Destination management organizations
- Specialized agencies/organizations involved in tourism business
- Private sector
- Local communities

Different laws on tourism determine the principles, regulations and measures on the establishment, activities and administration of tourism, with the aim to promote, develop and extend different forms of tourism such as cultural, historical and natural tourism in sustainable ways. Main objectives of these laws are to transform tourism industry into a modern service industry, to contribute to national protection and development, and to promote mutual understanding, peace, friendship and cooperation in international development.

The impact of tourism is both positive and negative. Tourism brings many positive benefits to tourists such as enjoyment, relaxation, recreation, recuperation, widening of horizons and social contacts and change of environments. It also upgrades the standard of living and values, preserves cultural heritage and fosters international understanding. Haphazard and improper planning of tourism may also bring some negative impacts such as social tension, distortion of lifestyle and cultural decay. Globalization of tourism also leads to inevitable commercialization of ethnic arts and crafts, cheapening of the artistic values and the pattern of consumption in the host population. Instances of social problems like prostitution, pedophilia, immoral traffic, gambling, drug trafficking, human trafficking theft, smuggling of antiques, etc., increase crime resulting in deteriorating the social values. Uncontrolled inflow of tourists of different cultures often breaks down traditional, social and cultural values in the destination.

There are certain laws which regulate tourist movement and activities, especially tourist immigration, frontier formalities, travel, accommodation, behaviour and so on. Sometimes there are also certain restrictions on tourist movement in certain areas of the country. There are certain specific laws which prohibit tourists from doing certain things. A sound knowledge of various laws regarding tourists, travel agencies, immigration, passport, visa, customs and so on is essential for every stakeholder of the tourism industry.

11.2. The Purposes of Tourism Laws

Tourism laws generally refer to either the general government regulations or specific travel and hospitality industry laws. They are mainly a combination of state, federal and international laws that regulate various aspects and functions of the travel industry. For example, travel laws may involve anything from hospitality to employment to public health regulations.

According to **UNWTO**,

The main purpose of travel legislation is to provide a regulatory framework for the proper development and management of tourism activities. Ideally, this will help in the conservation of natural resources and the preservation of cultural traditions. As an added benefit, travel consumers and organizations receive basic legal protection. (https://www.besthospitalitydegrees.com/faq/what-is-tourism-law)

The main purpose of tourism laws includes the following:

- Protect and conserve the natural resources, culture and customs, which serve as the foundation of the tourism sector
- Govern the development of the tourism sector in a sustainable manner effectively to reduce poverty
- Ensure and promote the quality of tourism services in the state/country through the introduction of a quality assurance system by providing security, safety and comfort and by increasing tourists' satisfaction
- Minimize negative impacts and maximize positive impacts of the tourism sector
- Seek markets and enhance publicity with participation of both the public and private sectors
- Develop human resources in the tourism sector
- Contribute to the development of international friendship and understanding through the tourism industry

11.3. Role of Legislation in Tourism Development

Tourism legislation helps in identifying the roles and responsibilities of various government and private agencies at different levels (international, national, regional and local) in tourism planning and development. It is always necessary to have consensus while formulating legislation for tourism at different levels. This can be achieved by maintaining consistency with national tourism and development policy, reviewing of existing regulations, reviewing of existing classification guidelines, finding core legal issues and building quality assurance and increasing professionalism including facilitating business development.

The draft tourism law should be prepared based on these aforementioned factors, which will lead to the achievement of sustainable development, management and regulation of the tourism industry, which will cater to the needs of the government, industry suppliers and consumers for determining their rights and obligations.

Since a self-regulatory mechanism is not enough to ensure sustainable development to control negative practices of the tourism industry, a specific and comprehensive legislative enactment is compulsory for the benefit of the tourism industry. Therefore, a specific tourism law is necessary for developing tourism in relation to the standards, licensing requirements and inspection procedures for different players of tourism and hospitality industry such as hotels and restaurants, travel agencies, tour operation business, tourist guides and other professionals.

11.4. Consumer Protection Law in Tourism (1986)

The Consumer Protection Act and its implications in general have been discussed before at various levels at various places, but the impact of the law relating to the consumer protection on a specific sector such as tourism and travel is unique.

Players in Consumer Protection Law in Tourism

As we all know the aim of the existing legislation is to provide redressal to the complaints of tourists against their exploitation by the **unscrupulous shopkeepers, tourist guides, taxi drivers, unauthorized travel agents and tour operators** and so on. The problem usually faced by the tourists (both foreign and domestic) because of the unfair practices done by service providers such as cancellation of airlines reservations, not providing of the facilities, etc., can also be checked by the existing legislation.

Features of Consumer Protection Law

The Consumer Protection Act (1986) categorizes the 'consumer' in two broad classes: consumers of goods and consumers of services. Buyers of goods for noncommercial purposes are in one class, and those who hire or avail any services including the beneficiary of the services with approval of the person who has hired or availed of the services are in the other class. Under the Act complaint could be in respect of an unfair trade practice or a restrictive trade practice alleged to have been avowed by a trader, the goods bought by the consumers or agreed to be bought by a consumer suffered from one or more defects, the service hired or availed of or agreed to be hired or availed of by a consumer suffered from deficiency in any respect, charging of price in excess of the price fixed by or under any law for the time being in force or displayed on the goods or a package, containing such goods by the trader which will be hazardous to life and safety been offered for sale to the public in contravention of the provisions of law for the time being in force, requiring trader to display information in regard to the contents, manner and effect of use of such goods.

Defect has been defined to mean any fault, imperfection or shortcoming in the quality, quantity, potency, purity or standard which is required to be maintained by or under any law for the time being in force or under any contract, express or implied or as is claimed by the trade in any manner whatsoever in relation to any goods.

Deficiency has been defined to mean any fault, imperfection, shortcoming or inadequacy in the quality, nature and manner of performance which is required to be maintained by or under any law for the time being in force or to be undertaken pursuant to the contract or otherwise in relation to any service. One has to bear in mind that the act does not impose any additional liability on any one and does not confer any additional right on anyone.

Whatever rights are available and liabilities are imposed under the existing general law or under the contract between the parties are the only basis on which the provision of the Act could be invoked. The only difference is that the Act provides an alternate forum of disputes redressal to the normal machinery of resolution of disputes through law courts. This alternative mechanism dispute resolution is expected to be a speedier and easier remedy.

Aim

The Act aims to achieve the protection of the consumers in two ways. One is preventive and the other is remedial. The preventive aspect of consumer protection is sought to be achieved by establishment of consumer protection council under Chapter II of the Act. Under the Act there has to be one consumer protection council at the national level and one state consumer protection council at the state level.

The objectives of these councils are to promote and protect the rights of the consumer such as the right to be protected against the following:

- Marketing of goods and services which are hazardous to the life and property
- The right to be informed about the quality, quantity, potency and standards
- The price of goods and services as the case may be, so as to protect the consumer against unfair trade practices
- The right to be assured, wherever possible, of access to a variety of goods and services at the competitive price
- The right to be heard and assured that consumers' interests will receive due consideration at appropriate forums
- The right to seek redressal against unfair trade practices or restrictive trade practices or unscrupulous exploitation of consumers and the right to consumer education

Thus, the function of promoting and protecting the right of the consumer has been assigned to the consumer protection councils set-up under this act.

Remedial Measures

So far as the remedial part of it is concerned, a three-tier system for resolution of consumer disputes has been set up.

1. At the lowest rank is the District Consumer Disputes Redressal Forum.
2. At the state level there is a State Consumer Disputes Redressal Commission.
3. At the national level there is a National Consumer Disputes Redressal Commission.

Disputes not exceeding the valuation (in India) of ₹5 lakh are recognizable by the District Forum. Disputes of valuation of above ₹5 lakh and up to ₹20 lakh are recognizable by the National Commission. The State Commission has an appellate jurisdiction over the District Forum and National Commission has an appellate jurisdiction over the State Commission. Besides, in deserving cases revisional powers can be exercised by the State Commission and the National Commission.

Application in the Field of Tourism

When we view the problems of a consumer in the field of tourism and travel in the background of the aforesaid provisions of law, it would be clear that so far as the remedial part of the Consumer Protection Act, namely the consumer dispute redressal agencies is concerned; there would hardly be any difference in the problem of the consumer in general and the consumer in the field of tourism and travel. The preventive part of the Act has set up Consumer Protection Councils with the avowed object of promoting and protecting the right of the consumers in specific consumer areas. Thus, the consumer protection councils may take steps for proper exercise by a consumer of his rights to be informed about the quality, quantity, potency, purity, standards and the price of goods and services to protect the consumer against unfair trade practices. The consumer protection council may also ensure that the proper exercise by a consumer of his rights to be assured, access to a variety of goods and services at competitive prices. Similarly, it is for the consumer protection councils to ensure that the consumers' interest will receive due consideration at the appropriate redressal forum. Problems faced by the consumers in different fields of trade or services are bound to differ in detail. For example, the complaints of tourists against their exploitation by the unscrupulous shopkeepers, guides, taxi drivers and unauthorized travel agents though not very different from the complaints of the consumers in the other fields, require special measure to be taken for redressal because what differentiates the case of a tourist as a consumer from that of a normal consumer is that a tourist consumer purchases goods and hires services at a place different than the place of his normal residence and is mostly a one-time buyer or a one-time hirer of service at a particular place, from a particular shopkeeper or a person who gives services on hire. Such a consumer is all the more vulnerable because as soon as he leaves the place where the goods were bought or services were hired by him, because of constraints of long distances he cannot seek redressal easily and mostly has to suffer in silence. This is the most encouraging factor for the unscrupulous shopkeepers and lenders of services to cheat the tourist consumer with the sense of impunity.

Remedial Measures

So far as the foreign tourist is concerned, he or she is the most gullible and vulnerable to these malpractices. Remedial measures can be taken in the shape of the following:

- Recognition
- Licencing
- Registration of specific shops at the various tourist centres where standardized goods and services at fixed rates would be available

The tourist can be advised to buy goods from such registered and licenced shops only to avoid cheating. The licence conditions may provide for an arbitration clause for resolving the disputes relating to complaints of the tourists. Failure to comply with the licence condition should result in cancellation of the licence and the registration.

Similar arrangements can be made to regulate the charging of fees by guides and fares by taxi drivers and so on. Standardization of rates and fees for guides, and charging of fares by the taxi drivers would go a long way in curbing the malpractices. For example, the fixed fare taxi service introduced not so long ago at the major airports of the country has archived very good results in saving the tourists from cheating by unscrupulous taxi drivers. So far as the problems of both foreign and domestic tourists regarding cancellation of airline reservation and so on are concerned, standard rules and standard terms of contract could be provided so that no one is in the dark about what exactly is expected of him. Deviation from such standard rules could then easily be taken as deficiency in services. The present rule of cancellation of reservations in airlines as also in the railways, prima facie appears to be expropriator and confiscatory in nature. If a passenger with a confirmed ticket on a flight does not turn up before a specific time prior to departure of flight, according to the present rules he loses the entire cost of ticket. In his place the airline can take a passenger on a waitlist ticket. Thus, the airline get a passenger in lieu of a passenger who has not reported in time and are not at any loss but the passenger with a confirmed ticket losses his/her entire money. The airlines get doubly paid for the same seat. Is it not the case of unjust enrichment? Similar is the case with the rules of cancellation for the loss suffered by the railways and has become a penalty on the passenger for not turning up in time or not getting the tickets cancelled within a specified time. Appropriate measures by amending rules or laws can be taken to redress these grievances.

Conclusion

Most of the problems of a tourist have their roots in the absence of any standard, universally accepted norms regulating the trade. If the standard of the quality of service and the rate at which it shall be available are laid down and revised periodically as per market exigencies, everyone would be clear about whether in a particular case the service was deficient or not. The lender of the services shall also be clear in his/her mind as to what is expected of him/her. This will lead to reduction in number of cases of deficiency in services and increase the number of cases settled mutually between the parties without intervention of dispute redressal agencies.

11.5. Passports Act (1967)

This is an Act to provide for the issue of passports and travel documents, to regulate the departure from India of the citizens of India and for other persons and for matter incidental or ancillary thereto. It was enacted by the Parliament in the 18th year of the Republic of India as follows:

1. Short Title and extent

    a. This Act may be called as Passport Act, 1967.
    b. It extends to the whole of India and applies also to the citizens of India who are outside India.

2. Definitions

The context which has been used is defined as follows:

    a. *Departure:* Means departure from India by water, land or air
    b. *Passport:* Means a passport issued or deemed to have been issued under this Act
    c. *Passport authority:* Refers to an officer or authority empowered under rules made under this Act to issue passports or travel documents and includes the Central Government
    d. *Prescribed:* Means the rules which are prescribed under this Act
    e. *Travel documents:* Are those which are issued or deemed to be issued under this Act

3. Classifications of passport/travel documents

    a. The following types of passports may be issued under this act namely:
        A. Ordinary/general passport
        B. Official passport
        C. Diplomatic passport
    b. The other travel documents which are necessary and are issued under this Act are as follows:
        A. The emergency certificate authorizing a person to enter India
        B. Certificate of identity for the purpose of establishing the identity of the person
        C. Such other certificates or documents as may be prescribed
        D. The central government can prescribe any document as required.

Following information is essential for the passport application form:

File Number (For Office Use Only)

GOVERNMENT OF INDIA, MINISTRY OF EXTERNAL AFFAIRS
PASSPORT APPLICATION FORM

Please read the Passport Instruction Booklet carefully before filling the form. Fill this form in CAPITAL LETTERS using blue/ black ink ball point pen only. Furnishing of incorrect information/ suppression of information would lead to rejection of the application and would attract penal provisions as prescribed under the Passports Act, 1967. Please produce your original documents at the time of submission of the form.

1. Service Required

1.1 Applying for ☐ Fresh Passport ☐ Re-issue of Passport

1.2 If re-issue, specify reason(s)

☐ Validity Expired within 3 years/ Due to Expire ☐ Exhaustion of Pages

☐ Validity Expired more than 3 years ago ☐ Lost Passport

☐ Change in Existing Personal Particulars ☐ Damaged Passport

1.3 If change in existing personal particulars, specify reason(s)

☐ Appearance ☐ Signature ☐ Given Name

☐ Surname ☐ Date of Birth ☐ Spouse Name

☐ Address ☐ Delete ECR ☐ Others, Please specify

Please paste your unsigned recent colour photograph with white background of size 4.5cm X 3.5cm. [Not needed for applicants submitting the application at Passport Seva Kendra]

Signature/ Left Hand Thumb Impression of Illiterate Applicant and Minors who cannot sign.

1.4 Type of Application ☐ Normal ☐ Tatkaal

1.5 Type of Passport Booklet ☐ 36 Pages ☐ 60 Pages

1.6 Validity Required ☐ 10 Years ☐ Up to age 18
(For minors between 15 and 18 years)

2. Applicant Details

2.1 Applicant's Given Name (Given Name means First name followed by Middle name (If any))(Initials not allowed)

Surname

2.2 Are you known by any other names (aliases)? ☐ Yes ☐ No
If yes, provide details in Column 1 of Supplementary Form

2.3 Have you ever changed your name? ☐ Yes ☐ No
If yes, provide details in Column 2 of Supplementary Form

Page 1 of 6

2.4 Date of Birth (DD-MM-YYYY) ⬜⬜ - ⬜⬜ - ⬜⬜⬜⬜

2.5 Place of Birth (Village or Town or City)

⬜⬜⬜⬜⬜⬜⬜⬜⬜⬜⬜⬜⬜⬜⬜⬜⬜⬜⬜⬜⬜⬜⬜⬜⬜⬜⬜⬜⬜⬜

District (If born in India)

⬜⬜⬜⬜⬜⬜⬜⬜⬜⬜⬜⬜⬜⬜⬜⬜⬜⬜⬜⬜⬜⬜⬜⬜⬜⬜⬜⬜⬜⬜

State/ UT (If born in India)

⬜⬜⬜⬜⬜⬜⬜⬜⬜⬜⬜⬜⬜⬜⬜⬜⬜⬜⬜⬜⬜⬜⬜⬜⬜⬜⬜⬜⬜⬜

Country (If born abroad) If born before 15/08/1947 in a place now in Pakistan or Bangladesh, write "Undivided India"

⬜⬜⬜⬜⬜⬜⬜⬜⬜⬜⬜⬜⬜⬜⬜⬜⬜⬜⬜⬜⬜⬜⬜⬜⬜⬜⬜⬜⬜⬜

2.6 Gender ⬜ Male ⬜ Female ⬜ Transgender

2.7 Marital Status ⬜ Single ⬜ Married ⬜ Divorced ⬜ Widow/ Widower ⬜ Separated

2.8 Citizenship of India by ⬜ Birth ⬜ Descent ⬜ Registration/ Naturalization

2.9 PAN (If available)   **2.10 Voter ID (If available)**

⬜⬜⬜⬜⬜⬜⬜⬜⬜⬜   ⬜⬜⬜⬜⬜⬜⬜⬜⬜⬜⬜⬜⬜⬜⬜⬜⬜

2.11 Employment Type

⬜ PSU ⬜ Government ⬜ Statutory Body ⬜ Retired Government Servant ⬜ Self Employed

⬜ Private ⬜ Homemaker ⬜ Not Employed ⬜ Retired-Private Service ⬜ Student

⬜ Others ⬜ Owners, Partners & Directors of companies which are members of CII, FICCI & ASSOCHAM

2.12 If employed in Government/ Statutory Body/ PSU, specify organization name

⬜⬜⬜⬜⬜⬜⬜⬜⬜⬜⬜⬜⬜⬜⬜⬜⬜⬜⬜⬜⬜⬜⬜⬜⬜⬜⬜⬜⬜⬜

⬜⬜⬜⬜⬜

2.13 Is either of your parent (in case of minor)/ spouse, a government servant? ⬜ Yes ⬜ No

2.14 Educational Qualification

⬜ 7th pass or less   ⬜ Between 8th and 9th Standard

⬜ 10th pass and above   ⬜ Graduate and above

2.15 Are you eligible for Non-ECR category? ⬜ Yes ⬜ No For details, see Column 2.15, section B of Instruction Booklet

2.16 Visible Distinguishing Mark

⬜⬜⬜⬜⬜⬜⬜⬜⬜⬜⬜⬜⬜⬜⬜⬜⬜⬜⬜⬜⬜⬜⬜⬜⬜⬜⬜⬜⬜⬜

⬜⬜⬜⬜⬜

2.17 Aadhaar Number ⬜⬜⬜⬜⬜⬜⬜⬜⬜⬜⬜⬜

3. Family Details

3.1 Father's Given Name (Given Name means First name followed by Middle name (If any)) (Initials not allowed)

Surname

3.2 Mother's Given Name (Given Name means First name followed by Middle name (If any)) (Initials not allowed)

Surname

3.3 Legal Guardian's Given Name (If applicable) (Initials not allowed)

Surname

3.4 Spouse's Given Name (Given Name means First name followed by Middle name (If any)) (Initials not allowed)

Surname

3.5 If applicant is minor, provide following details

Parent's Passport Details (If passport has been applied for but not received, give File Number)

Father/ Legal Guardian's File/ Passport Number   Father/ Legal Guardian's Nationality, if not Indian

Mother/ Legal Guardian's File/ Passport Number   Mother/ Legal Guardian's Nationality, if not Indian

4. Present Residential Address Details (Where applicant presently resides)
4.2 House No. and Street Name

Village or Town or City

District

Police Station

State/ UT

PIN

Mobile Number

Telephone Number

E-mail ID

4.3 Is permanent address same as present address? ☐ Yes ☐ No If no, provide details in Column 4 of Supplementary Form

5. Emergency Contact Details

Name and Address (Mention address only if different from present residential address)

Mobile Number

Telephone Number

E-mail ID

7. Previous Passport/ Application Details

7.1 Details of latest held/ existing/ lost/ damaged Ordinary Passport/ Identity Certificate

Passport/ Identity
Certificate Number   Date of Issue (DD-MM-YYYY)   Date of Expiry (DD-MM-YYYY)

Place of Issue

If you have held/ hold any diplomatic/ official passport, provide details in Column 6 of Supplementary Form

7.2 Have you ever applied for passport, but not issued? ☐ Yes   ☐No If yes, provide the following
                                                                                          details
File Number   Month and Year of applying

Name of passport office where applied

8. Other details

	Yes	No
8.1 Have you ever been charged with criminal proceedings or any arrest warrant/ summon pending before a court in India?	☐	☐

  If yes, fill Column 7.1 of Supplementary Form

8.2 Have you at any time during the period of 5 years immediately preceding the date of this application been convicted by a court in India for any criminal offence & sentenced to imprisonment for two years or more?   ☐ Yes   ☐ No
If yes, fill Column 7.2 of Supplementary Form

8.3 Have you ever been refused or denied passport?   ☐Yes   ☐ No
If yes, give reason for refusal or denial of Passport in Column 7.3 of Supplementary Form

8.4 Has your Passport ever been Impounded or Revoked?   ☐Yes   ☐ No
If yes, provide details in Column 7.4 of Supplementary Form

8.5 Have you ever applied for/ been granted political asylum to/ by any foreign country?   ☐Yes   ☐ No
If yes, provide details in Column 7.5 of Supplementary Form

8.6 Have you ever returned to India on Emergency Certificate (EC) or were ever deported or repatriated?   ☐Yes   ☐ No
If yes, provide details in Column 7.6 of Supplementary Form

9. Fee Details (Not to be filled by applicants submitting the application at Passport Seva Kendra)

9.1 Fee amount in (Rs)   **9.2 If paid by Demand Draft (DD), provide the following details**

DD Number

DD Issue Date   DD Expiry Date

Bank Name

Branch

10. Enclosures

1.		6.
2.		7.
3.		8.
4.		9.
5.		10.

11. Self Declaration

I owe allegiance to the sovereignty, unity & integrity of India, and have not voluntarily acquired citizenship or travel document of any other country. I have not lost, surrendered or been deprived of the citizenship of India and I affirm that the information given by me in this form and the enclosures is true and I am solely responsible for its accuracy, and I am liable to be penalized or prosecuted if found otherwise. I am aware that under the Passports Act, 1967 it is a criminal offence to furnish any false information or to suppress any material information with a view to obtaining passport or travel document.

Place

Date (DD-MM-YYYY)

Signature/ Left Hand Thumb Impression of Applicant (If applicant is minor, either parent to sign)

Page 5 of 6

4. Refusal of passport and travel documents

a. The passport authority shall refuse to make endorsement for visiting any foreign country under Clause (b) or Clause (c) of Subsection (2) of Section 5 on any one or more of the following grounds:

  A. That the applicant may, or is likely to, engage in such country in activities prejudicial to the sovereignty and with that or any other country.

  B. That the opinion of the Central Government the presence of the applicant in such country is not in the public interest.

b. The passport authority shall refuse to issue a passport and other travel documents for visiting any foreign country under Clause (b) or Clause (c) of Subsection 2 of Section 5 on any one of the more on the following grounds:

  A. Anyone is trying to disrupt the integrity of India.

  B. That the presence of the applicant in such country may, or likely to, be detrimental to the security of India.

C. That the applicant is not a citizen of India.
D. That the applicant may or likely to, engage outside India in activities prejudicial to the sovereignty and integrity of India.that the departure of the applicant from India may, or is likely to, prejudice the friendly relations of India with any foreign country.
E. That the applicant has, at any time during the period of 5 years immediately preceding the date of application, been convicted by a court in India for any offence involving moral turpitude and sentenced in respect thereof to imprisonment for not less than 2 years.
F. That proceedings in respect of an offence alleged to have been committed by the applicant is pending before a criminal court in India.
G. That a warrant or summons for the appearance, or a warrant for the arrest, of the applicant has been issued by a court under any law for the time being in force or that an order prohibiting the departure from India of the applicant has been made by any such court.
H. That the applicant has been repatriated and has not reimbursed the expenditure incurred in connection with such repatriation.
I. That in the opinion of the Central Government, the issue of a passport or travel document to the applicant will not be in the public interest.

5. Duration of the Travel Documents

A passport or travel document shall, unless revoked earlier, continue in force for such period as may be prescribed and different periods may be prescribed for different classes of passports or travel documents or for different categories of passports or travel documents under each such class.

Provided that a passport or travel document may be issued for a shorter period than the prescribed period:

a. If a person by whom it is required so desires; or
b. If the passport authority, for reasons to be communicated in writing to the applicant, considers in case that the passport or travel documents should be issued for a shorter period.

6. Extension of period of passport

When a passport is issued for a shorter period than the prescribed period under Section 7 such shorter period shall, unless the passport authority for reasons to be recorded in writing otherwise determines, be extendable for a further period (which together with the shorter period shall not exceed the prescribed period) and provision of this Act shall apply to such extension as they apply to the issue thereof.

7. Conditions and forms of passports and travel documents

The conditions subject to which, and the form in which, a passport or travel document shall be issued or renewed shall be such as may be prescribed:

a. Provided that different conditions and different forms may be prescribed for different classes of passports or travel documents or for different categories of passports or travel documents under each such class.

b. Provided further that a passport or travel document may contain in addition, to the prescribed conditions such other conditions as the passport authority may, with the previous approval of the Central Government, impose in any particular case.

8. Variation, impounding and revocation of passports and travel documents

a. The passport authority may, having regard to the provisions of Subsection (1) of Section 6 or any notification under Section 19, vary or cancel the endorsements on a passport or travel document or may, with the previous approval of the Central Government, vary or cancel the conditions (other than the prescribed conditions) subject to which a passport or travel document has been issued and may, for that purpose, require the holder of a passport or a travel document, by notice in writing, to deliver up the passport or travel document to it within such time as may be specified in the notice and the holder shall comply with such notice.

b. The passport authority may, on the application of the holder of a passport or a travel document, and with the previous approval of the Central Government also vary or cancel the conditions (others than the prescribed conditions) of the passport or travel document.

c. The passport authority may impound or case to be impounded or revoke a passport or travel document:

A. If the passport authority is satisfied that the holder of the passport or travel document is in wrongful possession thereof.

B. If the passport or travel document was obtained by the suppression of material information or on the basis of wrong information provided by the holder of the passport or travel document or any other person on his behalf.
(Provided that if the holder of such passport obtains another passport the passport authority shall also impound or cause to be impounded or revoke such other passport.)

C. If the passport authority deems it necessary to do so in the interests of the sovereignty and integrity of India, the security of India, friendly relations of India with any foreign country, or in the interests of the general public.

D. If the holder of the passport or travel document has, at any time after the issue of the passport or travel document, been convicted by a court in India for any offence involving moral turpitude and sentenced in respect thereof imprisonment for not less than 2 years.

E. If proceedings in respect of an offence alleged to have been committed by the holder of the passport or travel document are pending before a criminal court in India.
If any of the conditions of the passport or travel document has been contravened.

F. If the holder of the passport or travel document has failed to comply with a notice under Subsection (1) requiring him to deliver up the same.

G. If it is brought to the notice of the passport authority that a warrant for the arrest, of the holder of the passport or travel document has been issued by a court under any law for the time being in force or if an order prohibiting the departure from India of the holder of the passport or other travel document has been made by any such court and the passport authority is satisfied that a warrant or summons has been so issued or an order has been so made.

d. The passport authority may also revoke a passport or travel document on the application of the holder thereof.

e. Where the passport authority makes an order varying or cancelling the endorsements on, or varying the conditions of, a passport or travel document under sub-section (1) or an order impounding or revoking a passport or travel document under sub-section (3), it shall record in writing a brief statement of the reasons for making such order and furnish to the holder of the passport or travel document on demand a copy of the same unless in any case, the passport authority is of the opinion that it will not be in the interests of the sovereignty and integrity of India, the security of India, friendly relations of India with any foreign country or in the interests of the general public to furnish such a copy.

f. The authority to whom the passport authority is subordinate may, by order in writing, impound or cause to be impounded or revoke a passport or travel document on any ground on which it may be impounded or revoked by the passport authority and the foregoing provisions of this section shall, as far as may be, apply in relation to the impounding or revocation of a passport or travel document by such authority.

g. A court convicting the holder of a passport or travel document of any offence under this Act or the rules made there under may also revoke the passport or travel document:

> Provided that if the conviction is set-aside on appeal or otherwise the revocation shall become void.

h. An order of revocation under Subsection (7) may also be made by an appellate court or by the High court when exercising its powers of revision.

i. On the revocation of a passport or travel document under this section the holder thereof shall, without delay, surrender the passport or travel document, if the same has not already been impounded, to the authority by whom it has been revoked or to such other authority as may be specified in this behalf in the order of revocation.

9. Appeals

a. Any person aggrieved by and order of the passport authority under Clause (b) or Clause (c) of Subsection (2) of Section 5 or Clause (b) of the proviso to Section 7 or Subsection (1), or Subsection (3) of Section 10 or by an order under Subsection (6) of Section 10 of the authority to whom the passport authority is subordinate, may prefer an appeal against that order to such authority (hereinafter referred to as the appellate authority) and within such period as may be prescribed:

b. No appeal shall be admitted if it is preferred after the expiry of the period prescribed therefore:

> Provided that an appeal may be admitted after the expiry of the period prescribed therefore if the appellant satisfies the appellate authority that the he had sufficient cause for not preferring the appeal within that period.

c. The period prescribed for an appeal shall be computed in accordance with the provisions of the Limitation Act, 1963 (36 of 1963) with respect to the compilation of the periods of limitation there under.

d. Every appeal under this section shall be made by a petition in writing and shall be accompanied by a copy of the statement of the reasons for the order appealed against where such copy has been furnished to the appellant and (by such fee as may be prescribed for meeting the expenses that may be incurred in calling for relevant records and for connected services).

e. In disposing of an appeal, the appellate authority shall follow such procedure as may be prescribed:

> Provided that no appeal shall be disposed of unless the appellant has been given a reasonable opportunity of representing his case.

f. Every order of the appellate authority confirming, modifying or reversing the order appealed against shall be final.

10. Offences and penalties

a. Whoever
    A. Contravenes the provisions of Section 3.
    B. Knowingly furnishes any false information or suppresses any material information with a view to obtaining a passport or travel document under the Act or without lawful authority alters or attempts to alter or causes to alter the entries made in the passport or travel document.
    C. Fails to produce for inspection his passport or travel document (whether issued under this Act or not) when called upon to do so by the prescribed authority.
    D. Knowingly uses a passport or travel document issued to another person.
    E. Knowingly allows another person to use a passport or travel document issued to him, shall be punishable with imprisonment for a term which may be extended to (two years with fine which may be extended to five thousand rupees or both) or with both.
b. Whoever abets any offence punishable under Subsection (1) or Subsection (1A) shall, if the act abetted is committed in consequence of the abetment, be punishable with the punishment provided in that subsection for that offence.
c. Whoever contravenes any condition of an passport or travel document or any provision of this Act or any rule made under for which no punishment is provided elsewhere in this Act shall be punishable with imprisonment for a term which may extend to three months or with fine which may extend to five hundred rupees or with both.
d. Whoever, having been convicted of an offence under this Act shall be punishable with double the penalty provided for the latter offence.

11. Power to arrest

a. Any officer of customs empowered by a general or special order of the Central Government in this behalf and any (officer of police or emigration officer) not below the rank of a sub-inspector may arrest without warrant any person against whom a reasonable suspicion exists that he has committed any offence punishable under Section 12 and shall, as soon as may be, inform him of the grounds for such arrest.
b. Every officer making an arrest under this section shall, without unnecessary delay, take or send the person arrested before a magistrate having jurisdiction in case or to the provisions of (Section 57 of the Code of Criminal Procedure, 1973) shall, so far as may be, apply in the case of any such arrest.

12. Power of search and seizure

a. Any officer of customs empowered by a general or special order of the Central Government in this behalf and any (officer of police or emigration officer) not below the rank of an sub-inspector may search any place and seize any passport or travel document from any person against whom a reasonable suspicion exists that he has committed any offence punishable under Section 12.

b.   The provisions of the Code of Criminal Procedure, 1973, relating to searches and seizures shall, so far as maybe, apply to searches and seizures under this section.

13. Issue of passports and travel documents to persons who are not citizens of India

Notwithstanding anything contained in the foregoing provisions relating to issue of a passport or travel document, the Central Government may issue, or cause to be issued, a passport of India if the government is of the opinion that it is necessary so to do in the public interest.

11.6. Tourism Bill of Rights and Tourist Code (1985)

Tourism Bill of Rights and Tourist Code was the outcome of the General Assembly of UNWTO at its sixth ordinary session held at Sofia (Bulgaria) from 17 to 26 September 1985. In that session the Tourism Bill of Rights and Tourist Code were discussed in detail. Altogether 14 articles were framed in that session. Articles 1–9 comprise tourism bill of rights and articles 10–14 were tourist code.

Following resolutions were taken in the General Assembly meeting at Sofia in 1985:

1.   Aware of the importance of tourism in the life of the peoples because of its direct and positive effects on social, economic, cultural and educational sectors of national society and the contribution it can make, in the spirit of the United Nations Charter and the Manila Declaration on World Tourism, to improving mutual understanding, bringing peoples closer together and consequently, strengthening international cooperation.

2.   Recalling that, as recognized by the General Assembly of the United Nations, The World Tourism Organization has a central and decisive role in the development of tourism with a view to contributing in accordance with Article 3, paragraph I of its statute 'to economic development, international understanding, peace, prosperity and universal respect for and observation of human rights and fundamental freedom for all without distinction as to race, sex, language or religion.'

3.   Recalling the Universal Declaration of Human Rights adopted by the General Assembly of the United Nations on 10 December 1948 and in particular Article 24 which provides that 'Everyone has the right to rest and leisure, including reasonable limitations to working hours and periodic holidays with pay.' As well as the International Covenant on 'Economic, Social and Cultural rights adopted by the General Assembly of the United Nations on 16 December 1966, which invites states to ensure for everyone rest and leisure, including reasonable limitations to working hours and periodic holidays with pay, as well as remuneration for public holidays.'

4.   Considering the resolutions and recommendations adopted by the United Nations Conference on International Trade and Tourism (Rome; September 1963) and particularly those aimed at promoting tourism development in the various countries and at simplifying government formalities in respect of international trade.

5.   Drawing its inspirations from the principles set forth in the Manila Declaration on World Tourism adopted by the World Tourism Conference on 10 October 1980, which has

emphasized the true human dimension of tourism, recognizes the new role of tourism as an appropriate instrument for improving the quality of life of all peoples and as a vital force for peace and international understanding and defines responsibilities of states for developing tourism and, in particular, for fostering awareness of tourism among the peoples of the world and protecting and enhancing the tourism resources which are part of mankind's heritage, with a view to contributing to the establishment of a new international economic order.

6. Solemnly affirming, as a natural consequence of the right to work, the fundamental right of everyone, as already sanctioned by the Universal Declarations of Human Rights, to rest, leisure and periodic holidays with a pay and to use them for holiday purpose, to travel freely for education and pleasure and to enjoy the advantages of tourism, both within the country of residence and abroad.

7. Invites the states to draw inspiration from the principles set forth below substituting the Tourism Bill of Rights and Tourist Code, and to apply them in accordance with the procedures prescribed in the legislation and regulations of their own countries.

Tourism Bill of Rights

Article I

- The right of everyone to rest and leisure, reasonable limitation of working hours, periodic leave with pay and freedom of movement without limitation, within the bounds of the law, is universally recognized.
- The exercise of this right constitutes a factor of social balance and enhancement of national and universal awareness.

Article II

As a consequence of this right, the states should formulate and implement policies aimed at promoting the harmonious development of domestic and international tourism, and leisure activities for the benefit of all those taking part in them.

Article III

To this end the States should:

- Encourage the orderly and harmonious growth of both domestic and international tourism.
- Integrate their tourism policies with their overall development policies at all levels—local, regional, national and international—and broaden tourism cooperation within both bilateral and multilateral frameworks including that of the World Tourism Organization.
- Give due attention to the principles of the Manila Declaration on World Tourism and the Acapulco Document while formulating and implementing, as appropriate, their tourism policies, plans and programmes, in accordance with their national priorities and within the framework of the programme of work of the World Tourism Organization.
- Encourage the adoption of measures enabling everyone to participate in domestic and international tourism, especially by a better allocation of work and leisure time, the

establishment or improvement of systems of annual leave with pay and the staggering of holiday dates and by particular attention to tourism for the young, elderly and disabled.

- In the interest of present and future generations, protect the tourism environment which being at once human, natural, social, cultural, is the legacy of all mankind.

Article IV

The States should also:

- Encourage the access of domestic and international tourists to the heritage of the host communities by applying the provisions of existing facilitation instruments issuing from the United Nations, the International Civil Aviation Organization, the International Maritime Organization, the Customs Co-operation Council or from any other body, the World Tourism Organizationin particular, with a view to increasingly liberalizing travel.
- Promote tourism awareness and facilitate contact between visitors and host communities with a view to their mutual understanding and betterment.
- Ensure the safety of visitors and the security of their belongings through preventive and protective measures.
- Afford the best possible conditions of hygiene and access to health services as well of the prevention of communicable diseases and accidents.
- Prevent any possibility of using tourism to exploit others for prostitution purposes.
- Reinforce, for the protection of tourists and the population of the host community, measures to prevent the illegal use of narcotics.

Article V

The States should lastly:

- Permit domestic and international tourists to move freely about the country, without prejudice to any limitative measures taken in the national interest concerning certain areas of the territory.
- Not allow any discriminatory measures in regard to tourists.
- Allow tourists prompt access to administrative and legal service and to consular representatives, and make available internal and external public communications.
- Contribute to the information of tourists with a view to fostering understanding of the customs of the populations constituting the host communities at places of transit and sojourn.

Article VI

- The populations constituting the host communities in places of transit and sojourn are entitled to free access to their own tourism resources while fostering respect, through their attitude and behaviour, for their natural and cultural environment.
- They are also entitled to expect from tourists understanding of and respect for their customs, religions and other elements of their cultures which are part of human heritage.
- To facilitate such understanding and respect, the dissemination of appropriate information should be encouraged on:
  - The customs of host communities, their traditional and regional practices, local taboos and sacred sites and shrines which must be respected.
  - Their artistic, archaeological and cultural treasures which must be preserved.
  - Wild life and other natural resources which must be protected.

Article VII

The populations constituting the host communities in places of transit and sojourn are invited to receive tourists with the greatest possible hospitality, courtesy and respect necessary for the development of harmonious human and social relations.

Article VIII

- Tourism professionals and suppliers of tourism and travel services can make a positive contribution to tourism development and to implementation of the provision of this Bill of Rights.
- They should conform to the principles of this Bill of Rights and honour commitments of any kind entered into within the context of their professional activities, ensuring the provision of quality products so as to help affirm the humanist nature of tourism.
- They should in particular refrain from encouraging the use of tourism for all forms of exploitation of others.

Article IX

Encouragement should be given to tourism professionals and services by granting them, through appropriate national and international legislation, the necessary facilities to enable them to:

- Exercise their activities in favourable conditions, free from any particular impediment or discrimination.
- Benefit from general and technical training schemes, both within their countries and abroad, so as to ensure the availability of skilled manpower
- Cooperate among themselves as well as with the public authorities, through national and international organizations, with a view to improving the coordination of their activities and the quality of their services.

Tourist Code

Article X

Tourists should by their behaviour foster understanding and friendly relations among peoples, at both the national and international levels, and thus contribute to lasting peace.

Article XI

- At places of transit and sojourn tourists must respect the established political, social, moral and religious order and comply with the legislation and regulations in force.
- In these places tourists must also:
  - Show the greatest understanding for the customs, beliefs and behaviour of the host communities and the greatest respect for their natural and cultural heritage.
  - Refrain from accentuating the economic, social and cultural differences between themselves and the local population.
  - Be receptive to the culture of the host communities, which is an integral part of the common human heritage.
  - Refrain from exploiting others for prostitution purposes.
  - Refrain from trafficking in carrying or using narcotics and/or other prohibited drugs.

Article XII

During their travel from one country to another and within the host country, tourists should be able, by appropriate government measures, to benefit from:

- Relaxation of administrative and financial controls.
- The best possible conditions of transport and sojourn that can be offered by suppliers of tourism services.

Article XIII

- Tourists should be offered free access, both within and outside their countries, to sites and places of tourist interest and subject to existing regulations and limitations, freedom of movement in places of transit and sojourn.
- On access to sites and places of tourists interests and throughout their transit and sojourn, tourists should be able to benefit from:
    - Objective, precise and complete information on conditions and facilities provided during their travel and sojourn by official tourism bodies and suppliers of tourism services.
    - Safety of their persons, security of their belongings and protection of their rights as consumers.
    - Satisfactory public hygiene, particularly so far as accommodation, catering and transport are concerned, information on the effective prevention of communicable diseases and accidents and ready access to health services.
    - Access to swift and efficient public communications, both internal and external.
    - Administrative and legal procedures and guarantees necessary protection of their rights.
    - The practice of their own religion and use of existing facilities for that purpose.

Article XIV

Everyone is entitled to make their needs known to legislative representatives and public authorities so that they may exercise their right to rest and leisure in order to enjoy the benefits of tourism under the most favourable conditions and, where appropriate and to the extent consistent with law, associate with others for that purpose.

11.7. Classification and Star Gradation of Hotels in India

Introduction

Classification of hotels is one of the most important assignments performed by the Department of Tourism, Government of India. Hotel and Restaurant Approval Classifications Committee (HRACC) is the competent authority under the Ministry of Tourism which provides star classifications of hotels in India. There is a great deal of confusion/controversy regarding the number of rooms as well as the highest star category of hotels in India. In India officially 5-star deluxe is the highest star categorization available. No doubt in India we sometimes rate a hotel property as seven stars (7–star) in which the additional feature of helipad facility is there. Important information regarding star categorization of hotel is that for heritage hotels the classification criteria are different in relation to normal hotels. There is also no standard hard and fast rule to classify the hotels on the basis of number of lettable rooms available in a hotel. Star categorizations of hotel are made on the basis of three criteria. These include:

1. General features
2. Facilities
3. Service availability

Hotels in 5-Star Deluxe Category

This is a qualitative extension of the 5-star category, while quantitatively the basic features are as of 5-star category. The standard of service and amenities are of a very superior quality.

Hotels in 5-Star Category

1. General features

The façade, architectural features: general construction of the building should have distinctive quality of a luxury hotel. Other features include:

- Adequate parking space
- Immediate approach should be suitable
- 25 lettable bedrooms, all with attached bathrooms
- Modern shower chambers
- 24 hours hot and cold water services
- Public and private rooms are fully air conditioned, except in hill stations, where heating arrangements must be there
- Superior quality of carpets, curtains, furniture's, fittings and so on
- Deployment of professional, qualified and experienced interior decorators
- Adequate number of lifts if more than two storied including ground floor with 24 hours services

2. Facilities

- Swimming pool
- Lobby
- Ladies and gentleman's cloak rooms of the highest standards
- Receptions
- Cash and information counter attended by qualified and experienced personnel
- Conference facilities
- Banquet/conference room
- Private dining room
- Book stalls
- Beauty parlour
- Barbour shop
- Travel counter

- Money changing and safe deposit facilities
- Left luggage room
- Florist
- Medicine stalls on the premises
- Telephone in each room
- Telephone for the use of guests and visitors
- Provision of music and radio in each room
- Well-equipped dining room
- Restaurant on premises
- Well-equipped bar/permit room
- Pantry and cold storage should be professionally designed

3. Services

- Offer both international and Indian cuisine
- Food and beverage services should be of the highest standard
- Trained, professional qualified and experienced staff
- Clean uniform
- Understand and speak English
- Staff should also have knowledge of foreign language and continental language and should be on duty at all time
- Functioning of 24-hour service of reception, information, telephone and so on
- Housekeeping of highest standard
- Housekeeping department should supply good quality linen, blankets, towels and so on
- Each room should be provided with vacuum jug, thermos flask with ice-cold and boiling drinking water
- Provision for music and dancing should be there

Hotels in 4-Star Category

1. General features

- 25 lettable bedrooms all with attached bathrooms
- 50 per cent should have long bath with modern facility
- 24 hours hot and cold water facility
- All public and private rooms should be air conditioned, except in hill stations, where heating arrangements are there
- Carpets, furniture, fittings should be of best quality
- Provision for lifts and lobby
- Toilet for ladies and gents
- Provision of cloak rooms

2. Facilities

- Receptions
- Cash counters
- Information counters
- Well-trained staff

- Travel counters
- Book stalls
- Money exchange counter
- Safe deposit locker
- Telephone in each rooms
- Music, TV and radio in each room

- Well-equipped bar/permit rooms
- Kitchen
- Pantry
- Cold storage should be professionally designed

3. Services

- Hotel should offer both Indian and international cuisine
- Food and beverage service should be of highest standard
- Trained and qualified staff deployment
- Staffs should understand and speak English or foreign language/continental language
- 24 hours service of reception and telephone
- Provision of laundry and dry-cleaning facilities
- Housekeeping facilities of the hotels should be of the highest standard
- Provision of best quality of cutlery, glass wire, vacuum jug/thermos flask with ice-cold and boiling drinking water
- Special restaurants/dining room where facilities for music and dancing are provided

Hotels in 3-Star Category

1. General features

- Adequate parking facilities
- 20 lettable bedrooms all with attached bathrooms with bathtub/showers
- 50 per cent of the rooms should be air conditioned (except in hill stations)
- Adequate number of lifts
- Good lounge
- Ladies and gentlemen's cloak room

2. Facilities

- Reception
- Information counter should be attended by qualified staff
- Provision of laundry and dry-cleaning facilities
- Housekeeping of good standards

3. Services

- Staff should be experienced and qualified
- Staff should be courteous, efficient and in clean uniform
- Supervisory staffs should understand and speak English
- Provision of laundry and dry-cleaning service
- Superior quality supply of linen, blankets, towels and so on
- Each room provided with hot and cold/boiling water

Hotels in 2-Star Category

1. General features

- The building should be well constructed and the locality and environments including the approach should be suitable for a good hotel
- 10 lettable bedrooms
- 75 per cent should have attached bathroom with shower, or bathroom for every four of the remaining rooms
- 25 per cent of the rooms should be air conditioned
- Well-furnished lounge

2. Facilities

- Reception counters with telephone facility
- Telephone call bell in each room
- Separate telephone connection
- Well-maintained and air conditioned dining room/restaurants
- Provision of serving good, clean and wholesome food
- Clean and hygienic, and well-equipped kitchen and pantry

3. Services

- Staff should be experienced
- Staff should be courteous, efficient and in clean uniform
- Supervisory staffs should understand and speak English
- Provision of laundry and dry-cleaning service
- Housekeeping of good standard
- Provision of good quality linen, blankets and towels
- Crockery and glassware of good quality

Hotels in 1-Star Category

1. General features

- 10 lettable bedrooms
- 25 per cent with attached bath
- Rooms with shower facility in every four remaining rooms
- 25 per cent of the room should be provided with western style commode
- Modern sanitation with cold and hot water with proper ventilation

2. Facilities

- Reception counter
- Telephone use for both guests and visitors
- Clean, modern toilet
- Well-equipped dining room/restaurants
- Provision of clean wholesome food

3. Services

- Staff should be experienced and courteous
- Efficient and knowledge of good English
- Housekeeping of good standard
- Provision of good quality of linen, blankets and towels
- Crockery, cutlery and glassware should be of good quality

11.8. Manila Declaration in Tourism

Introduction

The World Tourism Conference which was held at Manila, Philippines, in October 1984, considered the nature of tourism phenomenon in all its aspects and the role tourism is bound to play in a dynamic and vastly changing world. Convened by the World Tourism Organization, the conference also considered the responsibility of various states for the development and enhancement as more than a purely economic activity of nations and peoples.

Aim and Significance

The participants in the World Tourism Conference stressed the significance of tourism particularly to the developing countries was discussed at length. From the beginning, only the conference pronounced on this subject itself. It stated its conviction:

> That the world tourism can contribute to the establishment of a new international economic order that will help to eliminate the widening economic gap between developed and developing countries and ensure steady acceleration of economic and social development and progress, in particular of the developing countries. (Bhatia 2006)

The Manila Declaration on World Tourism considered almost all aspects of the tourism phenomenon. Besides the economic aspect, social, cultural, spiritual aspects were also considered. The conference was also convinced that world peace can provide the moral and intellectual bases for international understanding and interdependence.

The Declaration states:

1. Tourism is considered an activity essential to the life of nations because of its direct effects on the social, cultural, educational and economic sectors of national societies and their international relation. Its development is linked to the social and economic development of nations and can only be possible if men have and enjoy the freedom to travel, within the framework of free time and leisure whose profoundly human character it underlines. Its very existence and development depend entirely on the existence of a state of lasting peace, to which tourism itself is required to contribute.

2. On the threshold of the twenty-first century in view of the problems facing mankind, it seems timely and necessary to analyse the phenomenon of tourism, in relation

fundamentally to the dimensions it has assumed to annual paid holidays, moved tourism from a restricted elitist activity to a wider activity to a wider activity integrated into social and economic life.

3. States recognizing that tourism plays an important role within the range of human activities, have entrusted the World Tourism Organization with the task of ensuring harmonious and sustained development of tourism, in cooperation, in appropriate cases, with specialized agencies of the United Nations and other international organizations concerned.

4. The right to use of leisure, and in particular, the right to freedom of travel and tourism, a natural consequence of the right to work recognized as an aspect to the fulfilment of the human needs by the Universal Declaration of Human Rights, as well by the legislation in many nations, it entails for society the duty of providing for its citizens the best practical, effective and non-discriminatory access to this type of activity. Such an effort must be in harmony with the priorities, institutions and traditions of each individual country.

5. There are many constraints on the development of tourism, and groups of nations should determine and study those constraints, and adopt measures aimed at removing their negative influence.

6. The share tourism represents in national economies and in international trade makes it a significant factor in world development. Its consistent major role in national economic activity, in international transactions and in securing balance of payments equilibrium makes it one of the main activities of the world economy.

7. Within each country, domestic tourism contributes to an improved balance of the national economy through redistribution of the national income. Domestic tourism also heightens the awareness of common interest and contributes to the development of activities favourable to the general economy of the country. Thus, the development of tourism from abroad should be accompanied by a similar effort to expand domestic tourism.

8. The economic returns of tourism, however real and significant they may be, do not and cannot constitute the only criterion for the decision by states to encourage this activity. The right to holidays, the opportunity for the citizen to get to know his own environment, a deeper awareness of his national identity and of the solidarity that links him to his compatriots, and the sense of belonging to a culture and to people are all major reasons for stimulating the individual's participation in domestic and international tourism through access to holidays and travel.

9. The importance that millions of our contemporaries attach to tourism in the use of their free time and in their concept of the quality of life makes it a need that governments should take into account and support.

10. Social tourism is an objective which society must pursue in the interest of those citizens who are least privileged in the exercise of their right to rest.

11. Through its effects on the physical and mental health of the individual practising it, tourism is a factor that favours social stability, improves the working capacity of communities and promotes individual as well as collective well-being.

12. Through a wide range of services needed to satisfy its requirements, tourism creates new activities of considerable importance which are a source of new employment in this respect; tourism constitutes a positive element for social development in all the countries where it is practiced irrespective of their level of development.

13. With respect to international relations and the search for peace, based on justice and respect of individual and national aspirations, tourism stands out as a positive and ever-present factor in promoting mutual knowledge and understanding, and as a basis for reaching a greater level of respect and confidence among all the peoples of the world.

14. Modern tourism results from the adoption of a social policy which led to the workers gaining annual paid holidays and represents the recognition of a fundamental right of the human beings to rest and leisure. It has become a factor contributing to social stability, mutual understanding among individuals and peoples, and individual betterment. In addition to its well-known economic aspects, it has acquired a cultural and moral dimension which must be fostered and protected against the harmful distortions which can be brought about by economic factors. Public authorities and the travel trade should accordingly participate in the development of tourism by formulating guidelines aimed at encouraging appropriate investments.

15. Youth tourism requires the most active attention, since young people have less adequate income than others for travelling or taking holidays. A positive policy should provide youth with the utmost encouragement and facilities. The same attention should be provided for the elderly and the handicapped.

16. In the universal efforts to establish a new international economic order, tourism can under appropriate conditions, play a positive role in furthering equilibrium, mutual understanding and solidarity among all countries.

17. Nations should promote improved conditions of employment for workers engaged in tourism, and confirm and protect their right to establish professional trade unions and collective bargaining.

18. Tourism resources available in various countries consist, at the same time, of space, facilities and values. These are resources whose use cannot be left uncontrolled without running the risk of their deterioration or even destruction. The satisfaction of tourism requirements must not be prejudicial in tourist areas, to the environment and above all to natural resources, which are fundamental attraction of tourism, and historical and cultural site. All tourism resources are part of the heritage of mankind. National communities and the entire international community must take the necessary steps to ensure their preservation. The conservation of historical, cultural and religious sites represents at all times, and notably in time of conflict, one of the fundamental responsibilities of states.

19. International cooperation in the field of tourism is an endeavour in which the characteristics of peoples and basic interests of individual states must be respected. In this field, the central and decisive role of the World Tourism Organization, as a utilizing and harmonizing body, is obvious.

20. Bilateral and multilateral technical and financial cooperation cannot be looked upon as an act of assistance, since it constitutes the pooling of the means necessary for the utilization of resources for the benefit of all parties.

21. In the practice of tourism, spiritual elements must take precedence over technical and material elements. The spiritual elements are essentially as follows:
    a. The total fulfilment of the human being
    b. A constantly increasing contribution to education
    c. The affirmation of the originality of cultures and respect for the moral heritage of peoples.

22. Preparation for tourism should be integrated with the training of the citizen for his civic responsibilities. In this respect, governments should mobilize the means of education and information at their disposal and should facilitate the work of individuals and bodies involved in this endeavour. Preparation for tourism, for holidays and for travel, could usefully form part of the process of youth education and training. For these reasons, the integration of tourism into youth education constitutes a basic element favourable to the permanent strengthening of peace.

23. Any long-term analysis of man's social, cultural and economic development should take due account of national and international tourist and recreational activities. These activities now form an integral part of the life of modern national and international societies. Bearing in mind the acknowledged values of tourism which are inseparable from it, the authorities will have to give more increased attention to the development of national and international tourists and recreational activity, based on an ever wider participation of peoples in holidays and travel, as well as the movement of persons for numerous other purposes, with a view of ensuring the orderly growth of tourism in a manner consistent with the other basic needs of society.

24. The conference urges the World Tourism Organization to take all necessary measures, through its own international machinery and, where appropriate, in cooperation with other international, inter-government and non-governmental bodies, so as to permit the global implementation of the principles, concepts and guidelines contained in this final document.

The rapid transition and the swift developments that are occurring not only in technology but also in the social structures and relations, in customers and in behavioural patterns will have profound effects on the travel and tourism in years to come. Because of the vast transformations which society is undergoing presently, there are bound to be changes in the travel and tourism scene. The forms of travel as a result of changes in transport and information technology, increased income resulting in availability of more money for travel and increased leisure time are going to have effect on tourism activity in the future.

11.9. Tourism Convention: Legal Aspects

Warsaw Convention (1929)

To facilitate the legal problem faced by the airline companies arising due to loss of property or life due to accident and/or mishandling, one international convention was organized at Warsaw (Poland) in 1929. In that conference, one international agreement was made to limit the liabilities of the airlines for the loss of or damage to baggage (baggage unaccompanied) and injury or death of passenger on most international flights (including domestic portion of international flights).

As a result of this agreement, airlines normally accept the liability for accidents up to a set limit and claimants do not have to prove negligence and excess value.

The main guidelines of the Convention are as follows:

- All the airline companies operating in commercial route should have the specified technical requirements in their carrier.
- All airlines operating for passengers (specially international or international +domestic) routes should have tri-party insurance coverage for life.

- The maximum limit for loss of or damage to checked baggage is set at US$1,500 unless specified.
- Any baggage (both checked and unchecked) of excess value which is declared at the time of check-in by the airline staff and by which one payment of a fee is made to the airline.

The possible compensation in the event of baggage loss or damage is increased. Excess value is applicable for both checked and unchecked baggage. But it is not insurance. The airlines will not necessarily compensate the full amount and negligence has to be proved on its part.

Chicago Convention (1944)

The Chicago Convention on International Civil Aviation was concluded at an international meeting among the governments in Chicago (United States of America). Nearly all the countries active in international air transport are parties to it. It governs the relations between the states on both technical and commercial subjects concerning international air transport such as:

- Flying over territory of contracting states (air services, customs, rules of air, spread of disease, charges, discriminations and so on)
- Nationality of the aircraft, facilitations (customs, accident investigation and so on)
- Documents (Recognition of certificates, licences and so on)
- International standards and practices including those of carriage of dangerous goods
- Statistics, finance and technical assistances, and so on
- In addition to this, the Convention also founded an organization named as International Civil Aviation Organization. This is a part of United Nations and its current membership is comprised of more than 187 states

The Chicago Convention does not itself grant rights to operate international air services, but it makes provision for the manners in which such rights may be granted. It draws a distinction between the scheduled and non-scheduled services.

Bilateral Agreements

Under these bilateral agreements each state designates its scheduled air carrier. Sometimes designation of three more carriers is permitted. The agreements specify the rights that such designated carriers will enjoy in the other country.

Freedom of Air

- **Overfly:** The right of an airline to carry passengers, mail and cargo, and overfly a country or different countries while flying from one country to another country.
- **Technical stopover:** The right of an airline to carry passengers, mail and cargo, and stopover in any country/place due to some technical problem provided it should not involve in any commercial activity at the stopover point. Technical stopover may be in the form of refuelling or any technical problem associated with the airlines and so on.
- **Home country to foreign country:** To set down passengers, mail and cargo from home country to foreign country.

- **Foreign country to home country:** To set down passengers, mail and cargo from foreign country to home country.
- **Between two foreign countries:** The right of an airline to carry passengers, mail and cargo between two foreign countries.
- **Between two foreign countries via foreign country:** The right of an airline to carry passengers, mail and cargo between two foreign countries via home country.
- **Wholly within a foreign country:** The right of an airline to carry passengers, mail and cargo between two foreign countries via home country.

11.10. Global Code of Ethics for Tourism

The Global Code of Ethics for Tourism (GCET) has been adopted by the representatives of world tourism industry, delegates of the states and territories including enterprises, bodies and institutional members of the World Tourism Organization (UNWTO) who had gathered for the general assembly at Santiago, Chile on 1 October 1999.

GCET sets a frame for the responsible and sustainable development of world tourism at the dawn of the millennium; it draws inspiration from many similar declarations and industry codes that have come before it. It adds a new thinking that reflects our changing society at the end of 20th century; with international tourism forecast to nearly triple in volume over the next 20 years, members of the World Tourism Organization believed that GCET is needed to help minimize the negative impacts of tourism on the environment and on cultural heritage while maximizing the benefits for residence of tourism destination.

The Code was called for in a resolution for the WTO General Assembly meeting in Istanbul in 1997. After 2 years, a special committee for the preparation of the global code of ethics was formed and a draft document was prepared by the Secretary-General and Legal Advisor of WTO in a consultation with WTO Business Council, WTO regional commissions and WTO Executive Council.

The United Nation Commission on Sustainable Development meeting in New York in April 1999 endorsed the concept of the Code and requested WTO to seek further input from the private sector, non-governmental organizations and labour organizations. Written codes were received from more than 70 WTO member states and other entities. The resulting 10-point global code was approved unanimously by WTO General Assembly meeting in Santiago in October 1999.

The code includes nine articles outlining the 'rules of the game' for destinations, government, tour operators, travel agents, developers, workers and travellers themselves. Article 10 involves the redressal of grievances and marks the first time a code of this type will have a mechanism for enforcement. It will be based through the creation of a World Committee of Tourism Ethics made up of representatives of each region of the world and representatives of each group of stake-holders in the tourism sector—governments, the private sector, labour and non-governmental organization.

GCET, reproduced on the following pages, is intended to be living documents, read it, circulate it widely, participate in its implementation; only with your cooperation can we safeguard the future of the tourism industry and expand the sector's contribution to economic prosperity, peace and understanding among all the nations of the world.

The General Assembly

Recalling

- That it has provided in its Istanbul session in 1997 for the formation of a special committee for the preparation of GCET and that this committee met at Cracow, Poland on 7 October 1998, in conjunction with the quality support committee meeting, in order to consider an outline of the said Code.
- That based on this initial consideration, the draft GCET was prepared by the secretary-general, with the assistance of the legal advisor to WTO and was studied by the WTO Business Council at the 16th session, all of which were invented to formulate their observation.
- That the WTO members were invited to communicate in writing the remarks for suggestions that they could not make at those meetings.

Noting

- That the principle for GCET aroused great interest among the delegations that participated in the 7th session of the Commission on Sustainable Development (CSD) in New York in April 1999.
- That after the CSD session additional conclusions were undertaken by the secretary-general with institutions representative of the tourism industry and the workers, as well as the various non-governmental organizations interested in this process.
- That as a result of these discussions and consultations, many written contributions were received, by the secretary-general, which have so far possible been reflected in the draft submitted to the assembly for consideration.

Reaffirming

The aim of the GCET was to establish a synthesis of the then available documents, codes and declarations of the same kind or with comparable aspirations that were published over the years, to complement them with new considerations reflecting the development of society and thus to serve as a frame of reference for the stakeholders in the tourism world at the dawn of the 21st century and millennium.

Reasserting

The aims set out in Article 3 of the Statutes of the World Tourism Organization, and aware of the 'decisive and central' role of this organization, as recognized by the General Assembly of the United Nations, in promoting and developing tourism with a view to contributing to economic development, international understanding, peace, prosperity and universal respect for, and observance of, human rights and fundamental freedoms for all without distinction as to race, sex, language or religion.

Firmly believing

That through the direct, spontaneous and non-mediatized contacts it engenders between men and women of different cultures and lifestyles, tourism represents a vital force for peace and a factor of friendship and understanding among the people of the world.

In keeping

With the rationale of reconciling environmental protection, economic development and the fight against poverty in a sustainable manner, as formulated by the United Nations in 1992 at the 'Earth summit' of Rio de Janeiro, and expressed in Agenda 21, is adopted on this occasion.

Taking into account

The swift and continued growth, both past and foreseeable, of the tourism activity, whether for leisure, business, culture, religious or health purposes, and its powerful effects, both positive and negative, on the environment, the economy and the society of both generating and receiving countries, on local communities and indigenous peoples, as well as on international relations and trade.

Aiming

To promote responsible, sustainable and universally accessible tourism in the framework of right of all persons to use their free time for leisure pursuits or travel with respect for the choices of society of all peoples.

But convinced

But convinced that the world tourism industry as a whole has much to gain by operating in an environment that favours the market economy, private enterprise and free trade, and that serves to optimize its beneficial effects on the creation of wealth and employment.

Also firmly convinced

That provided a number of principles and a certain number of rules are observed, responsible and sustainable tourism is by no means incompatible with the growing liberalization of the conditions governing trade in services and under whose aegis the enterprises of this sector operate and that it is possible to reconcile in this sector economy and ecology, environment and development, openness to international trade and protection of social and cultural identities.

Considering

That with such an approach, all the stakeholders in tourism development—national, regional and local administrations, enterprises, business associations, workers in the sector, non-governmental organizations and bodies of all kinds belonging to the tourism industry, as well as host communities, the media and the tourists themselves—have different albeit interdependent responsibilities in the individual and societal development of tourism and that the formulation of their individual rights and duties will contribute to meeting this aim.

Committed

In keeping with the aims persuaded by the World Tourism Organization itself since adopting resolution 364(XII) at its General Assembly of 1997 Istanbul, to promote a genuine partnership between the public and private stakeholders in tourism development, wishing to see a partnership and cooperation of the same kind extend, in an open and balanced way, to the relations between generating and receiving countries and their respective tourism industries.

Following up on

The Manila Declaration of 1980 on World Tourism and of 1997 on the social impact of tourism, as well as on the Tourism Bill Rights and the Tourist Code adopted at Sofia at 1985 under the aegis of WTO.

But believing

That these instruments should be complemented by a set of independent principles for their interpretation and application on which the stakeholders in tourism development should model their conduct at the dawn of the 21st century.

Using

For the purpose of this instrument, the definition and classifications applicable to travel, and especially by concept of 'visitor' and 'tourism' as adopted by Ottawa International Conference, held from 24 to 28 June 1991 and approved, in 1993, by the United Nations Statistical Commission at its 27th session.

Article 1

Tourism's contribution to mutual understanding and respect between peoples and societies

1. The understanding and promotion of the ethical values common to humanity, with an attitude of tolerance and respect for the diversity of religious, philosophical and moral beliefs, are both the foundation and the consequence of responsible tourism; stakeholders in tourism development and tourists themselves should observe the social and cultural traditions, and practices of all peoples, including those of minorities and indigenous peoples and recognize their worth.
2. Tourism activities should be conducted in harmony with the attributes and traditions of the host regions and countries, and in respect for their laws, practices and customs.
3. The host communities on the one hand and local professionals on the other hand should acquaint themselves with and respect the tourists who visit them, and find out about their lifestyles, tastes and expectations; the education and training imparted to professionals contribute to a hospitable welcome.
4. It is the task of the public authorities to provide protection for tourists and visitors and their belongings; they must pay particular attention to the safety of foreign tourists owing to the particular vulnerability they may have; they should facilitate the introduction of specific means of information, prevention, security, insurance and assistance consistent with their needs; any attacks, assaults, kidnappings or threats against tourists or workers in the tourism industry, as well as the wilful destruction of tourism facilities or of elements of cultural or natural heritage should be severely condemned and punished in accordance with their respective national laws.
5. When travelling, tourists and visitors should not commit any criminal act or any act considered criminal by the laws of the country visited and abstain from any conduct felt to be offensive or injurious by the local populations, or likely to damage the local environment; they should refrain from all trafficking in illicit drugs, arms, antiques, protected species and products and substances that are dangerous or prohibited by national regulations.

6. Tourists and visitors have the responsibility to acquaint themselves, even before their departure, with the characteristics of the countries they are preparing to visit; they must be aware of the health and security risks inherent in any travel outside their usual environment and behave in such a way as to minimize those risks.

Article 2

Tourism as a vehicle for individual and collective fulfilment

1. Tourism, the activity most frequently associated with rest and relaxation, sport and access to culture and nature, should be planned and practised as a privileged means of individual and collective fulfilment; when practised with a sufficiently open mind, it is an irreplaceable factor of self-education, mutual tolerance and for learning about the legitimate differences between peoples and cultures and their diversity.
2. Tourism activities should respect the equality of men and women; they should promote human rights and, more particularly, the individual rights of the most vulnerable groups, notably children, the elderly, the handicapped, ethnic minorities and indigenous peoples.
3. The exploitation of human beings in any form, particularly sexual, especially when applied to children, conflicts with the fundamental aims of tourism and is the negation of tourism; as such, in accordance with international law, it should be energetically combated with the cooperation of all the states concerned and penalized without concession by the national legislation of both the countries visited and the countries of the perpetrators of these acts, even when they are carried out abroad.
4. Travel for purposes of religion, health, education and cultural or linguistic exchanges is particularly beneficial form of tourism, which deserve encouragement.
5. The introduction into curricula of education about the value of tourist exchanges, their economic, social and cultural benefits, and also their risks, should be encouraged.

Article 3

Tourism, a factor of sustainable development

1. All the stakeholders in tourism development should safeguard the natural environment with a view to achieving sound, continuous and sustainable economic growth geared to satisfying equitably the needs and aspirations of present and future generations.
2. All forms of tourism development that are conducive to saving rare and precious resources, in particular water and energy, as well as avoiding so far as possible waste production, should be given priority and encouraged by national, regional and local public authorities.
3. The staggering in time and space of tourist and visitor flows, particularly those resulting from paid leave and school holidays, and a more even distribution of holidays should be sought so as to reduce the pressure of tourism activity on the environment and enhance its beneficial impact on the tourism industry and the local economy.
4. Tourism infrastructure should be designed and tourism activities programmed in such a way as to protect the natural heritage composed of ecosystems and biodiversity and to preserve endangered species of wild life; the stakeholders in tourism development, and especially professionals, should agree to the imposition of limitations or constraints on their activities when these are exercised in particularly sensitive areas: desert, polar or high mountain regions, coastal areas, tropical forests or wetlands, propitious to the creation of nature reserves or protected areas.

5. Nature tourism and eco-tourism are recognized as being particularly conducive to enriching and enhancing the standing of tourism, provided they respect the natural heritage and local populations and are in keeping with the carrying capacity of the sites.

Article 4

Tourism, a user of the cultural heritage of mankind and a contributor to its enhancement

1. Tourism resources belong to the common heritage of mankind; the communities in whose territories they are situated have particular rights and obligations to them.
2. Tourism policies and activities should be conducted with respect for the artistic, archaeological and cultural heritage, which they should protect and pass on to future generations; particular care should be devoted to preserving and upgrading monuments, shrines and museums as well as archaeological and historic sites which must be widely open to tourist visits; encouragement should be given to public access to privately owned cultural property and monuments, with respect for the rights of their owners, as well as to religious buildings, without prejudice to normal needs of worship.
3. Financial resources derived from visits to cultural sites and monuments should, at least in part, be used for the upkeep, safeguard, development and embellishment of this heritage.
4. Tourism activity should be planned in such a way as to allow traditional cultural products, crafts and folklore to survive and flourish, rather than causing them to degenerate and become standardized.

Article 5

Tourism, a beneficial activity for host countries and communities

1. Local populations should be associated with tourism activities and share equitably in the economic, social and cultural benefits they generate, and particularly in the creation of direct and indirect jobs resulting from them.
2. Tourism policies should be applied in such a way as to help raise the standard of living of the populations of the regions visited and meet their needs; the planning and architectural approach to and operation of tourism resorts and accommodation should aim to integrate them, to the extent possible, in the local economic and social fabric; where skills are equal, priority should be given to local manpower.
3. Special attention should be paid to the specific problems of coastal areas and island territories and to vulnerable rural or mountain regions, for which tourism often represents a rare opportunity for development in the face of the decline of traditional economic activities.
4. Tourism professionals, particularly investors, governed by the regulations laid down by the public authorities, should carry out studies of the impact of their development projects on the environment and natural surroundings; they should also deliver, with the greatest transparency and objectivity, information on their future programmes and their foreseeable repercussions and foster dialogue on their contents with the populations concerned.

Article 6

Obligations of stakeholders in tourism development

1. Tourism professionals have an obligation to provide tourists with objective and honest information on their places of destination and on the conditions of travel, hospitality and

stays; they should ensure that the contractual clauses proposed to their customers are readily understandable as to the nature, price and quality of the services they commit themselves to providing and the financial compensation payable by them in the event of a unilateral breach of contract on their part.

2. Tourism professionals, insofar as it depends on them, should show concern in cooperation with the public authorities for the security and safety, accident prevention, health protection and food safety of those who seek their services; likewise, they should ensure the existence of suitable systems of insurance and assistance; they should accept the reporting obligations prescribed by national regulations and pay fair compensation in the event of failure to observe their contractual obligations.

3. Tourism professionals, so far as this depends on them, should contribute to the cultural and spiritual fulfilment of tourists and allow them, during their travels, to practise their religions.

4. The public authorities of the generating states and the host countries, in cooperation with the professionals concerned and their associations, should ensure that the necessary mechanisms are in place for the repatriation of tourists in the event of the bankruptcy of the enterprise that organized their travel.

5. Governments have the right—and the duty—especially in a crisis, to inform their nationals of the difficult circumstances, or even the dangers they may encounter during their travels abroad; it is their responsibility, however, to issue such information without prejudicing in an unjustified or exaggerated manner the tourism industry of the host countries and the interests of their own operators; the contents of travel advisories should therefore be discussed beforehand with the authorities of the host countries and the professionals concerned; recommendations formulated should be strictly proportionate to the gravity of the situations encountered and confined to the geographical areas where the insecurity has arisen; such advisories should be qualified or cancelled as soon as a return to normality permits.

6. The press, and particularly the specialized travel press and the other media, including modern means of electronic communication, should issue honest and balanced information on events and situations that could influence the flow of tourists; they should also provide accurate and reliable information to the consumers of tourism services; the new communication and electronic commerce technologies should also be developed and used for this purpose; as is the case for the media, they should not in any way promote sex tourism.

Article 7

Right to tourism

1. The prospect of direct and personal access to the discovery and enjoyment of the planet's resources constitutes a right equally open to all the world's inhabitants; the increasingly extensive participation in national and international tourism should be regarded as one of the best possible expressions of the sustained growth of free time, and obstacles should not be placed in its way.

2. The universal right to tourism must be regarded as the corollary of the right to rest and leisure, including reasonable limitation of working hours and periodic holidays with pay, guaranteed by Article 24 of the Universal Declaration of Human Rights and Article 7.d of the International Covenant on Economic, Social and Cultural Rights.

3. Social tourism, and in particular associative tourism, which facilitates widespread access to leisure, travel and holidays, should be developed with the support of the public authorities.
4. Family, youth, student and senior tourism and tourism for people with disabilities, should be encouraged and facilitated.

Article 8

Liberty of tourist movements

1. Tourists and visitors should benefit, in compliance with international law and national legislation, from the liberty to move within their countries and from one state to another, in accordance with Article 13 of the Universal Declaration of Human Rights; they should have access to places of transit and stay and to tourism and cultural sites without being subject to excessive formalities or discrimination.
2. Tourists and visitors should have access to all available forms of communication, internal or external; they should benefit from prompt and easy access to local administrative, legal and health services; they should be free to contact the consular representatives of their countries of origin in compliance with the diplomatic conventions in force.
3. Tourists and visitors should benefit from the same rights as the citizens of the country visited concerning the confidentiality of the personal data and information concerning them, especially when these are stored electronically.
4. Administrative procedures relating to border crossings whether they fall within the competence of states or result from international agreements, such as visas or health and customs formalities, should be adapted, so far as possible, so as to facilitate to the maximum freedom of travel and widespread access to international tourism; agreements between groups of countries to harmonize and simplify these procedures should be encouraged; specific taxes and levies penalizing the tourism industry and undermining its competitiveness should be gradually phased out or corrected.
5. So far as the economic situation of the countries from which they come permits, travellers should have access to allowances of convertible currencies needed for their travels.

Article 9

Rights of the workers and entrepreneurs in the tourism industry

1. The fundamental rights of salaried and self-employed workers in the tourism industry and related activities should be guaranteed under the supervision of the national and local administrations, both of their state of origin and of the host countries with particular care, given the specific constraints linked in particular to the seasonality of their activity, the global dimension of their industry and the flexibility often required of them by the nature of their work.
2. Salaried and self-employed workers in the tourism industry and related activities have the right and the duty to acquire appropriate initial and continuous training; they should be given adequate social protection; job insecurity should be limited so far as possible; and a specific status, with particular regard to their social welfare, should be offered to seasonal workers in the sector.
3. Any natural or legal person, provided he, she or it has the necessary abilities and skills, should be entitled to develop a professional activity in the field of tourism under existing

national laws; entrepreneurs and investors—especially in the area of small and medium-sized enterprises—should be entitled to free access to the tourism sector with a minimum of legal or administrative restrictions.

4. Exchanges of experience offered to executives and workers, whether salaried or not, from different countries, contribute to foster the development of the world tourism industry; these movements should be facilitated so far as possible in compliance with the applicable national laws and international conventions.

5. As an irreplaceable factor of solidarity in the development and dynamic growth of international exchanges, multinational enterprises of the tourism industry should not exploit the dominant positions they sometimes occupy; they should avoid becoming the vehicles of cultural and social models artificially imposed on the host communities; in exchange for their freedom to invest and trade, which should be fully recognized, they should involve themselves in local development, avoiding, by the excessive repatriation of their profits or their induced imports, a reduction of their contribution to the economies in which they are established.

6. Partnership and the establishment of balanced relations between enterprises of generating and receiving countries contribute to the sustainable development of tourism and an equitable distribution of the benefits of its growth.

Article 10

Implementation of the principles of the Global Code of Ethics for Tourism

1. The public and private stakeholders in tourism development should cooperate in the implementation of these principles and monitor their effective application.

2. The stakeholders in tourism development should recognize the role of international institutions, among which the World Tourism Organization ranks first, and non-governmental organizations with competence in the field of tourism promotion and development, the protection of human rights, the environment or health, with due respect for the general principles of international law.

3. The same stakeholders should demonstrate their intention to refer any disputes concerning the application or interpretation of GCET for conciliation to an impartial third body known as the World Committee on Tourism Ethics.

Observation on the Code

Five general categories of literature deal with ethical issues in tourism that are reflected in the Code of Ethics adopted by the General Assembly of WTO in 2000. At a seminar at Tel Aviv, it was claimed that tourism was a harbinger of peace in two ways, it creates direct contact between tourist and host, and tourism operates in a region bound by a common interest in promoting tourism. On the success and friendly relations between people will depend the profitability of tourism. Ethical issues are related to ecological impacts, marketing, sustainable development, humanistic and social concerns, and education. Tourism educational material does not reflect the negative side of tourism or deals with ethical issues of tourism; therefore, it was felt that educational material needed an infusion of the ethical point of view. To ensure that tourism goods and services are marketed to meet accepted standards and practices in the industry, such as truthful advertising, honest classification of services and the various distribution channels that deliver the service, a best practice kind of approach was taken.

The Code of Ethical Conduct has been viewed as a voluntary code, and not to be implemented by zealous moral reformers, it is for this reason that a draft protocol for implementation was to be decided by the WTO General Assembly by 2001. The WTO condemned ill-conceived, ill-executed and opportunistic tourism development and decided to work to remove health and safety hazards that selfish tourism development had brought about. They identified drug abuse, sex tourism, child exploitation and environmental degradation amongst the visible problems created by the tidal wave of tourism all over the world. Sixty-four governments met in Manila in May 1997 and decided to work towards a code of ethics. In 1998 several NGOs joined issue with governments on the labour practices and remuneration for works in the tourism sector, the rights of local communities and indigenous people and rights of women and children. They also suggested a mechanism whereby the offenders could be punished. They felt that the growth in global tourism had brought about problem and complications, some of which were serious enough to threaten social consensus and the ecological equilibrium of communities.

The difference in the approach of industry and NGOs, and the WTO is reflected in the promotion of the International Year of Ecotourism, 2002; while NGOs feel this is a form of tourism, which penetrates into regions that are most endangered and peoples are most threatened, the UN organization believes that this form of tourism should be promoted, with certification safeguards, as it is the most sustainable. The campaign to rethink the year of eco-tourism has brought about some revisions of manner in which the WTO had planned a series of events to highlight the event. There is also a decision to ensure the participation of the concerned people from the south, who will be the most affected. There is a difference between NGOs of the north and south too.

Big business-oriented NGOs such as Conservation International and International Ecotourism Society are for promoting eco-tourism since it is their field of operation. Much international aid and consultancy will flow from such promotions for such NGOs. The southern NGOs such as Third World Network, TIM-Team and Equations, along with ECTWT have opposed the concept of eco-tourism being imposed from above. They want a clarification of the objectives and the definition before any promotion is allowed.

11.11. The Wild Life (Protection) Act, 1972

The term 'wild life' applies to all biotic elements that comprise every species of plants and animals excluding man and domesticated animals. But in practice it is mostly used for limited number of species, mostly game animals. The term 'wild life' as defined by the Wild Life (Protection) Act, 1972, of India includes 'any animal, bees, butterflies, crustacean, fish and moths and aquatic or other land vegetation which form part of any habitants.'

The **Wild Life (Protection) Act, 1972,** is an act of the Parliament of India enacted for protection of plant and animal species. The Government of India enacted this Act with the objective of effectively protecting the wild life of this country and to control poaching, smuggling and illegal trade in wild life and its derivatives. The Act was amended in January 2003, and punishment and penalty for offences under the Act have been made more stringent. The Ministry of Environment, Forest and Climate change has proposed further amendments in the law by introducing more rigid measures to strengthen the Act. The objective is to provide protection to the listed endangered flora and fauna and ecologically important protected areas. This is an Act to provide for the protection of wild animals, birds and plants and for matters connected therewith. It has six schedules which give varying degrees of protection. Schedule I and part II of Schedule II provide absolute protection—offences under these are prescribed the highest penalties. Species listed in Schedule III and Schedule IV are also protected, but the penalties are much lower. Schedule V includes the animals which may be hunted. The plants in Schedule VI are prohibited from cultivation and planting. For hunting, the enforcement authorities have the power to compound offences under this Schedule.

Wild Life in India

Till 1972, there was absence of any scientific assessment of all endangered and threatened species of wild life flora and fauna on a national level in India. However, a total of 253 species and sub-species of wild fauna (mammals, aves, reptiles, amphibians and invertebrates) have been included in Schedule I of the Wild Life (Protection) Act, 1972, in order to afford total protection of these species. As regards to flora, about 2,000 species of flowering plants alone are reported to suffer from one kind of threat. An inventory of 135 threatened species and sub-species of rare and endangered plants has been prepared by the Botanical Survey of India.

Threats to Wild Life

At present, wild life all over the world is vanishing rapidly, India is thus no exception. The pressure of modernization along with an unprecedented growth of human population and commercial exploitation of forest have been the prime causes for the decline of wild life in India.

Wild Life Action Plan

With the large-scale deforestation in India wild animals such as elephants, deer and wild boar began to enter in the agricultural areas in search of food. The big predators such as tiger and leopards began to lift the cattle and occasionally man. The result was large-scale destruction of wild life. The situation worsened during the 1950s and 1960s which witnessed a depletion of the country's biological heritage at a massive scale.

To meet the prevailing and future challenges, the Indian Board of Wild life (IBWL) was constituted, headed by the prime minister of India as chairperson. Broadly speaking, IBWL is a prospectus of action to be taken with regard to wild life conservation in India.

Conservation Objectives

There are three specific objectives of living resource conservation; obviously there are also three objectives in the establishment of protected areas which include the following:

- To maintain essential ecological processes and life support system
- To preserve genetic diversity
- To ensure the sustainable utilization of species and ecosystem

National parks, wild life sanctuaries, tiger reserves and biosphere reserves are the protected areas.

Wild Life (Protection) Act

A comprehensive central legislation was enacted in 1972, called the Wild Life (Protection) Act, for providing special legal protection to our wild life and to endangered species of fauna in particular. It has a provision for setting up of national parks and sanctuaries where our wild life can receive fullest protection. For infringement of the provision of this Act, very stringent punishments have been provided. This act has been adopted by all states and union territories of the country except the states of Jammu and Kashmir and Nagaland. The former have enacted their legislation largely on the same line as the central Act, while the latter has been addressed to adopt the Act as early as possible.

An expert committee set up by IBWL has questioned the needed amendments to the Wild Life Act. The most significant amendment will bring under the Wild Life Act hitherto neglected plant life. Thus, the endangered species of plants are also being included in the schedules. There is also provision for control of trade in plants and plant products. A new section for creation of biosphere reserves has been incorporated enabling the Central Government to declare appropriate areas as biosphere reserves in consultation with the concurrence of the concerned state governments.

Amendments

- The Wild Life (Protection) Amendment Act, 2013
- The Wild Life (Protection) Amendment Act, 2006 (No. 39 of 2006 [03/09/2006])
- The Wild Life (Protection) Amendment Act, 2002 (No. 16 of 2003 [17/01/2003])
- The Wild Life (Protection) Act 1972, as amended in 1993

Bills

- Wild Life (Protection) Amendment Bill, 2013

Content of Wild Life (Protection) Act, 1972

Chapter I

1. Short title, extent and commencement

a. This Act may be called the Wild Life (Protection) Act, 1972.
b. It extends to the whole of India, except the state of Jammu and Kashmir.
c. It shall come into force in a state or union territory to which it extends, on such date as the Central Government may, by notification, appoint, and different dates may be appointed for different provision of this Act or for different states or union territories.

2. Definitions under the Wild Life (Protection) Act

a. 'Animal' includes amphibians, birds, mammals, and reptiles, and their young, and also includes, in the cases of birds and reptiles, their eggs.
b. 'Animal article' means an article made from any captive animal or wild animal, other than vermin.
c. 'Captive animal' means any animal, specified in Schedule 1, Schedule II, Schedule III or Schedule IV, which is captured or kept or bred in captivity.

d. 'Circus' means an establishment, whether stationary or mobile where animals are kept or used wholly or mainly for the purpose of performing tricks or manoeuvres.
e. 'Habitat' includes land, water, or vegetation which is the natural home of any wild animal.
f. 'Hunting', with its grammatical variations and cognate expressions, includes:
    i. Capturing, killing, poisoning, snaring and trapping or any wild animal and every attempt to do so.
    ii. Driving any wild animal for any purposes specified in subclause of Wildlife (protection) Act 1972
    iii. Injuring or destroying or taking any part of the body of any such animal, or in the case of wild birds or reptiles, damaging the eggs of such birds or reptiles, or disturbing the eggs or nests of such birds or reptiles.
g. 'Land' includes canals, creeks, and other water channels, reservoirs, rivers, streams and lakes, whether artificial or natural, marshes and wetlands, and also includes boulders and rocks.
h. 'Livestock' includes buffaloes, bulls, bullocks, camels, cows, donkeys, goats, horses, mules, pigs, sheep and yak, and also includes their young.
i. 'Manufacturer' means a manufacturer of animal articles.
j. 'Meat' includes blood, bones, sinew, eggs, fat and flesh, whether raw or cooked, of any wild animal other than vermin.
k. 'National park' means an area declared, whether under Section 35 or Section 38 or deemed, under Subsection (3) of Section 66 to be declared, as a national park.
l. 'Reserve forest' means the forest declared to be reserved by the state government under Section 20 of the Indian Forest Act, 1927 (16 of 1927).
m. 'Sanctuary' means an area declared, whether under Section (26[A]) or Section 38, or deemed, under Subsection (3) of Section 66 to be declared, as a wild life sanctuary.
n. 'Taxidermy', with its grammatical variations and cognate expressions, means the curing, preparation or preservation of trophies.
o. 'Trophy' means the whole or any part of any captive animal or wild animal, other than vermin, which has been kept or preserved by any means, whether artificial or natural, and includes:
    i. Rugs, skins, and specimens of such animals mounted in whole or in part through a process of taxidermy.
    ii. Antler, horn, rhinoceros horn, feather, nail, tooth, musk, eggs, and nests.
p. 'Uncured trophy' means the whole or any part of any captive animal, other than vermin, which has not undergone a process of taxidermy, and includes a (freshly killed wild animal ambergris, musk and other animal products.)
q. 'Wild life' includes any animal, bees butterflies, crustacean, fish and moths; and aquatic or land vegetation which forms part of any habitat.
r. 'Zoo' means an establishment, whether stationary or mobile, where captive animals are kept for exhibition to the public but does not include a circus and an establishment of a licensed dealer in captive animals.

Chapter II

Chapter II deals with authorities to be appointed or constituted under the Act.

Appointment of Director and other officers: The Central Government may, for the purposes of this Act, appoint:

1. A director of wild life preservation
2. Assistant directors of wild life preservation
3. Other officers and employees as may be necessary

The state government may, for the purposes of this Act, appoint:

1. Chief wild life warden
2. Wild life wardens

Chapter III (hunting of wild animals)

Chapter III deals with hunting of wild animals

Prohibition of hunting: No person shall hunt any wild animal specified in Schedules I, II, III and IV except as provided under Section 11 and Section 12.

Hunting of wild animals to be permitted in certain cases:

1. Notwithstanding anything contained in any other law for the time being in force and subject to the provisions of Chapter IV:

   The chief wild life warden or the authorized officer may, if he is satisfied that any wild animal specified in Schedule I, Schedule II, Schedule III, or Schedule IV has become dangerous to human life or is so disabled or diseased as to be beyond recovery, by order in writing and stating the reasons therefore, permit any person to hunt such animal or cause such animal to be hunted.

2. The killing or wounding in good faith of any wild animal in defence of oneself or any other person shall not be an offence: Provided that nothing in this subsection shall exonerate any person who, when such defence becomes necessary, was committing any act in contravention of any provisions of this Act or any rule or order made there under.

3. Any wild animal killed or wounded in defence of any person shall be government property.

Chapter IIIa (Protection of Specified Plants)

No person shall:

1. Wilfully pick, uproot, damage, destroy, acquire or collect any specified plant from any forest land and any area specified, by notification, by the Central Government.
2. Possess, sell, offer for sale, or transfer by way to gift or otherwise, or transport any specified plant, whether alive or dead, or part or derivative thereof.

Chapter IV (Sanctuaries, National Parks and Closed Areas)

Declaration of Sanctuary

The state government may, by notification, declare its intention to constitute any area comprised within any reserve forest or the territorial water as a sanctuary if it considers that such area is of adequate ecological, faunal, floral, geomorphologic, natural or zoological significance, for the purpose of protecting, propagating or developing wild life or its environment.

Declaration of National Parks

Whenever it appears to the state government that an area, whether within a sanctuary or not, is, by reason of its ecological, faunal, floral, geomorphologic or zoological association or importance, needed to be constituted as national park for the purpose of protecting, propagating or developing wild life therein or its environment, it may, by notification, declare its intention to constitute such area as a national park.

Declaration of Closed Area

The state government may, by notification, declare any area closed to hunting for such period as may be specified in the notification. No hunting of any wild animal shall be permitted in a closed area as per Wildlife (protection) Act 1972.

Chapter V (Trade or Commerce in Wild Animals, Animal Articles and Trophies)

Wild animals and so on to be Government property:

Every—(a) wild animal, other than vermin, which is hunted under Section 11 or Subsection (1) of Section 29 or Subsection (6) of Section 35 or kept or [bred in captivity or hunted] in contravention of any provision of this Act or any rule or order made there under or found dead, or killed by mistake

(b) animal article, trophy or uncured trophy or meat derived from any wild animal referred to in Clause (a) in respect of which any offence against this Act or any rule or order made there under has been committed

(c) ivory imported into India and an article made from such ivory in respect of which any offence against this Act or any rule or order made there under has been committed

(d) vehicle, vessel, weapon, trap or tool that has been used for committing an offence and has been seized under the provision of this Act, shall be the property of the state government, and, where such animal is hunted in a sanctuary or national park declared by the Central Government, such animal or any animal article, trophy, uncured trophy or meat shall be the property of the Central Government.

Chapter VI (Prevention and Detection of Offence)

Power of entry, search, arrest and detention

1. Notwithstanding anything contained in any other law for the time being in force, the director or any other officer authorized by him in this behalf or the chief wild life warden or the authorized officer or any forest officer or any police officer not below the rank of a sub-inspector, may, if he has reasonable grounds for believing that any person has committed an offence against this Act.

Chapter VII (Miscellaneous)

1. Officers to be public servants.
2. Protection of action taken in good faith. No suit, prosecution or other legal proceeding shall lie against any officer or other employee of the Central Government or the state government of anything which is in good faith done or intended to be done under this Act.
3. Declaration of certain wild animals to be vermin.
4. Rights of scheduled tribes to be protected.

11.12. Constitutional Provisions of Tourism Legislation in India

Tourism legislation has its foundation in the Constitution of India. Although in the Constitution the word 'tourism' is not found anywhere, elements related to tourism are in the 'Directive Principles of State Policy', 'Distribution of Legislative Power' and 'Fundamental Duties of Citizens.'

Under 'Distribution of Legislative power' there are three lists: Union List, State List and Concurrent List. In these lists also the word 'tourism' does not appear anywhere, but there are certain points directly or indirectly related to tourism. These are as follows:

Union List

1. (13) 'Participation in internal conferences, associations and other bodies and implementing of decisions made thereat.'
2. (19) 'Admission into, and emigration and expulsion from India; passports and visa.'
3. (20) 'Pilgrimages to places outside India.'
4. (22) 'Railways'
5. (23) 'Highways declared by or under law made by Parliament to be national highways.'
6. (24) 'Shipping and navigation on inland waterways declared by Parliament by law to be national waterways, as regards mechanically propelled vessels; the rule of the road on such waterways.'
7. (25) 'Maritime shipping and navigation, including shipping and navigation on tidal waters; provision of education and training provided by states and other agencies.'
8. (29) 'Airways, aircraft and air navigation; provision of aerodromes; regulation and organization of air traffic and of aerodromes; provision for aeronautical education and training and regulation of such education and training provided by states and other agencies.'
9. (30) 'Carriage of passengers and goods by railways, sea and air or by national waterways in mechanically propelled vessels.'
10. (62) 'The institutions known at the commencement of this Constitution as the National Library, the Indian Museum, the Imperial War Museum, the Victoria Memorial and the Indian War memorial, and any other like institution financed by the Government of India wholly or in part and declared by parliament by law to be an institution of national importance.'
11. (67) 'Ancient and historical monuments and records, and archaeological site and remains, declared by or under law made by Parliament to be of national importance.'

State List

1. (5) 'Local government, that is to say, the constitution and powers of municipal corporation, improvement trusts, district boards, mining settlement authorities and other local authorities for the purpose of local self-government or village administration.'
2. (6) 'Public health and sanitation, hospitals and dispensaries.'
3. (7) 'Pilgrimages, other than pilgrimages to places outside India.'
4. (12) 'Libraries, museums and other similar institutions controlled or financed by the State; ancient and historical monuments and records other than those declared by or under law made by parliament to be of national importance.'
5. (13) 'Communications, that is to say, roads, bridges, ferries and other means of communication not specified in List I: Municipal tramways, ropeways, inland waterways and traffic thereon

subject to the provisions of List I and List III with regard to such waterways; vehicles other than mechanically propelled vehicles.'
6. (31) 'Inns and innkeepers'
7. (33) 'Theatres and dramatic performances; cinemas subject to the provisions of Entry 60 of List I; sports, entertainments and amusement.'

Concurrent List

1. (17A) 'Forests.'
2. (17B) 'Protection of wild animals and birds.'
3. (18) 'Adulteration of foodstuffs and other goods.'
4. (31) 'Ports other than those declared by or under law made by parliament or existing law to be major ports.'
5. (40) 'Archaeological sites and remains other than those declared by or under law made by parliament to be of national importance.'

Under Fundamental Duties of Citizens, tourism related duties are as follows:-

1. (f) To value and preserve rich heritage of our composite cultures.
2. (g) To protect and improve the natural environment including forests, lakes, rivers, wild life and to have compassion for living creatures.

The Constitution of India has highlighted the basics of tourism and also provided future guidelines for its growth. After understanding the provisions of the Constitution, the next step is to review the important existing legislations, dealing directly or indirectly with tourism.

Conclusion

Future role of tourism is very challenging. With accelerated changes taking place throughout the globe, there will be emergence of new role of tourism. The future of the human society is techno-transient by character. Rapid changes in human institutions of society, family and other organizations will give rise to urgent necessity of shaping social experiences to maintain and improve the quality of life. Developing legal and regulatory framework is essential for the sustainable development and management of tourism, protection and conservation of natural and cultural resources, and facilitation of the involvement of private sector and local communities in tourism development activities. It reflects the roles and responsibilities of all stakeholders, ensures the rights of international/local tourists, and ensures the rights and obligations of participating businesses, inbound and outbound tour operators and all other stakeholders in the tourism field. Tourism laws refer to a combination of state, federal and international laws that regulate various aspects and functions of the travel industry.

This chapter mainly deals with various legal and ethical aspects of tourism used in the world scenario in general and Indian context in particular. Some important legal issues such as consumer protection law in tourism, Passports Act, 1967, rules and regulations regarding the star classifications of hotels, Manila Declaration on tourism, some conferences related to legal issues on tourism such as Warsaw Convention, Chicago Convention, apart from the Wild Life (Protection)

Act, Tourism Bill of Rights and Tourist Code are also dealt with in this chapter. The laws governing tourism tend to be disorganized and non-standardized. However, every tourism law attempts to protect travel consumers and organizations.

MODEL QUESTIONS

1. Discuss the areas in which consumer protection law is applicable in the tourism industry.
2. Critically examine the application of consumer protection law in tourism in detail.
3. Discuss different methods of addressing various issues involved in consumer protection law in tourism.
4. Describe in detail about the main features of Passport Act, 1967.
5. State and explain the general features, facilities and services required to declare a hotel as 5- star hotel.
6. Discuss in detail about the main guidelines provided by the Warsaw Convention.
7. What are the main features of Chicago Convention?
8. Write a note on bilateral agreement.
9. Write a note on 'Freedom of Air'.
10. Why is Manila Declaration so significant in tourism?
11. Briefly explain Tourism Bill of Rights and Tourist Code.
12. Examine the objectives and characteristic features and significance of Wild Life (Protection) Act, 1972.

Student Activities

1. Find out different types of passport and visa issued by different countries and also find out the validity of types visa for different countries with the help of Travel Information Manual.
2. Find out different endemic yellow fever zones and list out the different countries where yellow fever vaccinations are necessary before visiting those countries.

Suggested Readings

Andreck, L. K., & Vogt, A. C. (2000). The relationship between residents' attitude towards tourism and tourism development options. *Journal of Travel Research*, *39*, 27–36.

Batra, G. S., & Chawla, A. S. (1995). *Tourism management: A global prospective*. New Delhi: Deep and Deep Publications.

Baum, T. (2006). *Human resource management for tourism, hospitality and leisure: An international* perspective (pp. 224–227). London: Thomson Learning.

Bhatia, A. K. (2006). *The business of tourism concept and strategies* (pp. 30–36). New Delhi: Sterling Publications.

Budowski, G. (1977). Tourism and conservation: Conflicts, coexistence and symbiosis. *Parks, 1*, 3–6.

Butler, R. W. (1974). The social implications of tourism developments. *Annals of Tourism Research, 2*(2), 100–111.

Caves, R., & Gosling, G. (1999). *Strategic airport planning*. Oxford: Pergamon.

Chawla, R. (2004). *Heritage tourism and development*. New Delhi: Sonali Publications.

Clarke, M. (2002). *Contracts of carriage by air*. London: Lloyd's of London Press.

Cohen, E. (2003). Contemporary tourism and host community in the less developed areas. *Tourism Recreation and Research, 28*(1), 1–9.

Cordato, J. (1990). *Australian travel and tourism law*. Sydney: Butterworth.

Dickerson, T. (1981–2002). *Travel law*. New York, NY: Law Journal Seminar Press.

Dinn, K. (1988). Social and cultural impacts of tourism. *Annals of Tourism Research, 15*(4), 563–566.

Fladmark, J. M. (Ed.). (1993). *Heritage: Conservation, interpretation and enterprise*. London: Donhead Publishing.

Geoffrey, W. (2000). Sustainable development. In J. Jafari (Ed.), *Encyclopedia of tourism*. London: Routledge.

Gunn, C. (1985). *Tourism planning*. New York, NY: Taylor & Francis.

Holden, A. (2008). *Environment and tourism* (2nd ed.). London: Routledge.

Inskeep, E. (1991). *Tourism planning: An integrated and sustainable development approach*. New York, NY: Van Nostrand Reinhold.

International Union of Official Travel Organization (IUOTO). 1976. *The impact of international tourism on the economic development of developing countries*. Geneva: World Tourism Organization.

Laws, E. (1995). *Tourist destination management: Issues, analysis and policies*. London: Routledge.

Leiper, N. (1990). *Tourism systems: An interdisciplinary perspective* (Occasional Paper 2, Massey University, Department of Management System). New Zealand: Palmerton North.

Mill, R. C., & Morrison, A. M. (1992). *The tourism system: An introductory test*. Englewood Cliffs, NJ: Prentice Hall.

Motiram (2003). *International tourism: Socio-economic prospective*. New Delhi: Sonali Publications.

Norval, A. (1936). *The tourism industry: A national and international survey*. London: Pitman.

Page, J. S., & Connell, J. (2009). *Tourism: A modern synthesis* (3rd ed.). Hampshire: South-Western Cengage Learning.

Prentice, R. (2004). Tourism motivations and typologies. In A. Lew, C. M. Hall & A. Williams (Eds.), *A companion to tourism*. Oxford: Blackwell.

Pruthi, R. K. (2004). *International tourism: Potential measurement and prospects*. New Delhi: Rajat Publications.

Ranga, M., Gupta, P., & Chandra, A. (2004). *Legal prospectives in Indian tourism*. New Delhi: Abhijeet Publications.

Saggerson, A. (2000). *Travel law and litigation*. Welwyn Garden City: CLT Professional Publishing.

Sharma, P. S. (2004). *Tourism education: Theories and practices*. New Delhi: Kanishka Publications.

Sharpley, R. (1994). *Tourism, tourist and society*. Huntingdon: Elm.

The Consumer Protection Act, 1986: Bare act.

The Environmental (Protection) Act, 1986: Bare act.

The Passports Act, 1967: Bare act and rules

The Wild Life (Protection) Act, 1972: Bare act.

World Tourism Organization. (1985, 17–26 September). *Tourism bill of right and tourist code A/6/11(a) adopted by the sixth General Assembly*. Sofia, Bulgaria: Author.

Tribe, J., Font, X., Griffith, N., Vickery, R., & Yale, K. (2000). *Environmental management for rural tourism and recreation*. London: Cassel Publication.

Turner, R. K., Pearce, D., & Bateman, I. (1993). *Environmental economics: An elementary introduction*. Baltimore: The Johns Hopkins University Press.

Vrancked, P. (Ed.). (2002). *Tourism and the law in South Africa*. Port Elizabeth: Butterworth.

World Travel and Tourism Council, World Tourism Organization and the Earth Council. (1996). *Agenda 21 for the travel and tourism industry: Towards environmentally sustainable development*. London: World Travel and Tourism Council.

Young, G. (1973). *Tourism: Blessings or bright?* Harmondsworth: Penguin.

Suggested Websites

United Nations World Tourism Organizations: www.world-tourism.org
World Travel and Tourism Council Report: www. wttc.com
World Travel and Tourism Council: www.wttc.org

Bibliography

Adams, K. (1990). Cultural commoditization in Tana Toraja, Indonesia. *Cultural Survival Quarterly, 14*(1), 31–34.

Andreck, L. K., & Vogt, A. C. (2000). The relationship between resident's attitude towards tourism and tourism development options. *Journal of Travel Research, 39*, 27–36.

Balsdon, J. P. D. (1969). *Life and leisure in ancient Rome*. London: Bodley Head.

Banister, D. (1995). *Tourism and urban development*. London: Spon Press.

———. (2002). *Transport planning* (2nd ed.). London: Spon Press.

Banks, J. H. (2002). *Introduction to transportation engineering*. New York, NY: McGraw-Hill.

Bansal, S. P., Sushma, S. K., & Mohan, C. (2002). *Tourism in new millennium*. Chandigarh: Abhishek Publications.

Batra, G. S., & Chawala, A. S. (1995). *Tourism management: A global prospective*. New Delhi: Deep and Deep Publications.

Baum, T. (2006). *Human resource management for tourism, hospitality and leisure: An international perspective* (pp. 224–227). London: Thomson Learning.

Baumol, W. J. (1982). Contestable markets: An uprising in the theory of industry structure. *American Economic Review, 72*, 1–15.

Beamon, B. M. (1999). Measuring supply chain performance. *International Journal of Operations & Production Management, 19*, 275–292.

Belisle, F., & Hoy, D. (1980). The perceived impact of tourism by residence: A case study in Santa Marta, Columbia. *Annals of Tourism Research, 8*(10), 83–100.

Bell, P., & Cloke, P. (1990). *Deregulation and transport: Market forces in the modern world*. London: Fulton.

Bhaumik, P. K. (2002). Regulating the domestic air travel in India: An umpires game. *Omega, 30*, 33–44.

Black, A. (1995). *Urban mass transportation planning*. New York, NY: McGraw-Hill.

Blake, A., & Sinclair, M. T. (2003). Tourism crisis management: US responses to September 11. *Annals of Tourism Research, 30*(4), 813–832.

Bramwell, B., & Lane, B. (1993). The concept of a tourist—area cycle of evolution and implications for management. *The Canadian Geographer, 24*(1980), 5–12.

Brendon, P. (1990). *Thomas Cook: 150 years of popular tourism*. London: Secker.

Britton, S. G. (1982). A conceptual model of tourism in a peripheral economy. In D. G. Pearce (Ed.), *Tourism in South Pacific: The contribution of research to development and planning*. Christchurch: University of Canterbury.

Burkart, A. J., & Medlik, S. (1974). *Tourism—past, present and future*. London: ELBS-Heinemann.

———. (1981). *Tourism—past, present and future*. London: ELBS-Heinemann Professional Publishing.

Budowski, G. (1977). Tourism and conservation: Conflicts, coexistence and symbiosis. *Parks, 1*, 3–6.

Buhalis, D. (1998). Information technology. In R. Cooper & S. Wanhill (Eds.), *Tourism: Principles and practices* (pp. 409–421). London: Pitman.

———. (2000). *E-tourism: Information technology for strategic tourism management*. Harlow: Pearson Education (reprinted in 2003).

Bull, A. (1995). *The economics of travel and tourism* (2nd ed.). Melbourne: Longman.

Burgess, A., & Frances, H. (1967). *The age of grand tour*. London: Paul Elek.

Butler, R. W. (1974). The social implications of tourism developments. *Annals of Tourism Research, 2*(2), 100–111.

———. (1980). The concept of tourist area cycle of evolution: Implications for management of resources. *Canadian Geographer, 14*, 351–384.

Button, K., Haynes, K., & Stough, R. (1998). *Flying into the future: Air transport policy in the European Union*. Cheltenham: Edward Elgar.

Button, K. J. (1993). *Transport economics* (2nd ed.). Aldershot: Edward Elgar.

Button, K. J., & Gillingwater, K. (Eds.). (1983). *Future transport policy*. London: Routledge.

Button, K. J., & Stough, R. (2000). *Air transport networks: Theory and policy implications*. Cheltenham: Edward Elgar.

Calder, S. (2002). *No frills: The truth behind the low-cost revolution in the skies*. London: Virgin Books.

Cartwright, R., & Baird, C. (1999). *The development and growth of the cruise industry*. Oxford: Butterworth–Heinemann.

Casson, L. (1974). *Travel in the ancient world*. London: John Hopkins.

Caves, R., & Gosling, G. (1999). *Strategic airport planning*. Oxford: Pergamon.

Chadwick, R. (1994). Concepts, definitions and measurement used in travel and tourism research. In J. R. B. Ritchie & C. Goeldner (Eds.), *Travel, tourism and hospitality research: A handbook for managers and researchers* (2nd ed.). New York, NY: John Wiley & Sons.

Chamberlin, E. H. (1933). *The theory of monopolistic competition*. Cambridge, MA: Harvard University Press.

Chapman, K. (1979). *People, pattern and process: An introduction to human geography*. London: Edward Arnold.

Chawla, R. (2004). *Heritage tourism and development*. New Delhi: Sonali Publication.

Chopra, S., & Meindl, P. (2001). *Supply chain management: Strategy, planning and operations*. Upper Saddle River, NJ: Prentice-Hall, Inc.

Cobin, J. M. (1999). *A primer on modern themes in free market economics*. Parkland, FL: Universal Publishers.

Cohen, E. (1972). Towards a sociology of international tourism. *Social Research, 39*(1), 64–82.

———. (1979). Rethinking the sociology of tourism. *Annals of Tourism Research, 6*(1), 18–35.

———. (2003). Contemporary tourism and host community in the less developed areas. *Tourism Recreation and Research, 28*(1), 1–9.

Coltman, M. M. (1989). *Introduction to travel and tourism: An international approach*. New York, NY: Van Nostrodam Reinhold.

Connell, J. (2004). The purest of human pleasure: The characteristics and motivations of garden visitors in Great Britain. *Tourism Management, 25*(2), 229–247.

Connell, J., & Page, S. J. (2005). Evaluating the economy and spatial effects of an event: The case of the world medical and health gains. *Tourism Geographic, 7*(1), 63–85.

Cook, A. R., Yale, J. L., & Marqua, J. J. (2012). *Tourism: The business of travel* (3rd ed.). New Delhi: Pearson.

Cooper, C., & Wanhill, S. (1997). *Tourism developments: Environmental and community issues*. Sussex: John Wiley & Sons.

Cooper, C. P., Fletcher, J., Gilbert, D., Wanhall, S., & Shepherd, R. (1998). *Tourism: Principles and practice* (2nd ed.). London: Longman.

Craven, J. (1990). *Introduction to economics* (2nd ed.). Oxford: Blackwell.

Dalen, E. (1989). Research into values and consumer trends in Norway. *Tourism Management, 10*(3), 183–186.

Dann, G. (1981). Tourist motivation: An appraisal. *Annals of Tourism Research, 6*(4), 187–219.

———. (1988). Tourism: Peace, and classical disruption. *Tourism: Vital force for peace*. Montreal: L.J. D'Amore and Associate.

Davidson, R. (1993). *Tourism* (pp. 129–197). London: Pitman Publishing House.

Dinn, K. (1988). Social and cultural impacts of tourism. *Annals of Tourism Research, 15*(4), 563–566.

Dogan, H. (1989). Forms of adjustment: Socio cultural impacts of tourism. *Annals of Tourism Research, 16*(2), 216–229.

Doganis, R. (2001). *Airline business in the 21st century*. London: Routledge.

———. (2002). *Flying off course: The economics of international airlines*. London: Routledge.

Doswell, R. (1997). *Tourism, how effective management makes the difference* (pp. 107–163). Great Britain: Butterworth–Heinemann.

Douglas, N., & Douglas, N. (1996). Tourism in the Pacific: Historical factors. In C. M. Hall & S. J. Page (Eds.), *Tourism in the Pacific: Issues and cases* (pp. 19–35). London: Thomson Learning.

———. (2000). Tourism in South East and South Asia: Historical dimensions. In C. M. Hall & S. J. Page (Eds.), *Tourism in South and South East Asia: Issues and cases* (pp. 178–194). Oxford: Butterworth–Heinemann.

Dowling, R., & Newsome, D. (Eds.). (2005). *Geotourism: Sustainability, impacts and management*. Oxford: Butterworth–Heinemann.

Doxey, G. (1976). When enough's enough: The natives are restless in old Niagara. *Heritage Canada, 2*(2), 26–27.

Dwier, L., Forsyth, P., & Spurr, R. (2004). Evaluating tourism's economic effects: New and old approaches. *Tourism Management, 25*(3), 307–317.

Faulkner, B., Moscardo, B., & Laws, E. (2000). *Tourism in the 21st century*. London: Continuum.

Feifer, M. (1985). *Going places: The way of the tourists from imperial Rome to the present day*. London: Macmillan.

Fennel, D. (1999). *Ecotourism: An introduction*. London: Routledge.

Fladmark, J. M. (Ed.). (1993). *Heritage: Conservation, interpretation and enterprise* (pp. 114–124). London: Donhead Publishing.

Fletcher, J., & Snee, H. (1989). Tourism in South Pacific Island. In C. Cooper (Ed.), *Progress in tourism, recreation and hospitality management* (Vol. 1). London: Belhaven.

Frechting, C. D. (1996). *Practical tourism forecasting*. Oxford: Butterworth–Heinemann.

Gartner, C. W. (1996). *Tourism development: Principles, processes and policies*. New York, NY: Van Nostrand Reinhold.

Gee, C. Y. (1988). *Resort development and management*. East Lansing, MI: American Hotel and Motel Association Educational Institute.

———. (1994). *Sustainable tourism development: A strategic issue for the Asia Pacific region*. Presented before the Commission on Asia and the Pacific of the World Tourism Organization, Kuala Lumpur.

Gee, C. Y., Dixter, J. L., & Makens, J. C. (1984). *The travel industry* (pp. 110–115). Westport, CT: Avi.

Gee, C. Y., Makens, J. C., & Choy, D. J. L. (1997). *The travel industry*. New York, NY: Van Nostrand Reinhold (a division of International Thomson Publishing).

Geoffrey, W. (2000). Sustainable development. In J. Jafri (Ed.), *Encyclopedia of tourism* (p. 155). London: Routledge.

George, B. P. (2005). Measuring tourist attachment to holidays: Some preliminary results. *Tourism, 52*(3), 229–246.

George, B. P., Inbakaran, R., & Poyyamoli, G. (2010). To travel or not to travel: Towards understanding the theory of nativistic motivation. *Tourism, 58*(4), 395–407.

Goeldner, C. R., & Ritchie, J. R. B. (2009). *Tourism: Principles, practices, philosophies*. Hoboken, NJ: John Wiley & Sons.

Goeldner, C. R., Ritchie, J. R. B., & McIntosh, R. W. (2000). *Tourism: Principles, practices and philosophies*. New York, NY: John Wiley & Sons.

Graham, A. (2001). *Managing airports: An international perspective*. Oxford: Butterworth–Heinemann.

Gray, H. P. (1970). *International tourism: International trade*. Lexington: Lexington Books.

Guerrier, Y. (1999). *Organisational behaviour in hotels and restaurants: An international perspective*. New York, NY: Wiley.

Gunn, C. (1985). *Tourism planning*. New York, NY: Taylor & Francis.

Hall, C. M. (2003). *Introduction to tourism: Dimensions, and issues* (4th ed.). Melbourne: Addison Wesley Longman.

Hall, C. M., & Page, S. J. (2002). *The geography of tourism and recreation: Environment, place and space* (2nd ed.). London: Routledge.

Hanlon, P. (1999). *Global airlines: Competition in a transnational industry*. Oxford: Butterworth–Heinemann.

Hernandez, A. S., Cohen, J., & Garcia, H. L. (1996). Resident attitudes towards an instant resort enclave. *Annals of Tourism Research, 23*(4), 755–779.

Hibbert, C. (1974). *The grand tour*. London: Spring Books.

Holden, A. (2008). *Environment and tourism* (2nd ed.). London: Routledge.

Holloway, J. C. (1994). *The business of tourism* (4th ed.). London: Pitman Publishing.

———. (2001). *The business of tourism* (6th ed.). London: Pearson Education.

Holloway, J. C., & Robinson, C. (1995). *Marketing for tourism*. Harlow: Longman.

Hoogvelt, A. (2001). *Globalization and the postcolonial world* (2nd ed.). Basingstoke: Palgrave.

Hunt, J. D., & Layne, D. (1991). The evolution of travel and tourism terminology and definitions. *Journal of Travel Research, 29*(4), 7–11.

Hunziker, W., & Krapf, K. (1942). *Algemeine frendenverkehrslehre*. Zurique: Berna University.

Inskeep, E. (1991). *Tourism planning: An integrated and sustainable development approach*. New York, NY: Van Nostrand Reinhold.

International Union of Official Travel Organization (IUOTO). (1976). *The impact of international tourism on the economic development of developing countries*. Geneva: World Tourism Organization.

Jafri, J. (1989). Tourism as a factor of change: An English language literature review. In J. Bystrzanowski (Ed.), *Tourism as a factor of change: A socio cultural study* (pp. 17–60). Vienna: European Coordination Centre for Research and Documentation in Social Science.

Jovicic, Z. (1999). *Osnovi turizmologije* (fundamentals of tourismology). Banjaluka: PMF.

Jud, G., & Krause, W. (1976). Evaluating tourism in developing areas. *Journal of travel Research, 15*(2), 1–9.

Kotler, P., Bowen, J., & Makens, J. (1999). *Marketing for hospitality and tourism* (2nd ed.). Upper Saddle River, NJ: Prentice Hall.

Krippendorf, J. (1982). *The holidaymakers: Understanding the impacts of leisure and travel*. London: Heinemann.

———. (1987). *The holidaymakers: Understanding the impacts of leisure and travel*. London: Heinemann.

Lapide, L. (2000, 15 April). What about measuring supply chain performance? In *Achieving supply chain excellence through technology* (Vol. 2). San Francisco, CA: Montgomery Research.

Latham, J., & Edwards, C. (2003). The statistical measurement of tourism. In C. Cooper (Ed.), *Classic review in tourism*. Clevedon: Channel View.

Laws, E. (1995). *Tourist destination management: Issues, analysis and policies*. London: Routledge.

Leiper, N. (1990). *Tourism systems: An interdisciplinary perspective* (Occasional Paper 2, Massey University, Department of Management System). New Zealand: Palmerton North.

———. (2004). *Tourism management* (3rd ed.). Frenchs Forest, NSW: Pearson.

———. (2008). Why the 'tourism industry' is misleading as a generic expression: The case for plural variations, 'tourism industry'. *Tourism Management, 29*(2), 237–251.

Lickorish, L. J., & Jenkins, C. L. (Eds.). (1997). *An introduction to tourism.* Oxford: Butterworth–Heinemann.

Lickorish, L. J., & Kershaw, A. G. (1958). *The travel trade.* London: Practical Press.

Liu, Z., Siguaw, J. A., & Enz, C. A. (2008). Using tourist travel habits and preferences to assess strategic destination positioning: The case of Costa Rica. *Cornell Hospitality Quarterly, 49*(3), 258–281. doi: 10.1177/1938965508322007.

Lowry, L. L. (1994). What is travel and tourism and is there a difference between them: A continuing discussion. *New England Journal of Travel and Tourism, 5*, 28–29.

Lumsdon, L. (1997). *Tourism marketing.* London: Thomson International Business Press.

Macleod, V. L. D. (2004). *Tourism, globalisation, and cultural change: An island community perspective.* London: Channel View Publications.

Maslow, A. H. (1943). A theory of human motivation. *Psychological Review, 50*, 370–396.

———. (1954). *Motivation and personality.* New York, NY: Harper and Row.

Mathieson, A., & Wall, G. (1982). *Tourism: Economic, physical and social impact.* Harlow: Longman.

McConnell, D. (1990). *The tourist* (2nd ed.). New York, NY: Schocken.

McIntosh, R. W., & Goeldner, R. C. (1984). *Tourism: Principles, practices and philosophies* (pp. 113–133, 137–142). New York, NY: Wiley.

Medlik, S. (1991). *Managing tourism.* Oxford: Butterworth–Heinemann.

Medlik, S., & Middleton, V. T. C. (1973). The tourism product and its marketing implications. *International Tourism Quarterly, 3*, 28–35.

———. (2001). *Marketing in travel and tourism* (3rd ed.). Oxford: Butterworth–Heinemann.

Meethan, K. (2001). *Tourism in global society: Place, culture, consumption.* Basingstoke: Palgrave.

Mentzer, J. T., DeWitt, W., Keebler, J. S., Min, S., Nix, N. W., Smith, C. D., & Zacharia, Z. G. (2001). Defining supply chain management. *Journal of Business Logistics, 22*(2), 1–25.

Middleton, V. T. C., & Clarke, J. (2001). *Marketing in travel and tourism* (3rd ed.). Oxford: Butterworth–Heinemann.

Mill, R. C., & Morrison, A. M. (1985). *The tourism system: An introductory text.* Englewood Cliffs, NJ: Prentice-Hall.

———. (1992). *The tourism system: An introductory test* (2nd ed.). Englewood Cliffs, NJ: Prentice-Hall.

Morgan, N., & Pritchard, A. (2001). *Advertising in tourism and leisure.* Oxford: Butterworth–Heinemann.

Motiram. (2003). *International tourism: Socio-economic prospective.* New Delhi: Sonali Publications.

Moutinho, L. (1987). Consumer behaviour in tourism. *European Journal of Marketing, 21*(10), 3–44.

Mowforth, M., & Munt, I. (1998). *Tourism and sustainability: New tourism in the third world.* London: Routledge.

Murphy, P. E. (1985). *Tourism: A community approach* (pp. 17–26). New York, NY: Methuen.

Nash, D. (1979). The rise and fall of an aristocrat tourist culture: Nice, 1763–1936. *Annals of Tourism Research, 6*, 61–76.

Negi, J. (1990). *Socio-economic and eco-environmental impact of tourism in the developing countries.* New Delhi: Metropolitan.

Norval, A. (1936). *The tourism industry: A national and international survey.* London: Pitman.

Ogilvie, F. W. (1933). *The tourist movement. Journal of the Royal Statistical Society, 96*(4), 686–688.

OntarioBuys. (2006). *Performance measurement: A report by the hospital supply chain metrics working group* (pp. 1–30). French Forest, NSW: Hospitality Press.

Opperman, M., & Chon, K. (1997). *Tourism in developing countries.* London: Thompson Business Press.

Page, S. J. (1999). *Transport and tourism.* Harlow: Addison-Wesley Longman.

———. (2003). *Tourism management: Managing for change* (1st ed.). Oxford: Elsevier Ltd.

Page, S. J., & Connell, J. (2009). *Tourism: A modern synthesis* (3rd ed.). Hampshire: South-Western Cengage Learning.

Page, S. J., & Hall, C. M. (2003). *Managing urban tourism.* Harlow: Prentice Hall.

Pearce, D. (1995). *Tourism today: A geographical analysis* (2nd ed.). Harlow: Longman.

Pearce, P. (2005). *Tourist behaviour: Themes and conceptual schemes.* Clevedon: Channel View.

Pearce, P. L. (1982). *The social psychology of tourist behavior.* Oxford: Pergamon.

———. (1993). Fundamentals of tourist motivations. In D. G. Pearce & R. W. Butler (Eds.), *Tourism research: Critics and challenges* (pp. 113–134). London: Routledge.

Pearce, P. L., Moscardo, G. M., & Ross, G. (1996). *Understanding and managing the tourism community relationship.* London: Elsevier.

Pearson, C. S. (2000). *Economics and the global environment.* Cambridge: Cambridge University Press.

Peck, H., Payne, A., Christopher, M., & Clark, M. (1999). *Relationship marketing: Strategy and implementation.* Oxford: Butterworth–Heinemann.

Pender, L. J. (2001). *Travel trade and transport: An introduction*. London: Continuum.

Perreault, W. D., Dorden, D. K., & Dordon, W. R. (1979). A psychological classification of vacation life-styles. *Journal of Leisure Research, 9*, 208–224.

Pitts, R. E., & Woodside, A. G. (1986). Personal value and travel decisions. *Journal of Travel Research, 25*(1), 20–25.

Pizam, A. (1978). Tourism impacts: The social cost to destination communities as perceived by its residents. *Journal of Travel Research, 16*(4), 8–12.

Plog, S. C. (1973, November). Why destination areas rise and fall in popularity. *Cornell HRA Quarterly, 42*(3), 13–16.

———. (1974). A carpenter's tools: An answer to Stephen L. J. Smith's review of psycho centrism/allocentrism. *Journal of Travel Research, 28*(4), 43–45 (reprinted in 1990).

———. (1987). Understanding psychographics in tourism research. In J. R B. Ritchie & C. R. Goeldner (Eds.), *Travel, tourism and hospitality research: A handbook for managers and researchers* (pp. 203–213). New York, NY: John Wiley.

———. (1990). A carpenter's tools: An answer to Stephen L. J. Smith's review of psycho centrism/allocentric. *Journal of Travel Research, 28*(4), 43–45.

Plumb, J. H. (1959). The grand tour. *Horizon, 2*(2), 73–105.

Poon, A. (1993). *Tourism, technologies and competitive strategies*. Wallingford: CAB International (reprinted in 1994).

———. (2003). Competitive strategy for a new tourism. In C. Cooper (Ed.), *Classic review in tourism*. Clevedon: Channel View.

Porter, E. M. (1980). *Competitive strategy: Techniques for analyzing industries and competitors*. New York, NY: The Free Press.

Prentice, R. (2004). Tourism motivations and typologies. In A. Lew, C. M. Hall & A. Williams (Eds.), *A companion to tourism* (pp. 261–279). Oxford: Blackwell.

Pruthi, R. K. (2004). *International tourism: Potential measurement and prospects*. New Delhi: Rajat Publications.

Quinet, E., & Vickerman, R. (2004). *Principles of transport economics*. Cheltenham: Edward Elgar.

Ranga, M., & Chandra, A. (2003). *Tourism and hospitality industry in 21st century*. New Delhi: Discovery Publishing House.

Rauscher, M. (1997). *International trade, factor movements, and the environment*. Oxford: Oxford University Press.

Ray, N., & Ryder, M. (2003). E-abilities' tourism: An exploratory discussion of the travel needs and motivations of the mobility disabled. *Tourism Management, 24*(1), 57–72.

Robinson, H. (1976). *A geography of tourism*. London: MacDonald and Evans.

Roday, S., Biswal, A., & Joshi, V. (2009). *Tourism operation and management*. New Delhi: Oxford University Press.

Rowling, M. (1971). Everyday life of medieval travellers. London: B. T. Batsford.

Rugof, M. (1960). *The great travelers*. New York, NY: Simon and Schuster.

Ryan, C. (1991). *Recreational tourism: A social science perspective*. New York, NY: Routledge.

Ryan, C. (Ed.). (1997). *The tourist experience*. London: Cassell.

Ryan, C., & Page, S. J. (Eds.). (2000). *Tourism management: Towards new millennium*. Oxford: Pergamon.

Schiefelbusch, M., Jain, A., Schafer, T., & Muller, D. (2007). Transport and tourism: Roadmap to integrated planning developing and accessing integrated travel chains. *Journal of Transport Geography, 15*(2), 94–103.

Schwartz, K., Tapper, R., & Font, X. (2008). A sustainable supply chain management framework for tour operators. *Journal of Sustainable Tourism, 16*(3), 298–314.

Seaton, A. V., & Bennett, M. M. (1996). *The marketing of tourism: Concepts, issues and cases*. London: International Thomson Business Press.

Sessa, A. (1983). *Elements of tourism*. Rome: Cantal.

Sharma, P. S. (2004). *Tourism education: Theories and practices*. New Delhi: Kanishka Publications.

Sharpley, R. (1994). *Tourism, tourist and society*. Huntingdon: Elm.

———. (1996). Tourism and consumer culture in postmodern society. In M. Robinson, N. Evans, & P. Callaghan (Eds.), *Proceedings of the tourism and culture: Towards the 21st century conference* (pp. 203–215). Sunderland: Centre for Travel and Tourism/Business Education Publishers.

Shaw, G., & William, A. (1994). *Critical issues in tourism*. Oxford: Blackwell.

Shih, D. (1986). VALS as a tool of tourism research: The Pennsylvania experience. *Journal of Travel Research, 24*(4), 2–11.

Sinclair, T. M., & Stabler, M. (1997). *The economics of tourism*. London and New York, NY: Routledge.

Smith, D. M., & Krannich, S. R. (1998). Tourism dependence and residents attitude. *Annals of Tourism Research, 25*(4), 783–802.

Smith, S. (1982). The state of art of tourism research: A theoretical perspective. In J. Fridgen & D. Allen (Eds.), *Michigan tourism: How can research help?* (Special report#6, Agricultural Experimental Station) East Lansing: Michigan University.

Smith, S. J. L. (2007). The measurement of global tourism: Old debates, new consensus and continuing challenges. In A. Lew, C. M. Hall & A. William (Eds.), *A companion to tourism* (pp. 23–25). Oxford: Blackwell.

Smith, V. L. (1977). *Hosts and guests: The anthropology of tourism*. Philadelphia: University of Pennsylvania Press.

Stephen, L., & Smith, J. (1995). *Tourism analysis: A handbook* (2nd ed.). UK: Longman Book.

Stewart, C. D., & Calantone, R. J. (1978). Psychographic segmentation of tourists. *Journal of Travel Research, 16*(3).

Stock, J. R., & Ellram, L. M. (1998). *Fundamentals of logistics management*. Boston, MA: Irwin/McGraw-Hill.

Stringer, P. (1981). Hosts and guests: The bed and breakfast phenomenon. *Annals of Tourism Research, 8*(3), 357–376.

Sumption, J. (1975). *Pilgrimage: An image of mediaeval religion.* New Jersey, NJ: Bowman and Littlefield.

Swarbrooke, J., & Horner, S. (1999). *Consumer behavior in tourism* (1st ed.). Great Britain: Butterworth–Heinemann.

———. (2001). *Business travel and tourism.* Oxford: Butterworth–Heinemann.

———. (2007). *Consumer behavior in tourism* (2nd ed.). Boston: Elsevier/Butterworth–Heinemann.

Tapper, R., & Font, X. (2004). *Tourism supply chains* (report of a desk research project for the Travel Foundation). Leeds: Leeds Metropolitan University.

Teare, R., Moutinho, L., & Morgan, N. (Eds.). (1994). *Managing and marketing tourist services in the 1990s.* London: Cassel.

Telfer & Sharpley. (2008). *Tourism development in the developing world.* London: Routledge.

Theobald, F. W. (1994). *Global tourism.* Oxford: Butterworth and Heinemann.

Thornton, P., Shaw, G., &Williams, A. (1997). Tourist group holiday decision making and behaviour: The influence of children. *Tourism Management, 18*(5), 287–298.

Tinsley, H. E. A., & Kass, R. A. (1978). Leisure activities and need satisfaction: A replication and extension. *Journals of Leisure Research, 10*(3), 191–202.

World Tourism Organization. (1985, 17–26 September). *Tourism bill of right and tourist code A/6/11(a) adopted by the sixth General Assembly.* Sofia, Bulgaria: Author.

Towner, J. (1996). *A historical geography of recreation and tourism in the western world: 1540–1940.* Newcastle: University of Northumbria.

Tribe, J. (1995). *The economics of leisure and tourism.* Oxford: Butterworth–Heinemann.

Tribe, J., Font, X., Griffith, N., Vickery, R., & Yale, K. (2000). *Environmental management for rural tourism and recreation.* London: Cassel Publication.

Turner, R. K., Pearce, D., & Bateman, I. (1993). *Environmental economics: An elementary introduction.* Baltimore: The Johns Hopkins University Press.

Twain, M. (1869). *The innocents abroad.* New York, NY: Harper.

Urry, J. (1990). *The tourist gaze: Leisure and travel in contemporary societies.* London: SAGE Publications.

Uysal, M., & Jurowski, C. (1994). Testing the push and pull factors. *Annals of Tourism Research, 21*(4), 844–846.

Vellas, F., & Becheral, L. (1995). *International tourism.* London: Macmillan Press.

Waggle, D., & Fish, M. (1999). International tourism cross elasticity. *Annals of Tourism Research, 26*(1), 191–194.

Wahab, S., & Cooper, C. (2001). *Tourism in the age of globalisation.* London: Routledge.

Wahab, S., & Pigram J. J. (Eds.). (1997). *Tourism development and growth: The challenges of sustainability.* London: Routledge.

Walker, J. R. (2004). *Introduction to hospitality management* (1st ed., pp. 40–52). New Jersey, NJ: Pearson Education .

Wall, G., & Ali, M. (1977). The impact of tourism in Trinidad and Tobago. *Annals of Tourism Research, 4*(4), 43–49.

Walmsley, D. J. (2004). Behavioural approaches in tourism research. In A. Lew, C. M. Hall, & A. Williams (Eds.), *A companion to tourism.* Oxford: Blackwell.

Waters, S. R. (1995). *Travel industry World Year Book 1994–94.* New York, NY: Child and Waters.

Weaver, D. (2001). Ecotourism as a mass tourism: Contradiction or reality, *Cornell Hotel and Restaurant Administration Quarterly, 40*(2), 102–112.

Weinstein, A. (1987). *Market segmentation: Using niche marketing to exploit new markets.* Chicago: Probus Publishing Company.

Werner, C. (1985). *Spatial transportation modeling.* Beverly Hills, CA: SAGE Publications.

Wheatcroft, S. (1994). *Aviation and tourism policies: Balancing the benefits.* London: Van Nostrand Reinhold.

Wight, P. (1996). North American ecotourism markets: Motivations, preferences and destinations. *Journal of Travel Research, 35*(1), 3–10.

Williams, G. (1993). *The airline industry and its impact of deregulations.* UK: Ashgate.

Williams, S. (1998). *Tourism geography.* London: Rutledge.

———. (2009). *Tourism geography: A new synthesis.* London: Routledge.

Witt, S. (1991). Tourism in Cyprus: Balancing the benefits and costs. *Tourism Management, 12*(1), 37–46.

Witt, S. F., & Witt, C. A. (Eds.). (1992). Tourism demand: Literature review and econometric model specification. In *Modeling and forecasting demand in tourism* (pp. 16–29). San Diego, CA: Academic Press Inc.

World Travel and Tourism Council, World Tourism Organization and the Earth Council (1996). *Agenda 21 for the travel and tourism industry: Towards environmentally sustainable development.* London: World Travel and Tourism Council.

World Tourism Organization (WTO). (1983). *Definition concerning tourism statistics.* Madrid: WTO.

Yale, P. (1990). *From tourist attractions to heritage tourism.* Huntington: ELM Publications.

Yilmaz, Y., & Bitici, U. S. (2006). Performance measurement in tourism: A value chain model. *International Journal of Contemporary Hospitality Management, 18*(4), 341–349.

Young, G. (1973). *Tourism: Blessings or bright?* Harmondsworth, England: Penguin.

Zhang, X., Song, H., & Huang, G. Q. (2009). Tourism supply chain management: A new research agenda. *Tourism Management, 30*, 345–358. World Tourism Organization (16 January, 2012

Zivadin, J. (1999). *Osnovi turizmologije (fundamentals of tourismology)*. Banjaluka: PMF.

Zuzanek, J., & Mannel, R. (1983). Work leisure relationships from a sociological and social psychographical perspective. *Leisure Studies, 2*(3), 327–344.

Suggested Websites

http://www.texaschapbookpress.com/magellanslog15/grandtourmap.htm

League of Nations: Wikipedia, 2005.

World Travel and Tourism Council Report: www.wttc.com

United Nations World Tourism Organization: www.world-tourism.org

Index